Do-it-Yourself

HOME MAINTENANCE MANUAL

INVEST IN LIVING

Do-it-Yourself

HOME MAINTENANCE MANUAL

EP Publishing Limited
1980

Published 1980 by EP Publishing Ltd, East Ardsley, Wakefield, West Yorkshire WF3 2JN

Reprinted 1981

Printed in Brighton England by G. Beard & Son Ltd

Acknowledgements

The authors and publishers are grateful to the following for permission to include copyright photographs:

ICI Ltd.: pp. 89, 91 and cover
Wolf Electric Tools Ltd.: p. 90 (2 pictures)
Cement and Concrete Association: p. 91
S. Marshall & Sons Ltd.: p. 92
Stanley Tools Ltd.: pp. 93, 94 (5 pictures) and 95 (4 pictures)
Record Ridgway Tools Ltd.: pp. 96 (2 pictures), 236 (2 pictures) and 237
Midland Electric Manufacturing Co. Ltd.: p. 235 (2 pictures)
Formica Ltd.: p. 236
Doulton Sanitaryware Ltd.: p. 238
Chloride Shires Ltd.: p. 239
Aga Infrared Systems: p. 240
Everest Double Glazing: p. 241 (3 pictures)
Grattan Warehouses Ltd.: p. 242
Cape Insulation Services Ltd.: p. 242
Yorkshire Electricity Board: p. 242 (2 pictures).

In addition, we should like to express our thanks to the following manufacturers for the information which they have so willingly provided:

Asbestos Information Committee
Bartol Plastics/Plastidrain Ltd./ members of the Plastics Division of Hepworth Ceramic Holdings
BP Aquaseal Ltd.
Brick Development Association
British Insulated Callender's Cables
British Standards Institution
Camping Gaz International
Cement and Concrete Association
Colas Products Ltd.
Conex Sanbra Ltd.
Craft Department of Myers Grove School, Sheffield
Cuprinol Ltd.
Deltaflow Ltd.
ICI Paints Division
ICI Plastics Division
London Brick Co. Ltd.
Magnet Joinery Sales Ltd.
Marley Ltd.
S. Marshall & Sons Ltd.
Metrication Board
Midland Electric Manufacturing Co. Ltd.
National Water Council
Polycell Holdings Ltd.
Rabone Chesterman Ltd.
Rawlplug Co. Ltd.
Record Ridgway Tools Ltd.
Spear & Jackson (Tools) Ltd.
Stanley Tools Ltd. and Stanley Education Services
Timber Research & Development Association
Unibond Ltd.
Wavin Plastics Ltd.
Wolf Electric Tools Ltd.
Yorkshire Imperial Metals Ltd.
Yorkshire Water Authority.

Contents

INVEST IN LIVING

Part I

MAINTENANCE
& OUTDOOR REPAIRS

by

Tom Pettit

Introduction

This book has been written as a practical guide for all householders. Nationally we are being faced by ever-increasing costs of materials and labour. By necessity, more and more men and women who have invested considerable amounts of money in their homes are maintaining their property in good repair at reasonable costs by doing much of the work themselves. Often work which was previously considered to demand the expertise of the professional is now being carried out quite expertly by the householder who is prepared to learn and to make a study of what is required of him or her in order to remedy some particular fault. Not only this, but by careful attention to methods, many are making considerable improvements to their property at a modest outlay and thereby adding considerably to its overall value.

The emphasis in the book is largely, but not entirely, concerned with the out-of-doors aspect of the structure, this being due to the very nature of a building. Repair and maintenance are the chief concerns, but where necessary basic practices are described so that repairs may be carried out with diligence. Every effort should be made to ensure that work is carried out to precise standards, particularly where these are required by law.

The aspects of maintenance and improvements are dealt with in a direct and practical way, as are those chapters giving advice on recommended tools and materials. Personal safety which is so important is also included in the text wherever appropriate.

Whilst every effort has been made by the author to ensure that information provided in the book is correct and that within the limits of the space available, accepted procedures are sufficiently detailed, results cannot be guaranteed since the conditions under which the work is carried out are beyond the control of the publishers or the author.

A sincere attempt has been made throughout to assist the reader with property care, making this a concise and worthwhile addition to the practical bookshelf.

About the Author

Tom Pettit has taught woodwork, metalwork and technical drawing for thirty years and is at present Head of the Craft and Design Faculty at Aireville Secondary School, Skipton. He participated in the School's Council Craft and Design Curriculum Development Project from which has developed the School's national reputation for Community Service in craftwork. He is a founder member of the Craft Teachers' Centre in Burley in Wharfedale which was the first of its kind to be set up in the country.

1 Metric Information

Information for the handyman on metric materials, tools and components now available.

Remember

● More and more goods are now marked in metric.
● When working use metric tapes. Measure and order in metric. There is no need for difficult conversions.
● Mixing is still done on a ratio basis. There should be no added complications when working in metric. A bucketful is still a bucketful.

Metric Units of Measurement

	UNIT	SYMBOL
Length	**metre**	m
	1 m is approximately	
	3 ft 3 in (39·37 inches)	
	centimetre	cm
	100 cm = 1 m	
	millimetre	mm
	1000 mm = 1 m	
Area	**square metre**	m²
	1 m² is approximately	
	1⅕ sq yd (1·20 sq yd)	
	10 000 m² = 1 hectare	
Volume	**cubic metre**	m³
	1 m³ is approximately	
	1⅓ cu yd (1·31 cu yd)	
	litre	l
	1 l is approximately	
	1¾ pints (1·76 pints)	
	1000 l = 1 m³	
	millilitre	ml
	1000 ml = 1 l	

Weight	**kilogram**	kg
	1 kg is approximately	
	2 lb 3½ oz (2·20 lb)	
	50 kg are approximately	
	1 cwt (110·23 lb)	
	gram	g
	25 g are approximately	
	1 oz (0·88 oz)	
	1000 g = 1 kg	

Imperial equivalents in brackets are correct to two places of decimals.

Tins of Paint

Paint is sold in metric quantities in a standard range of tin sizes agreed by the industry.

● 5 litres
● 2·5 litres
● 1 litre
● 500 millilitres
● 250 millilitres

A litre is the same as 1000 millilitres.

Old brushes fit the new tins.

Some manufacturers also supply paint in larger and smaller sizes than this standard range. Not all manufacturers make nor all shops stock the full range of standard sizes.

LABELLING

Metric marked tins of paint must, by law, also show the quantity in imperial.

A typical label:

2·5 litres 0·55 gallon

COVERAGE

METRIC TIN SIZES	Approximate spreading capacity in square metres on non-porous surfaces		
	PRIMER	GLOSS	EMULSION
5 litres	60	75	90
2·5 litres	30	37	45
1 litre	12	15	18
500 ml	6	$7\frac{1}{2}$	9
250 ml	3	$3\frac{1}{2}$	$4\frac{1}{2}$

1 square metre is approximately 1·20 square yards.

Spreading capacities are approximations.

Tools and Fasteners

TOOLS

Rules, tapes and gauges for measuring in metric are readily available. The dimensions of many hand tools are now given in metric. In most cases the metric description does not, for practical purposes, involve any change in the actual size.

Metric spanner sizes are described by the *across flats* dimension in millimetres of the bolts or nuts on which they are to be used. Details are given in the tables opposite.

A wide range of engineer's twist drills are available in metric sizes. Number (gauge) and letter sizes have been obsolete for several years; metric equivalents are available.

FASTENERS

Bolts, screws and nuts: for general purposes the ISO Metric Coarse Thread Series is being adopted in place of BA, BSW, BSF, UNC and UNF. Tables overleaf show bolt/screw sizes. The number following the letter **M** indicates the thread diameter in millimetres.

NAILS AND WOODSCREWS

Wire nails are now metric in length and diameter but self-tapping screws and wood screws remain unchanged for the time being.

ISO METRIC BOLT/SCREW DATA

BOLT SCREW SIZE	THREAD DIAMETER	COARSE PITCH	DRILL DIAMETER		SPANNER SIZE
			TAPPING	CLEARANCE	
	mm	mm	mm	mm	mm
M2	2	0·40	1·60	2·4	4
M2·5	2·5	0·45	2·05	2·9	5
M3	3	0·50	2·50	3·4	5·5
M4	4	0·70	3·30	4·5	7
M5	5	0·80	4·20	5·5	8
M6	6	1·00	5·00	6·6	10
M8	8	1·25	6·80	9·0	13
M10	10	1·50	8·50	11·0	17
M12	12	1·75	10·20	14·0	19
M16	16	2·00	14·00	18·0	24
M20	20	2·50	17·50	22·0	30
M24	24	3·00	21·00	26·0	36

ISO METRIC	BA	BSW	BSF	UNC	UNF
M2	9			2	2
	8				
M2·5	7			3	3
	6				
				4	4
M3	5	$\frac{1}{8}$		5	5
	4			6	6
M4	3	$\frac{5}{32}$		8	8
	2			10	10
M5		$\frac{3}{16}$	$\frac{3}{16}$		
	1			12	12
M6	0	$\frac{1}{4}$	$\frac{1}{4}$	$\frac{1}{4}$	$\frac{1}{4}$
M8		$\frac{5}{16}$	$\frac{5}{16}$	$\frac{5}{16}$	$\frac{5}{16}$
		$\frac{3}{8}$	$\frac{3}{8}$	$\frac{3}{8}$	$\frac{3}{8}$
M10					
M12		$\frac{7}{16}$	$\frac{7}{16}$	$\frac{7}{16}$	$\frac{7}{16}$
M16		$\frac{1}{2}$ $\frac{9}{16}$	$\frac{1}{2}$ $\frac{9}{16}$	$\frac{1}{2}$ $\frac{9}{16}$	$\frac{1}{2}$ $\frac{9}{16}$
M20		$\frac{5}{8}$	$\frac{5}{8}$	$\frac{5}{8}$	$\frac{5}{8}$
M24		$\frac{3}{4}$ $\frac{7}{8}$	$\frac{3}{4}$ $\frac{7}{8}$	$\frac{3}{4}$ $\frac{7}{8}$	$\frac{3}{4}$ $\frac{7}{8}$
		1	1	1	1

ISO METRIC BOLT/SCREW LENGTHS

mm	10	12	16	20	25	30	35	40	45	50
in	$\frac{3}{8}$	$\frac{1}{2}$	$\frac{5}{8}$	$\frac{3}{4}$	1	$1\frac{1}{4}$	$1\frac{3}{8}$	$1\frac{1}{2}$	$1\frac{3}{4}$	2

mm	55	60	65	70	75	80	90	100
in	$2\frac{1}{4}$	$2\frac{3}{8}$	$2\frac{1}{2}$	$2\frac{3}{4}$	3	$3\frac{1}{4}$	$3\frac{1}{2}$	4

Wood and Board

Softwood and to an increasing extent hardwood come from the mills in standard metric lengths and sections and are being sold in metric measures. Where you used to think of lengths in feet think now in **metres (m)** and where you thought of inches for sections think now of **millimetres (mm)**. It can be misleading to make conversions between imperial and metric. It is better to measure in metric from the start.

LENGTHS

Sawn Softwood
The standard range of lengths supplied from the mills begins at 1·8 metres and increases in steps of 300 millimetres (300 mm) to 6·3 metres. Shorter and longer lengths can be obtained.

Sawn Hardwood
The standard range begins at 1·8 metres and increases in steps of 100 millimetres (100 mm). Some hardwoods are imported in lengths shorter than 1·8 metres. Retailers who cut to special requirements will normally continue to do so.

STANDARD SECTIONS
Metric standard sections are slightly smaller than customary inch sizes.

Sawn Softwood
The smaller metric sizes are as follows and larger thicknesses and widths are also available.

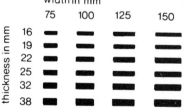

Sawn Hardwood
Thickness in mm
19   25   32   38   50   63   75   100
Widths are normally 50 mm and up in steps of 10 mm. Additionally widths of 63, 75 and 125 mm are available.

SMALL SECTIONS
Small sections for the home handyman are re-sawn from standard sections.

Nominal sizes are
25 mm × 25 mm   25 mm × 50 mm
25 mm × 38 mm   50 mm × 50 mm

REMEMBER
Planed timber will always measure less than sawn sizes (nominal sizes). Allowance should be made for this when stating your requirements.

BOARD AND SHEET MATERIALS
These materials are also now sold in metric lengths, widths and thicknesses. For practical purposes, the dimensions are no different from those you are used to; for example, 8 ft × 4 ft sheet is now described as 2440 mm × 1220 mm.

Bricks

The format of the standard metric brick, including the mortar joint, is 225 × 112·5 × 75 millimetres. The work size is 215 × 102·5 × 65 mm. *Work size* is the size of the brick itself and is subject to tolerance.

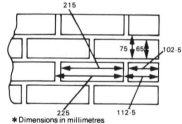

* Dimensions in millimetres

The metric brick is only slightly smaller than the imperial one. **It can be used with existing brickwork by slightly increasing the mortar joint.**

COMPARISON OF METRIC/ IMPERIAL BRICK FORMAT

	Metric		Imperial	
	mm	(in)	in	(mm)
Length (incl. joint)	225	(8·86)	9	(228·6)
Width (incl. joint)	112·5	(4·43)	4½	(114·3)
Height (incl. joint)	75	(2·95)	3	(76·2)
Typical joint	10	(0·39)	⅜	(9·5)

This is how the standard metric brick may be used with metric concrete blocks.

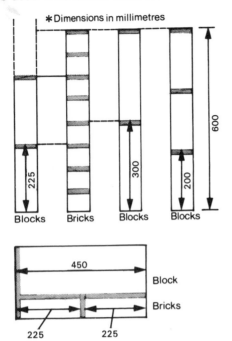

*Dimensions in millimetres

Blocks   Bricks   Blocks   Blocks

Several manufacturers are producing modular metric bricks. The most common sizes are 200 × 100 × 100 mm and 300 × 100 × 100 mm. Bricks to these sizes are being used in some building projects.

Concrete Building Blocks

There is a range of 16 dimensionally co-ordinated sizes of concrete blocks.

Purchases are made by reference to the co-ordinating size which includes the mortar joint. Of these sizes the following are most in demand:

Co-ordinating size (mm)	Work size (mm)
400 × 100	390 × 90
400 × 200	390 × 190
450 × 200	440 × 190
450 × 225	440 × 215
450 × 300	440 × 290

Work size is the size of the block itself and is subject to tolerance.

A total range of seven thicknesses (work size) is available from 60 mm to 215 mm, but not all block sizes are manufactured in all thicknesses.

Concrete blocks of work size 448 mm × 219 mm (18 in × 9 in including mortar joint) and 397 mm × 194 mm (16 in × 8 in including mortar joint) are available for maintenance and repair work.

These are near enough to the metric sizes to be within normal tolerances.

Central Heating and Plumbing

METAL PIPES

Fractional and Metric Pipe Sizes

NOMINAL FRAC-TIONAL SIZES	IRON/STEEL	COPPER	LEAD
	NOMINAL INSIDE DIAMETER mm	OUTSIDE DIAMETER mm	INSIDE DIAMETER mm
$\frac{3}{8}$	10	12	10
$\frac{1}{2}$	15	15	12
$\frac{3}{4}$	20	22	20
1	25	28	25
$1\frac{1}{4}$	32	35	32
$1\frac{1}{2}$	40	42	40
2	50	54	50

Note: Metric copper pipe is measured externally.

For practical purposes there is no change in the physical sizes of lead and iron/steel pipes. The sizes of copper pipes have changed slightly.

TOOLS

Tools suitable for use with metric copper tubing are available, e.g. pipe benders and pipe bending springs.

PIPE FITTINGS

Only fittings for use with copper pipe are affected by metrication: metric compression fittings are interchangeable with imperial in some sizes, but require adaptors in others.

INTERCHANGEABLE SIZES		SIZES REQUIRING ADAPTORS	
mm	in	mm	in
12	$\frac{3}{8}$	22	$\frac{3}{4}$
15	$\frac{1}{2}$	35	$1\frac{1}{4}$
28	1	42	$1\frac{1}{2}$
54	2		

Metric capillary (soldered) fittings are not directly interchangeable with imperial sizes but adaptors are available.

Pipe fittings which use screwed threads to make the joint remain unchanged. The British Standard Pipe (BSP) thread form has now been accepted internationally and its dimensions will not physically change. These screwed fittings are commonly used for joining iron or steel pipes, for connections on taps, basin and bath waste outlets and on boilers, radiators, pumps, etc. Fittings for use with lead pipe are joined by soldering and for this purpose the metric and inch sizes are interchangeable.

PLASTIC PIPES

A wide range of plastic pipes and fittings in metric sizes for non-pressurized services is generally available.

Miscellaneous Materials

WALLPAPER

Since 1963 standard rolls of finished wallpaper have been in nominal lengths of 10·05 metres (approximately 11 yards) and in nominal widths of 530 mm (approximately 21 inches).

ELECTRIC CABLE, ETC.

The electric cable industry changed to metric British Standards in 1969. The practice since then has been to specify conductor sizes by their nominal cross-sectional areas in square millimetres. Examples of sizes of flexible cords are:

0·5   0·75   1·0   1·5   2·5 mm²

Examples of wiring cables for domestic fixed installations are:

1·0   1·5   2·5   4·0 mm²

FURNITURE

Fitted kitchen units are available in metric. The standard sizes for sinktops and worktops are 900 mm high and 600 mm from back to front. Other furniture is also in metric.

PLASTIC RAINWATER PIPES AND GUTTERS

These are available in standard metric lengths of 2 and 4 metres. Cross section sizes are described in millimetres.

GLASS

The thickness of flat glass is now defined in millimetres — no longer by weight. Examples are: 2 mm replaces 18 oz, 3 mm (24 oz), 4 mm (32 oz). 6 mm replaces $\frac{1}{4}$ inch plate.

Lengths and widths are specified in millimetres.

TILES

Expanded polystyrene and other ceiling tiles are produced in metric sizes, so are carpet and PVC floor tiles and PVC flooring. Mosaics are available in 300 mm squares. Ceramic wall and floor tiles are also produced in metric sizes.

AGGREGATES, CEMENT, PLASTER

Most sand and gravel has been sold retail by the cubic metre for some time, as has ready-mixed concrete. Cement, sand, sand/cement mix and plaster are sold in prepackaged metric quantities, e.g. 5 kg, 25 kg and 50 kg bags.

CONCRETE PAVING SLABS

Precast slabs are available in the following sizes: 600 × 450 mm, 600 × 600 mm, 600 × 750 mm and 600 × 900 mm. They are available in thicknesses of 50 or 63 mm.

2 An Outdoor Tool Kit

Here are suggestions for a minimum number of hand tools which will enable considerable outdoor work to be accomplished successfully. They are basic tools many of which will be useful elsewhere, and the list is by no means exhausted. Electric power tools are dealt with in a separate chapter.

1. (a) Folding rule × 1 m
   (b) steel tape × 2 m
   (c) builder's tape × 20 m
2. Combination square × 300 mm
3. Single marking gauge
4. Spirit level × 250 mm and 900 mm
5. Awl × 3 mm
6. Screwdrivers × 100, 150, 250 mm
7. Chisels – (a) woodworking × 6, 13, 20, 25 mm
   (b) cold 155 × 13, 205 × 19, 230 × 25 mm
   (c) brick bolster 230 × 75 mm
   (d) plugging chisel
8. Nail punch 100 × 8 × 2 and 100 × 8 × 3 mm
9. Hammers – (a) claw 455 gm
   (b) Warrington 340 gm
   (c) club 1135 gm
   (d) brick 500 gm
10. Mallet – wooden – head size 115 mm
11. Saws – (a) tenon – Spearior × 250 mm, chrome vanadium steel blade
    (b) hand – fleam tooth – G104 H.P. Black Prince Hard Point. Induction hardened teeth for long cutting life. Blade coated with rust-resisting Teflon* S
    (c) general purpose – cuts wood, mild steel, non-ferrous metals, laminates. Five blade positions
    (d) hack saw – adjustable tubular frame. Die-cast handle, takes 239, 250 or 300 mm blades
12. Pincers – ball and claw handles × 180 mm
13. Pliers – combination type × 175 mm – insulated
14. Brace × 250 mm sweep
15. Wood boring bits – (a) long auger bits × 6, 8, 10, 13 mm
    (b) centre bits × 13, 16, 20, 25 mm
    (c) countersink × 13 mm
16. Plane – smoothing
17. Adjustable spanner
18. 'Lockjaw' vice – new design – portable suction pad secures to non-porous surfaces – optional G-clamp fixes to any fixtures up to 65 mm thick – self-adjusting jaws hold irregular shapes – body of strong shatterproof non-corrosive alloy
19. Trowels – (a) brick × 250 mm
    (b) pointing × 125 mm
    (c) concreting 275 × 113 mm
20. Pick – chisel and point × 3·2 kg – hickory handle recommended
21. Shovel – square mouth 320 × 255 mm
22. Paint stripping knife 38 and 65 mm
23. Putty or stopping knife × 115 mm
24. Tool box – 610 mm long × 203 mm wide × 216 mm high – in sheet steel
25. Ladder – wooden or aluminium extension ladder of suitable length.

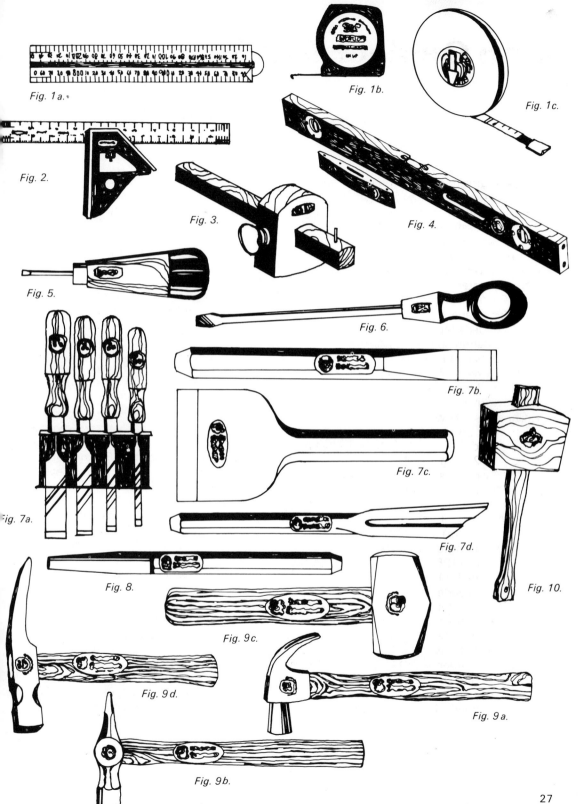

Fig. 1a.

Fig. 1b.

Fig. 1c.

Fig. 2.

Fig. 3.

Fig. 4.

Fig. 5.

Fig. 6.

Fig. 7a.

Fig. 7b.

Fig. 7c.

Fig. 7d.

Fig. 8.

Fig. 9a.

Fig. 9b.

Fig. 9c.

Fig. 9d.

Fig. 10.

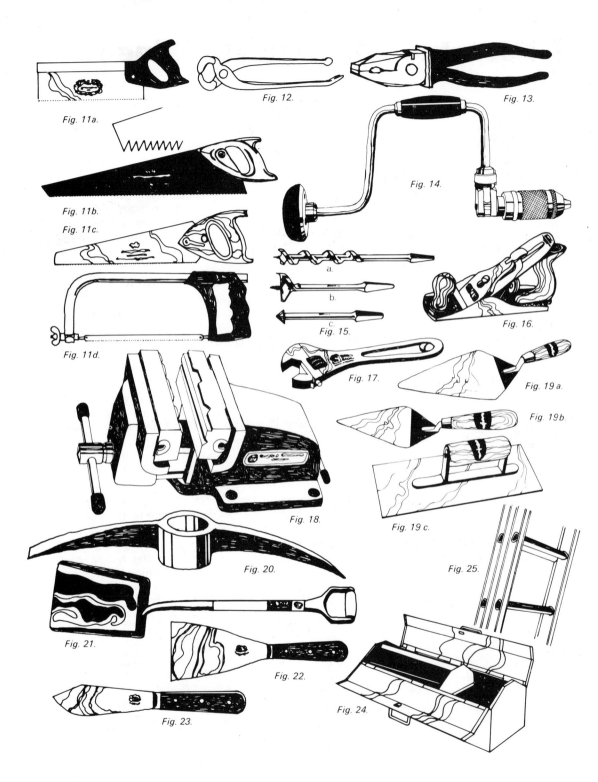

Fig. 11a.

Fig. 12.

Fig. 13.

Fig. 11b.

Fig. 11c.

Fig. 14.

a.

b.

c.

Fig. 15.

Fig. 16.

Fig. 11d.

Fig. 17.

Fig. 19 a.

Fig. 19b.

Fig. 18.

Fig. 19 c.

Fig. 25.

Fig. 20.

Fig. 21.

Fig. 22.

Fig. 24.

Fig. 23.

3 Portable Electric Machines

Modern power tools, which speed up many of the time-consuming tasks confronting the practical householder, are readily available at what are still reasonable prices. Although a considerable amount of money may be saved by buying a power drill and a range of attachments to fit it, the author is of the opinion that in the long term it is advisable to purchase power tools which are specifically designed for one purpose only. In the main, they are more robust and will give better service. In terms of outdoor use a plain drill, a rotary percussion drill and a saw will meet most requirements, with an angle grinder having specialised application.

The design of power tools has improved tremendously during the past few years, manufacturers paying particular attention to insulation, a point to which a would-be purchaser must give considerable consideration. The best of these tools are now built on the 'double-insulation' principle which is a system of insulating a power tool so that the motor and other 'live' parts are isolated from those parts which the user might handle. A non-conductive material is used for the machine body and handle in addition to the internal insulation. Even the drill chuck spindle is insulated from the electrical mechanism so that the inside of the machine is totally isolated from the outside, and therefore only a two-wire supply is required, the earth wire being eliminated.

From 1908 to 1964 the Factories Act required all portable electrical tools to be earthed, but while acknowledging that a properly earthed system was absolutely safe, industry became aware that hazards

to safety occurred due to incorrect connection of the earth wire, or other faults in the earthing system. Because of this, two methods of advanced safety not dependent upon earthing, i.e. Double-Insulation and All-Insulation were pioneered by Wolf Electric Tools. In 1964 the British Standards Institution issued a revised Safety Standard Specification BS 2769 giving for the first time official recognition to these much safer methods. Power tools satisfying the stringent tests carried out by the British Standards Institution now bear the Kite Mark and are authorised for use without earthing. *(Fig. 1.)* The tests include aspects of quality and safety protection against electric shock, overheating, insulation resistance and electrical strength, conduct under careless and abnormal operation, moisture resistance, internal wiring and strength of external flex. It is interesting to note that Messrs Wolf were the first company to hold the Kite Mark for a complete range of tools.

Careful thought must be given to the selection of the tools, paying particular attention to quality and the nature of the work for which the machine is required.

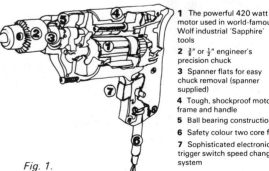

1 The powerful 420 watt motor used in world-famous Wolf industrial 'Sapphire' tools

2 $\frac{3}{8}$" or $\frac{1}{2}$" engineer's precision chuck

3 Spanner flats for easy chuck removal (spanner supplied)

4 Tough, shockproof motor frame and handle

5 Ball bearing construction

6 Safety colour two core flex

7 Sophisticated electronic trigger switch speed change system

Fig. 1.

A drill is the obvious first choice for someone building up a tool kit. Drills are graded by the largest diameter hole which they will drill in mild steel. They consist of a powerful electric motor, the shaft of which is geared to a chuck into which the drill bit is fitted. The unit is held in the hand and is activated by finger pressure on the trigger switch which if necessary can be locked in the 'on' position. Cooling is by a built-in fan, which draws in air through slots in the body of the machine. At all times these must be kept clean and free of dust. Multi-speed drills controlled by an electrical device are available, as are speed reducers for single-speed drills. The author, however, does not recommend these and would advise the purchase of a two-speed drill, these being most efficient for most household purposes. The Sapphire 3521, for example, which is illustrated *(Photo A)* here has a maximum capacity in steel of 10 mm; hardwood 22 mm; hole saw up to 38 mm and light alloy up to 13 mm. Its no load/full load rpm is on low speed 950/650, and second speed 2050/1500. Using an appropriate bit it will also drill holes in masonry up to 16 mm diameter.

Plain drills are perhaps sufficient for drilling small-diameter holes in brickwork and masonry, but for ease and particularly for larger diameter holes the rotary percussion drills are superb. They may be used as a plain drill for conventional boring of steel and wood, etc., but by adjusting the selector may be used for rotary percussive drilling in masonry. For larger diameter holes their efficiency is still further improved if a small pilot hole is drilled first. A depth gauge and side handle are usually supplied with the machine. (The reader is referred to Chapter 14, Building a Car Port.)

Portable power saws are probably the

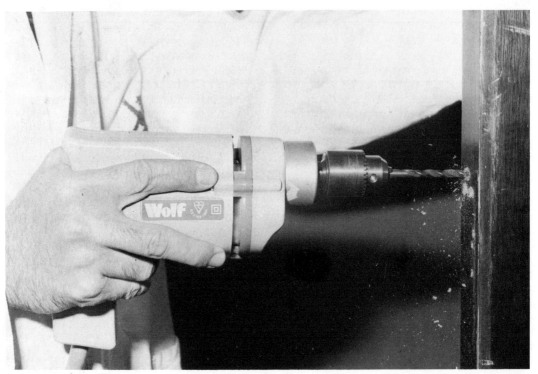

a. With the appropriate drill bit, holes may be made quickly and accurately in a variety of materials. Note how the palm-grip puts pressure in line with the bit, exactly where it is required

best example of the need to purchase purpose-built machines. The saw blade requires a great deal of power to drive it efficiently, more in fact than is generally supplied by a drill. Considerable practice in the use of these hand-held saws is necessary to ensure proficiency. The machine must always be started and allowed to reach its maximum revolutions before the blade is allowed to touch the wood. This high speed must be maintained to avoid damage to the motor, and therefore the blade must not be fed into the wood under too much pressure, nor must it be required to cut too deeply. 184 mm and 235 mm diameter blades make maximum vertical cuts of 58 mm and 84 mm respectively *(Photo B)*, their maximum bevel cuts at 45 degrees being 45 mm and 62 mm. *(Photo C.)* These machines are excellent for moderately heavy-duty use out of doors, making light of what would be lengthy, laborious work if done by hand. The timber being cut must have a straight edge, and care is necessary to begin the cut in the exact position.

This is made easier by looking directly down the blade from above the saw. It is often possible to nail a lath to the wood being cut which will act as a fence for the tool, thereby keeping the cut straight. The adjustable ripping fence which guides the saw parallel to the edge of the wood may also be used within certain limits of width.

Because circular saws of this type cut upwards through the timber the blade should always be set to the minimum depth possible, so flattening the angle at which it cuts. *(Fig. 2.)* Never at any time should an attempt be made to twist the blade in order to true the cut should it wander off the line. The saw must be withdrawn and the cut recommenced at the point of deviation. Saws such as those illustrated are supplied with Teflon* S coated combination rip and crosscut blades with a soleplate extension available as an extra. This is particularly useful for increased stability on narrow work. *(Photo B.)*

b. Deep sawing on the edge of a board. Note the use of the extension sole plate and how the saw dust is thrown clear of the work and the operator

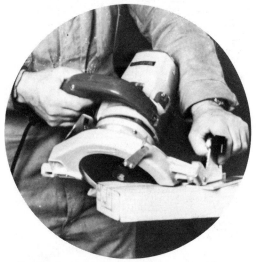

c. Sawing at an angle with the saw set at its maximum bevel cut. The wide sole plate sets the saw firmly on the wood and well designed handles ensure complete control

Fig. 2. The sole plate should be set so that the blade just breaks through the under surface

Special blades for crosscutting, and for sawing wallboard, aluminium, corrugated and flat steel, as well as abrasive discs are also available.

The sander/grinder is yet another machine tool worthy of serious consideration. It is very adaptable, having a number of accessories, coupled with a peripheral speed of 2570 on full load. This gives an excellent grinding performance and is also a suitable sanding speed. Photographs *D* and *E* give an indication of how versatile this machine really is. If such a tool is pur-

Cable Capacity			
Length	Nominal cross – sectional area of conductor	Current rating amps	Number and diameter of wires forming conductor
91 m	0·75 ²mm	6	24/0·20 mm
82 m	1·00 ²mm	10	32/0·20 mm
55 m	1·50 ²mm	15	30/0·25 mm

Fig. 3.

chased it is essential that it complies with the Abrasive Wheels Regulations 1970. Electrical safety has already been discussed, but it will be noted that the craftsman cleaning up the weld in *D* is wearing safety goggles. This is a worthwhile precaution when using any power tool, providing the vision is not obscured, as is the wearing of a simple dust respirator should this be necessary.

An extension cable is an essential accessory for the user of portable power tools, enabling the machine to be used at considerable distances from a power point. Standard cables are available, and the higher the current consumption of the machine, the thicker is the cable required. The cable should be wound on to a suitable portable drum fitted with sockets into which machines may be plugged. An indication of cable sizes as recommended by Wolf Electric Tools is given in *Fig. 3*.

Fitting a plug to double-insulated machines is made much simpler as there is no earth wire, and two-core cable is used, these being coloured brown – live, and blue – neutral. The insulation should be carefully pared off from the end of each, baring sufficient of the wire to fit round or into the terminal of the plug depending upon its design. Damage to the wire must be avoided, and this must then be twisted up tightly between finger and thumb. If the terminals are screw pattern fitted with a washer and slotted nut, the wire must be wound round the screw clockwise, so that it is not squeezed out when the nut is tightened down. If the wire fits into the terminal and space permits, the end should be doubled back so that an efficient contact is made. *(Fig. 4.)* The neutral wire

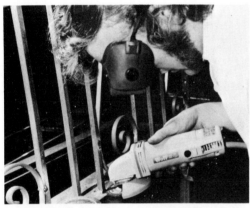

d. The sander–grinder being used to clean up a weld. For the increasing number of home craftsmen who have welding equipment this tool is a worthwhile acquisition

e. 'Chasing-out' for electrical wiring or pipe work can be done cleanly and efficiently

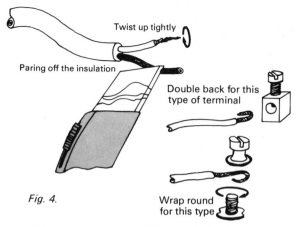

Twist up tightly

Paring off the insulation

Double back for this type of terminal

Wrap round for this type

Fig. 4.

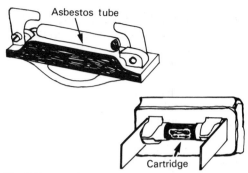

Asbestos tube

Cartridge

Fig. 5. Fuse carriers

should be connected first and the brown — live — then connected to the fused terminal. The cord grip of the plug should then clamp down over the outer sheath of the cable and not the inner wires, so taking the bulk of the strain. *(Photo F.)*

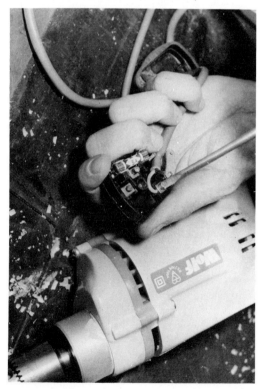

f. Wiring a 13 amp flat-pin plug with 2-core cable. The live wire — brown — goes to the fused terminal and the earth pin is not used

13 amp flat-pin plugs are fused so that if the circuit is overloaded in any way the fuse will melt, cutting off the current. There will be no other damage to the wiring or the appliance. In older property it is usual for each circuit to be fused. The fuse carriers may be of porcelain or moulded plastic, and should be labelled indicating which circuit is served by each fuse. *(Fig. 5.)* The modern household supply is fused at what is known as the 'consumer unit' which contains fuses in specially designed carriers and also miniature circuit breakers. In either case it is essential that a fuse is repaired with a cartridge or fuse wire of the correct amperage depending upon the design of the carrier. *Fig. 6* indicates a typical consumer unit.

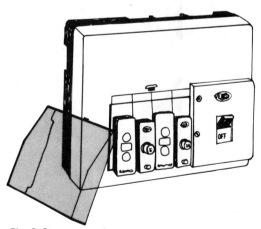

Fig. 6. Consumer unit

4 Hardware Outdoors

This usually falls into two simple categories, fasteners or fixing devices and door or gate furniture of metal. Corrosion and rust are the chief enemies of metals used out of doors. Because of this an effort should be made to obtain items made of metals which are corrosion- or rust-free, providing they are sufficiently strong to do the work required of them. Alternatively, if they are made of steel they should be 'sherardised' or zinc plated – galvanised to make them rust resisting.

Fasteners

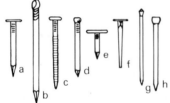

Fig. 1.

Nails (*Fig.1.*)

(*a*) flat-headed round wire nails – selection 20 to 150 mm long.

(*b*) oval wire nails – selection 20 to 100 mm long.

(*c*) ringed-shank nails – gripping power for fencing – selection 50, 65, 75 mm long.

(*d*) aluminium lost-head round nails – for cedar wood cladding or where resistance to staining is important – selection 38, 59 mm long.

(*e*) wire felt nails – extra large head – 20 mm.

(*f*) cut copper slate nails – selection 32, 38, 45 mm long.

(*g*) deep drive panel pins – inverted cone heads – selection 20, 25, 40, 50 mm long for light work.

(*h*) GKN hardened steel fixing pins – may be hammered directly into masonry, concrete, brickwork without previous drilling or plugging – 16 to 20 mm penetration should be allowed – light duty 25 mm diameter 20 × 60 to 65 mm long. Heavy duty 3·5 mm diameter 38, 45, 50, 65, 75, 90 and 100 mm long.

washers to suit light-duty and heavy-duty pins.

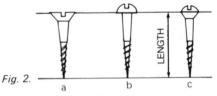

Fig. 2.

Wood Screws (*Fig. 2.*)

(*a*) countersunk headed, (*b*) round headed and (*c*) raised headed in various lengths and gauges as required.

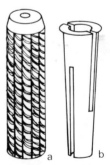

Fig. 3.

Rawlplug (*a*) fibre or (*b*) plastic plugs for light-duty fixing – lengths and size dependent upon work to be done. (*Fig. 3.*)

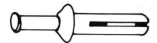

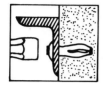

Fig. 4.

'Rawlplug Nailin'. A low-cost, one-piece component for through fixing. A flanged expansion sleeve of zinc alloy contains a nail-type expander. When driven home the nail expands the sleeve into the masonry. 4·7 mm diameter × 22 mm long and 6·5 mm diameter × 25, 32, 38 mm long. (*Fig. 4.*)

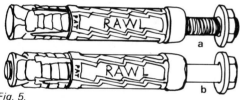

Fig. 5.

Rawlbolts for very heavy duty fixing to masonry etc. Two types are made, (*a*) bolt projecting and (*b*) loose bolt, each being available in a wide range of diameters and lengths from 6 × 38 mm to 16 × 110 mm. (*Fig. 5.*)

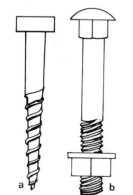

Fig. 6.

A selection of (*a*) coach screws and (*b*) coach bolts for heavy-duty fixing

of wood or metal to masonry, metal to wood or wood to wood. (*Fig. 6.*)

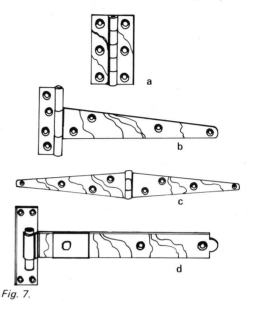

Fig. 7.

Door and Gate Furniture

Hinges (*Fig. 7.*)
  (*a*) butts in steel or brass
  (*b*) tee hinges — black japanned or self-colour
  (*c*) strap hinges — self-colour
  (*d*) steel hooks and bands — self-colour or galvanised

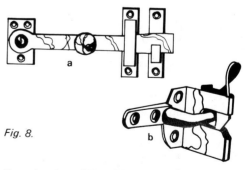

Fig. 8.

Gate latches (*Fig. 8.*)
  (*a*) traditional — many designs
  (*b*) automatic

Hinges and gate latches are available in various styles of 'antique ironwork'

35

Fig. 9.

Gate holders (*Fig. 9.*)
   to be built in – usually of black malleable iron

Fig. 10.

Barrel bolts (*Fig.10.*)
   various styles, some of which may be secured with a padlock

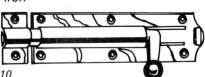

Fig. 11.

Hasps and staples (*Fig.11.*)
   safety pattern – galvanised steel

Fig. 12.

Padlocks (*Fig. 12.*)
   many designs – quality and efficiency varying depending upon cost

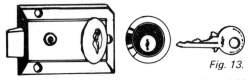

Fig. 13.

Cylinder Rim Latches and Locks (*Fig. 13.*)
   various patterns of the familiar 'Yale' (for fixing see Chapter 9)

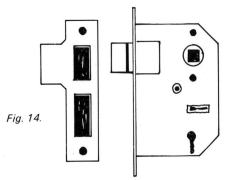

Fig. 14.

Mortice locks (*Fig. 14.*)
   for setting into the edge of doors – many patterns from which to choose

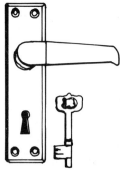

Fig. 15.

Lever handles (*Fig. 15.*)
   plain or with keyhole

Fig. 16.

Letter plates (*Fig.16.*)
   gravity flap action – plain or with 'postal knocker'

Miscellaneous hardware includes door chains, door knockers, door and gate return springs, cabin hooks and eyes, window stays and catches and house number or nameplates. Anti-burglar devices recently introduced by a number of manufacturers are also worthy of serious consideration.

Unitrol, a rustproofing agent manufactured by Unibond is now available in an aerosol container designed for home use. It may be applied to bare, clean metals as a pre-primer, or to firm rust on iron and steel. It then combines with the rust to form a coating which prevents further corrosion.

5 Exterior Painting and Decorating

Once the decision to redecorate externally has been taken, the householder is then faced with what may be quite a confusing array of modern paints, each of which offers its own particular benefits. Choosing the most suitable for the work in hand is important, and it is useful initially to appreciate just what protective paints consist of. There are three basic ingredients: pigment, binder and thinner.

The pigment gives the paint its colour and opacity, that is to enable it to hide the colour over which it is being applied. A wide variety of pigments are used in modern paints, some being obtained from metals, some from coloured earths and clays, but most are man-made dyes.

A binder is a resinous substance which binds together the particles of pigment. Most of the paints used externally will be oil-based.

Thinners are used to adjust the mixture of pigment and binder to the best consistency for application. Household paints are almost invariably supplied at the correct consistency, but if it is necessary to thin them, the maker's instructions will be on the can.

Modern synthetic resins which may be more precisely formulated to suit a particular job have replaced the natural resins which were previously used in oil-based paints. Alkyd resin is the most widely used of these, and the first building paint in this country to be so formulated was Dulux Gloss Finish. Of recent years polyurethane has been combined with Alkyd to produce greater toughness, and even more recently Silthane has been introduced. This is a combination of polyurethane and silicone which produces an even tougher and more durable finish for all domestic applications – wood, plastered surfaces and metal. Brushes and rollers which have been used to apply silthane paints may be simply washed out with hot water and detergents, a distinct advantage over ordinary oil-based paints.

There are characteristics common to oil-based paints in that they have a 'painty' smell during and for a little while after application. They may be thinned with white spirit and they normally need to dry overnight between coats. When a choice is finally made, remember that oil-based paints do need considerable preparatory work but give a very durable finish.

Exterior Woodwork – Preparing and Priming

New, unpainted timber should be rubbed down along the grain with a medium-grade abrasive paper to remove any roughness and all sharp edges. It should then be dusted off and a thin coat of knotting brushed over all knots. Any shakes in the timber, nail holes, or open joints should be filled with an exterior-grade filler.

Normal softwoods should then be given one coat of primer. For hardwoods, including oak, the primer should be thinned by the addition of 10 per cent white spirit to ensure good keying to the surface. Resinous woods should be given one coat of aluminium sealer followed by the priming coat.

If the old paint is flaking from previously painted woodwork, or if it is blistered or cracked and generally in a poor condition, it should be removed completely by burning off or with a paint remover. It should then be treated as new wood and primed as previously described. However, if the paint is sound and in good condition it should be washed with detergent, rinsed and allowed to dry, Minor areas of defective paint should be scraped off and the whole rubbed down with glasspaper. Faulty mastic around door jambs and window frames, between the woodwork and the masonry should be made good, as should putty round the glass. Again any necessary filling should be done with a proprietary filler. Any defective timber should be made good, and bare or filled areas primed as described earlier.

Any timber which has been previously treated with creosote or any similar preservative must not be painted until it has weathered for at least one year. It should then be treated as new wood and be given one or two coats of aluminium sealer followed by a coat of primer.

To finish, the woodwork should be given one coat of undercoat, followed by one or two coats of gloss paint. Two coats of gloss are recommended for extra protection on outside woodwork, but where the surface has been painted previously, and where there is no marked change of colour, one finishing coat may be sufficient. Extra coats may be required on strongly contrasting or rough surfaces.

Exterior Metalwork – Preparing and Priming

If the metal is new and unpainted it should be cleaned with white spirit to ensure that it is free from grease and oil. Individual metals should then be prepared as follows.

Iron and steel

All rust and loose scale must be removed with a wire brush or by scraping or rubbing with emery cloth. They may also be treated with a proprietary brand of rust inhibitor.

Galvanised iron

This is best left to weather and become dull before painting. If this is not possible it may be rubbed down lightly with medium-grade abrasive paper to form a key for the paint and then wiped clean with a cloth damped with white spirit.

Aluminium

This should be rubbed down with fine abrasive paper before any oxidisation takes place, and cleaned with white spirit on a cloth.

Once clean, all metals should then be primed with one coat of Dulux Chromate Metal Primer at the earliest possible moment to exclude the air.

On metal which has been painted previously, defective areas must be cleaned thoroughly down to the bare metal and then primed. Rust must be removed from iron and steel or it will continue to creep below the paint. Sound paint should be cleaned with white spirit and abraded lightly.

Any metalwork which has been bitumen coated should not be painted unless the coating is hard and well weathered. When painting is practicable it should be prepared as above and primed with one or two coats of aluminium sealer followed by a coat of wood primer.

Once the metal has been prepared it should then be given one coat of undercoat and two coats of gloss. Black bituminous paints should be applied on the inside of gutters.

Outside Walls

There are specialist masonry paints for decorating and protecting exterior brickwork, masonry, rendering, etc., the better brands of which contain their own mould inhibitor to prevent the growth of mould and algae. Some also contain cement or sand particles which make the paint look more substantial, but which also make them more difficult to apply. The particles also trap dirt which soon spoils the appearance of the wall, and where they are trapped below the surface the paint coating is thinner. As this surface wears away the particles tend to become loose, falling out and leaving tiny holes which hold water. If these freeze they will begin to break up the surface. Dulux Weathershield is a smooth-finish masonry paint not prone to this defect. If the wall is new or unpainted, it should be brushed down thoroughly with a stiff brush to remove all loose material. On older walls large cracks and defective pointing should be raked out and filled with a cement/sand mix of 1 part cement to 4 parts of clean, sharp sand. Minor cracks should be filled with an exterior-grade proprietary filler, and these must dry out before painting.

Mould and algae must be scraped and brushed off, applying domestic bleach solution – 1 part bleach to 4 parts water – to affected areas in dry weather, thereby killing any residual growth. This should be washed down after forty-eight hours and any residues scrubbed off.

If leaky gutters or pipes have caused stains, the defect must be traced and repaired, leaving the wall to dry out. A test coat of Weathershield should then be applied, left to dry overnight and then damped to see if the stain reappears. If so, a coat of Dulux Alkali Resisting Primer may be applied, allowing it to dry for twenty-four hours.

On sound, new or unpainted walls priming is not usually necessary for Weathershield, but if the surface is powdery, Dulux Masonry Sealer should be applied.

Walls previously painted with emulsion paint, cement paint or lime-wash will almost certainly require a coat of Masonry Sealer, first taking care to remove all loose flaking paint and powdery residues. To finish, in all cases apply two coats of Weathershield by brush or roller for maximum obliteration and durability.

Paint Required

It is possible to estimate quantities of paint quite accurately so that sufficient is purchased at the beginning of the work. This may well save the time and expense of returning to the dealer for more. Areas to be painted need to be calculated.

Doors

For modern flush doors, measure the height and width to the outside of the door frame and multiply together. If the door has heavy mouldings add 10 per cent. Glazed doors may need proportionately less.

Gutters, Fascia Boards, Eaves

Estimate the girth from the outside edge of the gutter, add on width of fascia board, or eaves. This can usually be done from a bedroom window, then at ground level measure the length. Multiply length by width.

Downpipes

Measure the girth with a steel tape and estimate the height by counting the number of joints which are usually about 2 m apart. Multiply height by girth.

Walls

The height may be estimated from downpipes, or for the average house allow 3 m per storey. Measure the distance round the walls and multiply by the height to obtain the area. Then deduct areas of doors and windows. The actual surface area of rough-cast or pebble-dashed walls will be greater than the measured area simply on account of their roughness. It may be that the area measured will have to be almost doubled.

Next the 'spreading rate' of the paint must be checked, and the area to be painted divided by the spreading rate to find the quantity required, bearing in mind that in some cases two coats will be necessary. The following table indicates the spreading rate of 1 litre.

Dulux Alumium Sealer	17 sq m
Dulux Metal Primer Chromate	11 sq m
Dulux Wood Primer	8 sq m

Dulux Undercoat	11 sq m
Dulux Gloss finish	17 sq m
Dulux Masonry Sealer	12 sq m
Dulux Weathershield	3–7 sq m

Before painting asbestos sheeting, vegetation such as moss, lichen or algae must be removed using a fungicidal wash. Several are marketed, such as Santo Brite, Shirlan Na, Blue Circle Fungicide and Heptasan. This should be applied in dry weather and the vegetation brushed off after twenty-four hours, or as the manufacturer recommends. It is advisable to wear a face respirator in view of the dangers of asbestos dust.

When re-painting, if the existing paint film is sound, standard painting practice should be followed, where possible using the same brand of paint. Solvent or alkaline strippers may be used if necessary but all residues must be washed off before the primer is applied. Sealapore, Brolac Primer Sealer and Ceramite Pigmented Sealer are recommended. For finishing, paints which have high alkali-resistance should be used, i.e. epoxy resin or polyurethane based paints, but cement paints or those containing chlorinated rubber also give good service. For rainwater systems, where gutters should be painted both inside and out, bituminous paints are advised. In every situation where asbestos cement materials may become damp the reverse side should also be painted.

It is good practice to begin by painting the highest portions first, barge boards, fascia boards and where necessary the gutters. If the walls are to be painted do these next, followed by the downpipes, protecting the newly painted wall with a sheet of thin card behind the pipe. Follow this with the windows and metal air grates. The glass in windows should be clean and the top coats of paint taken 3 mm beyond the putty into the glass to prevent rain creeping through. (See Reglazing a Window, Chapter 8.) Finally, paint the doors, taking particular care in view of their frequent use. Ladders will be necessary, or alternatively portable scaffolding may be used. It is possible to hire both if you do not have your own. In any case take particular care to avoid accidents when working at a height. Try to avoid placing the ladder against gutters and if necessary buy or hire a ladder stay to keep it off the wall and clear of the gutter. If possible secure the top of the ladder with rope and have someone to steady the bottom with a foot on one of the lower rungs, or tie it to a stake driven into the ground.

A paint kettle is more convenient than working straight from the can, in that it has a handle and will hold measured amounts of paint. In addition, a modest selection of brushes will be required, the author finding a 25 mm brush suitable for fine work such as glazing bars; a 50 mm one for all other woodwork, gutters and downpipes, and a 102 mm brush for walls. Whilst the work is in progress, brushes may be kept soft by suspending them in water – they should not stand on the bristles in case they are distorted. Once the job is completed, however, they should then be washed out thoroughly in the appropriate thinners or brush cleanser, and then washed in warm soapy water and rinsed. When dry they should be wrapped in newspaper and stored flat.

The timing of your painting is important, spring or late summer when the temperature is not too high being the usual periods. The woodwork must be dry and free from surface moisture due to fog, or dew which may be present in the early morning or late evening.

6 Timber Decay and Preservation

Of all the materials used in building a house, a large proportion is timber. Considering that during the past few years the price of timber has trebled, it is sound policy to ensure that it is protected against decay and insect attack. In general, timber will not decay if its moisture content is less than 20 per cent; however, being an organic material it can support the life of other organisms if conditions prevail which are suited to their growth. Houses which are well built and are well maintained are not likely to be subjected to decay except by accidental damage. If, on the other hand, because of lack of maintenance the property becomes subjected to dampness, then the timber may be liable to attack by wood-rotting fungi. These are plants which live on organic matter and can convert wood substance directly into food for themselves. The common cause of decay is excessive moisture and it is easy to conduct a survey of your home and check for external faults which may lead to internal dampness. Common sources are burst water or waste pipes, which may have been cracked by frost, faulty overflows, blocked gutters, especially if they are out of sight, broken or loose roof tiles, faulty flashing around chimneys and other abutments, faulty mastic pointing around doors and windows, blocked air bricks and the bridging-over of the damp-proof course by soil in flower beds. Internally, regular inspections should be made of loft spaces, underfloor cavities where this is possible, plumbing and central heating installations. Methods of correcting many of the above faults are dealt with elsewhere within the book, others are quite easily corrected.

New lengths of waste pipe or rainwater pipe may be inserted quite readily by simply releasing the damaged section, lifting out and fitting a new length, replacing any pipe clips and making good any joints with an appropriate sealing compound or solvent cement. (See Chapter 11, Repairs to Rainwater Systems.)

Blocked gutters should be cleared of debris, care being taken to avoid any of it falling into the downpipe. A garden trowel is useful for this purpose, the rubbish being deposited in a bucket hooked to the rung of the ladder.

The common cause of overflows from plumbing installations is a faulty ball-valve washer, the renewing of which is quite commonplace to most householders.

Airbricks which may be covered with soil or growth plants should be cleared, as should any soil which is above the level of the damp course.

Should any decayed timber be found during the course of your survey, the first step must be to locate and rectify the source of dampness. The decay of external timbers, i.e. door and window frames, is almost sure to be due to Wet Rot which may be caused by one of several individual fungi. The most common of these is the Cellar Fungus which darkens the wood and cracks it along the grain. Surface growth of the fungus is often totally absent, but when present consists of thin dark brown or black strands with a thin olive green fruiting body which darkens when old. Once the location has been dried out, the fungus will cease activity, but all decayed and infected wood must be cut out and burnt. All replacement and remaining sound timber must be treated with a suitable preservative.

Messrs Cuprinol recommend the following treatment:

1. Locate and cure the cause of damp.
2. Cut away and burn all infected timber to at least 0·5 m beyond the apparent extremity of the attack.
3. Remove any nearby debris which may contain strands of the fungus.
4. Ensure adequate ventilation to cavities, so permitting free circulation of air behind the timber.
5. Sound timber, framing, skirting and panelling in close proximity must be treated with three flowing brush or spray coats of a wood preservative on all surfaces. Paint varnish or other surface coatings must be removed before applying the preservative. Any of the sound wood which was damp must be allowed to dry before application.
6. All new wood must be well seasoned and be treated with a preservative. Three flowing brush or spray coats must be applied to all surfaces, and the end grain dipped, or the whole totally immersed for at least ten minutes. Second and third coats of brush or spray applications must be made before the previous coat is dry to ensure continuous penetration. It is important that every side of the timber is thoroughly treated and it is for this reason that immersion is preferred. Wherever possible, fresh surfaces exposed by cutting or drilling, etc., must be brush treated with preservative before final installation.

Moisture penetration of the structure because of external faults may also cause Dry Rot in the internal timbers, the fungus being *Merulis lacrymans*. This is a most virulent fungus requiring stringent and often costly measures to eradicate it. The rot usually starts where timber is in contact with damp masonry and may remain concealed until an advanced stage is reached. The failure of a floor board, or the appearance of a growing fruit body may be the first sign that something is wrong. If an attack is found there will be indications such as a damp musty smell, warping of skirting and floorboards and deep surface cracks will appear on the timber, particularly across the grain. Affected timber can easily be pierced by a knife or other sharp tool, or when struck does not ring as though it was sound. The spores of the fungus may also be present as a fine rusty red powder.

Before any form of treatment is commenced all surrounding timbers should be opened up and plaster knocked from the walls until the full extent of the attack has been determined. This is because the fungus can spread behind plaster and through walls into adjacent rooms, and this examination should be made for at least 1 m beyond the visible limits of the growth.

Recommended treatment is then as for Wet Rot, the first stage being to eliminate the source of moisture, ensure improved ventilation and *in addition* to irrigate all brickwork or masonry which was near to infected timber or had fungus strands growing on it. Downward sloping holes must be bored into the walls at 250 mm centres from 300 mm above and around the infected area. These holes should penetrate to within 50 mm of the other side of the wall, which if very thick should be drilled from both sides. The holes must be topped up with Dry Rot Killer for Brickwork and Masonry, and the surrounding area given brush or spray coatings until the wall is thoroughly saturated. Additionally, surrounding concrete floors, grounds or subsoil should also be sprayed freely.

It must be emphasised that removing decayed wood and sterilising infected walls must be carried out thoroughly if further outbreaks are to be avoided. In no case should untreated timber be used for repairs in a building where there has been dry rot.

Whenever wood becomes damp it may decay. In many instances, with such as fences, gates, garden furniture, seed-boxes, garden stakes, cladding and fascia boards this is inevitable. In all situations, therefore, wood is better preserved and in some it is essential if it is to give satisfactory service.

Creosote is still used extensively for the preservation of fencing timbers and outbuildings, but on new timbers the range of modern coloured wood preservatives — Transcolor by Cuprinol — may be used with advantage.

Insect attacks on timber are prevented by the use of these modern preservatives but attacks on old timbers may be eradicated by first cleaning away all dirt and debris, and then treating with two flowing applications of Woodworm killer, paying particular attention to joints, end grain and cracks.

7 Exterior Damp~proofing

Some of the reasons for dampness were indicated in the previous chapter. Dampness is, of course, more obvious internally because of the adverse effect it has on the décor, particularly plaster and wallpaper. But as it is almost invariably due to some structural fault it is better to look outside and treat the dampness at its source. This is better than making improvements internally which prove to be only temporary and still leave the wall damp.

In old property rising damp is a common problem often caused by a faulty damp-proof course or no DPC at all. Various methods of dealing with this are available, even to the extent of inserting a DPC. This may be done by sawing out a slot along the mortar using a special saw, or by knocking out a course of masonry over short distances at a time and then building in a DPC as the masonry is reinstated.

Electro-osmosis is yet another method by which copper rods are inserted at the level of where the DPC would normally be. These are then joined to an earthed copper strip. It is advisable to have professional advice regarding these methods.

One of the simplest ways is to impregnate the base of the wall with Aquaseal 66, Exterior Water Repellent. If the wall is of solid construction the work may be done from inside, but for cavity walls internal and external skins must be treated separately. The skirting board should be removed and the plaster/cement rendering knocked off to expose the lower courses. Ideally this should be done a few days before any treatment is carried out, all debris and mould, etc., being carefully

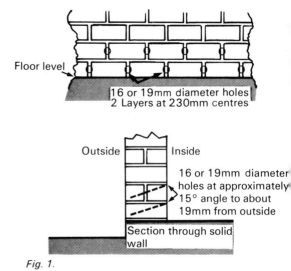

Fig. 1.

removed so that the wall can dry out to some extent. Holes should now be drilled as indicated *(Fig. 1),* taking care not to drill right through. A Wolf rotary percussion drill of the type already referred to, fitted with a depth indicator, makes light work of this part of the job. In stonework the holes should be as near to 230 mm centres as possible. Each hole should then be blocked with a cork or bung which has a small hole in its centre through which Aquaseal can be injected with a garden spray. The time taken to saturate the wall will vary depending upon its porosity, but the average is two to five minutes, when the Aquaseal will come to the surface making the wall look as though it is sweating. By using an electric pressure pump, saturation may be reached in a few seconds. After treatment the holes should be made good with a sand/cement mortar, and twenty-four hours later the impregnated wall given a brush coat of Aquaseal both internally and externally. Any soil should be dug away from the outside of the wall before the brush coating is applied. The wall should now be left for not less than one week before cement screed and plaster are replaced. It is advisable to fit new skirting boards treated with a suitable preservative. The quantity of Aquaseal 66 required to impregnate a wall will vary depending upon its porosity, but an average estimate is 3 litres per metre.

Aquaseal 66 contains silicones, complying with the test requirements of BS 3826 and may be used on all porous building surfaces. On brick, stone (siliceous and calcareous) concrete, and cement, asbestos/cement, building blocks and renderings it will preserve or provide a water-repellent surface. The surface is not sealed and the structure will still breathe, allowing any dampness present to dry out. Outer walls which are suspect should be treated overall, all dirt and loose material being first removed. Cracks or defective pointing should be made good with a suitable sand/cement mortar and when dry Aquaseal brushed on liberally working from top to bottom. Normally one application is sufficient but if the surface is very porous a second may be made after about six hours. One litre will treat 2–4 sq m, the best results being obtained when the wall has been dry for three to four days and rain is not imminent.

If it is considered necessary to seal the wall completely this can be achieved by applying Unibond HydrEpoxy 156. This is an Epoxy resin two-part system which may be applied by brush or spray, and dries to a hard, clear coating without concealing the original colour. It can be applied to dry, or to damp surfaces providing there is no running or standing water, but should not be applied to exterior surfaces if rain is probable within four hours.

Aquaseal 88 Bitumen Mastic will seal cracks and joints in roofs and gutters. The surface must be clean and dry when the mastic can then be applied by trowel, knife or hand to a thickness of 1·5 mm, overlapping adjoining surfaces by 50 mm each side. As the repair is made a reinforcing strip of thin roofing felt should be laid over the mastic, bedding the edges well in. This reinforcement should overlap the joint being sealed by 38 mm all round, and should then be covered completely by a further 1·5 mm coat of mastic. If the joint being sealed is between vertical and horizontal surfaces the reinforcement should extend 50 mm on to each. *(Fig. 2.)*

Fig. 2.

Aquaseal 88 mastic may be used for jointing metal guttering, but for asbestos/-cement, concrete or other porous material, the surfaces should first be primed using Aquaseal 44 Black Bitumen Paint. By using suitable reinforcement the mastic can be used as a repair over existing joints in such gutters.

The roofs of garages, sheds and other outbuildings may be waterproofed easily by brushing on Aquaseal 5. Cracks, holes or joints should first be sealed with mastic 88, then porous surfaces, hairline cracks, pinholes and other small imperfections will be effectively waterproofed by Aquaseal 5. It may be applied to asphalt, asbestos/-cement, concrete, corrugated iron, lead, zinc and roofing felt.

Fig. 3.

If concrete roofs are in very bad condition they may be covered completely with roofing felt secured with Aquaseal Firmafix Adhesive. The surface must be clean and if very absorbent, primed with Firmafix thinned with 10 per cent white spirit. The roofing felt should be cut to length and laid flat for twenty-four hours prior to fixing, and the Aquaseal applied at the rate of $1\frac{1}{2}$ litres per sq m. When tacky after about fifteen minutes, the felt should be positioned and pressed down to exclude all air. The first strip of felt should be laid at the eaves, working upwards with subsequent layers. Laps of 75 mm should be allowed, these also being stuck down with Firmafix.

If the roofing felt is laid on a boarded surface it is normal practice to fix it along the laps with felt nails, and it is a wise precaution to waterproof the laps with Firmafix before nailing down.

Simple repairs may be made to flashings of lead and zinc, etc., using Aquaseal Flashing. This consists of fine-gauge aluminium backed with a layer of flexible bituminous mastic with high self-adhesive properties. Available in rolls, it is applied by cutting to length, removing the release paper and pressing smoothly and firmly on to the surface to be repaired. Care must be taken to avoid damage to the aluminium facing, and to exclude all air.

Aquaseal Waterproofing tape is more flexible, consisting of an impregnated base fabric coated with a waterproofing compound. The tape must be pressed well down on to the surface to be waterproofed, excluding all air by smoothing down the centre of the tape first, then working outwards. It must be pressed well into angles when applying over glazing bars or any other angular sections, overlapping adjoining surfaces by a minimum of 6 mm each side. Where panes of glass or roofing sheets overlap, do not attempt to bridge the dip between them. A new strip of the tape should be used on the lower surface, and the top tape overlapped for 25 mm. Once the surface of the tape has weathered, normal paints can be applied, taking care to avoid over-brushing.

Faulty sealing between window and door frames and other surrounding walls may also be a source of dampness. Before repairs are made to any cracks, old and loose mastic should be raked out, the repair then being made with traditional mastic of red sand and linseed oil. Or, alternatively, there are several modern flexible compounds available which may be applied by pressure gun or knife.

8 Reglazing a Window

Modern 'float glass' is now used for most domestic and commercial glazing. It is a high-quality product being absolutely flat and free from the wavy distortions characteristic of so-called 'sheet glass'. It is manufactured by floating molten glass directly from the furnace over the surface of a bath of molten tin, so that irregularities melt out and the glass becomes uniform in thickness and has a lustrous, highly polished surface.

With these qualities it is now commonly used for ordinary windows within the home, 4 mm thickness being most suitable. However, for greenhouses, cold frames and other horticultural purposes where the superior qualities of float glass are of no practical advantage, cheaper 3 mm and 4 mm sheet glass is still readily available from merchants.

Removing broken glass from a window frame demands considerable care, and at all times when handling glass it is advisable to wear tough, supple gloves and wristbands. Garden gloves and surgical bandages will often suffice for occasional wear. Glass being brittle, serious cuts may happen when they are least expected and sensible precautions such as these are advisable. Broken glass should always be removed from the top of the frame downwards so that unsupported pieces do not fall out with possibly serious consequences. If the window being repaired is above ground level, then the area below should be made obviously 'out of bounds' to both other people and domestic animals. A much safer precaution of course is to take out the sash or frame and work at ground level. So that the broken glass may be removed easily, old putty should be chipped from the front of the glass preferably with a glazier's hacking knife, but failing this, an old chisel will suffice. *(Fig. 1.)* The glass will also be secured with a number of glazing sprigs or panel pins which should be removed as and when convenient. In the case of metal windows spring clips are used which hook into the frame and press on to the glass. It will be necessary to retain these for further use. Stubborn pieces of glass may be levered out with pliers, and the whole of the rebate then cleaned out thoroughly down to the bare wood. It should be noted that in box windows the upper edge of the glass in the lower sash is bedded in putty in a plough groove rather than a rebate. This is often particularly difficult to clean out and careful chiselling is necessary to clear away the old putty, and very often, small pieces of glass. *(Fig. 2.)* Once the rebate is clear it should be scraped with a sharp chisel and a coat of primer applied. This protects the timber and prevents it soaking up the oil in the putty which would allow it to crumble. *(Fig. 3.)*

At this stage a good sweep up of broken glass and putty is advisable, all being safely deposited as refuse. Measurements should now be taken from inside the rebate to determine the size of the replacement glass. From the overall size deduct 3 mm all round to give adequate clearance if the pane is more than 0·4 sq m.

Too tight a fit may result in the glass cracking due to expansion or movement of the timber. The amount of clearance may be reduced for smaller panes. *(Fig. 4.)*

Fig. 1. Removing old putty with the glazier's hacking knife

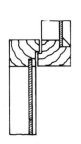

Fig. 2. Groove for glass in top of lower sash

Fig. 3. Applying primer to the rebate once it is thoroughly clean

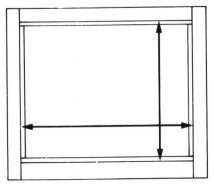

Fig. 4. Measurements for new glass, 3 mm is deducted from all sides

Fig. 5. Testing new glass for size

Fig. 6. Running putty into rebate with the thumb from a ball in the hand

Fig. 7. After the glass has been inserted it is retained by driving in sprigs, using a flat-sectioned bar

Fig. 8. Pointing off the strip of weather putty

Fig. 9. Cutting off surplus putty on inside of frame

As glass ages it becomes more brittle and is often difficult to cut. For this reason new glass is recommended and will be cut to the correct size by the merchant. If, however, it is necessary to cut your own, perhaps from an offcut left over from previous work, the procedure is as follows:

1. The glass must be placed on a smooth flat surface. Thin felt or blanket placed underneath will pad the glass and give further protection.
2. Thoroughly clean the glass.
3. Mark out its size with either a felt-tipped pen or chinagraph pencil. For this a steel tape, wooden straight edge and/or Tee-square are required. Rechecking the measurements before cutting is another sensible precaution!
4. Cutting is best done with a diamond, but modern steel-wheel cutters are quite satisfactory. In use these cutters should be lightly lubricated with a thin oil.
5. Place the straight edge, or Tee-square if convenient, 3 mm from the line on which the cut has to be made. This is to allow for the position of the cutter in relation to the straight edge.
6. Hold the cutter vertically by its handle between first and second fingers, with the thumb underneath for extra support; hold the straight edge steady and draw the cutter firmly and smoothly along the line. Only one cut should be made and you will hear the glass being scored.
7. Now place the straight edge under the glass so that its edge is immediately below the scored line.
8. With the fingers and thumb of each hand spread out, and placed at the near end on each side of the scored line, apply steady, even pressure until a clean break is made.
9. In cases where the waste glass is very narrow, once the scored line has been made it may be carefully snapped off with pliers. A flat-jawed type must be used to apply even leverage.
10. Once cut to size, the glass should be 'offered-up' to the frame in order to check for correctness. *(Fig. 5.)*

At all times care must be taken when handling and carrying glass for obvious reasons — it is fragile and can cause serious cuts. Small pieces may be carried under the arm, and if gloves are not worn, folded newspaper should be placed under the bottom edge. Similarly, if glass is leaned against a wall prior to use it should be padded with newspaper along its top and bottom edges to prevent chipping. Large panes of glass may be carried by holding underneath, leaning the glass on the shoulder and supporting the front edge with the other hand. Larger panes still will require the assistance of a second person.

Having checked the glass for size, a bedding strip of linseed oil putty 3 mm thick is laid round the rebate. This is made continuous by holding a ball of putty in the hand and feeding it into the rebate with the thumb. *(Fig. 6.)*

The glass is now placed into position by resting the bottom edge in the rebate and tipping the pane forward, pressing its edges firmly into the putty. On no account should pressure ever be applied to the centre. In the case of lower sashes the top edge of the glass must be pushed up into the groove first. It is then held there by small wooden wedges under its edge in the bottom rebate.

Now secure the pane with glazing sprigs at intervals of approximately 150 mm. These are held on the glass and driven into the sides of the rebate. In preference to using a hammer for this purpose — which could fracture the glass — the author uses 300 mm of bright mild steel 25 mm × 6 mm in section. Being flat this slides smoothly over the surface of the glass and is sufficiently heavy to drive in the sprigs. *(Fig. 7.)*

By feeding putty from the left hand and following with the putty knife tipped at 45 degrees in the right, a bead of 'weathering' putty is applied. This must be pressed well in and the corners made off to a neat mitre to shed water. Any tendency for the putty to stick to the knife may be prevented if it is moistened with water. *(Fig. 8.)*

Surplus putty is then cut off from the inside to give a neat finish. A period of several weeks should be allowed for the putty to harden before painting. The paint line should run just over the putty and on to the glass to complete the seal, preventing water creeping between the putty and the glass. *(Fig. 9.)*

On large windows, wooden glazing beads may be used instead of the weather strip of putty. These should be primed, allowed to dry and then bedded on to a thin layer of putty. They may be fixed either with rust-proofed panel pins, or raised-head brass screws with screw cups.

Metal-framed windows are glazed in basically the same way as wooden ones. All rust or corrosion must be removed and the metal treated with a rust-inhibiting paint (see Chapter 5), the putty being a special non-hardening mastic such as that made by Polycell Ltd. Small pieces of wood or plastic are bedded into the putty in the bottom rebate to allow for expansion and, as mentioned previously, the glass is held in place by special spring clips.

As an alternative to plain glass the reader may consider the use of tinted or patterned glass of which there is a range of several decorative styles. It should be remembered, of course, that these are intended to be used for special purposes or effect, being designed to obscure vision while still allowing the passage of light.

9 Replacing an Outer Door

You may consider it desirable to fit a new door to your home during the course of redecoration, so giving the property a face-lift; or it may be that a glazed door is preferable to let in more light, or that the existing door has become unserviceable due to age and decay. It was on account of this last reason that the author was recently called upon by friends to hang a new cottage door. Door openings have gradually over the years been made to standard sizes, so that now doors of 1981 mm × 686 mm; 1981 mm × 762 mm; 1981 mm × 838 mm and 2032 mm × 813 mm are available from manufacturers. Standard door frames are made to suit each size.

Since the cottage was built in 1757, it is hardly surprising that the door was not standard. Enquiries indicated that the present one had been fitted in the early 1930s, and therefore had had a useful life of over forty years in what is a very exposed situation. Difficulty in opening and closing the door had been experienced for some time due to damp causing the mortise and tenon joints between the bottom rail and stiles to fail, which in turn had allowed the bottom rail to drop causing it to scrape the floor. An attempt had been made by a previous occupant to reinforce this bottom rail by screwing a batten across the back of the door, but at last it had failed completely, splitting along its centre and falling away from the door along with the weather board. Examination proved that the condition of the door was such that complete replacement was necessary, so a visit was paid to the local branch of Magnet Joinery Ltd to see what was available. Good quality mass-produced doors may be purchased at a fraction of what it would cost in material, time and effort to make one by hand. It was decided that a framed, ledged and braced door would suit the property best, but there was the problem of size. 813 mm was a suitable width. Being a little oversize would allow for fitting, but the length of 2032 was 150 mm too much. Fortunately this was a little more than the depth of the bottom rail which could therefore be cut off completely and moved to a higher position.

The frame was of glued and wedged mortise and tenon construction, so we were presented with the problem as to how the rail should be removed. The eventual solution was to saw across the door from side to side, cutting off the bottom of the stiles just above the mortise and thereby releasing the rail. The short ends of boards were removed from its outer side and the tenons sawn off close up to their shoulders. This was achieved by cramping it between the stiles and boring four 12·5 mm dowel holes from the outer edge of each stile in to the rail, the holes being slightly staggered to avoid weakening the stile. It was also necessary to remove the diagonal brace so that the rail could be repositioned.

Cascomite 'One Shot' waterproof resin glue was then used to secure the rail and dowels, after which the brace was replaced. It is worth noting at this stage that such doors are made right or left hand depending from which edge they are to be hung. As wood is strong in compression, the brace, or braces, run diagonally across the door, the lower end being against the stile to which the hinges are applied, thereby preventing the door from sagging under its own weight. Due to the internal arrangement of the cottage it had been decided to hang the door from the left instead of the right as previously, so we had been careful to select a door of the correct hand.

These modifications to the door were carried out in the comfort of the workshop, but it had to be hung in situ at the cottage which proved on the day to be a very bleak hillside indeed. Completely lacking in electric power, all the work had to be done by hand, and as it was some distance from home, considerable time was spent in drawing up a list of all the tools and accessories likely to be required. This is sound advice if occasional work of this nature is undertaken.

Once on site the work proceeded in the following sequence:

1. The old door was removed, stubborn screws being released by having a red-hot bar (heated in the fire) pressed against the head. The heat softens any paint round the screw head and also by expansion and contraction eases the screw.

2. The bottom of the door jambs had also rotted, so these were cut back to sound wood and new pieces spliced in. The way this is done is very important so that water is shed away from the splice. *(Fig. 1.)* From

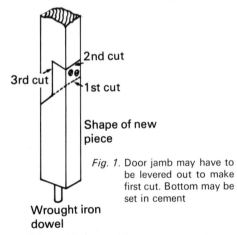

2nd cut

3rd cut **1st cut**

Shape of new piece

Fig. 1. Door jamb may have to be levered out to make first cut. Bottom may be set in cement

Wrought iron dowel

this stage onwards any exposed surface or new wood were treated with a preservative, the door itself having been treated by the manufacturers.

The new pieces of jamb were secured at the bottom by the original wrought-iron dowel, nailed (or they may be screwed) at the splice and also to wooden wedges driven into a seam in the stonework. *(Fig. 2.)*

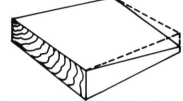

Fig. 2. The opposite corner is cut off underneath so that the wedge twists and tightens itself as it is driven home

3. The hardwood threshold was fitted between the jambs and with the aid of rawlplugs screwed to the stone step.

4. From inside the cottage the door was now 'offered up' to the opening, and by planing where necessary, the hinge stile and the top of the door were fitted to the frame.

5. Wooden wedges were used under the door to hold it in position so that the lower edge could be inspected to ensure that it was clear of and parallel to the floor. Any irregularities were marked and planed off.

6. By careful measuring, and use of the single marking gauge and try square the position of the hinges were marked on the door. From the photographs it will be seen that rise and fall butt hinges were used, and that only the leaf of the hinge is recessed into the door and the jamb. This type of hinge was chosen to ensure that the door was lifted over any irregularities in the floor as it was opened.

7. Similarly, by marking across from the door the hinge position was set out on the jamb. In each case recesses for the hinges were cut out with the bevel-edged chisel and mallet. *(Fig. 3.)* It is most important that at this

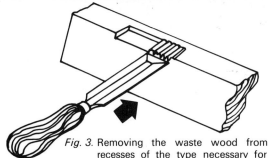

Fig. 3. Removing the waste wood from recesses of the type necessary for fitting hinges and locks

stage only one screw is used in each leaf of each hinge in case minor modifications to their positions are required to perfect the hanging of the door. It is also necessary to chisel a little from the top corner of the hinge stile to prevent it fouling the frame when the door rises as it is opened.

8. The door was lifted on to the hinges and closed against the door frame, waste wood on the lock stile being marked off with a pencil drawn down the inner edge of the rebate. *(Fig. 4.)* This can only be done from

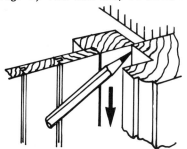

Fig. 4. Section through door and jamb showing how the door is marked to width

outside. The door was then stood on its edge and the waste removed with a try plane, the long sole ensuring accuracy, so that it now hung correctly and fitted the frame, the remaining screws being put into the hinges.

9. The Suffolk Latch was fitted to the door avoiding the joint between rail and stile; and the keep fitted to the jamb.

10. Next the cylinder lock and keep were fitted to door and jamb, recesses

being cut where necessary with mallet and chisel in a similar manner to those for the hinges. The distance from the outside of the lock casing to the centre of the cylinder was measured carefully and marked from the edge of the door. On a new lock this information may be supplied with the instructions. A 30 mm hole to accept the cylinder was drilled on this mark, care being taken to avoid splintering by drilling from each side. The rose and cylinder were now fitted and the backplate screwed to the back of the door. Next the lock casing was fitted over the backplate making sure the cylinder bar was engaged, and screwed into place. Now the door was closed, marking the position for the lock keep on the jamb. This was then fitted and screwed into place.

If a mortise lock is fitted, the short type should be used so that it can be recessed into the stile without having to cut into the middle rail to obtain sufficient depth, which would, of course, ruin the joint.

11. The weather board was cut to length and screwed in place, a piece of hardboard being used as a spacer between it and threshold to prevent binding. Care was taken to avoid screwing into the joints between boards.

12. The previous positions of hinges and lock in the door frame were filled with carefully prepared strips of wood fixed with oval wire nails. It is worth noting that the hinges, and all screws and nails used throughout the work, were zinc plated to avoid corrosion.

Finally the whole of the work was rubbed down with glasspaper, removing all sharp edges prior to painting. The reader is now referred to Chapter 5, Exterior Painting and Decorating.

a. b. c. d.

e. f. g. h.

i. j. k. l.

m.

Replacement of Outer Door
a. The defective door showing how the bottom rail had rotted and split away
b. Close up view of door bottom and rotted frame
c. The new piece spliced in
d. The threshold plugged and screwed into position
e. Gauging the position of the hinges on the door stile
f. The hinge recessed into the door stile
g. Fitting the hinges to the door frame
h. The door hung – note rise and fall hinges
i. Suffolk latch fitted to the door
j. Screwing the weather bar to the door
k. The door hung and fitted to the frame
l. Applying knotting prior to painting
m. Painted and complete

10 Roof Repairs

Byzes of Naxos is credited with the design of the first marble roofing tiles around 620 BC. The author had occasion recently to visit Athens and had the opportunity of visiting the Acropolis, circa second century AD. Like many thousands before he was quite awestruck by the magnificence of what still remains and the grandeur of the original concept. It is interesting to know that the Parthenon, the largest building on the site, was roofed with tiles having a flange on each side over which joint tiles were accurately fitted presaging the design of modern interlocking roof tiles. Bedded sandstone and slate are traditional natural materials for roofing. Fired clay tiles became very popular but had the disadvantage of delaminating, so during the late nineteenth century concrete was tried as a tile-making material. However, not until 1924 with the establishment of the Marley Tile Company did it really become established. Gradually the qualities and advantages of concrete tiles became known and trusted. They are impervious to frost damage, absorb far less moisture than clay and do not delaminate. They are still comparatively inexpensive and have a long life span. Aesthetically, they offer a wide range of profile, colour and surface texture, six patterns being in common use. *(Fig. 1.)*

Tiles are plain or interlocking, and usually have nibs protruding on the underside of the 'head' which is also provided with nail holes. These nibs hook over the supporting battens. *(Fig. 2.)* In practice,

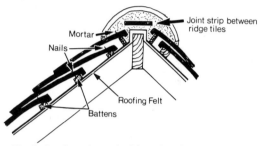

Fig. 2. Section through ridge showing top courses nailed to battens

unless the roof is in a very exposed position, not every course is nailed. The nails should be non-corrosive and copper or aluminium alloy are recommended. At the eaves, ridge and 'verge', i.e. at a gable end, the tiles are nailed to the supporting battens. Interlocking tiles engage with adjacent tiles each giving additional support to the others in addition to being nailed, usually on every other course. Aluminium clips nailed to a secondary batten are often used to give added support to the 'tail' of interlocking tiles, and where the roof is steep above 45 degrees, this is very necessary to prevent the possibility of chatter in high winds. There is little tendency for tiles to slip out of position, but occasionally one may be broken and has to be replaced. If it is a plain tile the bottoms or 'tails' of the two tiles directly above should be lifted with one hand and the broken tile wriggled out. If nailed, the unnailed tiles above may have to be lifted to

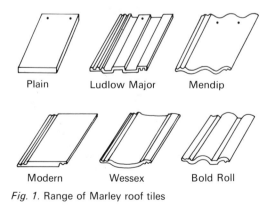

Plain   Ludlow Major   Mendip

Modern   Wessex   Bold Roll

Fig. 1. Range of Marley roof tiles

enable the nails to be withdrawn, when the new tile may then be slipped into place. *(Fig. 3.)* To remove and renew an

Fig. 3. Removing plain tile

interlocking tile the ones above and to the left should be raised and supported on blocks of wood until the new tile has been positioned. *(Fig. 4.)* Care must be taken

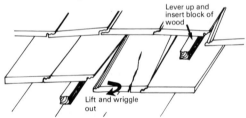

Fig. 4. Removing interlocking tile

during these operations to avoid damage to the underlying layer of roofing felt.

Modern roofs which are slated will also be felted, but older ones will be 'back-pointed'. *(Fig. 5.)* Slates are laid upwards

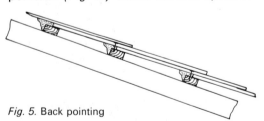

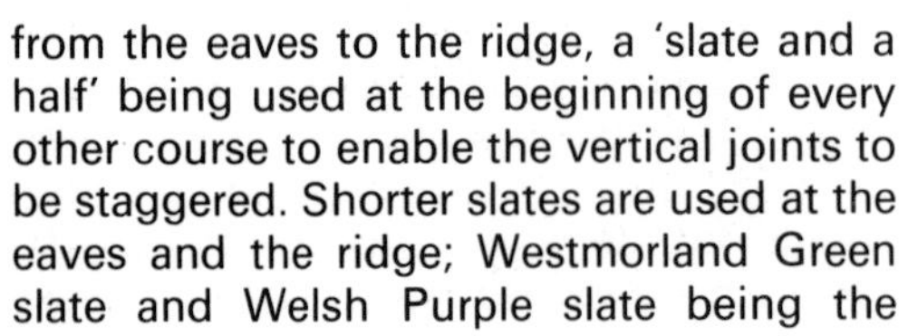

Fig. 5. Back pointing

from the eaves to the ridge, a 'slate and a half' being used at the beginning of every other course to enable the vertical joints to be staggered. Shorter slates are used at the eaves and the ridge; Westmorland Green slate and Welsh Purple slate being the main varieties used. *(Fig. 6.)* Slates are

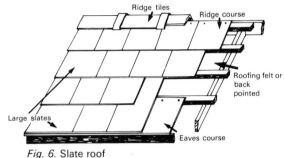

Fig. 6. Slate roof

strong, but are perhaps more susceptible to faults than tiles. If the fixing nails corrode they can slip out of position more easily; or if the nail holes were made too close to the edge they may break away. A small natural fault may in time develop into a crack due to the movement of the structure, sagging of the rafters or carelessness such as walking on the slates. If a faulty slate is still held by its nails a slate 'ripper' *(Fig. 7)* will be

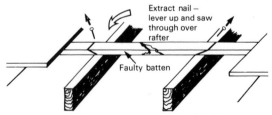

Fig. 7. Ripper

required to chop off or tug out the nails so that the slate can be pulled out. A variety of sizes of slates are used but your local builder should be able to cater for your needs. Before any tile or slate is replaced, the battens to which they are attached should be checked to ensure they are sound, any defective timber being replaced, the new and any adjacent timber being treated with a suitable preservative. This may necessitate removing other slates *(Fig. 8)* which can largely be nailed back

Fig. 8. Repairing slating battens. Avoid damage to roofing felt or make good the back pointing

into position, the last slate or slates being held in place with a copper clip which is nailed between two slates to the batten below *(Fig. 9.)* If the roof is back-pointed

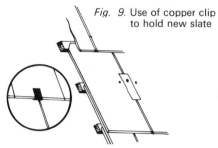

Fig. 9. Use of copper clip to hold new slate

this should then be made good with a mortar mix of 1 part cement to 5 or 6 of sand.

'Hips' and 'ridges' are made off with suitable angle or segmental tiles which may be overlapping or butt jointed, the bedding mortar being 1 part cement to 3 parts sharp sand. This should be pointed off as the work proceeds, the bedding mortar being solid at the butt joints and edge-bedded to the tiles. A galvanised hip iron should be fixed at the foot of each hip as a support. *(Fig. 10.)*

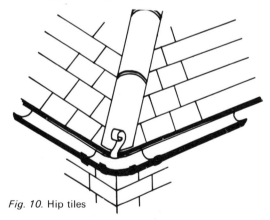

Fig. 10. Hip tiles

Where a pitched roof abuts on a vertical wall such as a chimney stack, flashings will be used to weatherproof the joint line between roof and wall. The flashings may be of lead or copper, or Nuralite which is a modern, purpose-made weatherproof sheeting composed of asbestos and

bitumen. One method is to fit 'soakers' to each course of slates or tiles with a cover flashing which is stepped where the wall is brickwork or otherwise suitably coursed. *(Fig. 11.)* The other is where soakers are

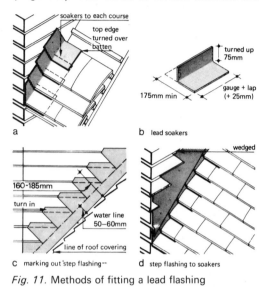

Fig. 11. Methods of fitting a lead flashing

not fitted but the cover flashing is dressed on the face of the tiles, slates or other roof coverings as an overflashing. *(Fig. 12.)* This method is not suitable for plain tiles or slates where there is a risk of rain being

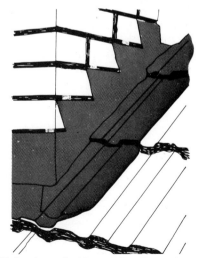

Fig. 12. Lead over flashing on tiles. The wedges holding the stepped flashing into the brickwork can be seen

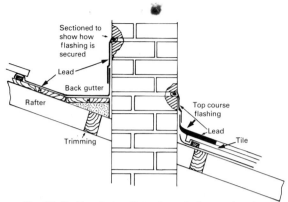

Fig. 13. Sectional elevation of an abutment showing a back gutter and top course flashing

driven under the edge, whereas with contoured tiles the edge is not so vulnerable to driving rain. So-called 'back gutters' and 'top course flashings' should be constructed as shown in *Fig. 13*. The gutter lining is supported on boards and the cover flashing let into the brickwork then lapped over the gutter lining. The top-course flashing should extend well down over the top tiles and be dressed into the pans, again being protected with an apron flashing set into the brickwork. At all abutments where tiling meets walls or chimneys an adequate flashing must be used to weather the junction. The method will vary depending upon the recommendations of the tile manufacturers and the style of tile used. Little should be required in the way of maintenance, but if rain does come in, the fitting in of the flashing to the masonry should be inspected first. The flashings should be wedged at intervals and the joint grouted in and pointed off with mortar. *(Fig. 14.)* Wedges for lead flashings are

made from folded off-cuts from the sheet and are driven in to secure the flashing. Nuralite may be secured in a similar fashion or with hardwood wedges. Should a wedge become loose through expansion and contraction the mortar joint may be cracked and water run down between the flashing and the brickwork. Replacing the wedge with a suitable flat-ended tool and remaking the mortar joint is quite within the scope of the practical householder. If other faults are suspected the aid of a professional roofing contractor should be sought.

It is worth noting that in conditions of severe exposure, or where chimney stacks penetrate a flat roof, the flashing may also form a damp-proof course — DPC. It is fitted over the appropriate course of stone or brickwork and the inner edge turned up inside the flue after which the remainder of the stack is built on it.

Safety in working on a roof is essential. Ladders must be secured at the eaves with a rope, either to rafters if they are accessible, or to a large screw driven into the fascia or soffit boards. Care must be taken to avoid damage to gutters with the ladder which must protrude at least 1 m above them. Work near the eaves may be done from the ladder, but for other work a cat ladder (which may be home made) will be necessary. It should be assembled with screws rather than nails and have an anchor block at the top end which hooks over the ridge. *(Fig. 15.)*

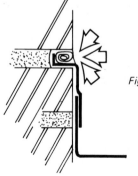

Fig. 14. Wedging flashing

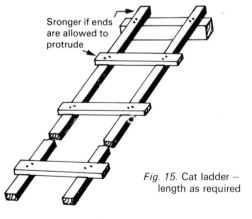

Fig. 15. Cat ladder — length as required

58

11 Repairs to Rainwater Systems

It is important to maintain gutters and rain-water pipes in good condition to avoid structural problems associated with dampness. Cracked or leaking gutters, or faulty pipes discharging water on to outside walls can have very adverse effects on the interior decoration of the house, or worse still, lead to timber decay. Gutters are easily clogged with leaves, small twigs and other debris from the roof. If this is allowed to accumulate rainwater will backup and spill over with detrimental effects on the fascia and soffit boards, and possibly rafter ends. In addition, fasteners and brackets will tend to corrode or rust away. The problem may be further aggravated by frost, the water expanding and doing further damage as it freezes. Periodical cleaning is therefore essential. A garden trowel will scoop out most of the waste, the remainder then being flushed away with the garden hose or buckets of water, finally making sure that the down spouts are clear. Blockages here can often be cleared away using a length of stiff wire, avoiding the need to dismantle.

On older property gutters may be of stone, wood or cast iron and it is quite common for leaks to occur at the joints. These can be effectively sealed using Aquaseal mastic and a reinforcement as indicated in Chapter 7, making sure that the surfaces are clean and dry. Wooden gutters also develop leaks along their length as the timber deteriorates, and these too may be repaired in a similar way. A common fault with cast-iron gutters occurs at the joint between sections due to the fixing screw rusting away, allowing the joint to spring open. In such cases the joint should be cleaned, coated with a sealing mastic and the two sections pulled together once more with a brass nut and bolt, which will not corrode. Surplus mas-tic should be wiped away, a little paraffin oil on a cloth usually being effective. The joint between lengths of wooden guttering is always vulnerable and at times it is necessary to joint in short lengths rather than replace the whole piece. This may be done using lap joints which are then secured with brass screws. *(Fig. 1.)* It is

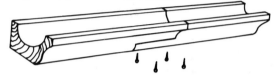

Fig. 1. Lap joint in wooden gutter

important that the wood is treated with a suitable preservative, and that the joint is packed with a sealing mastic before it is finally screwed up. Both wooden and iron gutters should be treated regularly on their inner surface with bituminous paint to prevent deterioration.

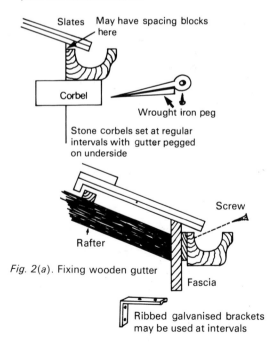

Fig. 2(a). Fixing wooden gutter

Figures 2(a) and (b) indicate some of the ways by which wooden and iron gutters are supported in case the reader is ever faced with the problem of removing and replacing whole lengths.

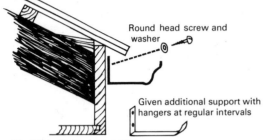

Round head screw and washer

Given additional support with hangers at regular intervals

Fig. 2(b). Fixing iron gutter

Some of the problems associated with cast-iron down pipes are shown in *Fig. 3*, which usually result in the need to replace

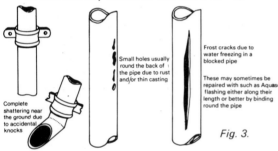

Complete shattering near the ground due to accidental knocks

Small holes usually round the back of the pipe due to rust and/or thin casting

Frost cracks due to water freezing in a blocked pipe

These may sometimes be repaired with such as Aquaseal flashing either along their length or better by binding round the pipe

Fig. 3.

the defective length or in some cases the whole pipe. When making replacements the joint between lengths should be made as in *Fig. 4.*

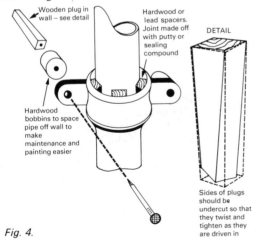

Wooden plug in wall – see detail

Hardwood or lead spacers. Joint made off with putty or sealing compound

DETAIL

Hardwood bobbins to space pipe off wall to make maintenance and painting easier

Sides of plugs should be undercut so that they twist and tighten as they are driven in

Fig. 4.

Many of the previous problems were overcome by the use of aluminium systems which have now been largely superseded by modern PVC rainwater systems, such as those manufactured by Bartol Plastics. Of the many advantages, long life, ease of fitting, freedom from rust and corrosion, and no need for painting are but a few. The system is available in either half-round or square-section profiles, finished in grey, white or black depending upon choice of shape. *(Fig. 5.)* The following fixing instructions are recommended for both systems. *(Fig. 6.)*

Half Round Rainwater Systems

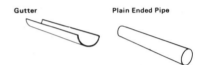

Gutter   Plain Ended Pipe

Square Section Rainwater Systems

Gutter   Plain Ended Pipe

Fig. 5.

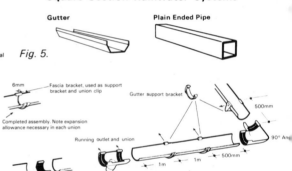

6mm   Fascia bracket, used as support bracket and union clip

Gutter support bracket

500mm

Completed assembly. Note expansion allowance necessary in each union

Running outlet and union

90° Angle

1m   1m   500mm

Fig. 6. Assembly of Half Round System

Gutter
1. Check that the fascia board is primed, glossed and secure.
2. Mark the position of the outlet or outlets. Ideally position over gully.
3. *For End Fixed Outlet – Gable Ends*
   a. Fix bracket to fascia board at opposite end to outlet as high as practical.
   b. Using a fall of 1 in 600 (25 mm in 12 m) from this point, screw fix the stopend outlet in position. The outlet should overlap the roof by 38 mm to ensure complete collection.

For Centre Fixed Outlet – Gable Ends
a. Fix brackets to fascia board at both ends of run as high as practical.
b. Using a fall of 1 in 600, screw fix the running outlet in position over centre gulley.

For Hipped Roof Installations
a. Determine high points in the system. This will depend on the position of the gulleys but care must be taken to ensure one outlet is not overloaded or isolated. Fix first bracket as high as practical. Where 90 degree angles are used, the support bracket must be fixed 100 mm from wall end to clear them.
b. Determine position of outlets and screw fix using fall of 1 in 600.

4. Fix line between bracket and outlet. Screw fix remaining gutter support brackets at maximum 1 m centres along line.
5. On gutter runs over 4 m determine position of gutter union to join two gutter lengths. Using line as guide, screw fix union bracket to fascia. If floating unions are used, ensure gutter bracket is clipped around recess provided in fitting.

Expansion Allowance
Table 1 gives recommended expansion allowances per socket between the gutter and the gutter stop moulded into the fitting

Table 1

GUTTER LENGTHS	Ambient Fixing Temperature		
	0–10°C	10–20°C	20–30°C
Up to 2m length	6·5mm	5·0mm	3·5mm
2m–4m length	9·5mm	6·5mm	3·5mm

6. Take gutter length and cut to allow expansion allowance at either end. *(Table 1.)* Ensure that the gutter is cut square and is deburred.
7. The gutter can now be snapped into position under retaining ribs of fittings and brackets. Pushing fittings and gutter together end to end may result in damage to the seal and is not recommended. *(Fig. 7.)*

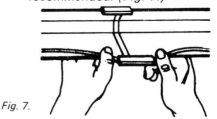
Fig. 7.

8. Wherever possible attach stopends and angles to gutter on the ground. Stopends to overlap roof edge by 38 mm to ensure collection.

Downpipe
1. Use offset to bring pipework back to wall from gutter outlet if required.
2. Push fit pipe to outlet fitting or offset.
3. Join pipe lengths using straight connectors, allowing 9·5 mm gap per length for expansion.
4. Downpipe must be supported by use of clips under the offset and at maximum 2 m centres. Additional socket clips must be used around connectors and shoes. If a hopper is incorporated in the system, this must be screw fixed to the wall.

If only part of the system is being replaced, fittings are available to enable plastic sections to be matched to metal.

12 Mixes for Mortar and Concrete

It is advisable that mortar mixes for masonry, brick and concrete-block laying should not be too rich or strong as this may make a wall too rigid, thereby localising the effects of minor movements within its structure. If these movements are not absorbed by the mortar and distributed in the joints, it may result in severe cracking, not only along the joints but of the building blocks themselves. Plain Portland cement should not be used, nor should concreting sand. This is a coarse washed sand without fine particles, sometimes known as sharp sand.

Recommended mortar mixes for brick, screenwalling, reconstructed stone or building with concrete blocks are shown in *Tables A* and *B*.

Dry ready-mixed mortar can be obtained from builders' merchants, and is ready for immediate use with the addition of water. This saves a lot of time and trouble, ensuring correct mix proportions combined with consistent strength, colour and workability. Standard pack sizes are 20 and 40 kilos, 20 kilos being sufficient to lay eighty bricks.

Special powders are usually available which may be added to the dry mix to produce various colours if required.

Whereas mortar is basically sand and cement, concrete contains an aggregate. The aggregate consists of small particles of stone or other inert material which is bonded together with a mineral solution of Portland cement and water. Cement forms a paste with water which hardens and gains in strength, bonding the particles of aggregate into a dense, strong and durable structural material.

After mixing, the concrete is plastic and can be positioned, compacted and levelled. Hardening commences quickly and within two hours, or less on a hot, dry day, the concrete will be too stiff to use. This is an important point to remember, as once hardening begins it cannot be reversed or slowed. The work must be planned so that the concrete can all be placed while it remains workable, even if this means breaking the job down into smaller stages.

Concrete must not be allowed to dry out too quickly, and must be covered with plastic sheeting or damp sacking particularly on hot days — or days when there is a drying wind. Should new concrete be allowed to dry out in this way it will be weakened, and to prevent this the sacking should be kept damp for at least three days. This slow drying out is referred to as curing. Similarly, newly laid concrete must be protected from frost either with straw under plastic sheeting, or with a layer of earth or sand.

Concrete mix *C* is suitable for foundations, floor slabs, in situ paving and other uses where the thickness of the concrete is 75 mm or more.

Concrete mix *D* is stronger and more suited to small units or thin sections.

A maximum aggregate size of 20 mm is suitable for general purposes, but for thin sections of 50 to 75 mm a smaller aggregate of 10 mm is advisable.

Cement mixes for mortar and concrete

Table A

Conditions	Proportions by Volume		
	Masonry Cement, Sand	Cement, Sand with Plasticiser	Cement, Lime, Sand
Blocks with severe exposure	1 : 4-4½	1 : 5-6	1 : 1 : 6
Blocks internally or with only moderate exposure	1 : 5-6	1 : 7-8	1 : 2 : 9

Note: 'Slaked' or hydrated lime must be used, **not** quicklime.

Table B

Type of Construction	Recommended Mortar Mix	
	Portland Cement Lime Dry Sand	Masonry Cement Dry Sand
Internal walls, Inner leaf of Cavity wall. Backing to External solid walls	1 : 2 : 8—9	1 : 5½—6½
Work below ground, work below D.P.C. External free standing walls	1 : 1 : 5—6	1 : 4—5
Bricks with minimum average compressive strength of 17·5 MN/m2 (2,500 lb/sq.in.) used for retaining walls	1 : ½ : 4½	—

Table C

	Ordinary Portland cement	Damp sand (concreting)	Coarse aggregate	Yield (approx.)
Proportion by volume	1	2½	4	5
Per bag of cement	1 bag	0·085m³	0·140m³	0·17m³
Per cubic metre (m³) of concrete	6 bags	0·5m³	0·8m³	1m³

Table D

Proportion by volume	1	2	3	4
Per bag of cement	1 bag	0·070m³	0·110m³	0·14m³
Per cubic metre (m³) of concrete	7 bags	0·5m³	0·75m³	1m³

13 Working in Brick and Reconstructed Stone

For the amateur craftsman bricklaying can be a very satisfying experience, and if undertaken carefully can produce nothing but worthwhile results providing adequate preparations have been made. It should also be borne in mind that some work may require the approval of the local authority.

Bricks are manufactured in three distinct forms: solid, frogged and perforated. The choice for domestic use will be from one of these forms in either 'common' for 'facing' grade. *(Fig. 1.)* Common bricks are most

Fig. 1. Forms of brick

suited for interior walls unless they are to be covered by cement rendering or weather boards. Facing bricks, as would be expected, are used where they will be seen, some being faced on all sides. The solid brick can therefore be used showing any of its six faces. Others are faced on the ends and one side only, the facing being a particularly moulded texture or of applied sand. Facing bricks are strong, weather resisting and of a more pleasing appearance than common bricks. Bricks with a frog are laid with the frog uppermost so that it is completely filled with mortar which, when set, keys the brick in place. Perforations serve the same purpose.

Brickwork should be designed and built using the 'nominal' dimensions. That is the 'work size' of the brick plus 10 mm — the thickness of one mortar joint. *(Fig. 2.)*

Bricks are laid in bonded patterns so that no matter what the purpose of the construction vertical joints do not coincide

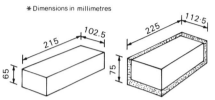

∗ Dimensions in millimetres

Fig. 2. 'Worksize' and 'Nominal dimensions'

either on the face of the wall, or in its thickness. Bonding in this way gives brickwork strength and its characteristic appearance.

Stretcher bond is the most common, but is only suitable for so called 'half-brick' walls. This, and other bonds are illustrated in *Figs. 3(a)*, *(b)* and *(c)*. Practice will be

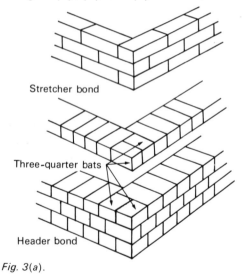

Stretcher bond

Three-quarter bats

Header bond

Fig. 3(a).

necessary in cutting bricks for these bonds and a recommended way is to scratch the line on which the cut is to be made, place the brick on a firm surface and with a bolster or cold chisel and hammer cut out a groove along the line 10–12 mm deep. Careful hammering will be necessary to do

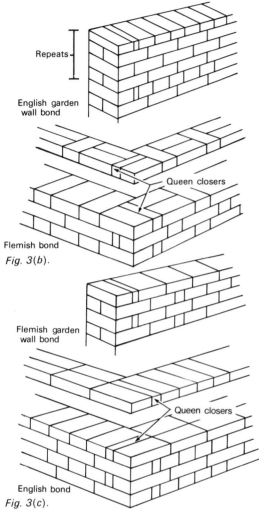

Repeats

English garden wall bond

Queen closers

Flemish bond

Fig. 3(b).

Flemish garden wall bond

Queen closers

English bond

Fig. 3(c).

During building, bricks should be stored on a clean, dry base, and should not be allowed to become saturated by rain before use. Similarly, bags of cement or bags of ready-mixed mortar should be under cover in the garage or garden shed. The mortar mixture should be 1 part cement to 4 parts sand and mixed as described in Chapter 14, Building a Car Port.

The preparation of the foundations for brickwork is important and the setting out must be done with care. The recommended mix for simple work of this nature is 1 part cement : $2\frac{1}{2}$ parts damp sand : 4 parts coarse aggregate, a thickness of 75–100 mm being suitable for light work. It is advisable to take out a trench of sufficient depth to allow for at least an equal thickness of well-rammed hardcore (brick or concrete rubble) to be placed in the bottom of the trench, over which the concrete is laid. This is then levelled and consolidated with a punner — a heavy board set at right angles to a stout shaft. *(Fig. 5.)*

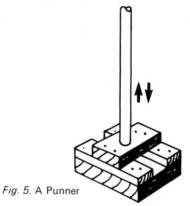

Fig. 5. A Punner

this. Then place the bolster firmly in the groove hitting it hard with the hammer and the brick will part. *(Fig. 4.)*

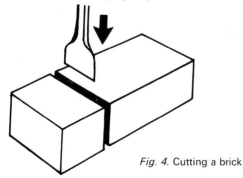

Fig. 4. Cutting a brick

In order to establish the level for the concrete, wooden pegs, which will later be removed, should be driven into the ground at each end of the trench. They should be levelled by spanning them with a straight edge on which the spirit level will stand. If the distance between the pegs is too great for a straight edge, use a hosepipe level. One end of a length of hose is tied to a peg at the required level, and the other end is held near the second peg. The hose is then charged with water and the free end raised or lowered, topping up as required until the water is at the top of the pipe at each end. The level may then be marked on the peg. *(Fig. 6(b).)* This method will work over any distance and also round corners.

Fig. 6(*a*). Levelling with straight edge and spirit level

Level marked

Fig. 6(*b*). Levelling with hosepipe

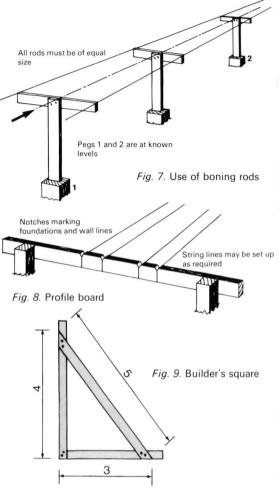

All rods must be of equal size

Pegs 1 and 2 are at known levels

Fig. 7. Use of boning rods

Notches marking foundations and wall lines

String lines may be set up as required

Fig. 8. Profile board

Fig. 9. Builder's square

Where it is necessary to have inter-mediate levelling pegs over a considerable distance, boning rods should be used. These are T shaped and of equal size. It is usual to paint one side of the top member white and the other side black to create a contrast when sighting along them. In use, once the levelling pegs have been posi-tioned at each end, the intermediate peg or pegs are partially driven in, a boning rod held vertically on the top of the two end pegs and the third rod held on the inter-mediate peg. The level of this is then adjusted with the hammer until the tops of all three boning rods are level when sighted from end to end. By this method any number of pegs may be set between the first two, or beyond them. In a similar way pegs may be set to a constant fall. *(Fig. 7.)* When building walls, trenches for the concrete foundations may be marked with pegs to which cross bars are nailed. From these, strings are run from notches indicating foundation and wall lines. *(Fig. 8.)*

A plain slab of concrete may be set out in the following way using string, lines and pegs, tape measure and builders' square. *(Fig. 9.)*

1. Locate one corner – *A* – from a known reference point. This may be an existing building or wall.
2. From *A* peg out first side – line 1.
3. Peg out line 2 at 90 degrees to line 1 using builders' square.
4. Establish *B* along line 1 by measuring, and peg out line 3 at right angles using the builders' square.
5. From *A* and *B* measure along lines 2 and 3 to establish points *C* and *D*, so positioning line 4.
6. Check the lengths of all sides with the tape, and the truth of each corner with the builders' square.
7. Measure the diagonals *AD* and *BC*. These must be equal. *(Fig. 10.)*

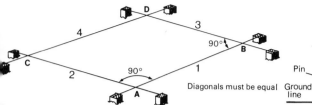
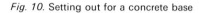

Fig. 10. Setting out for a concrete base

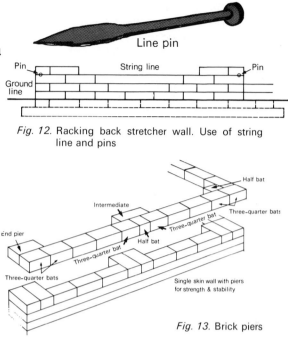

Line pin

Fig. 12. Racking back stretcher wall. Use of string line and pins

Fig. 13. Brick piers

If the setting out is for a small building set on strip foundations, 'profile boards' should be set up straddling the centre line of the walls. These are pairs of pegs with a board nailed across them as in *Fig. 8* which must be sufficiently long for the pegs to be outside the foundation line. Using a string line between temporary pegs as a centre line *(Fig. 10)*, mark the foundation and wall lines on the cross bars and notch them with a saw. The temporary string lines and pegs can be removed but the profile boards are left in position during the construction. String lines are run between the notches as and when required.

For simple work such as this — for garden walls, raised flower beds, etc., it is usual for the foundations to be set one

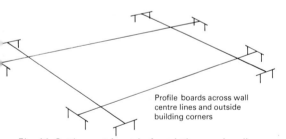

Profile boards across wall centre lines and outside building corners

Fig. 11. Setting out for strip foundations and walls

course of bricks below ground level. The ends or corners are then raised and a string run between them on line pins. This space is then bricked in, and the sequence repeated until the required height is reached. *(Fig. 12.)*

Half-brick walls in stretcher bond should be strengthened by piers at each corner, and if it is of considerable length at intervals of not more than 3 m along the wall. *(Fig. 13.)*

The actual laying of the bricks is not difficult, the first course being laid on a bed of mortar a little thicker than that to be employed later between courses which should then be 10 mm. Laying begins at the corners, the bricks being carefully set true with the wall lines and gently tapped down into position with the handle of the trowel. Before the succeeding bricks are laid, one end should be 'buttered' to make the vertical joint with the previous brick. As successive courses are laid they are racked back towards the corner, that is one brick fewer as in *Fig. 12.* Excess mortar is sliced off with the trowel as each brick is laid and the joint 'pointed'. How this is done has an important effect on the appearance of brickwork. 'Flush' joints are made by cutting the mortar roughly level with the bricks and when partly dry rubbed over with a piece of softwood or sacking to produce a smooth finish, care being taken not to stain the bricks with wet mortar. 'Weather-struck' pointing is formed with the trowel and ensures that the face of the wall drains well. So-called 'bucket-handle' joints are produced by recessing the mortar with metal cut from an old handle. It produces a pleasant shadowing effect. Recessed square pointing is raked out square with a suitable piece of steel or hardwood which produces a deep shadowing effect. This looks very attractive if used with textured bricks but is not suitable for walls subjected to heavy rain. *(Fig. 14.)* If the mortar joint between

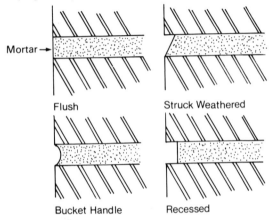

Fig. 14. Methods of Pointing

bricks is subsequently observed to be breaking away it should be 'repointed'. The joint must be raked out to a depth of 10–15 mm and then remade using a mixture of 1 part cement to 2 parts of sand, damping the wall before the mortar is applied.

'Glenstone' bricks are a modern product and are being used extensively for new developments. They are pre-cast from Dolomite limestone and are available in three finishes: Smooth Faced Facing bricks, Split bricks and Pitched Faced

bricks. All types are produced in four colours: Stainton Grey, Charcoal Grey, Golden Buff and Marigold. When building with these bricks it is important to use the correct mortar mix. Should the mortar be too strong this may lead to cracking of the finished work at a later date due to lack of flexibility.

'Marshalite' is a 'reconstructed' walling stone made from hard York stone aggregate. Large slabs are split in the factory into smaller blocks reproducing the rough pitched face typical of dressed natural stone. 'Tudor' stone is a similar 'reconstructed' walling stone manufactured in five colours: York stone, pink, brown, light and dark grey. It has the appearance of natural stone at a fraction of the cost. As each stone is flat bedded it is comparatively easy to erect really beautiful walls, suitable for houses, home extensions, garages, internal or external feature walls or landscape walls. Foundations should be the same as those for brick walls and mortar mixes similar to those for 'Glenstone' bricks. If used for earth-retaining walls — e.g. terracing — drainage holes should be left at 1 m intervals, with piers every 3–4 m for stability. Reconstructed stone may be cut in the same way as bricks.

With the above information to hand the following are suggested projects which the reader may care to design and build.

1. Flower beds and boxes
2. Garden shelf unit to hold seed boxes, young plants, tools, etc.
3. Barbecue unit
4. Bird bath
5. Compost pit
6. Pergola, screen wall and patio.

14 Building a Car Port ~ Plastic Roofing

Somewhat sadly, it was decided at the conclusion of my daughter's final year at her college that the old banger, which had served her faithfully, and at times not so faithfully during the previous three years, would have to go. Success in applying for a business post settled the matter, rapid enquiries were made of local garages and within days a bright new car appeared. Once the excitement of this had died down, serious thought had to be given to where it should be kept. Unlike its predecessor it should not be allowed to suffer the indignities of our climate when not in use. The design of our home precluded a second garage but the concrete area in front of the existing one could possibly be roofed over. It was bounded on one side by the garage and a short wall; to the north by the rear wall of our small outhouses, and to the south by two rather dense holly bushes; the house itself forming part of the fourth side which gives access to the drive. *(Fig. 1.)* If two pillars

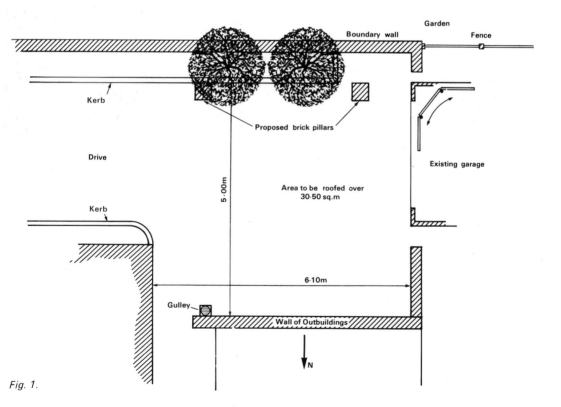

Fig. 1.

a

b

c

d

e

f

g

h

i

j

a. The area to be roofed, bounded on two sides by the garage and the wa
outbuildings. Supporting pillars to be built to the left

b. Timber and bricks delivered, and some tools accumulated

c. By careful measurement the positions of the pillars are marked with chalk.
for the centre reinforcing rods are drilled in the concrete with a rotary percu
drill

d. Mixing the mortar. 1 cement : 4 sand

e. A pillar completed – the ragbolt to secure the cross beam can be seen protr
from the top

f. The cross beam and rafters are positioned

g. Close up view of the pillar, cross beam and rafters

h. All the timber work has been painted and the PVC sheet is being applied

i. Drilling the wall of the outbuilding to secure metal ties by means of rawl

j. Completed – a general view

Sawing
k. The material must be well supported and a small-
▼ toothed saw used, being held at a very low angle

Drilling
l. Again support is essential. The drill should
be ground as for drilling metal and be 3 mm
▼ oversize in diameter

◄

Screwing
m. The recommended screws with plastic washers
and caps must be used. Screw holes must be
made through the crest of the corrugation for
roofing or the bottom of the groove between corrugations for vertical fixing. In the photograph a
foam eaves filler has also been fitted

71

could be erected on the south side a single pitch roof could be constructed, its lower end being supported by the outbuildings. Armed with these thoughts and a plan of the area, various builders' merchants were consulted regarding materials. The span of the roof was considerable and substantial timbers necessary to avoid sagging, if only from their own weight. The additional weight of the battens and cladding, and possibly of snow at times, had also to be considered. It was finally decided that rafters 75 mm thick and 175 mm deep would be sufficiently strong in the lengths required, providing the roofing chosen was not too heavy. Initially it was thought to build the pillars of concrete blocks, but on second thoughts facing bricks, manufactured by the London Brick Co, appeared more suitable and would produce a smaller-sectioned neater construction. The face texture of the bricks would harmonise happily with the existing stonework.

Several possible roofing materials were considered, both flat and corrugated but were rejected on account of weight. Also, as they were not transparent they would have made the car port very gloomy. It was obvious that a light, strong, transparent sheeting was essential, and that ICI's Novolux rigid profiled PVC sheeting would meet these requirements. It is manufactured in sheets of corrugated or box section 762 mm wide, by 1·83 m, 2·44 m and 3·05 m in length. It comes in colours and superclear; bronze tint transparent; yellow tint transparent and opaque deep white. The box section sheeting was rather more pleasing aesthetically and this was eventually chosen in bronze tint. Current Government Building Regulations permit the use of Novolux for any kind of roofing at least 6 m from the boundary of the site, this being regarded as extending to the centre of any street, river or canal butting on to the land. It may also be used for roofing less than 6 m from the boundary for a garage, conservatory or outbuilding so long as the floor area is not more than 40 sq m. This restriction is removed if the roof is for a balcony, veranda, open car port, covered way or swimming pool, whether or not the building is detached. Novolux is self-extinguishing since it ceases burning immediately the source of ignition is removed and also has a low fire rating. It should be remembered that some structures require the approval of the Local Planning Authority under Building and Planning Regulations.

When used for roofing Novolux needs adequate support even though it is extremely resilient, and in normal situations the battens to which it is fastened should be at 610 mm centres. If the situation is very exposed this distance should be reduced to provide additional support. When used for interior or vertical cladding the supports need only be at 1220 mm intervals. Novolux is secured by zinc-plated round-headed screws which are rust resisting. Each screw is fitted with a plastic washer which compresses snugly to the cladding forming a waterproof seal as the screw is tightened. Both are then covered with a weatherproof plastic cap. *(Fig. 2.)* For roofing, the screw is inserted

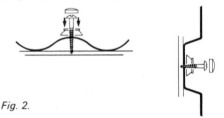

Fig. 2.

through the top of the corrugation and for vertical application through the bottom. In this case there is the added advantage that the screws are protected by the corrugations on each side of them. The recommended spacing of screws for corrugated and box-section sheet is indicated in *Fig. 3*, the sheet being screwed to each sup-

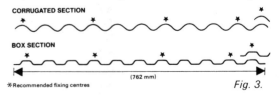

CORRUGATED SECTION

BOX SECTION

(762 mm)

*Recommended fixing centres

Fig. 3.

porting batten. Holes for screws should be made with metalworking twist drills and their diameter should be 3 mm oversize. This is to allow for expansion and contraction of the Novolux as the temperature varies. When drilling, the sheet must be firmly supported underneath to prevent splintering. This also applies when sheets are being cut, for which a very fine-toothed saw is essential. It must be held at a very low angle so that the maximum number of teeth are cutting at any one time. The author found that a pad saw fitted with a hacksaw blade of 32 TPI was ideal. The material is rather more flexible when warm and extra care is necessary when handling it during cold weather. Novolux should not be stacked in direct sunlight as the magnifying glass effect can create discoloration and distortion. If sheets are left in the open they should be laid flat upon battens and covered with tarpaulin.

As the sheets are laid they should always overlap one complete corrugation on each side, taking into account the direction from which the worst weather is experienced. End laps should be at least 150 mm but where the roof pitch is less than 10 degrees, 300 mm is advisable. A pitch of 5 to 10 degrees is recommended so that the sheet remains clear of silt and leaves when washed down with rainwater.

With this information made available from the manufacturer's leaflets, and advice from the merchants, preparations for the car port went ahead with confidence. Timber, bricks, sand and cement were delivered and with the addition of our own clutter of building tools, old buckets and stand steps the work began.

Positioning the pillars and building them had obviously to be done first. Their bases were marked out with chalk on the concrete, taking care that each was the same distance from the wall of the outhouses, and at the same time checking carefully that they were correctly placed with regard to the proposed arrangement of the roofing timbers of which a simple sketch had been made. *(Fig. 4.)* The pillars were to be further reinforced with mild steel rods down

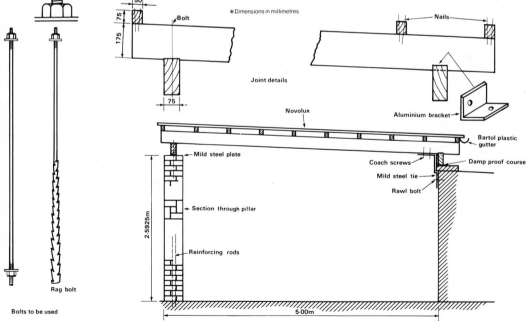

Fig. 4. Section and details of proposed structure

the centre cavity created by the coursing of the bricks, the reinforcements being sunk into the existing concrete to further stabilise the pillar. Holes for this purpose were made quickly and with little effort using a Wolf rotary percussion drill fitted with a suitable masonry bit. Cement was mixed in the proportion of 1 cement : 4 sand and the building of the pillars began.

Mixing the cement must be done carefully to the correct proportions, possibly by the bucketful depending upon the quantity required; the author finding an old ladling can of sufficient volume. The ingredients should be mixed thoroughly with the shovel whilst still dry, spread out slightly and a hollow scooped in the centre to which a little water is added. The mixture is then turned over repeatedly, more water being added from time to time until a working consistency is produced. The mixing should be done on a flat board where necessary to prevent an unsightly patch being left once the work is completed. Masonry cement was chosen on this occasion because of its resilience when set, being less brittle than normal cement. The first course of bricks was laid on a layer of mortar slightly thicker than the following jointing layers. This was to ensure that the bricks bedded firmly to the concrete which had been roughened with a hammer and chisel.

As the base of each pillar was built a simple right-angled triangular frame of wood was used to check verticality, but as the pillars became taller this was done with a builder's spirit level. Periodically the cavity was filled with a rough mix of sand, gravel, broken brick and cement so that the pillar became solid. A simple scaffold of bricks with a plank across and then finally a tall pair of steps were necessary to reach the work as it became higher, and while the last four courses were built up a rag bolt was cemented into the cavity. *(Fig. 4.)* This was to anchor down the beam carrying the main roof timbers. The bricks were laid using the bricklayer's trowel, and

throughout bed joints and vertical joints were maintained at 10 mm. They were weather pointed as the work proceeded. (The reader is referred to Chapter 13, Working in Brick.)

The main timbers for the roof were now prepared. By careful measurement, holes were marked and drilled through the beam for the rag bolts, and notches 25 mm deep cut in the appropriate positions along the edge of the timber selected as the wall plate which would be placed on the wall of the outhouses. Before this was positioned a length of damp-proof coursing was inserted between it and the coping stones of the wall.

The pillars had now had twenty-four hours or so in which to harden, so with the help of a friend the beam was lifted up and dropped neatly over the rag bolts. To give the beam further support on account of its cantilever design a piece of mild steel, suitably drilled and 1 m long by 75 mm × 18 mm in section was placed between it and the top of each pillar. The ends of this were then fixed to the underside of the beam with coach screws. From this stage rapid progress was made, the rafters lifted into place and suitably notched to fit on to the beams between the pillars. *(Fig. 4.)* Each was drilled at this point for its bolt, as was the beam, and bolted into place, the bolts being greased to help to delay rusting. The lower end of each rafter then fitted snugly into the notches in the wall plate. Short lengths of aluminium angle with a 50 mm web were then screwed to the wall plate and to each side of each rafter giving them further support. Battens of 75 mm × 50 mm section were then nailed across the rafters at the recommended spacing to carry the Novolux. Since each batten protruded 800 mm beyond the first and last rafter, a piece of similar section was notched and nailed to their ends completing the upper framework and giving firm support to the cladding. The whole of the timberwork was then painted white to match our existing colour scheme. (See Chapter 5, Exterior Painting and Decorating.) A coloured preservative could have been used as an alternative, but on no account should timbers which are in contact with the cladding be creosoted or staining will occur.

The Novolux was then screwed down as recommended previously without any particular problem arising. It is worth noting that the author found that providing the load was spread by using a wide board across the battens or in some cases a ladder laid along the corrugations, it was possible to kneel on the cladding whilst the next sheet was being applied. Naturally this was not necessary on every occasion and must always be done with care.

As a final note, a plastic eaves filler for use on structures where it is desirable to exclude draughts is available. So too, is a heavy-duty Novolux to suit asbestos, iron or aluminium corrugated sheeting. All types of Novolux are guaranteed for five years against damage which is a direct result of weather conditions, providing the recommended fixing instructions are observed.

The following diagrams indicate how versatile Novolux is, and some of its many possible applications which may be adapted freely to meet your own needs.

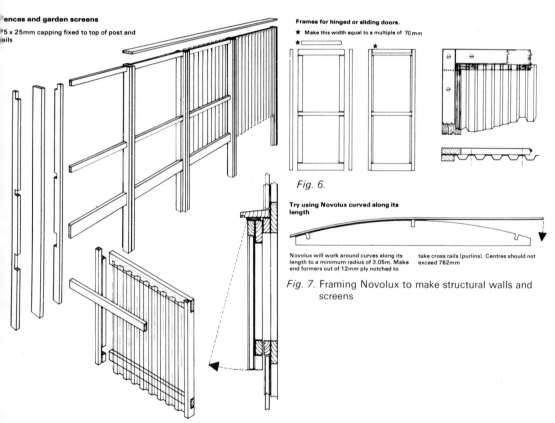

Fences and garden screens

75 x 25mm capping fixed to top of post and rails

Fig. 5. Fences and Garden Screens

Frames for hinged or sliding doors.

★ Make this width equal to a multiple of 70 mm

Fig. 6.

Try using Novolux curved along its length

Novolux will work around curves along its length to a minimum radius of 3.05m. Make end formers out of 12mm ply notched to take cross rails (purlins). Centres should not exceed 762mm

Fig. 7. Framing Novolux to make structural walls and screens

15 Laying Concrete

The Cement and Concrete Association advises that the following tools are common to many concreting jobs. It may well be that you already have many of them, some can be made as required, others will have to be purchased and it is sound advice to buy good quality heavy duty tools as they will last a long time. For example: a light-weight garden wheelbarrow which is ideal for carrying garden refuse is not likely to stand up to shifting loads of concrete for very long.

Steel or linen builder's tape measure — 15 m — for setting out.

Steel pocket tape — 2 m.

Builder's spirit level with vials for level and plumb.

Builder's steel square.

Builder's square made to required size. (See *Fig. 9*, page 66.)

String line and plumb line.

Hand saw, claw hammer for shuttering and other woodwork.

Timber straight edge, length according to the job.

Spade and fork for digging out foundations, footings, etc.

Tamper or garden roller for compacting soil and hardcore.

Square-ended shovels for mixing and handling concrete. One shovel should be retained for cement only if mixing from separate materials.

Heavy duty buckets or other containers for gauging materials (again one should be kept for cement only). All should be the same size — approximately 9 litres is an easy volume to handle.

Banker board (large sheet of plywood or other hard, waterproof material) for hand mixing or receiving loads from a small mixer.

Wheelbarrow for carrying fresh concrete or mortar.

Timber tamping beam for compacting in situ slabs or paving — made up as required.

Punner for compacting concrete in trenched foundations.

Pointed trowel for building with bricks, etc.

Steel trowel, wood float for surface finishing and rendering.

Raking and pointing tools for finishing mortar joints.

For suitable concrete-mix proportions the reader is referred to Chapter 12 and is advised, because of the very hard work involved, to mix only small quantities by hand, when the method is as follows:

1. Measure out coarse aggregate and concreting sand and heap them together.
2. Scoop out a hollow in the top of the pile and add the cement. (Plain Portland.)
3. Mix dry until the whole is a uniform grey colour. (Turning three times from one heap to another is usually enough.)
4. Hollow the top and add a little water.
5. Shovel dry material from the edge to the middle until the water has been absorbed.
6. Repeat until the concrete is thoroughly mixed and just wet

enough to be tamped into position. Too much water will weaken the concrete and too little will make it difficult to tamp down.

Ideally when the top of a pile of newly mixed concrete is tapped with a shovel it should smooth down without watery cement coming to the surface.

If a considerable quantity of concrete is required a small mixer should be hired, the mixing procedure being:

1. Arrange the machine and materials close to hand. Start the machine.
2. Load with coarse aggregate and some water.
3. Add half the sand.
4. Add the cement.
5. Add the remaining sand.
6. During mixing add extra water to produce the right consistency.
7. Run for a further two minutes before emptying.

Care must be taken to run at the correct speed and never to overload the machine, which must be cleaned thoroughly at the end of each day by running a little coarse aggregate and water through it to remove residues.

If even larger quantities are necessary it may be advisable to have ready-mixed concrete delivered to the site.

Laying a path or a drive for yourself is a real economy as the materials are still reasonably cheap, but the cost of labour is high. Although concrete may not be as aesthetically pleasing as some materials it is comparatively easy to lay and is hard wearing. The area to be concreted should be marked out with pegs and string lines (refer to Chapter 13, Working in Brick and Reconstructed Stone) allowing 75 mm each side for the formwork or shuttering. These are boards, held in position by wooden pegs driven into the ground. In turn the boards retain the concrete until it has set. The top soil should be dug away to a depth of 130 mm for paths and 230

mm for drives, or until a firm layer is reached. The bottom of the excavation should be checked for level with a spirit level on a board. Alternatively, if the finished surface is on a gradient, the slope should be checked by holding the level on a board which is tapered to the finished 'fall', i.e. angle of slope. The formwork should now be positioned, the boards being nailed to the pegs so that their top edges are at the height to which the concrete must be. *Fig. 1* gives a general

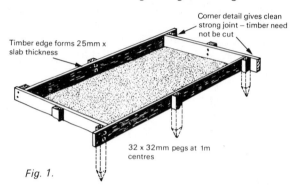

Corner detail gives clean strong joint – timber need not be cut

Timber edge forms 25mm x slab thickness

32 x 32mm pegs at 1m centres

Fig. 1.

indication of how the formwork should be arranged, large areas being divided into smaller bays and curves made with strips of hardboard, extra pegs being required for additional support. Pegs must never extend above the tops of the boards. Hardcore should be shovelled in and consolidated with the end of a heavy piece of timber until just sufficient depth is left below the edge of the boards for the required thickness of concrete – 50 mm for paths and 100 mm for drives. *(Fig. 2.)* It is

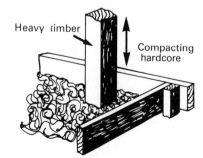

Heavy timber

Compacting hardcore

Fig. 2.

advisable to brush the inside of the form-work with a release agent (your builders' merchant will probably have several varieties) before the concrete is laid. It should be raked and shovelled into place, making sure that corners are completely filled, bringing the level over the whole area to slightly above that of the formwork. The concrete must then be tamped down, a suitable tamper being made from a length of 225 × 50 mm boarding used on edge and fitted with a simple handle at each end. The tamper should extend at least 150 mm beyond the formwork on each side, so that the concrete may firstly be consolidated across its full width by beating down with the tamper and then finally levelled by moving with a sawing motion along the full length of the slab. *(Fig. 3.)*

joint between them using a soft-wood board the full depth of the slab and 10 to 12 mm thick, treated with a suitable preservative. The board should be supported on one side by a length of formwork timber firmly pegged to the sub-base and concreted in level with its top edge. Concrete should also be added to the next bay almost up to the supporting formwork and pegs. These can then be removed and concrete added to complete the joint. The concrete must be compacted thoroughly on each side of the joint board, the resilience of which is sufficient to take up any expansion and contraction of the slab, preventing the development of a crack. *(Fig. 4.)* If the new concrete butts on to a building or an existing slab a joint may be formed between the two with a strip of thick bituminous felt.

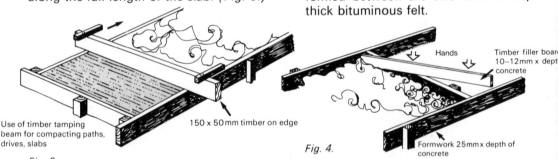

Use of timber tamping beam for compacting paths, drives, slabs

150 x 50mm timber on edge

Fig. 3.

Hands

Timber filler board 10–12mm x depth concrete

Fig. 4.

Formwork 25mm x depth of concrete

Different surface textures may be obtained using soft or hard brooms wooden float, shovel back or steel trowel. The texture in each case will vary depending to what extent the concrete has been allowed to harden, and before the whole surface is treated, experiments should be made at a corner until the desired result is obtained. A so-called 'exposed aggregate' finish can be obtained by washing away the fine material. The surface is wetted with water from a can with a fine rose and then brushed gently.

A one-piece slab should not be much more than 4 m in any direction nor should the length exceed twice the width. In fact, on a large area a length-to-width ratio of $1\frac{1}{2}$ to 1 is safer. If necessary divide the area into two or more slabs of equal size with a

Where the slab is forming a floor which must be dry, a membrane of 1000 gauge plastic sheeting should be laid over the hardcore allowing the edges to come up and over the formwork. Any necessary joints in the plastic sheeting should be double folds of at least 150 mm. If there is any danger of the hardcore piercing the membrane a layer of sand should be used to protect it.

On good level ground the floor slab and foundation for light walls, such as are necessary for a garage, may be combined. The slab should be 100 mm thick increasing to 300 mm over a 300 mm width at the edge. *(Fig. 5.)* Depending upon the length and width of the slab a joint may be necessary about mid-way using a soft-wood board 100 mm × 10 mm.

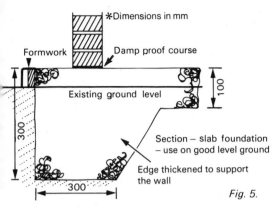

*Dimensions in mm

Formwork

Damp proof course

Existing ground level

300

100

300

Section – slab foundation
– use on good level ground

Edge thickened to support
the wall

Fig. 5.

Where the ground is poor, trench foundations will be needed, 600 mm deep in soft subsoils to 900 mm deep in clay. Pegs driven into the bottom of the trench mark the level of the foundation concrete, the pegs being removed as the concrete is poured. This will be below slab level and

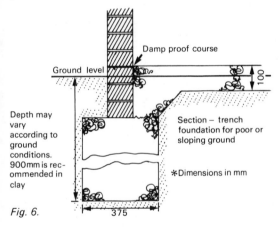

Damp proof course

Ground level

100

Depth may vary according to ground conditions. 900mm is recommended in clay

Section – trench foundation for poor or sloping ground

*Dimensions in mm

Fig. 6.

375

the concrete must be well compacted with a punner. The walls should now be raised to the floor level and after a suitable hardening period of three to four days the floor slab can be laid within the wall as described earlier. *(Fig. 6.)* The walls act as formwork and tamping guides.

Fig. 7.

Repairs to Concrete Paths

If the concrete has cracked, or has been badly chipped at the edges, all loose material should be chopped away with hammer and chisel, and, if necessary, extra hardcore should be added where the repair is to be made. Cracks may have to be chiselled out to a sufficient width to allow for the necessary mortar. Where possible simple formwork should be erected to contain the new material. *(Fig. 7.)* The prepared edges should now be coated with Uni-bond and when this is tacky the repair made with a mix as indicated in Chapter 12, its surface being finished to match the existing concrete. Any formwork should be left in place for several days and then carefully removed to avoid damage to the repair.

16 Screen Walling

Work of this kind is now almost invariably done with 'precast concrete' products which are made at a precasting works under conditions of strict quality control. Skilled workmanship ensures that the items are produced with care and that the 'curing' of the concrete is done efficiently.

Screen Walling

There are many styles of open-pattern blocks which are used for screen walling. Those in *Fig. 1* are typical designs having

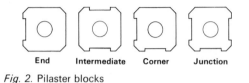

End Intermediate Corner Junction

Fig. 2. Pilaster blocks

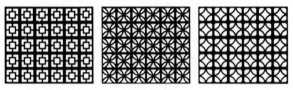

Fig. 1. 'Super Screen' walling blocks

numerous applications in the home or garden, and may be used for garden walls, to screen the patio or vegetable garden or for a car port. The open pattern provides an excellent screen, but allows the light through, avoiding the closed-in feeling of the traditional solid wall. They may be of grey or white cement, but white is particularly attractive and is quite suitable for interior use also. Standard size of block is 290 × 290 × 90 mm and average 105–130 per tonne depending upon pattern. Pilaster blocks are available to give additional support to screen walls and are manufactured with slots to fit the screen units. One slot for end pilasters, two for intermediate or corner use and three for a right-angled junction. *(Fig. 2.)* Three pilasters fit two courses of screen walling to give correct

bonding. Half pilasters, coping and pilaster caps are available for finishing off the wall. *(Fig. 3.)*

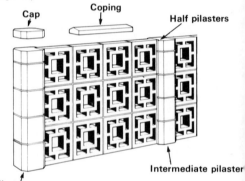

Cap Coping Half pilasters

End pilasters

Intermediate pilaster

Fig. 3. A typical arrangement

To wall with screening blocks a concrete foundation at least 200 mm wide and of a minimum thickness of 100 mm depending on ground conditions is required. This should be laid over a good layer of rubble, the mixture being 1 part Portland cement : $2\frac{1}{2}$ parts damp sand : 4 parts coarse aggregate. Some manufacturers suggest that to obtain an even more attractive appearance one or two courses of 'reconstructed stone' are laid before commencing with the screen walling blocks.

The truth of each course must be checked carefully with a spirit level, the mortar joints both horizontal and vertical being 10 mm thick.

Pilaster supports should be constructed for stability every 3 to $4\frac{1}{2}$ m depending upon the height of the wall. Vertical reinforcement of the pilaster blocks may be achieved by inserting a mild-steel bar extending into the foundations, then filling with weak concrete. Expanded metal reinforcement may be used, hidden in the joints for additional strength to long walls. *(Fig. 4.)* The mortar mix should be workable but not sloppy as it is important to

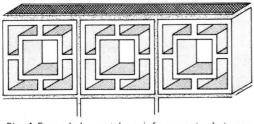

Fig. 4. Expanded metal reinforcement between courses

avoid spillage on the face of the block, and for this reason it is advisable not to build when it is raining. Recommended mix for mortar is 1 part masonry cement : $4/4\frac{1}{2}$ parts sand.

Slab Paving

Flags of natural riven stone were originally used for this purpose but increasing costs of material and labour have led to the almost universal use of precast concrete or cast stone paving slabs in their place. Manufactured to a high specification, the quality and uniformity of size of these man-made products makes the work of laying them so very much easier. 'Pennine Paving', for example, is unique with its attractive quarried face finish which simulates the surface texture of natural riven York stone. It is a versatile paving which may be used for paths, terraces, patios, pergolas, pool surrounds, etc. Four colours are available – brick red, light buff, light green and York brown – each in four sizes based on a module of approximately 230 mm square. *(Fig. 5.)* All are 38 mm thick and the paving weighs approximately

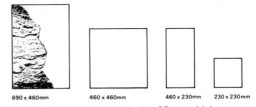

690 x 460mm   460 x 460mm   460 x 230mm   230 x 230mm

Fig. 5. Four colours – each size 38 mm thick

15 sq m per tonne. By using a combination of these sizes and colours a variety of patterns can be achieved. *(Fig. 6.)*

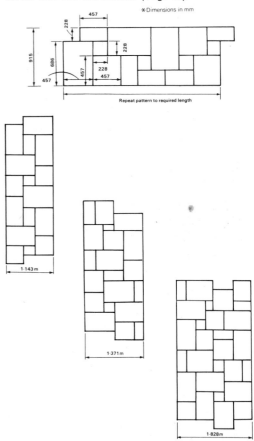

Fig. 6. Some examples of typical laying patterns

For areas which are only to be walked on, the foundations may be granular soil, sand or fine granular material which has been well compacted. The area to be laid should first be marked out with pegs and string, then excavated to the required level.

(Fig. 7.) Graded hardcore, or ashes can then be used to cover the base. *(Fig. 8.)*

Fig. 7. Digging out for paving foundations

Fig. 8. Adding hardcore

Fig. 9. Laying paving

The paving can then be laid directly on to a bed of sand, or if it is to carry heavy lawn mowers or wheelbarrows, it is advisable to lay the paving on a cement mortar bed spread evenly over the foundations to a depth of 25/38 mm, or by the traditional method of using a spot of mortar in each corner and one in the centre of each slab. When using a mortar bedding lay the mortar in position and tamp the paving down to the required level with a wooden trowel-handle or a piece of wood, making sure the paving does not rock. The mortar mix should be 1 part cement to 5 parts sand and not too wet. *(Fig. 9.)* It is not necessary to fill the joints as the paving has tapered sides and each slab should be butt

Fig. 10. Concrete in the garden

jointed at the base. Care should be taken to keep any mortar off the surface of the paving as this can leave a stain. A spirit level and straight edge should always be used to check the level of the paving. Cleaning should be done periodically every three to four months, using a stiff brush to scrub the whole surface with a mild detergent solution, washing off with plenty of clean water. The use of salt for the removal of snow and ice should be avoided. *(Fig. 10.)*

Stepping Stones

This is a further use for this pattern of paving. Produced as discs of 305, 380 and 460 mm diameter × 38 mm thick and available in red, green and buff they are both an attractive and functional item in the garden. The face has the natural quarried finish and this combined with the colour provides a pleasant and servicable path. If bedded in the lawn they should be set just below the mowing surface. *(Fig. 11.)*

Fig. 11. Stepping stones in a lawn

17 Macadam Drives and Paths

Resurfacing is now within anyone's scope. Three easy, quick DIY methods are available using Colas Path and Drive Emulsion, a brown bitumen solution which turns black as it sets. It is used as a 'tack' coat to bind the new surface to the old. The simplest method is 'surface dressing' — spreading chippings evenly over a base coat of the emulsion. Three colours of chippings are available — pink, green and grey-white and are supplied in 25 kg sacks, sufficient to dress approximately 3 sq m. The emulsion should be spread on to previous macadam surfaces at the rate of 4·5 litres to 3 sq m from a watering can with a spoon attached as a spreader. *(Fig. 1.)*

Fig. 1. Spreader

Wall grates, manhole covers, etc., should be masked; the emulsion brushed out lightly into an even film with a stiff-bristled broom always in one direction. Limited areas of 8–9 sq m should be treated at one time, the chippings being applied immediately so that they settle into the emulsion. The surface should now be rolled thoroughly with a garden roller, and with advantage twenty-four hours later, when any loose chippings should be lightly swept off and retained for future use. The overall appearance of the surface will then be that of the chippings.

The second method is resurfacing with macadam, a 25 kg sack covering approximately 1 sq m. Emulsion should be applied only to concrete or loose gravel, and is not necessary on previously macadamed areas. The Colascrete should be raked out to 19 mm thick — blocks of wood placed at intervals will help to determine the correct thickness — which will then compact by rolling to 13 mm. Before rolling, the surface may be 'tamped' with a board as for concreting to ensure even thickness. Rolling should be thorough and in several directions, keeping the roller wet to prevent the macadam adhering to it.

The surface appearance is enhanced by finally rolling in a light scattering of white marble chippings which are supplied in each sack.

Method number three is to apply Colas Carpet, an instant roll-out surfacing. This is a roll of fine 3 mm bitumen-coated chippings embedded in a high-strength fibre and bitumen backing, one roll of which will cover 4·1 sq m. A 'tack coat' of emulsion should be applied and after about thirty minutes the carpet may be laid on it and trodden down. A roller is not really essential unless the carpet is being laid on concrete indoors, say in a garage, where a tack coat may take a long time to set. It may be cut with a knife where fitting is necessary, and where lengths join it is better that they should butt rather than overlap.

The surface is hardwearing and will withstand considerable usage by foot and light traffic. It is an excellent non-skid surface if applied to concrete steps, etc.

Preparation for all methods is virtually the same. Levelling is most important, cracks and depressions in the old surface should be made good with 'tack' coat and infilling of macadam. Dust and other debris must be swept from the surface, weeds and grass removed and further growth prevented by dressing with a weed killer. The work should be done on a fine, drying day when the surface is free from moisture, and the tools required are simple and minimal. A roller, a rake, a length or two of board, an old stiff broom, a watering can and the odd bucket to collect loose chippings are probably all you will need.

18 Asbestos

Quite recently considerable publicity has been given to the danger to health of inhaling asbestos fibres.

Asbestos is a mineral fibre, unique in that it combines tensile strength and flexibility with resistance to fire, heat and corrosion. It is largely the fibrous nature of asbestos which gives it these properties. Unfortunately it is this fibrous nature which may cause disease if excessive dust is created. Research has revealed no evidence that swallowing fibre causes disease.

The principal types of asbestos are chrysotile (white), amosite (grey or brown in colour) and crocidolite (blue). As a result of inhaling substantial concentrations of airborne asbestos dust over a period of time, asbestosis may develop. This lung condition may develop into lung cancer, a liability which appears to be increased by cigarette smoking. The third disease is mesothelioma a rare form of malignant tumour affecting the lining of the chest or abdominal cavities. Many experts believe that mesothelioma is caused by 'blue' asbestos rather than 'white'. Specific regulations applying to any processes which give rise to dangerous amounts of dust were formulated in 1969, and in 1970 British manufacturers imposed a voluntary ban on the import of blue fibre.

So far as is known, nobody has contracted disease as a result of using asbestos-based products in the home or through home craftsmanship. It appears very unlikely for the home craftsman that harmful quantities of dust will escape in their normal use. Asbestos cement is one of the safest of all asbestos products. The sheets and pipes into which it is made present in themselves no health hazard, and are seven-eighths cement to one-eighth asbestos reinforcement. When in situ or being handled they do not present any danger.

Asbestos insulation board is an excellent form for fire protection as well as being an insulation. It is now always dust suppressed before leaving the factory, but in use it is sensible to cover any exposed surfaces with emulsion paint or size.

There are a few simple rules for the home craftsman to follow.

1. Damp the work with water. Wet dust does not become airborne and is not inhaled. For example, if scraping or wire-brushing asbestos products they should be damped. Nor should wall-plugging compounds be sanded unless damped.
2. Damp any dust which falls to the floor and pick it up as soon as possible by vacuum cleaner with disposable filter bag. Place it in a plastic bag and seal securely. It should then be marked *poisonous* for special waste disposal by the authorities.
3. Work in a well-ventilated space, if possible out of doors, when sawing, drilling, filing or sanding.
4. Use handsaws and hand drills, which produce less dust than power tools.

For paints suitable for use on asbestos-cement products the reader is referred to Chapter 5.

Further information with regard to the safe use of asbestos, or information regarding specific problems may be had from The Asbestos Information Committee, 2, Old Burlington Street, London W1X 2LH, or The Secretary, Environmental Control Committee, Asbestos Research Council, PO Box 18, Cleckheaton, West Yorkshire BD19 3UU.

19 Insulation

Although some insulation of the house is, of necessity, done from inside, much can be done externally. Cavity wall insulation is a job for the professional contractor, but draughts from around ill-fitting doors and windows account for considerable loss of heat. Cracks in the seal between door or window frames and the outer wall, allow cold air to penetrate into the wall with cooling effects. Rainwater too can find its way through these cracks causing further cooling, and also to the detriment of the woodwork and possibly the interior decoration. Such cracks can be effectively sealed with exterior Woodflex Polyfilla. This is a ready-mixed filler formulated for use outside the house and is particularly suited for filling round wood, but may be used on all outdoor surfaces. All loose material must be removed and the filler is then pressed into the crack with a suitable putty knife. *(Fig. 1.)* It should be smoothed

Fig. 1. Use of Woodflex Polyfilla

off carefully and when dry can be painted in the normal way. Draughts from around the outer door can be prevented by the use of self-adhesive PVC foam or rigid PVC strip. Polycell foam draught-excluder strip is 'skinned' on its outer surface, making it easy to clean and should be applied around the inside of the rebate of the door frame. Before application the woodwork should be wiped down with a damp cloth to remove all dust and then allowed to dry off so that positive adhesion is obtained. *(Fig. 2.)* With care PVC foam may also be

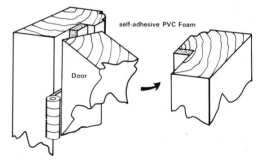

Fig. 2. Applying self-adhesive foam round a door frame

used round windows where appropriate. It is particularly effective when used below the bottom frame and above the top frame of sliding sash windows. If any gaps being sealed are particularly big a double layer may be used.

Draughts below a door which has been hung high, perhaps to clear a carpet, are particularly searching, and a draught excluder should be fitted, screwed either to the back of the door, or to the floor below it. These are available from merchants and DIY shops. *Fig. 3* indicates the principle upon which they work.

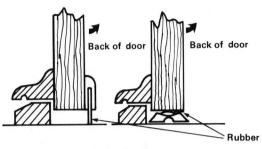

Fig. 3. Draught excluders for doors

Double glazing is the only effective way to stop all draughts from windows and at the same time conserve heat. Vacuum-sealed double glazing units are factory made and are expensive, and it is questionable whether they are a worthwhile proposition for the owners of old property, particularly where sash windows are fitted. Although considerable heat loss will be prevented through the glass, draughts around the frame will persist. Even in a new house, unless double glazing has already been fitted as standard, the practical householder would be well advised to consider either applying a second pane of glass to the existing sash, or frame in the case of a casement window. Sash windows differ slightly in construction and some difficulty may be experienced in fitting the necessary rebated frames to the sashes, particularly at the bottom. It may be found better to chisel out a rebate and set the glass into this. (Fig. 4.) Care is necessary to ensure that the sashes will still slide, and because of this it is necessary to put the second pane on the outside of the top sash, in which case it must be carefully weatherproofed. Sliding sash or casement windows provided with this form of double glazing are not vacuum sealed and are therefore liable to condensation. To some extent this may be overcome by drilling air holes, 13 to 16 mm in diameter through the bottom rails to

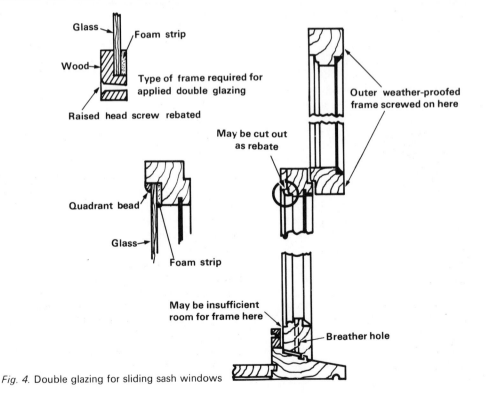

Fig. 4. Double glazing for sliding sash windows

provide ventilation, but this reduces efficiency due to the movement of air. If these holes are plugged lightly with a little glass wool (i.e. insulation material) dust and insects will be excluded. A further disadvantage, however, is that because of the extra panes, heavier counterweights may be required. Casement windows may be dealt with in much the same way, presenting fewer problems because the windows are hinged. Brass screws should be used throughout to avoid corrosion.

There are available on the market a number of DIY kits in aluminium or plastic. The latest one produced by Polycell in white matt-finished rigid PVC is particularly worthy of note. It is designed for sliding sash windows up to 1440 mm high and 1220 mm wide. The tracking can be fitted either to the inside of the window recess, that is to the casing, or to the face of the window frame itself. In either case each has to be at least 42 mm wide.

An an alternative to these applied frames, completely separate grooved frames for sliding panes may be set within the window space away from the existing frame. These have the advantage of providing some insulation against sound and also of effectively sealing off all draughts. And any tendency there may be for condensation may be overcome by placing a small bag of silica gel between the two. *(Fig. 5.)*

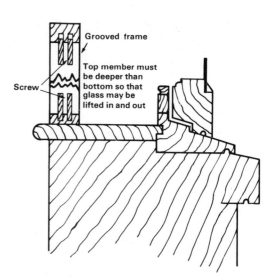

Fig. 5. Fitting separate ploughed frame for sliding panes

The actual style and design of double glazing decided upon will vary from house to house, depending upon requirements. It is a topic which provides scope for ingenuity and can be very worth while.

Approximately 10 mm between glass will provide good heat insulation if the air is still. With a gap of approximately 100 mm, moderate heat insulation and some sound insulation is provided.

For areas up to 1 sq m, glass of 3 mm thickness is sufficient; up to 2 sq m use 4 mm glass, and above this 6 mm float glass.

20 British Standards

The following British Standards will provide further information on many of the topics included in this book.

BS 743 : 1970.   Materials for damp-proof courses.

CP 102 : 1973.   Protection of buildings against water from the ground.

CP 112 : Part 2: 1971.   The structural use of timber.

CP 121 : Part 1: 1973.   Brick and block masonry.

BS 493 : Part 2: 1970.   Airbricks and gratings for wall ventillation.

CP 152 : 1972.   Glazing and fixing of glass for buildings.

BS 990 : Part 2: 1972.   Steel windows generally for domestic and similar buildings.

BS 4873 : 1972.   Aluminium-alloy windows.

BS 644 : Parts 1 and 2.   Wood casement/Double-hung sash.

CP 151 : Part 1: 1957.   Wooden doors.

BS 459 : Part 1 : 1954.   Panelled and glazed wood doors.

Part 2: 1962.   Flush doors.

Part 4: 1965.   Match-boarded doors.

BS 1567 : 1953.   Wood door frames and linings.

CP 142 : Part 2: 1971.   Slating and tiling.

CP 231 : 1966.   Painting of buildings.

CP 308 : 1974.   Drainage of roofs and paved areas.

BS 460 : 1964.   Cast-iron rainwater goods.

BS 4576 : Part 1.   Unplasticised PVC rain-water goods.

BS 4514 : 1969.   Unplasticised PVC soil and ventilating pipe, fittings and accessories.

BS 5255 : 1976.   Plastic waste pipe and fittings.

CP 301 : 1971.   Building drainage.

CP 302.200 : 1949.   Cesspools.

CP 2005 : 1968.   Sewerage.

BS 2760 : 1973.   Pitch-impregnated fibre pipes and fittings for below and above ground drainage.

BS 3656 : 1973.   Asbestos-cement pipes, joints and fittings for sewerage and drainage.

BS 6 and 540.   Clay drain and sewer pipes.

BS 1722 – Eleven parts – Fences.

BS 368 : 1971.   Precast stone flags.

BS 2028, 1364 : 1968.   Precast concrete blocks.

BS 3921 : 1974.   Clay bricks and blocks.

BS 680 : Part 2: 1971.   Roofing slates.

BS 473, 550 : Part 2.   Concrete roofing tiles and fittings.

BS 4203 : 1967.   Extruded rigid PVC corrugated sheeting.

BS 1331 : 1954.   Builder's hardware for housing.

BS 1926 : 1962.   Ready mixed concrete.

CP 98 : 1964.   Preservative treatments for constructional timber.

BS 2015 : 1965.   Glossary of paint terms.

BS 3827 – Four parts – Glossary of terms relating to builders' hardware.

Fig. 1. This terrace is protected from the elements by a roof of profiled PVC sheeting

Figs. 2 and 3. The basic electric drill can be used with different attachments to carry out a variety of maintenance and repair jobs (see pp. 29-33)

Fig. 4. The high gloss finish on this door is the result of careful preparation (see pp. 31-40)

Fig. 5. Another use for profiled PVC sheeting (see Chapter 14, Part 1)

Fig. 6. Making preparations for laying a stepped concrete path

Fig. 7. An attractive modern terrace. Screen walling provides reasonable privacy without the 'shutting-in' disadvantage of a solid wall (see pp. 80-82)

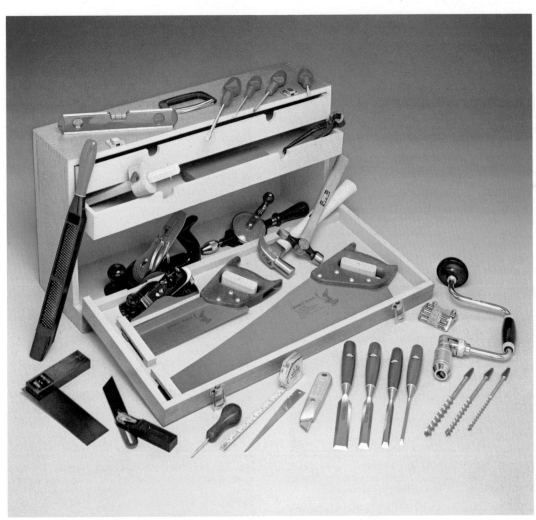

Fig 8. A suggested basic tool kit for home woodworkers

USING A SAW

Fig. 9. Use a sawing board (sometimes called a bench hook) to hold timber securely as it is sawn. This protects both the worker and the bench. Note the correct grip on the saw and timber

Fig. 10. Work is held low in the vice to avoid vibrations which would cause the saw to 'jump' from the work. The saw cut should be vertical

Fig. 11. NEVER attempt to stop vibration by supporting the work with your hand. If the saw slips out of control it will saw into your flesh

USING A CHISEL

Fig. 12. Both hands holding the chisel are safely behind the cutting edge, with the elbow supported on the bench. This gives extra control to the chisel movement. Use only tools which have been correctly designed and have comfortable handles

Fig. 13. For this operation work is held flat on a clean board to avoid damage to the bench surface. Both hands grip the chisel correctly. The lower hand also steadies the wood. The body is in a position to give pressure from the shoulder

◀ NEVER DO THIS

USING A CHISEL

Fig. 14. For some operations, work should be held securely on a solid part of the bench. For safety, use cramps for securing the work whenever possible. Use a mallet for striking chisels, never a hammer, as this may cause damage to the handle. This then becomes uncomfortable and unsafe to use

NEVER DO THIS ▲

Fig. 15. NEVER fix a cramp in the way. The tail of the cramp could cause serious face or eye damage to the operator as he/she bends forward to examine the work

SCREWDRIVERS

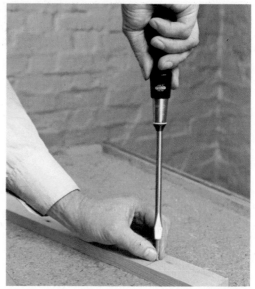

Fig. 16. Select the correct screwdriver for a screw. Drill the correct sized clearance and pilot holes for ease of entry. Using the wrong sized screwdriver causes sharp metal splinters to be left standing along the slot. These can cause either very nasty cuts or metal splinters in the flesh

Fig. 17. Using a hand drill

Fig. 18. A bench holdfast is useful for awkardly-shaped pieces of work that cannot easily be held in the vice

Fig. 19. 'G' cramps being used to hold a piece of work while the joint sets. Notice the small pieces of scrap wood that are placed under each face of the cramp to protect the work from damage

INVEST IN LIVING

Part II

WOODWORKING

by

Roy W. Draycon

Introduction

This section is primarily aimed at the young couple setting up home for the first time. It clearly describes materials, tools and techniques fundamental to home improvements, from such simple additions as shelving, through kitchen units to full room conversions. It is profusely illustrated and, throughout, relies on traditionally sound and technically correct procedures while utilising the latest materials, tools and accessories available for making even quite large projects comparatively simple for the amateur to carry out. Background information helps the reader to understand the nature of the materials and tools he is using, and an extensive Resources and Bibliography section encourages him to extend his skills and knowledge.

About the Author

Roy Draycon has devoted a long professional career to many aspects of design, craftwork and both internal and external carpentry, joinery and household conversions. While in the service of the Home Office for seventeen years, he organised courses in building, carpentry, joinery and cabinet-making.

He is a Fellow of the College of Craft Education and from 1968 to 1972, while in the service of the Inner London Education Authority, acted in an advisory capacity in Craft and Technical projects.

He also organised projects for young adolescents in some of the more deprived areas of London, in which old houses had their large rooms subdivided in order to accommodate families in more dignified conditions. Kitchens were redesigned and equipped with cupboards and storage areas and old floors etc. were restored to safe and hygienic conditions.

More recently, while in the service of the Northamptonshire County Council, he worked with young adolescent students on the conversion of obsolete double-decker buses into mobile play schools for the under-fives.

While with the Northampton Authority he also made teaching films showing boys and girls using man-made materials in the construction of household furniture and equipment, and these films are now widely used in Upper Schools and Colleges of Further Education.

Roy Draycon is particularly interested in all aspects of design in the home and in the problems of young people setting up home for the first time.

1 Basic Requirements

Recommended kit of hand tools. Suggestions for additional equipment for the more enthusiastic and experienced operator. Power tools. Advice on the selection and purchase of tools and equipment.

Most boys, and an increasing number of girls, have had some experience of woodworking during their schooldays and a very high proportion of them have enjoyed the time spent in this creative activity.

There is, however, at the present time, a further spur to the continuing development of these skills. Home repairs, the construction of simple furniture and units, the redesigning and conversion of kitchens, bathrooms, lofts, etc., even such simple things as the putting up of shelving, all now cost a small fortune if the professional is called in. So the day of the 'Do-it-Yourself' amateur is here and here to stay, well into the foreseeable future.

However, even if, by adopting DIY methods, you eliminate the high cost of labour, you are still faced with rapidly rising costs in the fields of timber, tools and equipment, so it is obvious that, in your own financial interests, you must develop your skills so that tools are used to their best advantage and all waste of materials is reduced to the absolute minimum. Tools have been highly developed over, in some cases, hundreds of years and, as with most things, there is a right and a wrong way of going about using them. Correct choice of materials and equipment is very important if your work is to prove efficient and economically viable.

Modern technology has developed many new materials, greatly increased the range and efficiency of tools, including portable electrical equipment, and advanced enormously the variety and efficiency of adhesives, finishes and accessories. This book sets out to help the amateur, of either sex, to take advantage of all these modern developments in a way which will save money, encourage pride in achievement, result in good, practical constructions and, it is hoped, stimulate the reader to develop his or her skills into a satisfying hobby.

Individual requirements, personal skills, economic conditions, physical circumstances and time available will all vary considerably from person to person but the book has been laid out to cater for all of those wishing to tackle the widest possible variety of jobs in the home.

Above all, make haste slowly! The acquisition of skill is a slow, progressive and methodical exercise. Never was the maxim more haste, less speed' better exemplified than in the art, craft and science of woodworking.

The best possible advice to the amateur contemplating the purchase of a kit of tools is simple and categorical: buy the best tools that you can afford, even if this means purchasing a very basic minimum. You can always add to this basic kit as experience and available cash make possible. A larger kit of cheap tools would lead to nothing but disappointment and frustration, particularly in the case of edged tools such as saws, chisels, planes, knives, scrapers and spokeshaves, which would not retain their sharpness. It cannot be stressed too often, or too vehemently, that blunt tools are dangerous tools. Sharp tools require far less effort in their manipulation and, in consequence, are far more controllable and hence safer.

Buy branded tools from well-known manufacturers; after-sales service on these far outweighs the heavier initial cost. Spare parts are more likely to be available and most of the better manufacturers run an advice service (see p. 166) which can be of considerable help. Assuming, therefore, a strictly limited budget, the following is a practical, basic kit with which the home woodworker could commence his activities.

Minimum Basic Kit

● 1 general purpose saw. This will cut wood, man-made boards, plastics and quite a few of the softer metals such as aluminium.

● 1 250 mm (10 in) tenon saw. Very useful in joinery.

● 1 smoothing plane (metal). Approximately 250 mm (10 in) long with a 50 mm (2 in) width blade. Since most wood for the amateur will be purchased 'planed all round', no larger plane would be necessary at this stage.

● 1450 g (16 oz) claw hammer. A good general purpose tool that will drive in and extract nails.

● 1 150 mm (6 in) screwdriver, preferably with a plastic (insulated) handle.

● 1 portable vice of the type that could be fixed by clamp to the kitchen table or bench, if one is available (fig. 1).

● 1 150 mm (6 in) try-square. Essential for

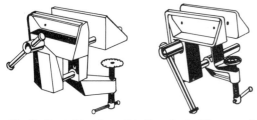

Fig. 1. Portable vice Excellent for holding wood and may be fixed to kitchen table or workbench. Two practical types are illustrated

'squaring' sides, ends and edges and for accurate 'marking out'.

● 1 2 m (6 ft) flexible metal tape rule: useful for all household measurements.

● 1 'Trimming Knife'. This is a multi-purpose tool which is useful for accurate marking out of joints and for a wide range of cutting jobs.

● 1 pair pincers, 180 mm (7 in).

● 1 nail punch.

● 1 'Surform' tool (flat).

● 1 'Surform' tool (half round).

● 1 hand drill capable of taking parallel shank drills up to 8 mm ($\frac{5}{16}$ in) diameter.

● 1 set of parallel shank drills: 3 mm, 4 mm, 6 mm and 8 mm diameters ($\frac{1}{8}$, $\frac{1}{6}$, $\frac{1}{4}$ and $\frac{1}{3}$ in).

● 1 set of bevelled-edged chisels: 6 mm, 12 mm and 18 mm blade width ($\frac{1}{4}$, $\frac{1}{2}$ and $\frac{3}{4}$ in).

● 1 wooden mallet (carpenter's, **not** carver's).

● 1 marking gauge.

● 1 combination oil stone (one side Coarse and one side Medium Grit) for sharpening plane blades, chisels and knives.

● 1 cabinet maker's scraper.

The cost of this basic kit will vary according to the circumstances of purchase: sometimes special offers on certain items can reduce the normal retail prices and you can occasionally be lucky enough to pick up a complete set of tools quite inexpensively through the second-hand columns in your local press – but be careful in such a circumstance to inspect the items carefully and to check for well-known brand names. Assuming, however, that you purchase the entire kit from your local tool merchant, at around 1980 prices you could expect to pay approximately £65.00.

Given a basic kit of this type, you will be able to carry out quite a wide range of operations but there will always be the occasion when special tools will have to be acquired in order to complete particular operations. These may be bought separately as required or, with luck, borrowed, but you may find that your local supplier operates a deposit/loan system on a wide range of specialist tools.

The most likely additions to your basic kit will be drills of different sizes, a smaller chisel (3 mm $-\frac{1}{8}$ in) and some form of saw for cutting round curved lines, such as a coping saw, padsaw, compass saw or the old-fashioned bowsaw (fig. 2).

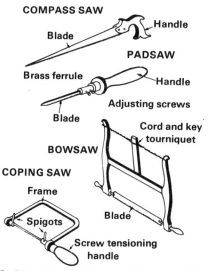

COMPASS SAW

PADSAW

BOWSAW

COPING SAW

Fig. 2. Saws for sawing round curves   A bowsaw is used for large curves in thick material; a coping saw will tackle tight curves and is better on thin material; a compass saw is used for internal curves of large radius; a padsaw (keyhole saw) is used on small internal radii

Growing enthusiasm, increased experience and mounting skill may lead you on to more advanced work, requiring additional tools and equipment. You can widen your scope very considerably by adding the following to your basic kit:

● 1 'G' cramp (150 mm; 6 in) (fig. 3).
● 1 sash cramp (1 m; 3 ft) (fig. 3).
● 1 ratchet brace, for holding bits (fig. 4).
● 1 set of centre bits for boring holes in thin wood – 10 mm ($\frac{2}{5}$ in), 12 mm ($\frac{1}{2}$ in), 15 mm ($\frac{3}{5}$ in), 18 mm ($\frac{3}{4}$ in) and 25 mm (1 in) diameter (fig. 4).
● 1 set of twist bits for boring deep holes in wood – 10 mm ($\frac{2}{5}$ in), 12 mm ($\frac{1}{2}$ in), 15 mm ($\frac{3}{5}$ in), 18 mm ($\frac{3}{4}$ in) and 25 mm (1 in) diameter (fig. 4).

● 1 rose countersink bit (12 mm; $\frac{1}{2}$ in).
● 1 mortice gauge (fig. 5).
● 1 set of mortice chisels – 6 mm ($\frac{1}{4}$ in), 9 mm ($\frac{3}{8}$ in) and 12 mm ($\frac{1}{2}$ in) blade width (fig. 6).
● 1 panel or hand saw (500 mm; 20 in) for cutting panels of plywood or hardboard among a wide range of other sawing duties.

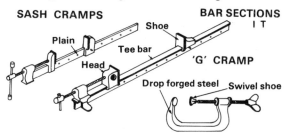

Fig. 3. Cramps   Sash cramps are used for cramping up frames and carcases. 'G' cramps are used for holding wood to the bench or holding small pieces of wood together

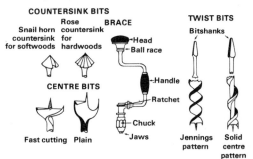

Fig. 4. Brace and bits   Centre bits are used for holes in thin wood, twist bits for deep holes, and countersink bits for cutting depressions to accommodate screw heads

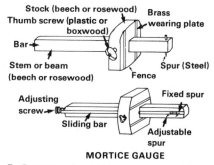

Fig. 5. Gauges   A marking gauge is used for marking single lines, and a mortice gauge for marking twin parallel lines in the direction of the grain

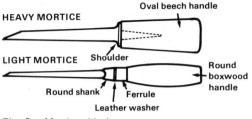

HEAVY MORTICE

Oval beech handle

LIGHT MORTICE   Shoulder

Round shank   Ferrule

Round boxwood handle

Leather washer

Fig. 6. Mortice chisels

The cost of this additional equipment, at 1980 prices, would be of the order of £40.00.

To widen still further your range of activities, and to increase your speed of working, with a reduction of physical effort, you may wish to consider adding to your hand tools by purchasing a power drill. You may buy one of these when economics allow, or you may suggest that they might form birthday or Christmas gifts from friends or relations. Such drills (fig. 7) have a wide variety of uses and many attachments may be purchased to increase still further the range of activities, including sanding, buffing, sawing and shaping. The most popular chuck sizes are 6 mm, 9 mm and 12 mm ($\frac{1}{4}$ in, $\frac{3}{8}$ in and $\frac{1}{2}$ in). Most

Fig. 7. Portable electric drill, single speed or two-speed

attachments are designed for use with the 6 mm size. If you are contemplating using your portable drill on masonry you will need special masonry drills and you would be well advised to purchase a two-speed drill at a little extra cost.

Your portable drill will accommodate a sander disc attachment (fig. 8) and these can be very helpful for removing old paint from flat surfaces, but before they can be used without leaving circular 'scores' on your work you would do well to practise

Fig. 8. A sander disc attachment The stem fits into the chuck of the portable drill. A rubber disc forms the base for sanding and buffing

on less important areas until you have acquired the necessary skill in manipulation.

Your second choice of a power tool could well be the sabre saw (fig. 9). This is a very useful tool indeed, since it can make the type of cuts no other saw can make. For this reason alone it deserves a high priority on your list of power tools. In principle it is a 'jig-saw'; these have a rapid

Fig. 9. A tilting base sabre saw

up-and-down motion. They have a range of blades, easily replaceable, giving an assortment of cuts. It will cut wood, metal and plastics if the appropriate blade is used.

It can be used horizontally and vertically, will cut flush to a surface and is excellent for coping with all manner of curved cuts.

If you want very smooth cuts you will need to use a blade with a very large number of teeth per 25 mm (inch) (approximately 10–12) but fewer, larger, teeth (6–8) will cut faster and are advised for use on softwood.

As the blade cuts on the up stroke, you will want the better side of your work facing downwards to avoid possible splintering on the surface. A good tip is to apply transparent adhesive tape over the line you wish to cut to; this will minimise any tendency to splintering at the edges of the cut.

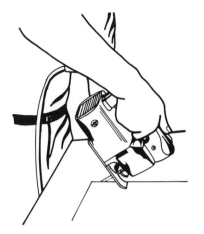

Fig. 10. Plunge cutting

An outstanding feature of the sabre saw is its ability to make 'plunge' cuts — a useful attribute if you want to make 'cut-outs' in a surface. To make your 'plunge' cut (fig. 10) you should tilt your saw forwards, keeping the forward edge of the shoe close to the surface of your wood. Now align the blade of your saw with the line you wish to cut, switch on the motor and lower the reciprocating blade into the surface of the material to be cut.

Having acquired the tools for your immediate needs, turn to Chapter 2 for practical help in the understanding of your basic material, wood, and for help in the selection of the best type for the job you have in mind.

Fig. 11. A typical portable power router

2 Materials

Hardwoods and softwoods. The nature and limitations of wood. Seasoning. Faults and diseases in timber. Man-made boards ... types and relative costs. Areas of use and abuse. The cheapest way to buy. How to order and estimate quantities.

Having acquired your basic kit of tools, you will now want to consider the other basic requirement – wood. There are more varieties of wood than there are days in the year, so no useful purpose will be served by confusing the DIY amateur with a full technical description of a wide range of varying timbers. Let us first look at the main divisions into which timber for home woodworking can be sensibly classified. There are three main divisions:

1. Softwoods
2. Hardwoods
3. Man-made boards.

Softwoods and hardwoods are, as their classification suggests, comparatively soft and hard respectively, but this is not always so. The classification 'softwood and hardwood' is, technically, a botanical one, the actual structure of the wood being quite different in each case. It is convenient to think of softwoods as, in the main, coming from evergreen trees. These are generally conifers, e.g. pine, fir and spruce, whereas hardwoods come from deciduous trees, i.e. those that lose their leaves in the winter, such as oak, beech, elm, chestnut and mahogany.

Softwoods

These are used in a very wide range of jobs. They form the bulk of the timber used in the building trades for roof and floor structures, doors, window frames, skirting boards, etc. In the home, softwoods make good shelving, framework for kitchen and other units and toys, and some of the better grade softwoods are becoming fashionable for a wide range of furniture including, even, dining-room suites. The following more popular softwoods are the most likely to be stocked by your local dealer:

Russian Red Deal (pine). Unless well seasoned, Russian Red Deal twists, cups and develops splits. The better grades are, however, quite satisfactory for general woodworking, e.g. framing for units, shelving, toys, etc. This is probably the cheapest natural wood currently available.

Douglas Fir. This wood has a straight, well-defined grain. It is a very strong wood and is almost entirely free from knots. It is used in building construction, high-class joinery and for making plywood (see p. 107) and is becoming popular for furniture.

Red Cedar. This is a reddish-brown timber which is very soft and rather weak structurally. It has an extremely high resistance to decay through damp. It works very easily but it is not ideal for joinery, except in the larger sections. It tends to corrode iron and steel. It is ideal for external carpentry and joinery in the form of garage doors, sheds, porches, sills and extensions to existing houses.

Hardwoods

Usually more expensive than softwoods, hardwoods are normally used for cabinet-making and furniture construction, although they have wide application in the building industry where durability, quality and appearance are more important than first cost.

They are, as a general rule, harder to work, partly because of their hardness but also because of their grain structure, which gives rise to different planing problems. Hardwoods, on the whole, are more attractive in appearance and are often sufficiently decorative in themselves to allow of transparent finishes which clearly show the natural grain features to good effect. Most hardwoods joint well and are durable if used externally. Some of the more popular hardwoods are:

Oak. There are many varieties of this popular timber but those you are most likely to find in your local merchant's yard are Japanese, American and English. Oak is excellent for furniture-making, decorative house doors, gates and other external structures.

Only brass screws should be used in oak as its acid content rapidly rusts steel screws. Since oak is hard and brass is a comparatively soft metal, a good clearance hole should be drilled in the top piece of wood, while the bottom piece should be well bradawled to avoid undue shear stresses on the screw. Use a well-fitting screwdriver on the slot in the screw head.

Teak. Teak is highly resistant to moisture, fire, attacks by insects, fungi and acids.

Teak veneers (see p. 107), are now very fashionable for radio and television cabinets.

It is moderately hard to work and you may come up against 'contrary grain' (see p. 152) which makes planing rather troublesome and 'finishing' an operation requiring more than usual care and concentration.

Beech. Supplies are available from Europe and Japan. It is pale brown in colour, hard, close-grained and of even texture. It is ideal for better quality kitchen furniture but is becoming fashionable for dining-room tables and chairs.

Ash. Ash is a pale wood with a coarse, straight grain. It is very tough but flexible and hard to work. It makes durable fencing but it is expensive for this purpose.

Chestnut. This can quite easily be mistaken for oak in appearance but it is much lighter in weight. For a hardwood, it is fairly easy to work. You can get a good surface finish and it polishes well. It is used in furniture-making and it is ideal for fencing and making gates.

Mahogany. There are many varieties of this wood. The best examples come from the Spanish Indies and Central America. There are an increasing number of varieties being imported from Africa but these are, almost without exception, of much poorer quality. The former varieties work excellently but samples of the latter can be very difficult to plane and 'finish' due to interlocking grain which makes the obtaining of a good surface very difficult.

All grades are used in the production of good quality furniture. In colour it is a 'reddish-brown' and it is very expensive.

Walnut. Fine-grained and, for a hardwood, easy to work. There is an Italian variety known as 'Black Walnut'. This is deep purple in colour and is highly prized for top-grade furniture-making.

Elm. Elm has a coarse, open grain that can twist very considerably, giving rise to severe warping in wide boards.

Elm is of a mid-brown colour and is quite difficult to work. It is highly resistant to moisture, shock and splitting. Well seasoned, it is excellent for refectory furniture, kitchen and dining-room chairs and it makes first-class garden furniture.

Whichever you choose, softwood or hardwood, you must remember one thing — timber, unlike metal, springs from a living organism. It grows from a seed, has an infancy, a youth, a middle and an old age and dies in due time. It suffers from diseases and, like human beings, has a clearly defined personality. All timber shrinks and swells with varying humidity and temperature, and uneven shrinkage leads to twisting and warping. To minimise, as far as possible, these undesirable characteristics, all timber must be seasoned.

Seasoning

Seasoning is a process whereby the natural content of water in a tree is reduced to an amount that will result in the least variation, through subsequent changes in humidity in the air, when the converted timber is used in the surroundings for which it is intended. There are two main ways of seasoning timber:

● **Natural Seasoning.** Air drying, out of doors but under roofing. Quite the best and most lasting results are obtained by this method.
● **Kiln Drying.** This is a highly sophisticated process of drying out a controlled amount of water from timber in days rather than years.

A great deal depends on how timber is actually sawn from the log. If it is converted to achieve the greatest possible amount of usable timber by 'flat sawing', then quite a high proportion of the resulting boards will be liable to warp and twist, since all timber tends to shrink away from the centre of the log (fig. 12a). If, on the other hand, the boards are cut radially (fig. 12b), there will be some waste but the resulting boards will be stable in use; they will, inevitably, be more expensive.

You must decide what your needs are and then consult your dealer, who will be pleased to help you if you tell him what you intend to do with the wood. Between

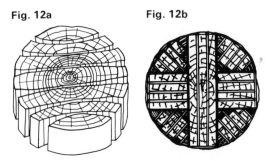

Fig. 12a. Shrinkage of timber away from the centre of the log Cutting straight across the log will give maximum yield but a high proportion of boards which will shrink and 'cup'

Fig. 12b. Radial cutting Boards cut radially from the log will not twist or warp. This method involves a fairly high proportion of waste and radially cut boards are expensive but very stable

'flat sawing' and 'radial sawing' there are a number of other cuts that can be made which produce compromise boards and it may well be that one of these will suit your purpose. Only an expert can advise you, when you define your objectives.

Faults and Diseases in Timber

All timber is susceptible to diseases and faults. The commonest likely to affect you in your purchase and use of timber are the following.

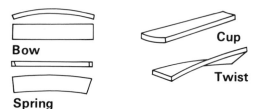

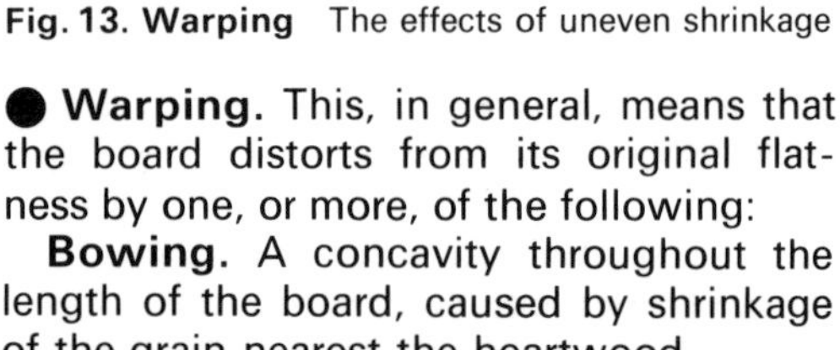

Bow

Cup

Twist

Spring

Fig. 13. Warping The effects of uneven shrinkage

● **Warping.** This, in general, means that the board distorts from its original flatness by one, or more, of the following:
Bowing. A concavity throughout the length of the board, caused by shrinkage of the grain nearest the heartwood.
Cupping. A hollowing across the width of the board, concave away from the 'heart' or centre of the log.

Springing. A hollowing over the length of the board.

Twisting. A spiralling from corner to corner over the length of the board.

● **Shrinkage.** A uniform diminution of the dimensions of a board, chiefly in width. This often seriously affects joints and most constructions must be so designed as to cater for the effects of the fault (see Chapter 6).

● **Shakes.** These are splits in the wood. They can arise through defects in the actual growth of the trees but often they are caused by poor seasoning.

● **Wet Rot.** This occurs in timber used externally. It causes a breakdown of the wood structure, characterised by a white, powdery residue.

● **Dry Rot.** Occurs mostly on timber used internally. It leaves a brown 'charred' appearance on the wood, which becomes decomposed.

● **Pests.** The commonest of these are the Furniture Beetle, the Death Watch Beetle and the Powder Post Beetle. They all bore into the wood, whether in furniture or house structures, and, in time, completely destroy its strength. There are proprietary solutions on sale which effect cures where there are mild attacks located early, but if the attacks are severe or of long standing, professional help must be sought in the case of structural damage. Where furniture is seriously affected, it should be burnt to avoid contamination spreading further. In mild attacks on furniture a solution of 50 per cent turpentine and 50 per cent paraffin, well brushed into any visible holes and repeated several times, can prove effective in stopping further deterioration.

● **Knots.** Although knots cannot strictly be classified as faults, diseases or pests, they nevertheless present certain difficulties in the working of your wood. Knots are formed when branches leave the trunk or main arms of the tree. They take the form of hard, round or elliptical brown areas of wood, often very resinous, contained within the wood structure.

Man-made Boards

Many of the faults that can be found in natural timber can be avoided by the use of man-made boards: the natural tendency of timber to 'cup', 'spring', 'twist' and warp, particularly in the wider widths, has been overcome by the introduction of these boards. They have eliminated the need to joint a number of boards together to give sufficient width for table tops, doors, carcase panels, etc., and, although they are not cheap, they may well work out cheaper in the end than the jointing together of a number of boards, particularly if you cost the labour time, the adhesive and such expensive equipment as sash cramps required to effect the necessary widths. The commonest of the man-made boards are:

Plywood

Plywood is made up of layers of veneer (ultra-thin sheets of wood) glued together so that alternate sheets have their grain directions at right-angles to each other. This arrangement eliminates both shrinkage and warping (fig. 14). Plywood sheets are

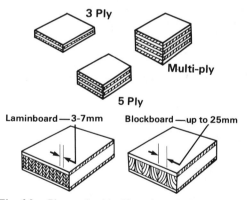

Fig. 14. Plywood, blockboard and laminboard. Note the odd number of plies in plywood

always manufactured in odd numbers, 3, 5, 7 and 9 plies, so that the external faces, both front and back, have their grains running in the same direction. Commercially, plywood sheets are graded A, B and BB. A is the best quality, being completely free from knots. It is most useful in 3–12 mm

$(\frac{1}{8} - \frac{1}{2}$ in) thickness. Above 12 mm plywood is costly to manufacture and difficult to come by: it can also be very heavy.

There is a special grade of plywood called 'Marine Plywood' which will stand up to immersion in boiling water for up to three days. The adhesive in this type of plywood is Phenolic Resin. Marine Plywood, as its name suggests, is used extensively in boat building.

Blockboard

Where thicknesses of 12 mm ($\frac{1}{2}$ in) or more are required, it is cheaper, and generally preferable, to use blockboard (fig. 14). This is a triple-sectioned board, the centre and largest section comprising softwood strips of up to 25 mm (1 in) wide, glued together edgewise. The two facing veneers are then applied to either side of this 'core', with the grain of the veneers running at right-angles to the line of the strips.

A wide variety of veneers can be applied to the 'core', making this type of board highly suitable for a large range of jobs from table tops to plain, painted doors. To disguise the blocks, visible on the end edges, a comprehensive range of edging strips can be obtained, some self-adhesive (see p. 158).

Laminboard

Very similar in general structure and application to blockboard. The core strips are, however, of hardwood and are generally thinner than those used in blockboard, never exceeding 7 mm ($\frac{1}{4}$ in) in width. They are normally used in high-class work and, in consequence of their construction, are more expensive than blockboard.

Particle Board

A cheaper alternative to either blockboard or laminboard, having a 'core' of wood chips and synthetic resin glue, bonded together under pressure. The general

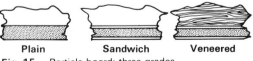

| Plain | Sandwich | Veneered |

Fig. 15. Particle board: three grades

name given to this type of board is 'chipboard'.

Fibreboards

Of little structural use but very valuable for unstressed panels, drawer bottoms and partitions. Fibreboards are made from wood fibres that are mixed with water and synthetic resin glues and compounded under pressure. A water-resistant version is manufactured and some are made with plasticised surfaces of varying types and designs. The two commonest examples of fibreboard are Hardboard and Tri-Wall. The latter is an American product currently manufactured in a thickness of 14 mm ($\frac{1}{2}$ in) and in standard boards of 1054 × 1270 mm (41 × 50 in) or 1524 × 1829 mm (60 × 72 in). Larger sizes can be supplied to special order. It can be used for the making of furniture, children's toys, stage scenery, etc. Little jointing is required, most structures being produced by slotting with a Stanley knife, folding and binding. Tri-Walls produce a work manual, which is listed on p. 166.

When purchasing man-made boards, it is far cheaper to purchase a whole board, since cutting small pieces to special order involves potential wastage and labour charges, both of which you pay for! Boards vary in size according to their country of origin; the commonest size is 1525 × 1525 mm (60 × 60 in) but 1220 × 2440 mm (48 × 96 in) is also readily available.

Jointing in man-made boards is limited and a different technique is required (see Chapters 6 and 7).

Buying Timber

In general, when buying softwoods, you order by the 'metre run', i.e. the total length of the wood that you require in any given thickness. You must also state the width that you need. On this latter dimension, you will do well to consult your local dealer, since softwoods now come in a limited range of widths and it can prove expensive to specify widths that are non-standard: you may well find yourself paying for a good deal of wastage or faced with a number of jointing jobs.

Example: If you are thinking of putting up, say, three shelves in the kitchen, one $2\frac{1}{2}$ m (8 ft) long, one 2 m (6 ft) and one $1\frac{1}{2}$ m (5 ft) and you want the width to be 200 mm (8 in), with a thickness of 18 mm ($1\frac{1}{2}$ in), then you would order 6 m 'run' of 200 × 18 mm Russian Red Deal. You must also specify 'planed one side' or 'planed all round' or 'rough sawn'. Naturally you will pay more for the first two alternatives than you will for the third, but you will save a great deal of work, time, mess and equipment costs.

If you are buying hardwood, you will be expected to estimate your requirements in square metres. If you take the above example, your calculation would be:

$Total\ length$ = 6 m
$Width$ = 200 mm = $\frac{1}{5}$ m
$Area$ = 6 × $\frac{1}{5}$ = 1·20 sq m

So you would order 1·20 sq m of 18 mm timber.

If, however, you were ordering large quantities of hardwood, you might be quoted in 'metres cubed'. In this case the area of timber required would be multiplied by the thickness (converted to a fraction of a metre). In the example given this would work out thus:

$\frac{6}{5}$ m × $\frac{18}{1000}$ m = 0·0216 cubic metres.

Such a small amount of timber as this would, however, more likely be quoted as 1·20 sq m of 18 mm thickness.

You will soon find that tools and timber, by themselves, are seldom enough. Fastenings and accessories come into almost every job that you tackle. Now turn to Chapter 3, where the commonest of these are fully explained and illustrated.

3 Fastenings and Accessories

Adhesives – types and typical uses. Screws, nails, pins, tacks and 'worms' – where and which to use. Hinges, locks, bolts, hasps and staples – types and applications.

Having collected together your tools and equipment and purchased your timber, you are now ready to proceed with the construction of the job you have in mind. Almost certainly you will require some form of adhesive, commonly called 'glue', when you come to the stage of fitting together the finished job and making it permanently 'fast'. A commonly held, but erroneous, idea is that a good 'dob' of glue will turn a poorly fitting joint into a good one. This is, quite definitely, not so. Adhesive has but one function: to bring two surfaces together in a permanently secure grip. It will turn a well-made joint into a strong, permanent fixture; it will stick veneer or plastic laminate to a base board and it will afford sufficient strength to join two boards, edge to edge, to give a wider surface.

Adhesives today are, technically, very advanced and highly sophisticated, clean in use and easy to handle. They are very strong. There is a wide range of types covering many specialised requirements. Below are listed the more popular types for home use.

● **Fish Glue.** Usually sold in tubes. Ideal for small repair jobs. Not economic or sufficiently strong for large work.

● **Casein Glue.** This is made from the protein in milk. You must follow the mixing instructions on the tin very carefully and be sure to mix in an earthenware container as it is affected by metal. Cramps have to be used on work glued with casein and these

should be left on for at least twenty-four hours. Casein glues have a tendency to stain certain woods, so they should be used carefully and sparingly.

● **Synthetic Glues:**

Resin Glue. This is usually sold in 1 lb tubes, ready mixed for immediate use. Resin glues are very clean to handle and they do not stain the wood. They require cramping but for less time than casein glues; in normal conditions of temperature and humidity, eight hours are sufficient.

You should remove any surplus glue with a damp cloth as soon as practicable after gluing up as it sets extremely hard and is then difficult to remove. Resin glue is completely waterproof. It lasts a long time in store.

Urea Formaldehyde Glue. This has two constituents, the glue and the hardener. It is manufactured in two forms:

(i) A thick liquid plus a hardener, also liquid.

(ii) A powder glue (to which water has to be added in precise proportions) plus a liquid hardener. Although two-part glues sound rather more bother than a resin type, which is ready to use, they afford the advantage of having an adjustable 'setting time', e.g. 'fast', five minutes; 'medium', ten minutes; and 'slow', fifteen minutes. No setting action will take place until the glue, applied to one surface, is brought into contact with the hardener on the other surface.

Cramps are needed for the duration of the hardening period.

Impact Glues. These require the surfaces to be joined to be evenly coated with the adhesive, using a spreader comb. They are then left to dry for about ten minutes until the surfaces feel dry to the touch. The two surfaces are then brought into contact, when fusion is immediate and permanent. The great advantage of impact adhesives is that no cramping is required but extreme accuracy is necessary in precisely locating the surfaces to be joined since, once they are in contact, no sliding adjustments can be made. The items glued together can be put into use immediately. This type of adhesive is commonly used in attaching plastic laminates to man-made boards for table tops, doors, cabinets, etc.

Screws

Adhesives provide a permanent joint, so that other means must be used where it might be found desirable for the structure to be dismantled and reassembled from time to time. When this arises, you will need to use one of the several types of screw on the market. The commoner types of screw in use are as follows.

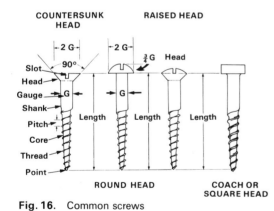

Fig. 16. Common screws

Countersunk Head

These are used where the screw is required to be flush with, or a little below, the surface of the wood. The wood through which the screw passes should be drilled large enough to take the plain shank of the screw; the 'recess' to take the head of the

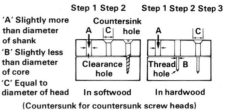

Fig. 17. Boring and countersinking for screws

screw should then be drilled into this hole with a countersink bit (fig. 17). The screw should then be started into the wood into which it is to be screwed by means of a bradawl. Countersunk-head screws are measured for length over the entire length of the shank, including the head. Countersunk-head screws are used on most hinges. They are usually made in mild steel (sometimes galvanised), brass and copper.

Round Head

This type has a hemispherical head which is flat underneath. They are used for holding jobs together and for attaching metal fittings such as 'T' hinges (fig. 26), surface locks and hasps and staples.

The length of a round-headed screw is taken from under the head, i.e. the hemispherical head is additional to the quoted length of the screw.

Raised or Oval Heads

These are a combination of the countersunk-head and the round-head screw. They are made from the same materials and have similar finishes but are often supplied with a chromium or cadmium finish. They are used in securing metal sheet and metal fittings to wood where strength in addition to decoration is required.

Coach Screws

A very strong form of screw made from mild steel only. They may be obtained galvanised. They are not driven into the wood with a screwdriver but have a square head on which a spanner is used, as with bolts.

Self-Tapping Screws

Made in toughened, hard steel, since their primary uses are in metal. They are, however, the only type of screw that can be used successfully in particle boards (see p. 108). They are also useful in attaching wood to metal. They have a special type of thread on them, sufficiently tough and hard to 'tap' or cut a thread into the wood or metal into which it is to be screwed, thus making the latter into a rudimentary 'nut'. A pilot hole, the size of the 'core' of the screw (i.e. the diameter of the bottom of the thread), is first drilled into the material into which it is to be screwed. Self-tapping screws are provided with a sharp point that is inserted into the pilot hole to start the screw off on its thread-cutting operation. Quite a lot of pressure is needed on the screwdriver for the first two or three turns: the action must be firm and positive and the screw must be maintained in an upright position.

The diameter of screws is defined by a gauge number. A screw of gauge number 5 is approximately 3 mm ($\frac{1}{8}$ in) in diameter. The higher the number (8–10–12), the larger the diameter. Typical sizes are: 12 mm ($\frac{1}{2}$ in) × 4, 18 mm ($\frac{3}{4}$ in) × 6, 25 mm (1 in) × 8, 37 m (1$\frac{1}{2}$ in) × 10 and 50 mm (2 in) × 12.

Screws derive their holding power by their threads becoming embedded in the fibres of the wood. They are much less effective in the end grain of wood as the thread tends to cut across the fibres which results in the screw tending to pull out easily. Self-tapping screws create the equivalent of a nut in the material into which they are screwed, thus producing a very strong bond.

Screws should be used in preference to nails

— when greater holding strength is necessary
— where superior decorative effects are required
— where nails might split or otherwise damage the wood
— where vibration or movement may detract from the holding power of nails
— when subsequent dismantling of the work may be a possibility (it helps if

the screws are waxed before inserting if this is likely).

Most screws have a narrow rectangular slot running across the diameter of the head, but a more recent development is the Phillips-head screw. This has a second groove at right-angles to the first, but neither groove extends to the full diameter

Slotted   Phillips   Pozidriv

Fig. 18. Types of screw head, viewed from above

of the screw head (see fig. 18). Understandably, the Phillips-head screw requires a specially shaped screwdriver to fit it. The use of a standard screwdriver on a Phillips head will rapidly damage it and nullify the more positive grip for which the correct screwdriver was designed.

Another screw, less commonly used, has the Pozidriv head. This has an even larger number of grooves in the head to provide even greater maximum driving force.

As a general guide to the correct length of screw to use, it is common practice to allow for a screw to be three times the thickness of the top piece of wood, providing that the lower piece will allow of this (fig. 23).

Nails

A very old method of holding pieces of wood together, yet one still very common today and, contrary to what you might think, one on which a great deal of technical development has been carried out. There is a very wide range of nails on the market today, each designed to do a specific job of work. Nails may be divided into two main types:
● Nails and brads
● Pins and tacks.
(See fig. 19.)

Nails and Brads
Round Wire Nails
These are strong nails made from round-

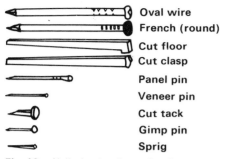

Oval wire

French (round)

Cut floor

Cut clasp

Panel pin

Veneer pin

Cut tack

Gimp pin

Sprig

Fig. 19. Nails, brads, pins and tacks

sectioned wire. They are pointed at one end and have a flat, circular head at the other. They are mainly used on coarse work in softwood carpentry. Smaller varieties are used to secure plywood or hardboard bottoms on to bottoms of boxes, since the large head can withstand fairly heavy loads and will not 'pull through' the material. Common sizes range from 20 mm to 150 mm ($\frac{4}{5}$–6 in) in length. Correctly driven, using the right hammer, the head may be driven marginally below the surface of the softwood (fig. 20).

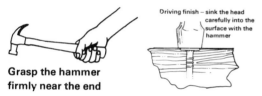

Driving finish – sink the head carefully into the surface with the hammer

Grasp the hammer firmly near the end

Fig. 20. The correct way to use a hammer

Oval Nails or Brads

These are made from steel wire of oval section, their primary function being to lessen the risk of splitting the wood, particularly when used near the end or close to the edge of a piece of wood (fig. 21). They have very small heads of oval section and

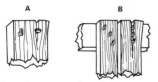

A   B

Fig. 21. How to use oval nails to prevent splitting of wood Turn the nails in line with the grain to prevent splitting (A). Whenever possible, stagger the nails to prevent splitting (B)

are used in the higher grades of carpentry and joinery. The special shape of the head allows the nail to be punched below the surface of the wood with a pin or nail punch. The resulting depression can then be filled in with a wood filler and, when the latter is dry, glasspapered down until virtually invisible (fig. 22).

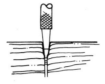

Fig. 22. Oval nail punched below the surface of the wood The small head allows the nail to be driven below the surface with a punch and hidden by a filling

Cut Nails or Flooring Brads

These are stamped out from sheets of mild steel and have heads that protrude on one side of the shank only. They are hammered in so that the flat surface of the shank is along the direction of the grain to minimise the possibility of splitting of the wood. The roughness of their edges contributes to their great gripping power.

Clout Nails

These are usually quite short, round-sectioned nails with large circular heads, approximately 12 mm ($\frac{1}{2}$ in) in diameter. Their chief use is in holding down roofing felt and, because of their exposure to the elements, they are invariably galvanised.

Pins and Tacks

Panel Pins

These are fine wire pins, about 1–1$\frac{1}{2}$ mm ($\frac{1}{25}$ in) in diameter, with very small heads, so that they may be pin-punched below the surface of the wood. They are used in cabinet work to secure mouldings and panels to framing. Sizes of from 10 mm to 35 mm ($\frac{2}{5}$ in to 1$\frac{2}{5}$ in) in length are common.

Veneer Pins

Even finer gauge pins for very delicate work, so called because they were, at one time, used to hold down veneers to base boards while the animal glue was drying.

Cut Tacks

Commonly called 'tin-tacks', these are cut from mild steel. They have round heads and are tapered all the way from directly under the head down to the very sharp point. For this reason, they are ideally suited to use in upholstery and for pinning down carpets to wooden floors. Common sizes are 9–18 mm ($\frac{1}{3}$–$\frac{2}{3}$ in) in length. They may be obtained in copper for use in boat building.

Sprigs

These are very sharp, headless, square-sectioned pins, 9–15 mm ($\frac{1}{3}$–$\frac{3}{5}$ in) in length. They are mainly used for securing backs to pictures and mirrors and for locating glass in windows before puttying.

Most nails are roughed for a short distance under the head to increase their grip on the wood. When deciding on the length of nail to use, a commonly used rule is that the length of nail shall be three to four times that of the thickness of the top piece of wood (fig. 23). Where possible, nails should be 'angled', or dovetailed, when driven into the wood, thus preventing too easy a removal (fig. 24).

For the rough joining of boards, 'worms' or 'wiggle' nails (fig. 25) are used. These are made of corrugated sheet steel. They are hammered into the end grain of adjacent boards.

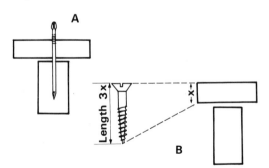

Fig. 23. Correct lengths of nails and screws to use for fastening wood to wood Where possible, the length of the nail should be 3 to 4 times the thickness of the top piece of wood (A). The length of the screw should be 3 times the thickness of the top piece of wood (B)

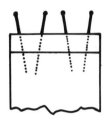

Fig. 24. Dovetail nailing

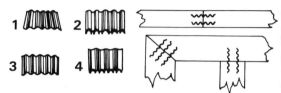

Fig. 25. 'Worms' or 'Wiggle' nails
1. Divergent corrugations with plain edge
2. Divergent corrugations with saw edge
3. Parallel corrugations with plain edge
4. Parallel corrugations with saw edge

Common Fixtures

Hinges

There are a great many types of hinge with specialist uses but the following are those commonly used by home woodworkers.

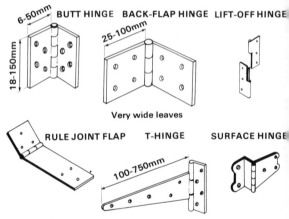

Fig. 26. Common types of hinge

● **Butt Hinges**. These are a general-purpose hinge for all types of doors, lids, flaps, etc. They are made in steel or brass, with a composite alternative of brassed steel to reduce the high cost of pure brass. Solid drawn brass hinges are the best, but the cheaper, pressed variety are quite satisfactory for light work.

● **Back-Flaps**. These are basically similar to butt hinges but each flap is longer from the knuckle of the hinge. They are used in heavy work and for hingeing the flaps on tables, writing desks, cocktail cabinets and similar structures.

● **'T' Hinges**. These are used wherever it is necessary to take heavy loads, as in the cases of gates, heavy doors and lids. They are usually made from mild steel and finished in black enamel.

● **Lift-off Hinges**. These are used where it is necessary, occasionally, to remove the door or flap from the main structure.

● **Rising Butt Hinges**. A heavily made butt hinge where one flap rides above the other as the hinge is opened. These are ideal for use on house doors so that they ride up and over thick carpets as the door opens and fall again to sill level when they are fully closed, thus obviating draughts.

● **Piano Hinges**. So called because they are invariably fitted to the lids on pianos of good quality. They are a continuous butt hinge and may be bought in long lengths.

The range of special hinges is now so great that if you have a problem or special requirement, consult your dealer who will always be pleased to advise you.

Locks

There are six main types of lock in common use:

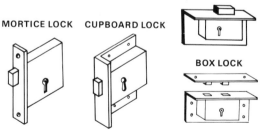

Fig. 27. Some common locks

● **Mortice Lock**. For use on substantial doors.

● **Cupboard Lock**. For general cupboard and utility quality cabinet use.

● **Till or Drawer Lock**. For good quality cabinet work.

● **Box Lock**. For high-class work such as jewellery boxes.

● **Yale Locks**. For use on doors where maximum security is required.

● **Padlocks**. These are for use with a hasp and staple. They come in many sizes and qualities. If they are to be used externally, you should make sure that they are made of brass or a non-rusting alloy.

All these locks except the padlock require fitting (fig. 104) with accurate marking out and careful workmanship. They offer much greater security than the 'screw-on' type of lock which is simply applied to the door and screwed to the surface of the wood (see Chapter 7). Locks may be supplied in steel, brass or alloy material and the more expensive ones can be very decorative.

Bolts

As with locks, there is a very wide range of bolts, catering for a variety of requirements. The commonest are:

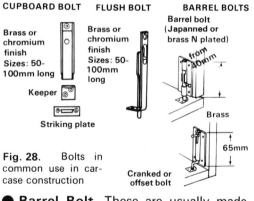

Fig. 28. Bolts in common use in carcase construction

● **Barrel Bolt**. These are usually made from mild steel and are commonly available from 50 mm to 200 mm (2 in to 8 in) in length. There is a locking variety that employs a padlock and these are ideal for use on gates, garage doors, sheds, etc.

● **Cranked or Offset Bolts**. These are barrel bolts that are cranked to allow the shaft to operate clear of the door to which it is attached and to allow of a greater area of wood around the hole into which the bolt locates, thus giving greater strength.

● **Flush Bolts.** These are fitted to the edge of one door when two doors are used. They are invisible when the second door is closed.

The better bolts are made in brass and most may be obtained with a chromium-plated finish.

Hasps and Staples

These are usually made from mild steel and have a black-japanned finish. This is a common form of fastening on tool boxes, shed and garage doors, and gates. A padlock is used for locking purposes. Sizes range from 25 mm to 150 mm (1 in to 6 in).

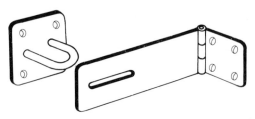

Fig. 29. Hasp and staple, used on garage and shed doors in conjunction with a padlock

As with tools, you usually get what you pay for. Always buy the best that you can afford; hinges, in particular, need to be strong and well made if applied to heavy, well-used doors and gates, and the same applies to locks.

4 Basic Joints

Butt, mitre, lap, housing, halving, mortice and tenon, bridle, dovetail, rubbed and dowelled joints. Tonguing and grooving. Layout and marking out. Techniques in making. Working to a drawing.

A high proportion of amateur DIY woodworkers have a totally unwarranted reluctance to tackle joints in their constructions. It is true that careful marking out and accurate sawing and chiselling are essential for successful jointing but, given care and unhurried application, the amateur can emulate the expert in practically everything but speed. So, the key to success is to take your time — never hurry your sawing or chiselling or try to set too rigid a timetable for any work involving joints.

Another tip is to choose a joint well within your limits of skill. There is such a wide range of joints, with a range of overlapping applications, that you will be able to choose one appropriate to your needs yet within the scope of your skill.

The following are the most commonly used and useful joints, and all fall within the skill capacity of the amateur woodworker.

Butt Joint

This is the simplest of all the joints. The basic, essential requirement is that all edges and faces to be joined shall be absolutely 'square' (i.e. at right-angles to each other) and flat. The butt joint is commonly used on rougher work, in softwood, in the construction of boxes, cases and such items as seed frames. The joint is generally nailed, preferably dovetailed (fig. 30b), but it can be glued too. Additional strength can be obtained by using softwood blocks glued into the corners (fig. 30c).

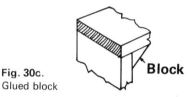

Fig. 30c.
Glued block
Block

Mitre Joint

This gives a very neat appearance, since no end grain is visible at all. The common mitre requires that the ends of the pieces of wood to be joined shall be sawn at an angle of 45°.

These joints can be marked out with a mitre square (similar to a try-square, but having the blade at 45° to the stock instead

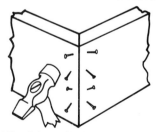

Fig. 31.   Mitre joint — this joint is generally pinned

of at 90°) and then sawn with a tenon saw. Alternatively, the joints may be sawn in a mitre block (fig. 32).

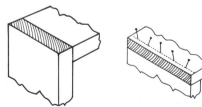

Fig. 30a.   Butt joint   Fig. 30b.   Dovetail nailing

117

Tenon or dovetail saw

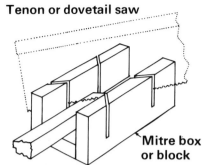

Mitre box or block

Fig. 32. Mitre block

A frame made with mitre joints is not very easy to nail or cramp together but if you use the simple blocks, with cord and tourniquet, as shown in fig. 33, you can glue and cramp them quite easily. When the adhesive is dry, you can dovetail pin the joint if you need the added strength. In some circumstances, it is possible to add glued blocks to the corners for added strength.

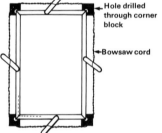

Hole drilled through corner block

Bowsaw cord

Fig. 33. Cramping up a mitre joint — the tourniquet method

Lap Joint

This is not a very strong joint, but it cuts down the amount of end grain showing. It provides a greater area of gluing surface. It is used on boxes, cheap drawer construction (in inexpensive kitchen units), simple cabinets and frames made from battens. It

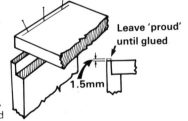

Leave 'proud' until glued

1.5mm

Fig. 34.
Simple lap joint, glued and nailed

can be nailed in addition to gluing and softwood blocks can be applied to the corners.

Housing Joint

There are a variety of these joints but the two commonest and most useful to the DIY amateur are:
- **The Through Housing**
- **The Stopped Housing.**

The through housing is very simple to make, but the joint shows on the edges. Where this is not desirable, the stopped housing should be used. If one piece of wood is narrower than the other (as with some shelves in cabinets or bookshelves), the stopped housing will automatically be used. Both joints are commonly used in

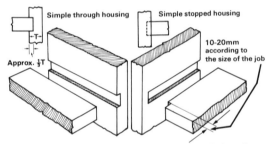

Simple through housing   Simple stopped housing

T

Approx. $\frac{1}{3}$T

10-20mm according to the size of the job

Fig. 35. Housing joints — simple through housing and simple stopped housing

cabinet construction, bookshelves and in the partitioning of trays and boxes. All edges to be sawn should be marked out deeply with a sharp marking knife and try-square. The depth of the groove (housing) should, in general, be about $\frac{1}{3}$ the thickness of the wood and a marking gauge is used to mark out the depth, giving a positive line for your final chisel cut.

The blind end of the stopped housing will have to be chiselled out, using your chisel across the grain, to the full depth of the groove and for a length of about 25 mm (1 in) to allow for the tip of the tenon to be started on the cut across the face of the wood.

It is usual to glue the joint, supplemented by nailing if greater strength is needed.

Halving Joint

Commonly used on light framework (see 'Wall Lining', p. 67). Broadly speaking, half the thickness of the timber is removed from one of the pieces to be joined and half from the second piece. There are three main versions:

● **The Cross Halving**
● **The 'T' Halving**
● **The Corner Halving.**

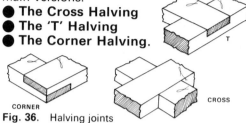

Fig. 36. Halving joints

These joints are normally glued. They may, additionally, be pinned or screwed for extra strength. They are commonly used in caravan construction and for wall battening. After sawing, all waste wood should be removed by chiselling half-way through from one edge, reversing the wood and chiselling half-way through from the other edge. This avoids splitting out and ensures that the depth of the joint is identical all the way through.

Mortice and Tenon Joint

This is the most widely used joint of all. There is a very wide range of these joints, each with a specific, technical application. The commonest and those mostly likely to be used by the DIY enthusiast are:

(a) The 'Through' Mortice and Tenon (fig. 37). Used in a wide variety of framed

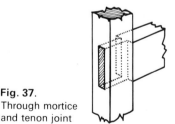

Fig. 37.
Through mortice and tenon joint

work, including all types of door. They are very strong joints and, to increase still further their holding capacity, they may be wedged or pegged (fig. 38). In general,

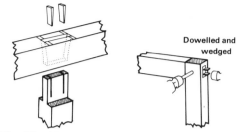

Dowelled and wedged

Fig. 38. Wedging and pegging a mortice and tenon joint

the tenon is marked out so that it is $\frac{1}{3}$ the thickness of the wood from which it is to be cut. It is good practice to mark the mortice to the chisel width that you will be using and not to some calculated amount. In accordance with the recommended $\frac{1}{3}$ proportion, use the chisel nearest to this size, erring on the side of extra width (up to $1\frac{1}{2}$ mm or $\frac{1}{16}$ in) (fig. 39).

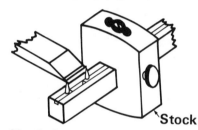

Stock

Fig. 39. Setting a mortice chisel between the 'spurs' of a mortice gauge

(b) The Stub (or Stopped) Mortice and Tenon (fig. 40). In this case the

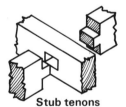

Stub tenons

Fig. 40. The stub or 'stopped' mortice and tenon joint

tenon does not go right through the wood in which the mortice is cut. No end grain shows and the joint is virtually invisible. This joint is used in stool and table construction where through joints would be unsightly and, technically, difficult to arrange. Where two stub joints meet inside a

119

The haunched and mitred
mortice and tenon joint

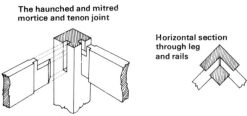

Horizontal section
through leg
and rails

Fig. 41. Stub tenons mitred inside the leg of a stool or table

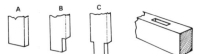

Fig. 42. A stopped, haunched mortice and tenon joint

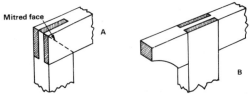

Fig. 43. Three typical bare-faced tenon joints
At A the mortice size equals the section of the upright. The single shoulder at B or double shoulders at C are more satisfactory

stool or table leg, the ends are mitred (fig. 41). They are also shouldered or 'haunched' so that the end of the upright piece does not reveal the tenon (fig. 42).

(c) Bare-faced Tenon (fig. 43). This tenon has only one shoulder. This type is sometimes used when the wood from which the tenon is to be cut is rather thin, possibly resulting in a weak joint if the $\frac{1}{3}$ proportion is adhered to and two shoulders are used.

Bridle Joint

Sometimes called an 'Open Mortice and Tenon'. It is weaker on corners than the mortice and tenon joint but it is quite

Fig. 44. Bridle joints An angle bridle (A) is used in frame construction; a 'T' bridle (B) is used in leg construction

strong when used as a 'T' joint in a frame. Gluing is essential and supplementary pinning or screwing is recommended.

Dovetail Joint

Like the mortice and tenon joint, this has several variations. Only the through dovetail need be considered by the home woodworker:

The Through Dovetail (fig. 45). Called a 'dovetail' because one of the two components is shaped like the tail of a dove. It is one of the few 'self-locking' joints. It is very strong and is used in the highest

Fig. 45. A through dovetail joint, suitable for boxes etc.

quality work for carcase construction, drawer-making and high-class cabinet work generally. It is used in both hard and softwoods. The slope of the dovetails is 1 in 6 for softwoods and 1 in 8 for hardwoods. The angle for the dovetails is set out in pencil (NOT a marking knife) and with an adjustable sliding bevel (fig. 46a) or dovetail template (fig. 46b). The latter may be made up quite simply from plywood and is advisable if you are making more than one or two dovetails.

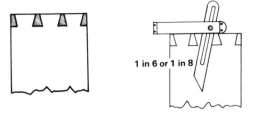

1 in 6 or 1 in 8

Fig. 46a. Setting out a dovetail joint using a sliding bevel. The correct dovetail slope is from 1 in 6 to 1 in 8

Template

Slope 1–6 1–8

Fig. 46b. Setting out a dovetail joint using a dovetail template

The sides of the dovetail are then sawn with a small tenon saw, or dovetail saw if you have one, and the bulk of the waste removed by means of a coping saw. The shoulders of the two end dovetails should be carefully cut with your tenon saw. The remaining waste is removed by using a suitably sized chisel (preferably a bevelled-edge type so as not to damage the sides of the dovetails) working half-way through from each side.

When this has been completed, the tails are positioned over the end grain of the second piece of wood (fig. 47) and their

Fig. 47. Marking out the pins

outline scribed on the end grain with a metal scriber or a long, pointed pencil. The cutting depth is then marked on the face of the wood. The cutting depth is the thickness of the wood on which the dovetails are made and the line is cut with a marking knife. Lines in pencil are then squared down from the scribed marks on the end grain to this depth line. These are called the 'pins'.

You are now ready to cut out your pins. Remember, when you are sawing, to saw touching your marked line but making sure that the actual saw cut (the 'kerf') is wholly within the waste material. The waste is removed from the pins in the same way as described for the dovetails. The two pieces of wood are then brought together and 'eased' to a fit, adjusting, where necesary, by very fine cuts from a sharp chisel.

Rubbed Joint

This, at first sight, is a simple joint. It is used to produce wide boards by gluing together two or more boards, edge to edge. To avoid undue movement through

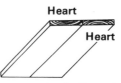

Fig. 48. Arrangement of alternate boards in 'rubbed joints' The alternate boards should have their annual rings concave and convex to minimise 'cupping' of the wide board

the inevitable shrinking and hollowing of the component boards, they should be arranged as shown in fig. 48, with the annual rings, as seen on the ends of the boards, arranged so that the alternate boards have the rings arranged in concave and convex profile. The edges of the boards are then carefully planed with a try-plane (a large plane of about 600 mm length) if you have or can borrow one, or with your Jack plane set finely. You should plane the edges so that they are very slightly concave at first and then take one or two final shavings through the entire length.

This plain joint is suitable for boards up to 1 m (3 ft 3 in) in length. With modern adhesives, which dry very quickly, it is essential to work quickly. A thin layer is spread on one edge only. This board is then placed, edge to edge, on the other board, which is best held in the vice, and rubbed to and fro once or twice, making sure that you keep the free board upright and steady. This action presses the adhesives into the surface of the wood and eliminates excess adhesive (fig. 49).

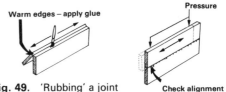

Fig. 49. 'Rubbing' a joint   Check alignment

If the boards are longer than 1 m, it is better to use sash cramps on them. Put two cramps under the boards with one over the top in the centre between the two lower cramps. Be sure to use wooden blocks between the faces of the cramps and the edges of the boards. This spreads the pressure and eliminates damage to the edges of the boards. Do not over-pressurise the cramps; this could cause 'buckling' of the boards, particularly if more than two boards are involved.

Dowelled Joints

Dowels are, really, wooden rods. Common diameters are 3 mm ($\frac{1}{8}$ in) to 25 mm (1 in) and the standard length is 1 m (3 ft 3 in). Dowelled joints can be used, in many instances, to replace mortice and tenon

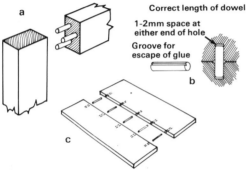

Fig. 50a. Dowelled joint, used in framing
Fig. 50b. Details of dowels
Fig. 50c. Dowels used to strengthen a joint when making wide boards

joints (fig. 50a and b). They are used extensively in chair construction. Another common use is to strengthen edge-to-edge joints used for the widening of boards (fig. 50c). Drilling holes for dowels entails the selection of the appropriate drill. The hole should be 3 mm ($\frac{1}{8}$ in) longer in each piece of the wood than the length of the dowel rod projecting into each piece. The dowel rod should be a snug push fit and slightly chamfered at each end for ease of entry into the hole. A saw cut should be made along the entire length of the dowel rod to allow trapped air and adhesive to escape. The hole into which the dowel rod is driven, by a wooden mallet to avoid 'burring' of the ends, should be slightly countersunk to accommodate excess adhesive and to allow the edges to fit closely together.

In all joints involving the use of dowel rods, accurate marking out is a prime essential and, if a large number of joints are

to be made, it could be worth your while to purchase a dowelling jig. These are mechanical aids to accurate drilling, centre points being located as desired by stops and gauges to ensure precise fitting.

Tongued and Grooved Joints

Used primarily to strengthen edge-to-edge joints when wide boards are required or, when applied to floor boards, to give a strong floor, allowing for natural movement of the timber over a large area without gaps appearing between the boards.

Information on laying and repairing floors is fully covered in another book in this series, *Home Decorating* (see p. 166).

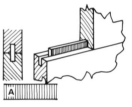

Fig. 51. Tongued and grooved joints. The tongue (A) is cross-grained hardwood or plywood

Layout and Marking Out of Joints

The key to good joinery is careful and accurate marking out. For basic marking out requirements the following tools are necessary:
1 300 mm (12 in) stainless-steel rule
1 steel tape (2 m, 6 ft 6 in)
1 150 mm (6 in) try-square
1 marking knife
1 marking gauge
1 carpenter's pencil (any hard pencil will do)
1 mortice gauge
1 mitre square (if mitre joints are to be made)
1 sliding bevel or dovetail template (the latter can easily be made from plywood)

All wood to be marked out must first be planed accurately to size and planed perfectly 'square', i.e. adjacent surfaces must

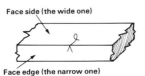

Fig. 52. Face side and face edge marks These are essential for the precise marking out of joints

be at right-angles to each other. All wood should be clearly marked with a face side and face edge (fig. 52). These are, respectively, the best side and best edge (i.e. free from flaws, knots, etc.) and they should be carefully and accurately planed to an included angle of exactly 90°. Subsequently, all marking out must be carried out from one or other of these two surfaces.

All marked lines indicating sawn or chiselled cuts must be incised with a sharp marking knife. Pencil lines should be used for this purpose only when:

● Cut lines are being transferred across faces where no cutting is to take place.

● Lines are required to run at a close angle to the direction of the grain, e.g. the marking out of dovetails and otherwise where a knife, so close to the grain direction, would follow this direction, thus ruining the marking out.

Lines, cut or pencilled, should be made across the surface of the wood using a try-square, with the stock of the try-square held tight against the face side or face edge of the wood (fig. 53).

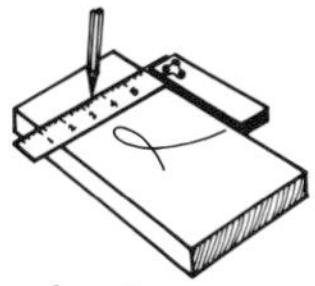

Fig. 53. The use of a try-square against the face side and edge

For cut lines parallel to the edge of the wood, in the direction of the grain, a marking gauge should be used (fig. 54). The 300 mm (12 in) stainless-steel rule is ideal for use with a marking gauge since it can be used directly against the stock of the gauge and the required measurement to the tip of the spur (the point) immediately set (fig. 55).

Dovetails of any number are best marked

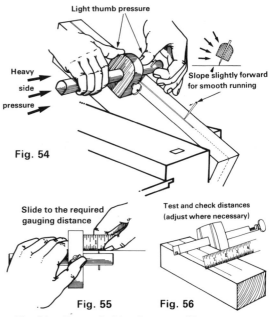

Light thumb pressure

Heavy side pressure

Slope slightly forward for smooth running

Fig. 54

Slide to the required gauging distance

Test and check distances (adjust where necessary)

Fig. 55   **Fig. 56**

Fig. 54. How to hold and use a marking gauge correctly

Fig. 55. Setting a marking gauge with a steel rule

Fig. 56. A mortice gauge in use

out from a template. These can be bought but are easily made from three-ply sheeting (fig. 57).

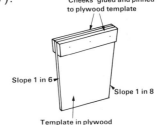

'Cheeks' glued and pinned to plywood template

Slope 1 in 6

Slope 1 in 8

Template in plywood

Fig. 57. A simple dovetail template made in plywood

When marking out items such as bookshelves, be sure to make your ends or sides in pairs — one left-hand and one right-hand. Mark your housing joints on the back edge of the two sides held together in the vice. Remove both pieces from the vice and open them **like the pages of a book** (fig. 58) and square your lines across the inside faces of the two pieces: in this way you will ensure that you have one left-hand side and one right-hand side.

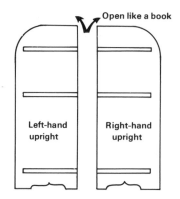

Open like a book

Left-hand upright

Right-hand upright

Fig. 58. Marking out the sides of a bookcase to ensure a right-hand pair Place the sides in the vice, face sides outside and face edges up. Mark out on the face edges. Remove from the vice and open like the pages of a book. Mark the housings across the two inside faces of the uprights. Gauge the 'stops' on the two outside edges

Whenever you have a number of items to be marked out, e.g. the lengths and widths of framing, the legs of stools or tables, or the partitions of boxes, always ensure exact similarity of length by putting them together in the vice or, if there are too many to go in the vice, by using a sash cramp to hold them together, and then marking them out together. This saves a great deal of time and ensures perfect equality in all members, but check your measurement at least twice — an error on this scale could be costly! This method is a must for any pieces of wood that have to be dowelled together.

Techniques in Making

Sawing (see p. 127) and chiselling are the keys to craftsmanship. Planing figures somewhat less largely than it did at one time since it is almost universal practice for the DIY woodworker to buy timber ready-planed for anything other than rough work. This saves a great deal of time, energy and cost of equipment. The small extra cost per metre for this service is well worth while since surfaces come prepared 'square', making joint-making much easier.

Successful joint-making, resulting in strong, good-looking products, relies to a great extent upon the understanding of the importance of the actual saw cut, the 'kerf' — where and how it is made. There are three ways of sawing in relation to a marked line:

Sawing ON a line
Alternate teeth are bent outwards on a saw blade, one to the left, one to the right. This is called 'set'. Set enables the tooth to present a sharp edge to the wood fibres, thus aiding easy cutting; it also ensures that the resulting 'kerf' is considerably wider than the thickness of the saw blade, thus eliminating 'jamming' in the cut. If a saw persistently jams, you can be sure of one of two things: there is too little 'set' or the blade is buckled; in a badly maintained saw it could be both. For the amateur, the best way to overcome these defects is to send the saw to a 'saw doctor' (your local hardware store can usually help you locate one of these) where, for a comparatively few pence, your saw can be put into perfect order. A 'kerf' can be as little as 1 mm ($\frac{1}{25}$ in) or as large as 4 mm ($\frac{1}{6}$ in) wide and this has to be taken into consideration when deciding how you are going to position your saw. Fig. 59a shows the saw

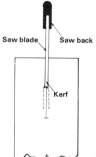

Saw blade   Saw back

Kerf

Fig. 59a. Sawing *on* a marked line The 'kerf' falls equally on either side of the line. Used where the wood is sawn in half

being used directly **on** the line. This will result in half the 'kerf' falling on one side of the line, while half falls on the other. Sawing **on** the line is, therefore, the way you would position your cut if you wished to saw a piece of wood into exact halves.

Sawing TO a line

Here your 'kerf' travels along your marked line, **touching** it all the way along its length, but the actual 'kerf' is wholly on one side of the line, into the waste wood. This position of the saw is used in all joint cutting, ensuring that the marked size of the joint is maintained in full on the wood – this is especially important in cutting tenons, dovetails, housing and halving joints. Cutting **on** the line or **to** the wrong side of the line will, inevitably, result in a slack fit and a poor joint. See fig. 59b.

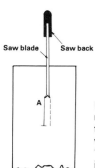

Saw blade   Saw back

A

Fig. 59b. Sawing *to* **a marked line** The 'kerf' touches the line all the way down but falls wholly to one side leaving piece 'A' full size. Used in sawing joints

Sawing FROM a line

In this cut, the saw is moving some 1–2 mm ($\frac{1}{25}$–$\frac{2}{25}$ in) away from the line into the waste, the 'kerf' travelling parallel to the marked line for its entire length. This cut is used when it is desired to leave a minimal amount of wood proud of the line so that it may be planed down to give a smooth, planed finish at line level (fig. 59c).

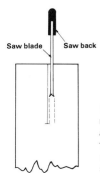

Saw blade   Saw back

Fig. 59c. Sawing *from* **a marked line** The 'kerf' falls away from the line but is parallel to it. Used where it is desired to plane down to the line to effect a smooth finish

Order of Making

The basic principles of constructing any frame or carcase are simple and straightforward.

1. Mark out lengths (assuming that the wood has been purchased planed to size all round).

2. Mark out joints.

3. Cut joints.

4. Fit joints.

5. Carry out any necessary shaping.

6. Clean up, with smoothing plane, scraper (if necessary), and glasspaper (see p. 58), all surfaces that cannot be reached after the structure has been glued up.

7. Glue and, if necessary, cramp up, removing any excess adhesive with a damp cloth before it dries (see p. 141).

8. When adhesive is dry, remove any cramps used and clean up the structure as described in 6.

9. Fit any special fittings such as hinges, locks, handles, etc.

10. Apply any surface finish required (see Chapter 8).

A tidy working area is essential and a planned procedure vital for success. Always allow plenty of time for these operations and, if your structure is of any real size, a companion is a great asset.

Work at a comfortable height and, when possible, in cool dry surroundings. You need plenty of light, preferably natural.

Working to a Drawing

Structures of even the simplest type should always be made from a drawing. This may not, of necessity, be a complex or technical piece of draughtsmanship. Drawings are thoughts expressed on paper, hence visual, practical and memory-jogging. It may not be necessary to record more than lengths, widths and thicknesses for items as simple as, for example, shelves. More complex structures will require more thought and greater detail – overall sizes, location of components, nature of joints to be used, rebates, panels, doors, drawers, etc., all should be planned and drawn out. Mistakes on paper are more easily rectified and are cheaper to put right. There are two ways of making such drawings:

● **Pictorial.** These are 'picture' views giving a three-dimensional representation of the structure to be made.
● **Orthographic Projection** (working or 'pattern' drawing).

Fig. 60 shows a pictorial drawing, in **isometric projection**, of a small box. All essential dimensions and details are given on this one drawing. Such drawings show a 'picture' of the finished article but the angles are distorted and no direct comparison of shape or sizes can be made by application of the object on the drawing. Such drawings are easily understood by the great majority of people and are very suitable for the simpler structures.

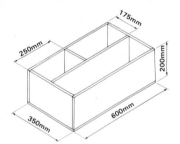

Fig. 60. Pictorial (isometric) projection of a small box

Fig. 61 shows an **orthographic projection** of the same box. You will see that there are three simple drawings of rectangles in precise positions in relation to one another. 'A' is a view looking down on top of the box, 'B' is a view looking on the front of the box, while 'C' shows the end of the box. The drawings are easy to make, much simpler, in fact, than the isometric projection, since they call only for vertical and horizontal lines in the main, easily drawn with a ruler. Like a pattern they may, with smaller jobs, be used for direct comparison of size and shape with the actual pieces of wood being shaped. Only two

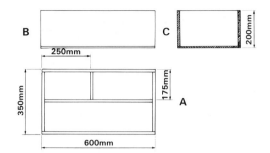

Fig. 61. Working drawing (orthographic projection) of the box in fig. 60, to the same scale

main dimensions can be given on any one view (length and width, length and height, or width and height) since each separate drawing is only two-dimensional. This being the case, not less than two of the views must be drawn for full dimensional coverage. If the ends require special treatment then it may be necessary to draw all three views.

Since most constructional jobs take considerable time, the committing of your ideas, dimensions, etc., to paper is essential for memorising details from one working spell to the next. Many snags could well be seen once your ideas are worked out on paper, thus eliminating much wasted time and material. Another useful feature of your drawing is its use in consultations with your timber and hardware merchants on quantities, qualities, sizes and types of timber and fitments to use. Advice and help in these matters are usually freely given.

If you work from diagrams in one of the many publications for DIY woodworkers (see p. 166) you will almost certainly be confronted with one or other of the drawings described, so you will be well advised to make yourself familiar with them. On p. 166 you will find the names of a number of publications that will help you to develop your drawing and to understand those that you may encounter in your favourite DIY magazine.

5 Techniques

Sawing, chiselling, planing, drilling, hammering and the use of the mallet and pincers.

Techniques are best described as the most effective ways of carrying out processes based upon a combination of experience, scientific research and acquired skills. It is true that some people are born with a special aptitude for certain activities; these could turn out to be the specialists, the artists and the experts. For most of us, the acquisition of skill will largely be the result of determination, hard work, extensive practice and prolonged experience. All of these will be helped to a great extent if we accept the guidance of experts, whose personal skills and wide experience have evolved a formula for success. You are interested in developing your skill in woodworking. The prime objective of this book is to help you do just that.

An understanding of the nature of wood and the mechanical principles underlying the tools we use is a vital contributing factor in the acquisition of skill. It will help you to choose the correct tools and the best woods for the job you have in mind. The following are the essential basic skills that must be acquired if success is to be achieved in your woodworking: sawing, planing, chiselling, drilling, hammering and the use of mallet and pincers.

Sawing

Saws may be divided into two main groups:

● Saws for sawing along straight lines
  (a) with the grain
  (b) across the grain
● Saws for sawing round curved lines.

Saws for Sawing in Straight Lines

These may be divided into two main groups: those for sawing along the direction of the wood grain and those for sawing across the grain. Those for sawing along the direction of the grain are called rip-saws. They meet with less resistance than those used for sawing across the grain since they do not have to cut across the tough fibres of the wood. Rip-saws have larger teeth, hence fewer, say 4–5, per 25 mm (inch) than do cross-cut saws and they may be likened to the use of high gear on a bicycle or car when the going is easy. They have only a small 'set' (see below) and the teeth are filed to a flat, chisel shape (fig. 62).

Saws for sawing across the grain are

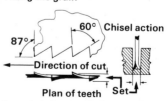

Along the grain

87° 60° Chisel action
Direction of cut
Plan of teeth Set

Fig. 62. Set and shape of rip-saw teeth A rip-saw is 660 mm long and has $3\frac{1}{2}$–$4\frac{1}{2}$ points per 25 mm

called 'cross-cut' saws and the two most common are the hand saw (6–8 teeth per 25 mm (inch)) and the panel saw (10–12 teeth per 25 mm (inch)). With cross-cut saws, the teeth have a greater 'set' and they are filed to points in order to sever the wood fibres (fig. 63).

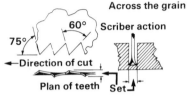

Fig. 63. Set and shape of cross-cut saw teeth
A cross-cut saw is 600 mm long and has 6–8 points per 25 mm

If you can only afford one saw at the beginning of your woodworking activities, choose the hand saw since this would saw along the grain direction, though somewhat slowly, as well as across it, whereas a rip-saw would certainly not be able to saw across the grain without a great deal of effort, accompanied by an extensive splitting of the wood. Panel saws are used for very fine work.

There is another important group of saws, mainly used on cross-grain cutting, called 'backed saws'. These have comparatively small, rectangular and rather thin blades (fig. 64). These thin blades are supported and strengthened by a brass or steel backbone along the top edge. The largest of these backed saws is called a tenon saw (14–16 teeth per 25 mm (inch)) and it is up to 300 mm (12 in) long. This saw is used for cutting tenon joints, particularly the 'shoulders' (see p. 120). There is a smaller version of this saw called a dovetail saw 200 mm (8 in) long which has 4–6 teeth per 25 mm (inch). This is used for the

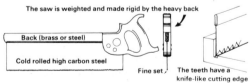

Fig. 64. Set and shape of backed saw teeth (tenon and dovetail saws) The saws are 200–250 mm long and have 10–15 points per 25 mm

cutting of dovetail joints (see p. 120) and other fine work. There is an even smaller variety, with a round handle, called a bead or gent's saw. This is used for very fine work.

When you have chosen the appropriate saw for the job you have in mind, you should practise your sawing on an odd piece of wood before starting on the real job. For the best results, you should follow these standard rules:

1. Make absolutely certain that you are standing comfortably, with the line you wish to cut to, the saw and your forearm all in one straight line. More poor saw cuts, off line and out of square, can be blamed on wrong stance than anything else.

2. Start your cut, wherever possible, on a corner so that you can see both lines – across the surface and down the edge (fig. 65).

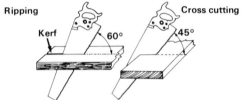

Fig. 65. Starting to saw – the correct angles

3. With your thumb steadying the saw, pull your saw backwards for your first stroke. Hold the saw tight and keep the blade vertical.

4. Take the weight **off** the saw and push forwards slowly. (If you push downwards and forwards you will meet with heavy resistance from the wood and your saw will probably jam.)

5. Use the full length of the blade on each forward and backward stroke.

6. Saw **slowly** – give the sawdust a chance to clear the saw-cut (kerf) to avoid 'build-up' and consequent jamming of the blade in the cut.

7. Keep your saw **vertical**.

8. Support your piece of wood so that the piece being sawn off does not split away as the cut severs it. Do not, however, lift it up, since this will tend to close the 'kerf' and thus jam the saw.

9. Never, under any circumstances, grease your saw blade. Grease of any kind will make your wood swell. This will cause it to grip the blade, resulting in jamming. If it does jam, check that the 'set' is correct and that the blade is not buckled. Some hardwoods have twisted fibres that sometimes cause the wood to move when the tension is removed by the saw-cut; this movement can result in the cut tending to close and grip the saw blade. If this happens, re-mark your line close to the original and saw down it again.

Saws for Sawing Round Curves

Most of your saw cuts will be in straight lines but, from time to time, you will need to saw round curves. For this purpose you will need one of the following saws.

Coping Saw (fig. 66). This has a one-piece metal frame that keeps a very fine, 150 mm (6 in) long, small-toothed blade

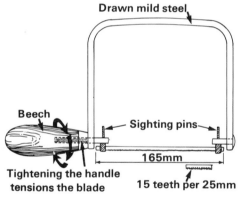

Fig. 66.   The coping saw

in tension. It is for use on small-radiused curves on comparatively thin wood. To avoid breaking the blade it is essential to:

● Make sure that the blade is not twisted.
● Keep sawing steadily while negotiating the curve.
● Keep your saw at right-angles to the direction of cut.
● Keep your saw blade in the horizontal plane.

● Use with one hand when possible but if two are necessary, keep them both on the handle. **Never** have one hand on the front of the saw frame.

Bowsaw (fig. 67). Gradually going out of fashion. It has a loosely joined frame made of beech wood. It has a blade 250–300 mm (10–12 in) long which is kept in tension by means of a tourniquet made

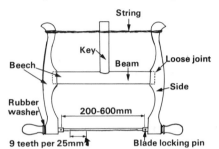

Fig. 67.   The bowsaw

from string and a wooden lever. It is used for larger curves and on thicker material than the coping saw. The rules for using the bowsaw are identical with those for the coping saw but the bowsaw is more robust and its blades less likely to fracture easily.

If it is necessary to remove waste wood from openings entirely inside the wood (e.g. the handle hole in a tea tray) one end of the blade must first be released from the frame, threaded through a 'starter hole' and then reconnected to the frame and reten-sioned. The bowsaw may be used for con-cave or convex curves. When it is not pos-sible to complete internal curves by these methods, one of the following saws should be used.

Padsaw ('Keyhole' saw) (fig. 68). This is used for small-radiused, internal curves. It has a malleable (soft) steel blade that can be retracted into the handle for easy and safe transportation. Malleable steel is used for the blade so that if, for example, it jams on a tight curve, it will 'give' rather than break. Any deformity of the blade as a result of such jamming can be corrected by simply bending it back straight again. A

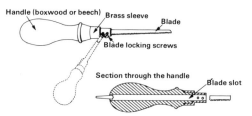

Fig. 68. The padsaw or keyhole saw

round pilot hole, sufficiently large to accept the blade, is drilled in the wood at a convenient point so that a start can be made on the internal saw cut.

Compass Saw (fig. 69). This is used on larger internal curves and can, in fact, be used on external curves. It has a normal, but open, saw handle with a fairly narrow blade, made from tool steel (unlike the soft steel of the padsaw). The blade tapers to a point for insertion into a 'starter hole'.

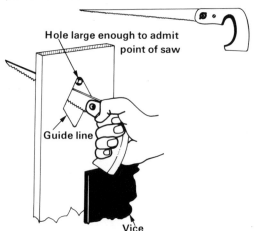

Fig. 69. The compass saw, for cutting curves and large holes

With coping, bow and pad saws, the blades are not resharpened but replaced with a new one, the cost of which amounts to only a few pence. It is, however, quite possible to resharpen and reset the blades of compass saws in the usual way.

If, at the start, when you may be spending quite a lot of money on setting up your initial tool kit, you wish to economise with a minimum loss of efficiency, you should purchase a 'general purpose saw'. This will

cover most of the work of all the straight line saws and also the majority of jobs that can be done by a compass saw, but you would be well advised to supplement it with a coping saw, which is quite inexpensive, for the smaller curved work. One saw which would do all the jobs for you is the portable, electric sabre saw (see p. 102).

Remember! Your saw is, perhaps, your most important tool. Look after it; grease it when not in use (remove the grease before use). Protect its cutting edge with a wooden guard strip. Buy the best you can afford and keep it sharp and properly set.

Chisels

After sawing, so often you will have to remove waste wood with a chisel. As with saws, there is a wide range of chisels covering a variety of work.

MORTICE CHISEL

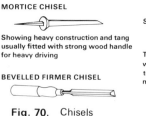

Showing heavy construction and tang usually fitted with strong wood handle for heavy driving

SQUARE-EDGED FIRMER CHISEL

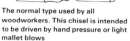

The normal type used by all woodworkers. This chisel is intended to be driven by hand pressure or light mallet blows

BEVELLED FIRMER CHISEL

Fig. 70. Chisels

Firmer Chisel. The 'maid-of-all work' chisel. As this is quite a strong chisel, it can be used for light work with a mallet (never a hammer!). Used for paring, joint cutting, particularly with housing and halving joints (see pp. 118-9). Sizes range from 3 mm to 50 mm ($\frac{1}{8}$ in to 2 in).

Bevelled-Edged Chisel. Broadly similar to the previous chisel, it has both edges bevelled off along the length of the blade. This makes it lighter in use but rather less robust. It is invaluable for getting into the corners of joints, such as dovetails (p. 120). Sizes range from 3 mm to 35mm ($\frac{1}{8}$ in to $1\frac{2}{5}$ in) in width.

Mortice Chisel. This is a much sturdier chisel with a very thick blade, an iron ferrule on the end of the handle and a thick leather or plastic shock-absorbing washer between the heavy duty shoulder of the blade and the handle. It is used primarily for cutting out mortices and is designed to take heavy blows from a mallet and the considerable strain of levering out the waste wood from the mortice.

Gouges (fig. 71). These are chisels used for making curved cuts. There are two types:

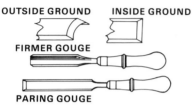

Fig. 71. Gouges Paring gouges are ground on the inside while firmer gouges are ground on the convex surface and are used for cutting grooves and hollow shapes

● Paring or Scribing Gouges. These are sharpened on the inside of the curved blade and are used for making concave cuts.
● Firmer or Carving Gouges. These are used for grooving, fluting or making dished surfaces. They are sharpened on the outside, or convex, surface of the blade.

In using any kind of chisel, remember that a blunt tool is a dangerous tool. Keep your chisels very sharp. A sharp chisel requires a great deal less physical effort to cut the wood, thus ensuring at all times that the edge is under your complete control. Make sure that, for whatever purpose you are using your chisel, **both hands** are always behind the cutting edge, making damage to the fingers impossible. When chiselling out joints to a given depth, always chisel from either end or side of the joint towards the centre, thus preventing splitting and ensuring similarity of depth at both extremities.

Remember, too, that several small, well controlled cuts are much more likely to produce good results than a few heavy

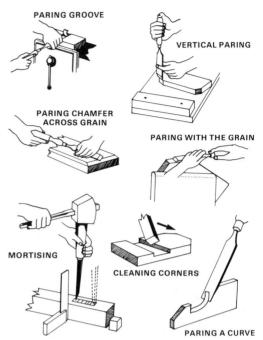

Fig. 72. Safe chiselling processes

cuts. Keeping the sharpened side of the chisel blade downwards to the surface being chiselled ensures easy and accurate control of the depth of the cut. A perfectly flat surface is better produced by using the flat side downwards but this requires considerably more skill and control.

Never attempt to use a chisel one-handed – this is a very dangerous practice at any time.

Planing

Far less planing is done today by the DIY woodworker since more amateurs purchase their timber planed all round and to size. This saves a great deal of time and energy and they are, generally, assuring themselves of 'square' surfaces and edges (i.e. at right-angles to each other), thus making marking out and joint-making easier (fig. 52). There always comes a time, however, when all woodworkers have to use a plane, if only to skim a surface level or smooth, to plane the edges of boards prior to jointing or to fit a drawer or door to a carcase. The ability to produce flat and 'square' surfaces is one that requires a great deal of practice and skill but the following tips will help you on your way:

● Always grip the plane firmly.

● Ensure that your stance allows you to keep the edge or surface being planed, your plane, your wrist and your arm in one continuous straight line. Standing too close to your work will tend to push the plane away from you, while standing too far away will drag the plane towards you, both faults resulting in 'out of square' planing. Nearly all poor planing stems from the wrong stance.

● Resulting from its own weight, your plane will tend to drop backwards at the start of your stroke and forwards at the end of it. Unless resolutely controlled, this will result in a convex surface to the wood being planed. Always press heavily on the nose (front) of the plane at the beginning of your stroke, with both hands during the middle part of the stroke, and on the heel (back) of your plane during the final part of the stroke. Put another way, your action should be akin to scooping the middle out of the piece of wood: this will give you the flattest surface.

● Wood is a living, natural material (see p. 104) and, like your hair, prefers to be 'groomed' in one particular direction; when dealing with wood, we say 'with the grain'. If you find that, despite having a perfectly sharp plane, you still get a rough surface, either turn the wood round or plane in the opposite direction. It may also be necessary to reduce the thickness of your cut. In any case, you will require a thinner cut on most hardwoods as these offer greater resistance and sometimes have very 'contrary' grain (see p. 105).

When planing end grain, you must take special precautions against splitting. Again, because it is a living, natural material, wood, unlike metal, works more easily in certain directions. Working across the grain, which is what planing end grain amounts to, is far harder than planing along the same direction as the grain 'flow'. There are two simple ways to avoid splitting the end grain when planing:

● Plane from one outer edge to the centre of the board only. Then reverse your direction of planing, coming from the other edge to the centre (fig. 73a).

Plane end grain halfway from each edge to avoid splitting

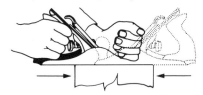

Fig. 73a. Planing end grain: Planing from the ends to the middle is one way to avoid splitting the wood

● Place a piece of wood, of exactly the same thickness as that which you are planing, tight up to the edge that you need to plane and cramp them together in the vice. You may then plane straight through to the supporting piece without damage to the piece you require (fig. 73b).

When planing end grain, using either of the above methods, it is essential to have your plane very sharp and very finely set. Half the battle in successful chiselling and planing is getting, and keeping, your cutting edges sharp. The sharpening of chisels and planes needs to be done very frequently, often several times during the cutting of one set of joints or the planing of one bundle of timber for a cabinet or

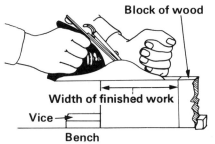

Fig. 73b. Planing end grain: An alternative way to plane end grain without splitting is to place a piece of wood of precisely the same thickness as that being planed tight up to your wood in the vice. You may then plane straight though without harm

box. This being so, the amateur must learn to master this art, for such it is.

It must, firstly, be realised (and you can do this by looking closely at a chisel or plane blade) that the sharp end is in two parts (fig. 74). The blade is, at first, ground

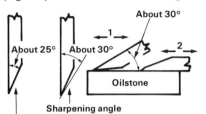

Fig. 74. Grinding and sharpening angles of the plane or chisel blade

on a grindstone to produce a slope of 25°. This, however, leaves a comparatively coarse edge which has to be brought to a fine cutting edge on an oilstone. To do this the blade is tipped up to an angle of 30° and rubbed to and fro over the flat surface of an oilstone. Fig. 75 shows the correct

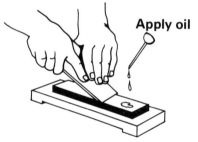

Fig. 75. Method of holding a plane blade when sharpening

way to hold the blade while sharpening it on the oilstone. 'Rocking' must be avoided at all costs, since this will result in a rounded edge which will never cut wood. The wrist and fingers must be kept absolutely rigid – this is the secret formula for success! The blade is then turned over and held absolutely flat while being rubbed over the surface of the oilstone (fig. 76). The slightest tipping up on this reverse side will completely ruin the cutting edge.

Oil should always be used on the surface of the stone to prevent the 'pores' becoming clogged, thus preserving its cutting

Fig. 76. Holding plane blade flat to remove 'burr' after sharpening

power on the steel blades. The best oils to use are sperm or neatsfoot but some of the thinner cycle-type mineral oils can be used satisfactorily. Always wipe the oil off the stone after use and keep the surface of the stone clean. The sharpening angle of chisels is usually a little greater than that for plane blades, up to 35°.

The sharpening of gouges is rather more difficult, special 'oilstone slips' (fig. 77)

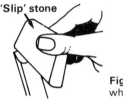

Fig. 77. Using a 'slip' stone when sharpening a gouge

being necessary to cope with the curved section of the blade. Paring gouges are flatted, on the convex side, by using a normal oilstone, while firmer or carving gouges are sharpened on the convex surface on an oilstone and flatted on the concave side by using a 'slip'. Great care must be taken to hold the 'slip' at a constant angle while in use.

Hammering

If there is one tool that everyone feels completely competent to use, it is the hammer. Such confidence is totally misplaced, for the hammer, like all tools, needs skill, patience and great care in use. Bruised wood, bent nails, nails through the sides of structures and even split wood, can all result from the incorrect use of the hammer.

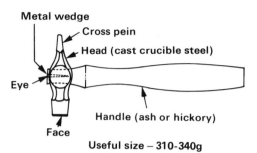

Metal wedge
Cross pein
Head (cast crucible steel)
Eye
Handle (ash or hickory)
Face

Useful size – 310-340g

Fig. 78. A Warrington hammer

It is important to choose the correct type of hammer for the job you have in mind. The Warrington style (fig. 78) is probably the best all-rounder. Sizes run in numbers, 00–12. A good weight will be given by a number 2 or 3, approximately 280 g (10 oz), but, in addition, a very light one, for driving pins, is a useful addition to your kit as soon as you can afford it. Another popular type is the claw hammer, weighing 220–900 g (8–32 oz) (fig. 79), which is used on heavier,

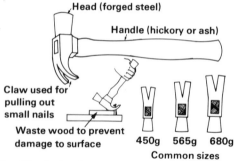

Head (forged steel)

Handle (hickory or ash)

Claw used for pulling out small nails

Waste wood to prevent damage to surface

450g   565g   680g

Common sizes

Fig. 79. A claw hammer

rougher work, and the 'claw' head is useful for removing nails from packing cases, etc.

To avoid marking the surface of the wood when driving the nail right into the surface of the wood, the hammer handle (the 'shaft') should be held right at the end remote from the head.

By holding the shaft in this way (fig. 80), the concave face of the hammer meets the surface of the wood perfectly flat-on, driving the nail head slightly below the surface of the wood without marking it. A very common error is to hold the hammer shaft close up to the hammer head. This results in the edge of the face coming into

Fig. 80. How to hold a hammer

contact with the surface of the wood as the mail is driven right home, causing an unsightly 'half-moon' to appear on the surface of the wood. With patience, this damage can often be removed by soaking the affected area with hot water. Several applications may have to be made. This causes the wood to swell up, eliminating the 'half-moon' but causing a mound on the wood which will have to be planed or glasspapered down. It is virtually impossible to drive a nail straight home without bending it or driving it out of the perpendicular if the shaft is held too close to the head.

Always ensure that the hammer head is tight on the shaft. In warm, dry conditions, the shaft may shrink a little, causing the head to loosen. There is a small steel wedge driven into the shaft where it emerges from the hole in the hammer head. Striking this wedge deeper into the shaft will usually cure a loose head but, if it does not, it will be necessary to soak the head end in water overnight. When buying a hammer, make sure that the shaft is made from ash or hickory and that the grain runs straight for the whole length of the shaft.

The Mallet

These are made from beech. Examine the face before purchasing. This is the end of the mallet with which you strike the chisel. Choose one that has the medullary rays (the thin, silvery streaks that cross the annual rings at right-angles) running straight up and down (parallel to the sides of the mallet).

Mallets are used exclusively for hitting wood or plastic. They are used for most of their lives on chisel handles, particularly

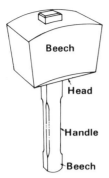

Fig. 81.   A mallet

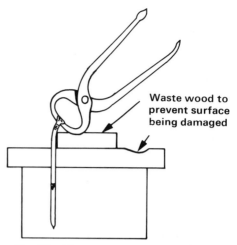

Fig. 82.   The correct way to use pincers, used for pulling out nails

mortice chisels. Never hit with the side face of the mallet, which is comparatively soft; always use the end face which presents end grain, which is hard and durable, to the object being struck. From time to time, it is advisable to wipe over both the head and the handle with a rag soaked in linseed oil. This will effectively prolong the life of the mallet and prevent the head from splitting.

Use of Pincers

These are commonly, but erroneously, called 'pinchers'. They are used, in the main, for extracting nails from wood. Fig. 82 shows the correct way to extract a nail from a piece of wood. A sheet of plywood or metal, 100 × 50 mm (4 × 2 in) is placed close up to the nail to be extracted, which is then gripped by the pincers. A rolling, levering action is then applied to the arms of the pincers, the whole being rotated on the rounded cheeks of the pincers. The ply or metal plate ensures that the surface of the wood is not damaged and the nail is effectively removed.

This chapter has covered the basic tech-

niques normally required to cover the range of activities likely to be undertaken by an amateur DIY woodworker. As your skill and experience grows and your structures take on a more ambitious nature, you will need more advanced advice and help. On p. 166 are the titles of some excellent publications that, bought or obtained on loan from your local library, will help you to further your techniques up to a point. When you have reached this stage, however, you would do well to consider joining a carpentry or cabinet-making class at your local Evening Institute.

A number of tool and material suppliers and manufacturers run their own advice services. Such services can be of considerable help since commercial firms may be relied upon to acquaint you with the latest and most efficient solution to your problems. You will find details of such services on p. 166.

6 Construction~Framed Stuctures

Stools and tables, doors and gates, frames. Order of procedure. Cleaning up. Cramps and cramping. Testing and 'squaring'.

Whether you are planning renovations, restructuring or making entirely new units, you will need to understand the basic principles of construction techniques. Broadly speaking, structures fall into two main groups:

● framed structures
● carcase constructions.

This chapter is concerned with the techniques underlying all framed constructions such as stools, tables, doors and windows, panelled structures such as cupboards and chests, picture frames and larger projects, such as greenhouses, garden sheds and gates of all types. Chapter 7 will deal with carcase constructions.

The following is a list of joints on which any framed constructions should be based:

● mortice and tenon – with its many varieties
● bridle
● halving
● dowelled ⎱ Sometimes used in combin-
● mitred ⎰ ation.

While the above, all described in detail in Chapter 4, form the basis of most framed constructions, other joints, such as the housing and the rebate (or lap) joint, are often combined with these. Let us now look at typical examples of framed structures.

Stools and Tables

These fall into two main groups:

(a) The more traditional type with four square-sectioned legs, joined by four rails, sometimes strengthened by rails near the bottoms of the legs.
(b) Those with batten-based frames utilising cross-halving and joints other than mortice and tenon. These come in a wide variety of shapes and are more commonly used for the smaller, casual-type table, such as the lounge coffee table.

Traditional Construction. Fig. 83 shows typical examples of tables in traditional

Fig. 83. Top: Table construction with top rails only. Bottom: Table construction with lower rails

construction, strengthened by rails near the bottom. If one thinks of a stool as a small table, then the general techniques of construction and procedures are identical. For this traditional construction, the mortice and tenon joint is first choice. Most people would regard as unsightly the end grain, inevitably exposed, in the through mortice and tenon, so a haunched, stopped and mitred tenon must be used. This variety is clearly shown in fig. 84. For the amateur of limited experience, it is safest to use the proportions

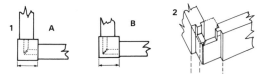

Fig. 84. Haunched mortice and tenon joint
1.   Corner leg and rail joint. At A the tenons are central in the rails. At B they are nearer the outside so that the tenons can have extra length
2.   Cutaway view showing how the tenon ends are cut on the mitre

shown in this diagram, with the rails inset from the face of the legs. One of greater experience and skill might prefer to have the rails flush with the outer surface of the legs. This brings the mortice much closer to the surface of the legs and calls for much greater control in execution – one false move and you could burst through the thin wall of the mortice.

For stools or tables of less than 400 mm (16 in) height no strengthening rails would be necessary under normal circumstances. Above this height much would depend upon the demands made on the structure in weight and possible movement. An extra-deep top rail might well prove sufficient if the legs were of substantial section; after all, most modern dining tables of medium size have no lower rails. Where, however, supporting rails are deemed to be necessary, these can be of two main types.

(a) Four smaller-sectioned rails than those used round the top, jointed in a similar way, but shouldered all round (fig. 85).
(b) Two end rails with centre rail or rails,

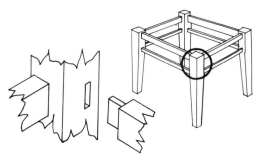

Fig. 85.   Left: Stub tenons, shouldered all round for lower rails of tables and stools. Right: Lower rails, shouldered all round

called 'stretchers'. No mitred tenons are necessary, all being 'stub' tenons into the legs and end rails (see figs. 40 and 86).

Fig. 86.   End rails with 'stretcher'

Batten Base Frames. These are made up from battens and the joints used are halving, lap, bridle or, for the more advanced woodworker, dovetails at the corners of the frames. Halvings or slotted joints are used at the cross-over points. Battens may be used on edge or flat. Fig. 87 shows a variety of under frames using batten construction.

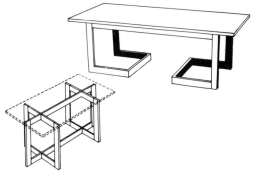

Fig. 87. Batten framed table construction   Battens may be joined by mortice and tenon, bridle, halving, butt or mitred dowelled or dovetail joints

The Fitting of Tops to Framed Structures

This operation falls into two main categories:

- where natural wood is used
- where man-made boards are used.

Natural Woods

As fully described on p. 106, natural wood shrinks and swells with varying conditions of humidity. The larger the area of the table top, the greater is the potential for movement. This being so, any attempt to fasten your table top rigidly to the underframe will result in either severe splitting or buckling of the top or damage to the underframe. Few people realise the enormous power of timber when it is shrinking or swelling and very extensive damage can be done if steps are not taken to counteract or allow for this movement. There are three standard methods employed to secure natural wood tops to tables, stools, dressing tables, chests of drawers, etc.

1. Buttoning. This is a traditional method (fig. 88a). A groove is cut in the rails around the frame, approximately 10–12 mm ($\frac{1}{2}$ in) from the top. The depth of the groove will vary with the width of the top, but between 6 and 9 mm ($\frac{1}{4}$ and $\frac{1}{3}$ in) is usually sufficient. Details of a single 'button' are given in fig. 88a, the best wood to use being beech. There should be a slight 'pull' on the button to give it a close fit but, at the same time, allowing necessary movement. Remember that wood shrinks most across the grain. Remember, too, that it swells, so that allowance must be made for the buttons to move into the groove as well as outwards. Buttons should be placed about 150–250 mm (6–8 in) apart.

2. Plating. This utilises a drilled and slotted metal plate, usually about 40 × 25 mm ($1\frac{3}{5}$ × 1 in) if flat (fig. 88a) or 25 × 25 × 25 mm (1 × 1 × 1 in) if bent at right-angles. The plates are firmly

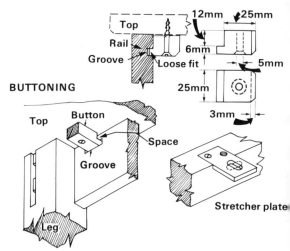

DETAIL OF TABLE TOP BUTTON

BUTTONING

Fig. 88a. Methods of fixing natural wood tops to underframe

screwed, either into the top of the rail, suitably inset to take the thickness of the plate, if a flat plate is used, or on to the inside of the rail if a right-angled plate is used. The 'free' end of the plate, in either case, is slotted and it is through this slot that a round-headed screw (see p. 111) is used to screw the top to the rails. The screw is screwed up tight and then unscrewed about half a turn to allow movement in the top along the groove or slot in the plate. There are usually two slots cut in one half of the plate at right-angles to each other: be sure to use the one that will allow movement across the width of the table top.

3. Slotted Holes. For small table tops or stool tops with narrow rails, economies can be effected by drilling slots right through the rails in the direction of movement of the top. It will only be necessary to drill these slots in the end rails. Slots may be made by drilling three holes slightly larger in diameter than the screw to be used and then sawing through them with a padsaw (p. 129), cleaning up with a small flat file. Screws are then screwed right up through the rails into the top, tightened up hard and then released half a turn to allow the top to move. The holes (slots) will need to be countersunk since countersunk-headed screws will be used in this operation.

Man-made Boards

These, as fully explained in Chapter 2, do not shrink or swell, twist or warp, so that the fairly elaborate methods described for fixing natural wood tops do not have to be used. There are three ways of attaching man-made boards to underframes.

Pocket Screwing (fig. 88b). A groove is cut in the rail of the underframe with a gouge (p. 131) and a hole of sufficient diameter to take the selected screw, is drilled upwards and at an angle in the end of the groove, so that it comes out, centrally, in the top edge of the rail. The top is

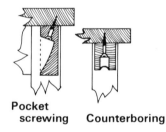

Pocket
screwing   Counterboring

Fig. 88b. Methods of fixing man-made boards to table underframe

screwed to the frame by screws, inserted into these 'pocketed' screw holes, tightened hard and left that way. Holes should be 150–250 mm (6–10 in) apart.

Counterboring. In this method, a larger hole, capable of accepting the head of any screw used, is drilled up through the rail to within 20 mm of the top edge. This precise distance can be marked on your drill by means of a band of masking or plastic tape. A smaller hole, large enough to admit the shank of the screw only this time, is drilled through the remaining width of the rail.

Screws inserted into the counterbored hole should be screwed down tight into the top; they should **not** be slackened off since no movement has to be allowed for.

Metal Plates. Although there is no call to use the slots for movement purposes, as for natural wood, this is a convenient and easy method for use with man-made boards. In this case the screws should be tightened right down.

Doors and Gates

Doors are, basically, frames with panels. There are two standard types.

Doors with fixed, unbreakable panels (fig. 89), grooved into the frame when it is assembled. Such frames have square-shouldered, haunched mortice and tenon

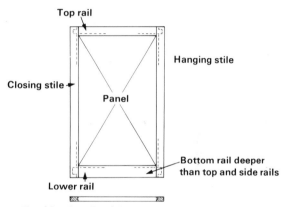

Fig. 89. Details of door with permanent panels

joints (Chapter 4) at the corners and, if there is a centre rail, at either end of this. Plain doors have a similar 'core' frame but can have a single sheet of plywood or hardboard applied directly to the frame on both sides.

All panels (fig. 90) should fit closely in the grooves and they should not be glued

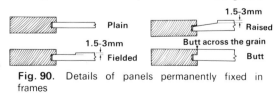

Fig. 90. Details of panels permanently fixed in frames

when assembled but they should be slightly smaller than the surrounding frame to allow for easy assembly.

Doors with semi-permanent or breakable (glass) panels. Such panels are not grooved (i.e. locked) into the frame but rebates are formed in the rails so that the panels may be inserted after the frame has been assembled and then held in place by fillets pinned to the main frame (see fig. 93). Frames to take this type of panel are

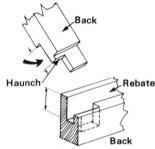

Fig. 91. Long and short-shouldered tenon, used in the construction of frames where a rebate is cut to house a semi-permanent panel (glass etc.)

jointed with long and short-shouldered tenons (fig. 91). Work on doors of this type should only be undertaken by the more experienced woodworker with above-average facilities and equipment.

Gates

Broadly, these follow the same basic structural pattern as doors, with morticed and tenoned frames. Large gates should have a diagonal strut to obviate 'lozenging' (dropping) due to the inbuilt weight of the structure. Gates for external use are best if constructed in hardwood and the joints should, preferably, be wedged (fig. 92).

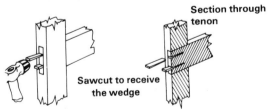

Fig. 92. Wedged mortice and tenon; the joint is wedged to make it stronger

Picture or Mirror Frames

Since these are constructed from comparatively small-sectioned wood, it is easier to use butt or, on larger frames, dowelled joints in the corners (see p. 122). Since end grain would be regarded as unsightly in most of these frames, you would have to mitre the corners. To take the glass and/or picture and backing board, a rebate would have to be cut in your wood before jointing. To avoid buying a rebate plane and learning to use it, it would pay you to buy ready-rebated timber; the additional cost if you only contemplate making one or two frames would be minimal. You could avoid rebating your wood by making a simple frame and pinning a bead around the inside edges of the frame, thus giving the same effect (fig. 93).

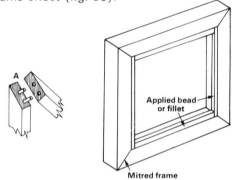

Fig. 93. Mitred and dowelled joint. Note the shorter dowel at A

Procedures

When you have constructed your frame, you should clean up all surfaces that cannot be reached when the structure is assembled and glued. First you should use a very finely set smoothing plane to remove all working marks and surface dirt. Follow this with coarse and fine glasspaper, used on a block (see p. 59). Always glasspaper in the direction of the grain otherwise you will severely scratch the surface of your wood. Always ensure that you assemble your structure in such a way that you are able to insert the last component. Give a lot of thought and pre-planning to your sequence of assembly and gluing up since nothing is more frustrating than to find that you cannot insert your final piece and have to dismantle the whole job, which, with modern resin glues, can be a difficult job as they partly set very quickly.

Always spread glue thinly. Most modern resin-based adhesives need only to be spread on one piece of the two to be glued. Do not use a brush to apply the adhesive, as with the old animal glues, unless you wash it out immediately after use in hot water, otherwise you will be left with a rock-hard head of bristles. Use a thin strip of softwood, approximately $150 \times 15 \times 3$ mm ($6 \times \frac{3}{5} \times \frac{1}{8}$ in) for spreading the adhesive on your wood. It should be tapered at one end to get into tight corners.

Cramps and Cramping

Cramps are a mechanical means of holding pieces of wood together, usually to exert pressure on them while the adhesive between them dries out or for the purpose of marking out a number of pieces of wood to identical lengths. They are often used to cramp pieces of wood to the surface of a bench while work is done on them. When gluing up structures, whichever type of cramp you use, always insert wooden blocks between the pads of the cramp and the surface of the wood being cramped. These spread the pressure and avoid possible damage to the surface of the wood (see top right). If you are using sash cramps on, say, a door, use one cramp per rail (i.e. on the cross-pieces) (fig. 94a), with alternate cramps under and over the structure, to minimise the chance of 'bowing' of the structure under pressure.

Checking for Squareness

To check for the 'squareness' of the corners (i.e. that they form true right-angles), it is possible to use a large (300 mm (12 in)) try-square, but it is much more accurate to use the diagonal measurement from opposite corners (fig. 94b). If the structure

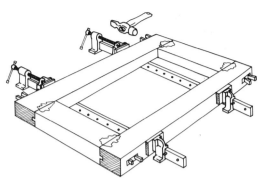

Fig. 94a. Cramping up a frame with sash cramps Note the use of wooden blocks between the pads of the sash cramp and the frame to spread the pressure and avoid possible damage to the frame

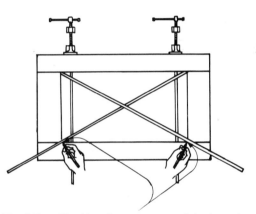

Fig. 94b. Checking the squareness of the frame by checking the diagonals with a 'squaring rod'. The framework is square when the diagonals marked on the squaring rod are equal

is truly 'square', the two diagonal measurements will be identical. Should one diagonal be longer than the other, the frame can be 'pulled' by moving the cramps at an angle across the frame and tightening up, measuring as you increase the pressure, until the diagonals are exactly the same length. Fig. 94c clearly shows the direction of movement of the cramps to effect the required correction. Be sure to keep the frame pressed tightly down on the bar of the cramps to avoid gluing up a 'winding' frame. (Winding is a diagonal twisting effect.)

When the glue is dry, remove the cramps

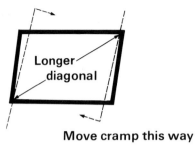

Move cramp this way

Longer diagonal

Move cramp this way

Fig. 94c. Pulling the frame square

and lightly skim over the surface of the wood to reduce all sides to the same surface level, while, at the same time, removing all working marks, superfluous glue, etc. Finish by glasspapering, using a block. Any further finishing required is fully dealt with in Chapter 8.

Cramping Mitre Joints

If you want to cramp a frame with mitred joints (i.e. joints at 45°) you will not be able to use sash cramps. You can buy special mitre cramps (fig. 95) for this purpose but you can manufacture your own mitre cramps by making four softwood

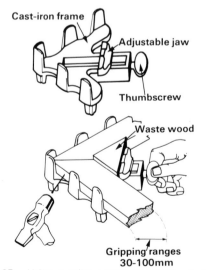

Cast-iron frame

Adjustable jaw

Thumbscrew

Waste wood

Gripping ranges 30-100mm

Fig. 95. Using a mitre square to cramp up mitre joints while gluing and nailing. A simple home-made tourniquet cramp for mitre joints is shown in fig. 33

blocks as shown in fig. 33. These blocks have 90° notches cut in them, as shown, and a small groove is cut in the back of the block. Several turns of strong twine are looped round the four blocks as they 'sit' on the four corners of the frame (fig. 95). Strips of hardwood (approximately $150 \times 18 \times 5$ mm ($6 \times \frac{2}{3} \times \frac{1}{5}$ in)) are then inserted between the strands of the twine and turned, as with a tourniquet. Opposite sides and ends are tightened together. Check for 'squareness' across the diagonals. If necessary, 'pulling' square may be achieved by varying the tightness of the opposing tourniquets. The need for this type of cramping is eliminated if dowel rods are used to strengthen the plain mitred corners. With these in use, sash cramps can be used with care if applied directly along the rails and on opposite sides of the frame. Take care not to impose undue pressure; too great a pressure could break the dowel rods.

Remember! Glue plus cramping does not make up for a poor joint. Undue stress by over-cramping may, temporarily, effect what appears to be a good joint but the inbuilt stresses will in time pull the joint apart. There is no substitute for accurate, careful work.

Garden Sheds, Greenhouses, Coal Bunkers, etc.

These are large projects, but their size alone need not deter you. If anything, the larger the structure, within reason, the easier it is to make. No two people will want the same shed or greenhouse. In any case, structures of this magnitude call for a complete working drawing (see p. 125). Study the drawing carefully before you make any attempt to start work and assure yourself that you fully understand what is entailed. Cutting lists for your timber usually accompany such working drawings. The basic principles of frame construction, dealt with in this chapter, will apply to your shed or greenhouse (or even a wooden garage). They are, invariably, made up in the form of four frames (two sides and two ends) one of which contains the door and one, at least, a window. These frames, separately constructed, are usually bolted together, but greenhouses, with their lighter framing, may be screwed together with angle brackets. Two further, but lighter, frames make up your roof which is, almost invariably, covered with a bituminous roofing felt, battened down with strips of wood and roofing nails (see p. 113).

Your plans (drawings) may be found in appropriate books in your local library or you may write to any one of the publishers of current DIY magazines who are, generally, quite ready to help. You might, in time, be bold enough to design your own structure, but stick to the principles laid down in these pages.

7 Construction~Carcase Construction

Boxes, shelves and cabinets. Layout and procedure. Gluing and cramping. Kitchen units, drawers, fitting locks.

Unlike framed constructions, carcase constructions use fairly large pieces of wood rather than battens or strips. Basically, carcase constructions cover all types of boxes, cabinets, bookshelves, cupboards, chests and various types of drawers. Although discussed separately, frame and carcase constructions are often complementary. Many carcase constructions are made up from an assembly of frames with panels and, of course, doors, which are frames, and are an integral part of many carcase constructions. The basic joints used in carcase constructions are:

● butt joints
● rebated (lap) joints
● tongued and grooved joints
● housing joints: through, stopped and dovetailed
● dovetailed joints, many varieties
● dowelled joints
● mitred joints, variously strengthened
● various commercially produced fasteners for use with man-made boards.

All of these joints are discussed in detail and illustrated in Chapter 4.

Of the joints recommended for carcase construction only the dovetail joint will cause the amateur any serious trouble. A great deal more skill and experience is required to make a success of the dovetail joint, even the comparatively simple through dovetail. Modern adhesives are of such strength and so simple and clean to use, that the simpler joints provide sufficient strength for all but the most highly stressed structures. Modern man-made boards keep their shape and may be bought in virtually any size, so that length, width and, to a lesser extent, thickness are no problem and the rather tedious and time- and skill-demanding processes of jointing boards of natural wood together to achieve a required width are eliminated. Such boards, however, require rather special jointing processes in a number of circumstances.

Box Construction

These are basically composed of two long sides, two shorter ends and, possibly, some internal partitions. A lid may be fitted. It should be taken as a general principle that the long sides go 'right through', while the ends tuck in between them; thus any visible end grain does not show on the long sides, usually recognised as the front or facing sides.

All wood should be accurately planed to size and ends should be perfectly square both ways, i.e. on the ends and on the thickness. Always be sure to allow for the thickness of the wood that you are using for the sides, ends and any partitions when calculating sizes. Unless the external dimensions are specially important (e.g. where the box has to fit into a special place or opening) you would do well to work on internal sizes and then add on the total number of thicknesses of wood used in sides, ends and partitions.

The most easily constructed joints for simple boxes are shown in fig. 96. When nails are used to supplement an adhesive, it is best if they are driven in at an angle as

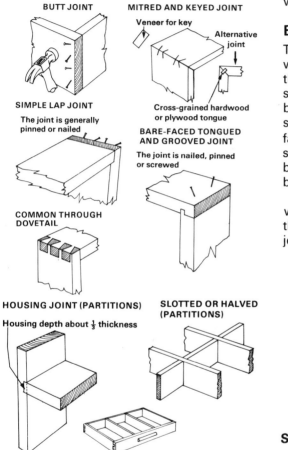

BUTT JOINT

MITRED AND KEYED JOINT

Veneer for key

Alternative joint

SIMPLE LAP JOINT

The joint is generally pinned or nailed

Cross-grained hardwood or plywood tongue

BARE-FACED TONGUED AND GROOVED JOINT

The joint is nailed, pinned or screwed

COMMON THROUGH DOVETAIL

HOUSING JOINT (PARTITIONS)

Housing depth about ⅓ thickness

SLOTTED OR HALVED (PARTITIONS)

Fig. 96. Joints used in box-making

shown — this is called 'dovetail nailing', a method which prevents easy separation of one piece from the other. The pins or nails should be as thin as possible and they should be pin-punched below the surface of the wood and the small hole left should be filled in with either a proprietary wood-filler or, better still and cheaper, one made up from a mixture of resin glue and some fine sawdust made from the actual wood being used. The holes should be firmly packed with the filler, not just given a superficial smear over the surface. The filler should be left a little 'proud' of the hole as it tends to shrink on drying. Surfaces thus treated may be lightly planed down and glasspapered, when the small nail holes will become virtually invisible.

Bookshelves

These are always popular with home woodworkers since they can be made to fit the exact requirements of the books to be stored and the space available — few bought bookshelves meet all of our personal requirements. Bookshelves generally fall into the following categories: (1) Free-standing. (2) Wall fixtures. (3) With fitted back. (4) Without back. (5) Flush top and bottom. (6) Proud top and bottom.

Here again, the amateur DIY enthusiast will be well advised to use the simplest of the alternative joints which are housing joints, through or stopped.

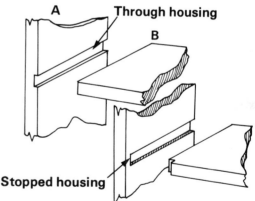

A   **Through housing**

B

Stopped housing

Fig. 97. Housing joints used in the construction of bookshelves
A shows a housed joint with groove taken right through
B shows a housed joint stopped at the front

Both through and stopped housings will have to be pinned through the uprights in most cases.

If a set of shelves with flush top and bottom is required then the top and bottom cross pieces will have to be glued and nailed to the uprights, using either a butt

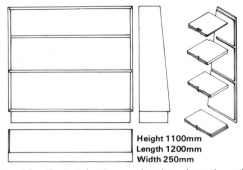

Height 1100mm
Length 1200mm
Width 250mm

Fig. 98. Typical bookcase showing through and stopped housing joints, with lapped joints top and bottom

joint or a rebate (lap) joint. A typical example of a bookcase of this type is shown in fig. 98.

It is possible to apply the plywood backing direct to the sides of the shelving and, in order to render it less conspicuous, it should be set back 2–3 mm ($\frac{1}{8}$ in) from the outer surface of the sides and lightly tapered down along its edges (fig. 99). It

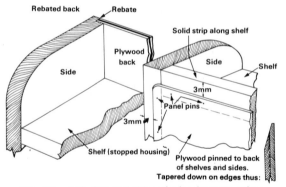

Fig. 99. Left: Rebated sides of a bookcase to take a plywood back. Right: Alternative method of attaching a back without rebating

should be pinned in place, using 10 mm ($\frac{2}{5}$ in) panel pins. This method is recommended, where acceptable, to woodworkers of limited skill and experience.

Cabinets

The same basic construction applies to bathroom, kitchen, first-aid and cocktail cabinets. Here again, the simple lap and housing joints can successfully be used by woodworkers of limited experience for the

four corners and any number of shelves required. Fig. 100 shows a variety of cabinets with alternative shelving arrangements. Doors for any of these cabinets can be framed, as described in Chapter 6, but simpler and very effective doors can be made from a single sheet of practically any

Fig. 100. Alternative designs for cabinets
Above: Through dovetails on corners with mitred plinth around the base. A blockboard door might complete the cabinet

Simple lapped joints used on the top and bottom corners. The shelf is stopped housed

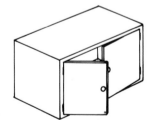

Plywood or laminboard doors with brass hinges and plastic spring catches

A simple cabinet, useful as a small cocktail cabinet. The drop arms are obtainable at a hardware store

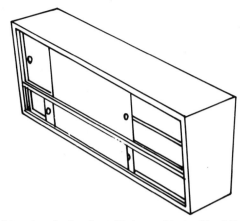

Attractive sloping front kitchen cabinet with sliding plywood doors at the top and decorative glass panels at the bottom. The plastic grooved strip for the runners is available at DIY stores

of the man-made boards, although plywood is not recommended as a first choice. Doors may be inset within the four sides of the cabinet or planted direct on to the front edges. The latter method is much the simpler for the amateur; it makes the fitting of the now universally used, spring-loaded plastic catch very easy. Full instructions for the fitting of these very inexpensive catches is given on the card or packet with it (see 'Hinges', p. 114).

Procedures

1. Prepare wood to size.
2. Make all joints and carefully fit them (see Chapter 4).
3. Clean up all surfaces that cannot be reached after assembly, using a finely-set smoothing plane followed by glasspaper (coarse, medium and fine) as described in Chapter 6.
4. Assemble dry (no glue). By using this preliminary, dry assembly, you will quickly discover any snags in the order and method of assembly; something that you will need to get right before the final assembly, using glue. It will also have your sash cramps 'set', with their wooden pressure blocks, ready for the final gluing up.
5. Glue up, using a wooden spreader.

Cramp up as described on p. 141 (fig. 101).
6. Check across diagonals for squareness (p. 141). As with framed construction, any deviation from perfect squareness can be

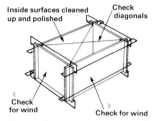

Fig. 101a. Cramping up a carcase If you can lay your hands on eight sash cramps then you can use them as shown above

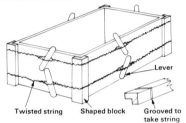

Fig. 101b. If, as is likely, you don't have eight sash cramps then you can, quite cheaply, set up the arrangement of string blocks and tourniquet levers to cramp up your carcase, as shown above

rectified by 'pulling' the carcase square by angling the cramps (fig. 94c, p. 142). Where possible, use at least two cramps across any shelving within the carcase.
7. Leave for adhesive to dry and then remove cramps after at least eight hours.
8. Where necessary, pin the joints and punch the nails below the surface of the wood. Fill any holes with wood filler and, when dry, clean off. Always use the thinnest pins possible consistent with strength but, in some cases, it will be necessary to use oval nails (p. 113). This is particularly the case in larger structures that carry considerable weight or are heavily stressed. The heads of the oval nails may easily be punched in as for panel pins.

When all cramps have been removed and pins punched well in and the holes filled, you can clean up the outside surfaces. It will help to strengthen the structure if any back is fitted before smooth-planing is carried out. A full and detailed description of finishing the surface is given in Chapter 8.

Kitchen Units

The shape, size and layout of kitchen units vary so much that only a broad, general outline of construction principles can be given. If, however, you have followed the instructions given in the preceding chapters for the construction of joints, frames and carcases and if you have understood the nature and use of man-made boards, you will be able to apply these general principles to your own particular problems. Fig. 102

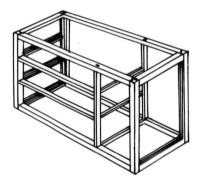

Fig. 102. **Basic framing for a kitchen unit** Depending upon the skill and inclination of the operator, the joints used in this basic kitchen unit can be stub mortice and tenon, halving butt and dowelled or housing. The unit could be completed by a blockboard door, three drawers and plywood panels

shows a typical structure for a framed-up kitchen unit. The joints used could be halving, bridle, mortice and tenon or dowelled.

If the unit were to be painted, the ends and back could be covered with 3–4 mm ($\frac{1}{8}$–$\frac{1}{6}$ in) plywood, glued and pinned to the framework. This would give great strength and stiffness. For many years this type of construction has been common practice in the caravan industry and it has stood up to hard wear very well indeed. A blockboard door could be fitted in or on the aperture at the right-hand end and drawers could be fitted into the three horizontal openings to the left.

Drawer Construction

The traditional construction for drawers requires dovetails of a fairly difficult type to make. These are called 'drawer dovetails' or lapped dovetails. With the advancement of adhesives, many commercially produced drawers utilise a much simpler construction that can be copied by the DIY woodworker, particularly if it is intended to paint the drawer fronts. Fig. 103 shows a simple

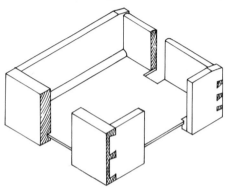

Fig. 103. **Lap dovetails used in a traditional drawer construction** A simplified construction could use lapped joints, glued and pinned at both the front and rear ends of the drawer

drawer construction using lap joints. The sides should be glued and pinned to the fronts, thus making a very strong and serviceable joint. A similar joint can be made at the back of the drawer but this time the lap is made on the sides with the end coming in between them. A plywood bottom is grooved into the front and sides, passing under the back, into which it is screwed. Two runners per drawer will be necessary for the drawer to slide on. Battens, 50 × 18 mm (2 × $\frac{2}{3}$ in) must be dowelled into the front cross-bars at either end of the openings and then screwed into the uprights at the back. Two thin strips of wood, 15 × 12 mm ($\frac{3}{5}$ × $\frac{1}{2}$ in) must be glued and pinned on to the surface of these battens (one on each) so that they are the width of the drawer apart, i.e. wide enough for the drawer to slide in and out between them. These are to prevent the drawer from slewing sideways and jamming.

Fitting a Top to your Unit

Your unit may now be completed by fixing a working top to the framework by means of the plates described on p. 138. There are proprietary brands of particle board or blockboard that are manufactured with a hard-wearing laminate surface on one or both sides. They are supplied in a variety of surface patterns and colours and one of these would provide an ideal working surface. Alternatively, you could fix a stainless-steel sink unit and draining board in place of the worktop but unless you are skilled in the necessary plumbing, you will be well advised to call on the services of a professional plumber at this stage.

Lock Fitting

It is almost certain that you will require some of the doors and drawers to be fitted with some sort of lock. Chapter 3 dealt in detail with the types of lock available and recommended to the DIY woodworker. The fitting of some of these locks calls for careful marking out and precise workmanship but nothing that patience and application cannot cope with. Fig. 104 clearly shows the steps in marking

out and cutting the necessary socket to take a cupboard lock. Similar procedures are used in the marking out and cutting for a drawer lock. Cupboard locks may be purchased either right-handed or left-handed. The stages in marking out and cutting are:

1. Mark out on the closing edge of the door. Ensure that the keyhole is above the centre and transfer this precise location to the reverse side of the door and then, using a marking gauge, mark in the distance from the centre of the keyhole to the edge of the door. Do this on both sides of the door.

2. Drill with appropriate sized drill, drilling half-way in from both sides. With a padsaw make the slot for the key.

3. Now carefully mark out a socket to take the rectangular portion of the lock mechanism, check again and cut out.

4. Putting the lock into the socket that you have cut, mark round the outside with a marking knife as shown.

5. Now set your marking gauge to the

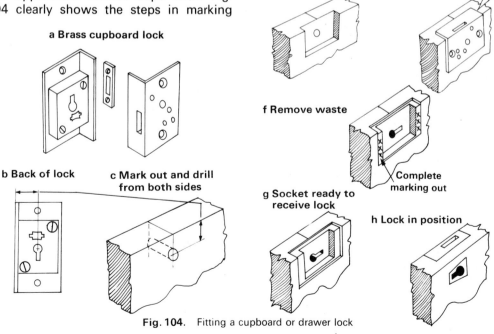

a Brass cupboard lock

b Back of lock

c Mark out and drill from both sides

d Cut out socket to take lock mechanism

e Mark round top edge with knife

f Remove waste

Complete marking out

g Socket ready to receive lock

h Lock in position

Fig. 104. Fitting a cupboard or drawer lock

width of the lock plate and gauge this width between the length marks in (4).

6. Gauge the thickness of the plate down the edge.

7. Now carefully remove the waste with a chisel.

8. Place the lock in position and, with a marking knife, cut round the outside of the back plate.

9. Remove the waste with a chisel, checking and fitting from time to time until the whole lock fits perfectly.

10. Screw lock into the socket prepared.

11. Close the door and put the key into the lock. Now turn the key several times, hard enough to make a mark against the side of the carcase. (You could put a piece of carbon paper between the bolt of the lock and the side of the carcase to make the mark more distinct.)

12. Cut out bolt slot to the correct depth, using a small, firmer or bevelled-edge chisel. Cut in the striker plate.

13. It is best if the keyhole is protected by an escutcheon plate as shown.

You may need to fit a mortice lock to an outside door or on to your garage side door. These offer an excellent degree of protection since all fixing screws are hidden when the door is shut. The stages for fitting a mortice are:

1. Mark the position of your lock on the edge of the door (fig. 105). It is usual to position the handle of a door about 1 m (3 ft 3 in) above the ground level and your lock should be close to this. Try to avoid any centre rail of a panelled door.

2. Gauge (with a mortice gauge, see p. 101) the width of the mechanism of the lock between the limits marked as indicated in (1).

3. Drill the majority of the waste wood from the mortice with a brace and bit (p. 101); the bit should be about 3 mm ($\frac{1}{8}$ in) smaller than the width of the required mortice to allow for a final cleaning up with a chisel (fig. 105). Mark the required depth on your bit by means of masking or plastic tape.

4. Insert the lock into the mortice and mark

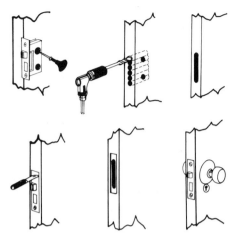

Fig. 105. Fitting a mortice lock When fitting a mortice, first hold the face of the lock against the edge of the door. Mark out with care and precision the exact length and width of the required mortice. Locate the knob spindle and keyhole and drill them out.
On the centre line of the mortice, drill out to the correct depth. When the mortice has been cleaned up with a sharp chisel, insert the lock and, with a sharp knife, mark round the sides of the plate. Chisel out the recess to house the face plate of the lock. Now put the lock into position, screw in the face plate, insert the spindle and attach all plates and knobs

round the cover plate and chisel out to the required depth.

5. Set a gauge from the cover plate to the keyhole centre and transfer this measurement to both sides of the door. Measure carefully from the key-hole centre to the edge of the lock and transfer this measurement on to the door on both sides.

6. Drill through from both sides of the door to the middle. Use a padsaw to complete the slot to take the key.

7. Put the lock into the mortice and screw into position.

8. Put the key into the lock and turn it several times till it makes a visible mark on the stile of the door frame. (You can use carbon paper between the bolt of the lock and the door frame to heighten the impression.)

9. Remove the required amount of wood to make the slot to house the bolt of the lock with a small mortice chisel.

10. Locate and screw the cover plate to the bolt mortice on to the door frame.

If you plan to fit a Yale type lock, you will find detailed fitting instructions in the container box, together with a location template. All that is required of you is complete accuracy and care in marking out.

Most other types of lock that you are likely to use are simple screw-on types and the fixing of these is self-evident.

Preceding chapters have now detailed a variety of framed and carcase constructions sufficient for you to be able to cope with the majority of home jobs. Remember that these two basic types of construction are seldom used in isolation — each complements the other.

Now go on to Chapter 8 for detailed instructions on 'finishing' your work. So often the only difference between the work of the amateur and that of the professional is in the 'finish'. In the construction, quite often the work of the amateur exceeds that of the commercially produced article but the commercial world knows the eye-catching appeal of a high surface finish. With a little more patience, the amateur can, at least, equal the performance of the professional — it is well worth it!

8 Finishing

The preparation of surfaces ... smoothing plane, glasspaper, scrapers. Painting, varnishing, waxing. The use of stain (dye). Coating with plastic laminates.

When you have completed the construction of your job you will, naturally, want to give it some form of surface finish. There are three main considerations at this stage:

● The physical conditions in which the structure will operate.
● The nature of the materials used in its construction.
● Aesthetic appeal.

Whatever the conditions, you will, first, have to prepare the surface of the wood to receive the final treatment. Here again, the extent of the preparation will depend to a large extent upon the nature of the ultimate surface finish. A hardwood, for example, with a fine grain that you wish to feature, would need a great deal more care in the preparation of its surface than, say, the softwood required for a kitchen shelf that you intend to paint. Remember, however, the better the surface preparation, the better the ultimate 'finish', whatever form it may take.

Surface Preparation

The first stage in the surface preparation of any wood is to remove working marks (fig. 52, p. 123) and any accumulated dirt by means of a very sharp, finely set smoothing plane, used in the direction of the grain. Most softwoods respond well to this initial planing but many hardwoods have a 'contrary' grain (p. 105), that results in rough patches being left on the surface of

the wood, no matter how sharp and finely set your plane may be or from which direction you plane. To overcome this uneven roughness, a cabinet-maker's scraper must be used. This consists of a rectangle of fine-quality steel, 100–150 mm (4–6 in) long × 50–60 mm (2–2½ in) wide and 1–1·5 mm ($\frac{1}{25} - \frac{1}{16}$ in) thick. These scrapers are flexible and cut by means of a 'burr' thrown up on the long sides. The scraper is held between the thumbs and fingers of

Fig. 106a. Cabinet scraper in use

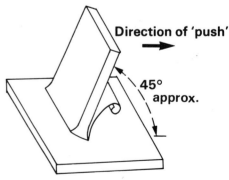

Direction of 'push'

45° approx.

Fig. 106b. Cutting action of scraper

both hands (fig. 106) and bent into a convex curve by pressure with the thumbs. It is then pushed over the surface of the wood where the rough patches occur, removing very fine scrapings from the rough patches until they are smooth. Scrapes succeed where the plane fails because their action is very local to the rough patches and they can be manipulated in the direction where they can be seen to be having the desired effect. The cutting or scraping is done by the leading (convex) edge of the scraper.

When you have prepared your surface with your plane and/or scraper, you are ready for glasspapering. For general work on softwood, you should glasspaper the surface, **in the direction of the grain**, with grade M2 (coarse) glasspaper wrapped round a cork block, for preference, or round a wooden block of an approximate size of 100 × 50 × 25 mm (4 × 2 × 1 in). Follow this with grade 1½ glasspaper. This should suffice for typical softwood finishes such as paint and varnish. For rougher work, the second rubbing down should be across the grain to give the surface of the wood a 'key' for the paint.

For hardwoods, M2 grade of glasspaper is rather too coarse to start with. Start with F2 and go on to use grade 1 and finish up with grade 0 or even 00 if a very high finish, highlighting the grain features, is required.

Applied Finishes

Bare wood soon discolours, absorbs moisture and collects dirt so, apart from purely aesthetic appeal, it is a physical necessity to apply a surface coating of some type. Another book in this series, *Home Decorating*, explains, in considerable detail, the best surface treatments to use in a wide variety of conditions. A correctly chosen and properly applied finish provides the surface of the wood with a protective coating that is hygienic and easily cleaned and maintained. Typical finishes for wood are:

Softwoods
Paint: internal and external uses.
Varnish: internal and external uses.
Creosote: external use only.
Proprietary wood protectors and finishes: mainly external use.

Hardwoods
Paint: whenever grain features are not of importance. Internal and external uses: some hardwoods, however (e.g. oak), tend to 'throw off' paint and it should not be used externally on these.
Varnish: particularly where grain is a feature. Internal and external use.
Wax. When grain is a feature: used internally and externally.
Linseed Oil. Enhances colour and is excellent externally. Hardwood is, however, seldom painted for internal uses.

Paint

Paint comes in three basic types:

● **Primer.** Use on new wood as a first, grain-filling coat. Acts as a 'key' between new wood and subsequent coats. Most primers contain some lead.
● **Undercoats.** A colour base and 'key' for subsequent coats. A 'flat', very opaque and non-gloss paint.
● **Gloss or Matt Finishing.** This provides a smooth, hard-wearing and easily cleaned surface. The gloss gives a high shine to the work, while the matt gives a low gloss, textured finish.
   The three types are used in the order given. For a really durable finish you will need one coat of primer, one of undercoat and two coats of gloss or matt finishing. Remember that you should apply your coats as thinly as possible consistent with complete cover. Lightly rub down the dry surface between coats with grade 0 glasspaper. Buy the best brushes that you can afford and do spend some time cleaning them, as instructed on the maker's instructions. No brushes are cheap and a little time spent on their cleaning will pay handsome dividends. Polyurethane paints are

now popular. They give a high gloss, hard surface and can be used with complete confidence on external work, areas of high stress and where heat might affect other paints.

Knotting. Some softwoods contain resinous knots (see p. 107) and, if left untreated, they can cause serious blistering of your paintwork. Before applying paint of any sort, these knots should be painted over with 'knotting'. You can buy proprietary brands of knotting or you can make your own up by dissolving shellac in methylated spirit.

Varnish

Varnish gives a transparent finish and is thus ideal for highlighting attractive grain in hardwood. It is equally suitable for use on softwoods, on which it provides a high resistance surface. Polyurethane varnishes provide a 'glass-hard' surface which is very durable and easily cleaned. The simplest way to apply is by brush, very sparingly. Thin coats dry hard and smooth; heavy coats tend to give wrinkles and 'runs'. Between coats, when they have dried hard, rub down lightly with grade 0 or 00 glasspaper, before applying further coats. Clean your brushes in the 'thinners' recommended for the varnish.

Wax

Suitable for hardwoods. After a high degree of surface finish has been obtained, wax, preferably beeswax based rather than paraffin-wax based, should be thoroughly rubbed into the grain, using a soft cloth, in a circular motion. It should then be allowed to dry off for five to ten minutes and then it should be rubbed vigorously with a clean, soft, cotton or linen cloth, free from fluff, along the direction of the grain (fig. 107). This process should be carried out at least three times; the more

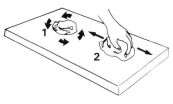

Fig. 107. Wax Polishing
1. With a cloth rub a small amount of wax evenly on the surface
2. Rub vigorously with clean linen
3. Repeat process as necessary

times it is repeated the better will be the finish.

Oil

Use either boiled or raw linseed oil. Oil improves the colour of most hardwoods. It should be applied with a fluff-free cloth and vigorously rubbed – this can be a hard and somewhat tedious process. The oil can be cut down with a little turpentine or white spirit in order to make the rubbing a little less arduous, but do not overdo the turpentine or you will spoil the result.

Creosote

A by-product of coal or the distillation of wood, it should only be used externally. Basic creosote is very dark brown in colour and it gives off a very pungent odour but it offers excellent protection against the effects of persistent damp and attacks by fungi and insects. It should be applied by brush but great care must be taken to avoid any possible splashing of the skin or eyes. More recently a refined version has been marketed that is lighter in colour and with a less pungent odour at the cost of some loss of protective quality.

Proprietary Wood Protectives

Some excellent wood protectives for external use are now marketed in a reasonable range of colours. They are lighter in substance than creosote and may be applied either by brush or by spray gun. For cedar wood, a special dressing is required. All of these proprietory preparations are, however, expensive in comparison with the more basic creosote.

Stains (Dyes)

If you wish to change the colour of your wood, or if you wish to heighten the existing colour, you can use a wood dye or stain. These can be obtained in three basic types:

1. Water stains, **2.** Spirit stains and **3.** Oil stains.

Water Stain

These may be purchased in powder or crystals. They are made up into a solution by adding warm water. Water stains are the cheapest but they have the fault of raising the grain of the wood, leaving the surface somewhat rough to the touch. To prepare the surface for polishing after staining with a water stain you will need to rub it down very lightly with well worn grade 0 glasspaper. Do not rub too hard or you may remove some of the stain. Water stains really need up to twenty-four hours to dry out before you attempt to use polish.

Spirit Stains

There is a fair range of proprietary spirit stains on the market. They are considerably more expensive than water stains but they penetrate deeply into the surface of the wood and they dry very quickly. The stain is normally applied by brush and this must be done fairly quickly to avoid unevenness in surface colouring. It helps if the fresh-stained surface is lightly rubbed over with a soft, fluff-free cloth; this evens out the colour. Most spirit stains contain an anti-fungus insecticide in their make-up. One very important advantage of spirit stains is that they do not raise the grain of the wood.

Oil Stains

These are more suitable for external structures but can be used generally. They flow on easily and do not promote patchiness. All surplus oil should be rubbed off to aid drying, which is normally rather slow. Oil stains do not raise the grain of the wood.

Techniques to Use when Staining

Either a brush or a rag may be used to apply the stain but if a brush is used the surface should be rubbed over with a soft rag before the stain has had time to dry off. Always try your stain on an odd piece of the actual wood you intend to stain. Leave the stain until it is quite dry before making any final decision since most stains dry out a different colour, not necessarily lighter. Remember, too, that any form of polish subsequently applied to the stained surface will, almost certainly, bring it up a shade or two darker, so you should allow for this or experiment first.

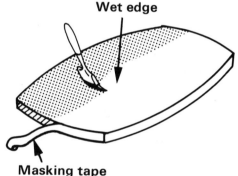

Fig. 108. Staining a surface Always keep the leading edge of the area being stained wet, or your results will be patchy. Tape up the end grain and stain it later with a weaker solution.

Always have a test run on a waste piece of wood of the same type that you intend to stain. Wait till it dries before making a final decision

Always use your brush or rag outwards towards the edges of your wood in order to avoid causing 'runs' down the edges. These are particularly hard to disguise if you have been using spirit stain. Always keep the advancing edge of your stained area wet, this will eliminate patchiness (fig. 108).

Wood Fillers

Some woods, having coarse, open grain, would, left untreated, absorb a great deal of dye and require an excessive number of finishing coats of polish. To avoid this and, in some instances, to highlight the beauty of the grain, a wood filler is used to fill the open pores of the wood. Many proprietary brands of wood filler are marketed but do not confuse these with so-called 'plastic wood', which is used, primarily, for filling holes and gaps in the timber or badly fitting joints. You require a 'grain filler' and you can make up your own much more cheaply by using household whitening and white spirit, mixed with a little gold size and suitable colouring. Mix to a consistency approximating to that of cold gruel.

Apply the mixture to the surface of the wood with a cloth and rub it hard into the grain with a felt pad. Before the mixture dries right off, wipe off any surplus with a cloth. Finally, even out the whole surface with a clean cotton or linen cloth and leave to dry. When the surface is completely dry, rub down with grade 0 glasspaper. A surface so treated will:

- Highlight grain pattern
- Reduce consumption of stain
- Reduce work on polishing
- Reduce total cost of finish.

Plastic Laminates

If you want a very hard and durable working top surface, capable of withstanding heat, damp and abrasion by knives, you would do well to consider the use of a plastic laminate. There are a number of good proprietary brands on the market and they come in a variety of colours, textures and patterns. They are usually about $1-1\frac{1}{2}$ mm ($\frac{1}{25}-\frac{1}{16}$ in) in thickness and are cheapest if purchased in the complete sheet, the sizes of which vary a little from manufacturer to manufacturer. If you ask for specially cut sizes to suit your own particular needs you must expect to pay rather more per square metre to cover wastage and labour.

Plastic laminates are stuck to the core top, usually a man-made board (see p. 108), but the technique is a special one which you would be well advised to follow carefully. Firstly, you must prepare your laminate very carefully by cutting and finishing it very accurately to the required size and shape of the core board. It may be sawn with a very fine-toothed saw, such as a dovetail saw, with not less than 14 teeth per 25 mm (inch). Smooth the edges down with grades 1 and 0 glasspaper. Any holes to be made should be drilled with a morse drill and not with a brace and bit.

The adhesive that you should use is what is called an impact adhesive (see p. 110). This type of adhesive should be spread thinly but evenly over both surfaces to be brought into contact. The surfaces should then be allowed to dry for at least ten minutes when they will feel dry to the touch. The next stage is the one calling for precision and care because impact adhesives grip immediately and very firmly the instant that the two surfaces are brought into contact. This being the case, there is absolutely no opportunity to slide or manoeuvre the laminate into its correct position on the core board once it has made contact with it; hence the need for absolute, first time precision in locating it. No cramps are needed but it can be helpful if weights are placed at strategic points around the edges of the laminate for an hour or so.

With growing skill and experience you may feel ready to tackle more ambitious projects and Chapter 9 outlines the basic principles underlying the making of kitchen and bedroom units and in the conversions of rooms and lofts into new and exciting accommodation.

9 Use of Man~made Boards

Plywood, hardboard, blockboard, laminboard, particle (chip) board, celotex and surfaced boards. Fixing, jointing, edging. Typical examples of redesigned and restructured kitchens and bedrooms. Loft conversions.

The advent of such man-made board as plywood, hardboard, blockboard, laminboard, particle (chip) board and the laminate surfaced boards has transformed the world of the DIY woodworker. Generally, most of them work out a little dearer than the cheaper, natural timbers but if one takes into account the time and labour and the advantageous physical features (see Chapter 2), they can be more economical in the long run. The beautifully finished proprietary makes of surfaced boards, using a particle board core, faced by a laminate or photo veneer, make cabinet-making little more than an assembly job.

These materials are widely, almost exclusively, used by the furniture, radio and television manufacturers for their contemporary cabinets, units and room dividers. They do away with a considerable amount of traditional frame and carcase construction procedures, provided that you are prepared to design your structures on a basically rectilineal format. Slabs of blockboard, laminboard or particle board, or any of the proprietary faced boards, may be joined together by simple angle brackets (fig. 112) to form carcase structures that would normally require lap, housed or dovetailed joints.

Normal wood screws may be used successfully with blockboard or laminboard but particle (chip) board tends to break up internally when penetrated by woodscrews. If particle board is used, you should use self-tapping screws as used by metalworkers (see Chapter 3). These get a very firm grip on the particle structure without damaging it. Self-tapping screws may be successfully withdrawn if the structure needs to be dismantled.

One of the drawbacks, at the present time, of the proprietary surfaced boards is their rather limited range of thicknesses. If you need to use a thickness outside the range of these boards, you can always use a basic blockboard or laminboard, whose thickness range is 15–25 mm ($\frac{3}{5}$–1 in), and use a plastic laminate on the surface. To disguise the end grain of the wood strips used in the construction of these boards, there is a wide variety of edging strips, some self-adhesive, that may be applied. They can be plain wood coloured, black or decorative, according to choice (fig. 110).

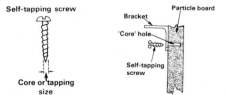

Fig. 109. Core or tapping sized hole for self-tapping screws

Fig. 110a. Lipping blockboard or laminboard to hide end grain blocks The edges of blockboard can be covered by a variety of lippings to hide the end grain

A softwood or semi hardwood lipping strip pinned and glued flush

A softwood or hardwood lipping grooved in and glued flush

A softwood or hardwood lipping grooved in and glued flush

A softwood or hardwood lipping with a tongue of ply, hardwood or plastic glued in

A metal or plastic angle screwed and glued on from the back of the panel

A softwood or hardwood capping nailed or screwed to a panel edge with punched or pelleted fixings

Fig. 110b. Alternative covers for the end grain of blockboard

Plywood is seldom used for carcase construction since at thicknesses above 12 mm ($\frac{1}{2}$ in) it becomes very expensive and less resistant to warping, twisting and distortion. It is most successfully used as panelling in framework, backs of units and for smaller type doors.

Techniques with Man-made Boards

Planing
No man-made boards should be planed on the surface since this is quite true and flat and consists of a thin veneer of wood over a core. You would quickly plane through this veneer and ruin the surface. The surface may be sanded to improve the quality of surface finish on untreated surfaces. The edges, however, are a different matter. Since your panels will almost certainly be cut from a larger sheet you will be left with rough-sawn sides and ends, which you will have to plane. Use a well sharpened, finely set smoothing plane for this job. On the ends where the core blocks show you must never plane straight across the top or you will, almost certainly, split out your wood, however sharp and finely set your plane may be (fig. 111). You should plane, as shown in the diagram, from each end, working into the middle. When planing along the other edges, however (the ones at right-angles to the end grain) you may safely plane straight through.

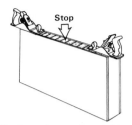

Fig. 111. Planing the ends of blockboard Always have a very sharp plane, finely set, and plane from both ends to the middle

Sawing
When sawing any man-made boards you should use a hand saw with rather smaller teeth than you would for a corresponding thickness in natural wood. A general guide is to use a saw with 10–12 teeth per 25 mm (inch).

Drilling
Unsurfaced plywood, blockboard and laminboard may be drilled with an ordinary carpenter's brace and bit. For a clean hole, you should drill through from one side until the point of the bit just breaks the surface on the opposite side. Withdraw the bit and, using the small hole on the opposite side to locate the centre point of the bit, drill through in the reverse direction to meet the partly drilled hole. If you have held the brace and bit level, you should have a clean hole. If, however, you are left with some roughness, then wrap some glasspaper round a piece of dowel rod and smooth up the inside of the hole with this simple tool. If your board is laminate or photo veneered, you must use a morse type drill for any holes required, where possible, drilling vertically, laminate side up, with a softwood block underneath to avoid any splitting out on the underside.

Commercial Qualities
Plywood, blockboard and laminboard are sold in the following categories relating to the quality of the facing veneers:

B Quality. For staining, clear sealing and high-class cellulose and paintwork. Free from all knots.

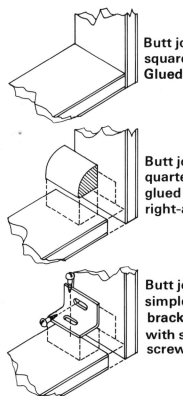

Butt joint, dead square on the ends. Glued and pinned

Butt joint with quartered block glued into right-angle

Butt joint with simple metal bracket screwed with self-tapping screws

Fig. 112. Methods of joining blockboards together

S Quality. Used on good-class work, especially where high-class paintwork is required.
BB Quality. Used for all jobs where a standard paintwork finish is sufficient. Used for overlay work.
WG Quality. These are for textured and aggregate finishes or for internal sheathing where appearance is not important.

It is quite possible to obtain boards with varying combinations of the face qualities, e.g. B on one side and BB on the other but, for all normal requirements, BB quality is quite satisfactory.

Commercial Sizes

Thickness: 12, 16, 18, 19, 22, 24, 25 mm.
Area:

1200 × 1200 mm	or	1500 × 1200 mm
1200 × 1500 mm		1500 × 1500 mm

1200 × 1800 mm	1500 × 1800 mm
1200 × 2100 mm	1500 × 2100 mm
1200 × 2400 mm +	1500 × 2400 mm +
1200 × 2700 mm	1500 × 2700 mm
1200 × 3000 mm +	1500 × 3000 mm +
1200 × 3600 mm +	1500 × 3600 mm +

Sizes marked + are normally stocked by local suppliers, although the other sizes are available.

Redesigning and Converting Kitchens, Bathrooms, Lofts, etc.

With house prices what they are today, many people, particularly young couples, are turning to older properties with a view to improving them over a period of time, largely by their own efforts. This has two advantages; a comparatively modest initial cost and an enhanced value as the conversions proceed. In this way a property becomes a real investment.

Improvement Grants

There are still a large number of people who are unaware that the Housing Act of 1969 gave Local Authorities greater freedom in the allocation of grants for the improvement and adaptation of older properties. These grants are now available to private owners and tenants. There are three types of grant for your improvements:

1. Discretionary. For improvements to a high standard or for conversions.
2. Standard. For the provision of certain standard amenities in existing buildings.
3. Special. For the provision of basic amenities in houses occupied by a number of families.

If you feel that the work you have in mind entitles you to any of these grants you should seek further information from your local council or read the appropriate leaflets published by the Ministry of Housing and Local Government.

Restructuring and Conversions

Whatever you have in mind in the way of restructuring or conversions, you need an imaginative eye or experienced help. The subject is so wide, the possibilities so great and the variations of such extent that no book of this size could possibly cover all the options. The general principles are, however, broadly similar in every case. The basic techniques outlined in this chapter will enable you to proceed with your own specific requirements.

If you are tackling the job with little or no professional help, you will be well advised to keep your requirements to a modest level in the first instance. For the restructuring or conversion of your kitchen you will need to consider sources of light, both natural and artificial — too sweeping changes here could well mean expensive professional involvement. The same comment could well apply to extensive changes in plumbing arrangements, since these invariably involve rather complicated regulations and by-laws.

Loft conversions usually give rise to lighting queries — will you be satisfied with artificial lighting or will you anticipate any natural lighting, such as a roof panel or dormer window? Unless you have above-average skill and experience you would do well to consult a local jobbing builder if you have the latter in mind. Assuming that you have thought carefully about these points, we can now look at some of the basic techniques underlying all reconstructions and conversions.

Floors

Replacement of Floor Boards and Provision of Floors in Roof Lofts

By using the grade of blockboard to suit your needs and the sizes to suit the area, much time and labour can be saved by laying full panels across the joists in random fashion (fig. 113). The end joints of panels will need no support, except where they meet the walls. When you are intending to renew completely a whole floor, you will

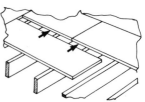

Plan showing joints unsupported

Panels with joints unsupported

Fig. 113. Panels used on floors with joints unsupported

find it economical to arrange your joists at centres to suit the panel length, thereby ensuring that the short joint is always supported (fig. 114).

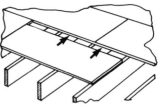

Panels with joints supported

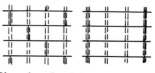

Plan showing joints supported

Fig. 114. Blockboard panels for flooring with joints supported When you are contemplating re-laying a whole floor, you will find it more economical to arrange your joists at centres to conform to the panel lengths. Always ensure that the short joint is supported

Overlaying Existing Floors

To save the labour and expense of taking up old and worn floor boards, blockboard panels may be laid over them where circumstances permit. They will provide a strong bridge over worn or damaged areas.

Tongued and grooved panels are available and are obviously the best solution to this problem but, of necessity, they come more expensive.

Internal Walls and Partitions

For partitions and walls required to sub-divide rooms and for wall linings in existing rooms, there is nothing better than plywood or blockboard. The use of these avoids any plastering and the walls made from either of these may be immediately painted or wall-papered. Wherever the Building Regulations dictate Class 1 surface spread of flame conditions, these boards can be treated with fire retardant paint or clear varnishes.

Wall Lining

Walls made from brickwork or breeze blocks can be lined with plywood sheets or panels of blockboard. Before covering the walls with such panelling, it is imperative to ensure that all possible sources of dampness are traced and eradicated. The walls must be properly prepared for lining with plywood. This will entail softwood battens, 50 × 18 mm (2 × $\frac{3}{4}$ in) being fixed in such a way that they present a true surface on which to fix the panels (fig. 115). These battens should be fixed to the

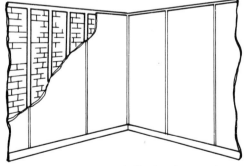

Fig. 115. Plywood panels fixed to battens that are screwed into wall plugs

walls by means of rawlplugs and sited at intervals of 400 mm (16 in). For this you will need a masonry drill. Full instructions for its use are given in the rawlplug packet,

including the size of the masonry drill required. You should use countersunk-head screws, 50 mm (2 in) long by 10 gauge in diameter (see Chapter 3).

A suitable thickness of plywood is 6·5 mm ($\frac{1}{4}$ in). These panels should be pinned to the battens at 150 mm (6 in) centres. You should plan your work so that the joints in the panels coincide with a batten. Your pins should be set in approximately 10 to 12 mm ($\frac{1}{2}$ in) from the edge of the plywood sheet, pin-punched in and filled with wood filler.

Partition Walls

For the DIY enthusiast, particularly if of limited experience, partition walls are best constructed as lightweight, single skinned structures, using blockboard. They are space saving and can be easily decorated. Three methods of constructing such partitions are shown in fig. 116.

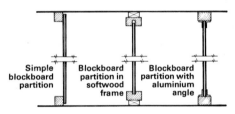

Fig. 116. Partition walls
Above: Alternative sections showing blockboard used in single-skinned partitions

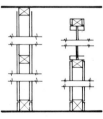

Alternative sections showing double-skinned ply-faced partitions, one glazed

Skirtings

These are easily constructed from plywood. They are very strong and give a fine decorative finish when painted. They can be used as part of a wall lining process or as a conventional skirting fixed direct to an existing wall (fig. 117).

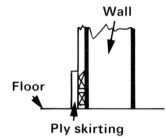

Fig. 117. Plywood used as a skirting board

Fixtures and Fittings

Most conversions rely heavily on a reorganisation of fixtures and fittings or adding these where none previously existed. Manmade boards reduce the need for framing to a very large extent. When designing your new fitments, you need to bear in mind the standard panel sizes and make use of them; this reduces costs. Fig. 118

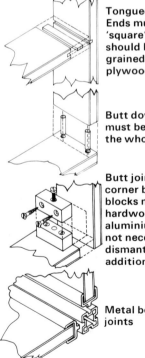

Tongued and grooved. Ends must be dead 'square'. The tongue should be either cross-grained hardwood or plywood

Butt dowelled. The ends must be dead 'square' and the whole joint is glued

Butt jointed with screwed corner blocks. These blocks may be of hardwood, plastic or aluminium alloy. If it is not necessary to dismantle the joint it may, additionally, be glued

Metal box-sectioned joints

Fig. 118. Methods of fixing blockboard panels. See also fig. 112

shows a variety of ways in which panels may be fixed together. Fig. 119 shows a typical conversion carried out on an old kitchen using a high proportion of man-made boards, while fig. 120 shows the modernising effect of blockboard and plywood used in a child's bedroom.

Loft Conversions

Fig. 121 shows a typical loft situation before any conversion has been attempted, while fig. 122 shows the same loft converted into a bed-sitter; ideal for a son or daughter who stops on at home for a while after leaving school. It could equally be used as a study, workshop or studio.

Detailed constructions for such conversions have not been attempted, since your personal requirements and the physical conditions of your accommodation will vary so much, but if you have followed the simple basic woodworking techniques described in this book, you will be able to apply them to your own particular circumstances and problems.

You can be helped a great deal by making use of the Technical Advice Services of the firms listed on p. 166. Many of the books listed will go into greater technical detail than is the brief of this publication but you must first gain the necessary skill and experience that the more advanced constructions and techniques outlined in these books require and towards which these pages can guide you.

Most Local Authorities run evening classes in Woodwork. You may feel that you could spare one evening each week and join one of these classes.

Whatever you decide, this book is a stepping stone to a new world — enjoy it!

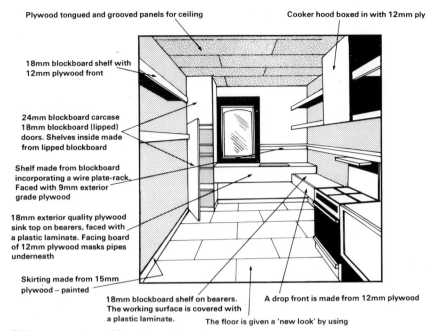

Plywood tongued and grooved panels for ceiling

Cooker hood boxed in with 12mm ply

18mm blockboard shelf with 12mm plywood front

24mm blockboard carcase 18mm blockboard (lipped) doors. Shelves inside made from lipped blockboard

Shelf made from blockboard incorporating a wire plate-rack. Faced with 9mm exterior grade plywood

18mm exterior quality plywood sink top on bearers, faced with a plastic laminate. Facing board of 12mm plywood masks pipes underneath

Skirting made from 15mm plywood – painted

18mm blockboard shelf on bearers. The working surface is covered with a plastic laminate.

A drop front is made from 12mm plywood

The floor is given a 'new look' by using

Fig. 119. Kitchen conversion with wall panels and new units

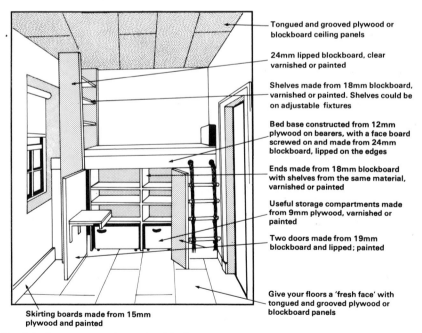

Tongued and grooved plywood or blockboard ceiling panels

24mm lipped blockboard, clear varnished or painted

Shelves made from 18mm blockboard, varnished or painted. Shelves could be on adjustable fixtures

Bed base constructed from 12mm plywood on bearers, with a face board screwed on and made from 24mm blockboard, lipped on the edges

Ends made from 18mm blockboard with shelves from the same material, varnished or painted

Useful storage compartments made from 9mm plywood, varnished or painted

Two doors made from 19mm blockboard and lipped; painted

Give your floors a 'fresh face' with tongued and grooved plywood or blockboard panels

Skirting boards made from 15mm plywood and painted

Fig. 120. Small bedroom conversion using block-board panels and new units

163

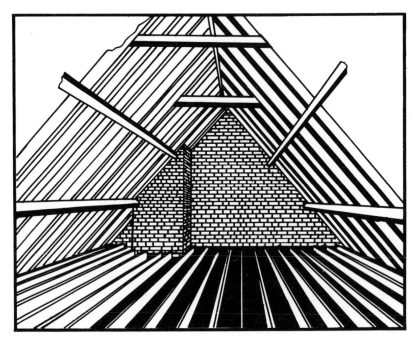

Fig. 121. Typical loft before conversion

Ceiling clad in plywood sheets
and then faced with cork board

Sloping ceiling covered
with plywood panels

The chimney breast
can be completely
covered in with
plywood sheets;
blockboard shelving
could be added as
required

Bookshelves and
support made from
birch plywood. They
can be varnished
or painted

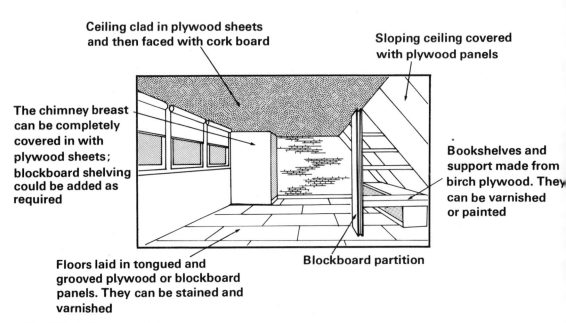

Floors laid in tongued and
grooved plywood or blockboard
panels. They can be stained and
varnished

Blockboard partition

Fig. 122. Loft converted into a bedsitting room

Glossary

Adhesive: A modern glue (*q.v.*), used for sticking structures together

Batten: A strip of wood of comparatively small section

Back-saw: Saw with a rectangular blade and a rib of brass or steel along the top edge, e.g. tenon saw or dovetail saw

Bit: A tool for making holes in wood; held in a brace (*q.v.*)

Brace: Cranked tool for holding a bit (*q.v.*) to make holes in wood

Brad: A small, round-sectioned nail

Cabinet scraper: A thin rectangular piece of tool steel, used for scraping wood with 'contrary' grain in order to obtain a smooth surface

Cramp: A device for holding. Used for holding wood to a bench, for holding structures together while the adhesive is drying out or for holding many pieces of wood together while they are being marked out

Combination plane: A set of planes combined in one main tool with a variety of accessories capable of performing a range of planing techniques

Coping saw: A small, framed saw for use on sharply curved lines

Compass saw: A saw for use on internal or external curved lines

Countersink: A depression in the surface of wood (or any other material) to take the head of a screw so that it is sunk just below the surface level

Dovetail joint: A joint used in good-quality carcase construction; self-locking in one direction and shaped like the tail of a dove

Dowel rod: A rod of circular section in hardwood (*q.v.*). Used to strengthen some joints

Filler: A paste used either to fill the open grain of wood before staining and polishing or to fill gaps in wood or poor joints

Fillet: A small sectioned strip of wood. Often used to retain panels of wood or glass in a main frame

Finishing: A process of preparing the surface of wood or of treating the surface to withstand damp,

abrasion or attack by fungus, insects or chemical action

Gauge: A marking-out tool, scribing single (Marking Gauge) or double (Mortice Gauge) lines on wood, parallel to the edge of the material

Glue: A generic title for adhesives (*q.v.*); usually understood now to refer to the virtually outdated animal glues

Gouge: A chisel with a blade of curved profile; used a great deal in carving

Grain: The effect seen on the surface of wood due to the natural structure of the timber; can be highly decorative in some hardwoods (*q.v.*)

Hand scraper: See Cabinet scraper

Hardwood: Usually from deciduous trees. Used in furniture making. Usually harder than softwoods to work and botanically different

Heartwood: The harder, centre section of a tree — the mature wood

Jack plane: A general-purpose hand plane, wood or metal. Usually with a 50 mm (2 in) blade and 300–350 mm (12–14 in) long

Key: A textured surface, provided to give grip (to paint, glue, etc.)

Keyhole saw (Padsaw): A saw with a thin blade that is flexible under stress. Used for sawing round sharp curves and in close situations, e.g. cutting keyholes

Knot. Hard area in wood, particularly softwoods (*q.v.*), caused by falling off tree of branch

Laminated wood: Man-made boards built up by strips of wood sandwiched between layers of veneer (*q.v.*). Plastic laminates are thin sheets of hard plastic material

Mallet: A wooden hammer; used on chisel handles. Made of beech

Mitre: A 45° cut or angle, e.g. a joint at the four corners of a picture frame, eliminating visible end grain

Mortice and tenon: A common joint used in all classes of framework, tables, chairs, doors, windows, etc.

Oilstone: A block of natural or man-made

stone for sharpening knives, chisels and plane blades

Paring: Hand chiselling

Pins (veneer, panel): Thin, circular-sectioned nails used on panelling and wherever no evidence of nailing is wanted

Plastic wood: A paste used for filling gaps in wood and joints

Punch (pin, nail): A metal tool, shaped to a flat-ended point, for punching nails and pins below the surface of wood

Rip-saw: A hand saw for sawing along the grain of wood. It has large teeth, about 4 per 25 mm (inch), with very little 'set'

Sapwood: The outer area of a tree trunk; wood that contains sap. It is soft and liable to shrink, twist and warp excessively. Works up rather roughly

Shrinkage: The effects of dehydration on wood; an even diminution of the dimensions of a board; greatest in width, least in length

Softwood: Usually from conifers. Used for roofs, floors, doors, shelves etc. Botanically different from hardwood and usually easier to work

Surform tool: Similar to a very rough file, but the abrasive surface is produced by a replaceable blade

Tongued and grooved: A term applied to the edges of boards or panels that fit snugly together so that gaps are not created when natural shrinkage occurs. There is a lip cut down one edge and a groove cut in the opposite edge. Adjacent boards are placed so that the lip on one fits into the groove in the other

Try-square: A testing and marking-out tool. Checks the 'squareness' of corners

Twist bit: A tool for drilling deep holes in wood. Held in a brace

Varnish: A transparent finish for a wood surface. Polyurethane varnishes are heatproof and waterproof and give a glass-hard surface

Veneer: A thin sheet of wood (1–1·5 mm thick). Often of choice grain figure for overlaying on wood of lesser quality

Vice: A device, usually attached to a bench, for holding wood while work is being done on it

Wire nails: Nails made from circular or oval-sectioned wire. An alternative to 'cut' nails, which are cut from sheet metal

Warping: The result of uneven shrinkage in wood, causing distortion of the board across the surface area

Bibliography

How to Work with Tools and Wood, Campbell & Mager (ed.) (Pocket Books, New York).

Stanley Home Comfort Cards: Sets 1, 2 and 3. Guide to DIY jobs (Queen Anne Press Ltd.).

Woodwork Joints, C. H. Hayward (Evans Bros.).

Designs for Home Storage, E. Winter (ed.) (Spectator Publications Ltd.).

Woodwork, J. Maynard (Hulton).

Pictorial Woodwork, Matthews and Kerr (Clowes and Son).

Home Decorating, R. W. Draycon (EP Publishing Ltd.).

Dampness in Buildings, R. T. Gratwick (Crosby Lockwood).

Floors and their Maintenance, J. Edwards (Butterworth).

Periodicals: *The Woodworker,* Antony Talbot (ed.) (Model & Allied Publications Ltd.).

Resources

Record Ridgway Education Services. Record Ridgway Tools Ltd., Parkway Works, Sheffield, S9 3BL.

Stanley Education Services. Stanley Works (G.B.) Ltd., Woodside, Sheffield, S3 9PD.

Finnish Plywood Development Association: for help with Conversions and Improvements, Broadmead House, 21 Panton Street, London, SW1Y 4DR.

The Timber Research and Development Association. Hughenden Valley, High Wycombe, Buckinghamshire.

Tri-Wall Ltd, Mount St., Berkeley Square, London W1.

INVEST IN LIVING

Part III

ELECTRICAL REPAIRS

by

L. R. Wakelin

Introduction

This book has been written as a practical guide for householders and do-it-yourself enthusiasts. It covers all aspects of home electrical repairs and maintenance.

Electricity is a household commodity which is normally taken for granted as it cannot be seen or heard, but it can be extremely dangerous if treated with contempt. An attempt has therefore been made to provide the reader with clearly written, safe and concise instructions in the repair and maintenance of his or her electrical installation or appliances.

The initial chapters deal with simple aspects of electrical work, for example, cables and flexes, and shows the difference between each and their applications. The need for fuses is dealt with comprehensively and it shows by simple calculation how fuse values are arrived at. Building on this basis, it goes on to explain how a two-way switch is connected and how dimmer switches are installed.

A large section of the book deals with the fault diagnosis of various electrical appliances and explains in general terms how these repairs can be carried out successfully.

The final chapters deal with the extension or installation of both lighting and power ring mains and the need for earthing, together with the purpose of the earth and its ultimate protection of the consumer.

The book has been written in such a way as to give as much practical knowledge as possible, whilst keeping the somewhat technical content of the subject to a minimum. In this way the reader will not have to be an expert in electrical theory in order to carry out the repairs and installations described.

About the Author

Les Wakelin worked for an electronics firm for a number of years as a test engineer, after which he joined the teaching profession. For the past six years he has taught Metalwork, Technical Drawing and Social Crafts in a Northampton Upper School. Being a keen handyman and house owner he has, at one time or another, carried out all the repairs and installations mentioned in his book.

1 A Simple Guide to Electricity Understanding

Voltage is the pressure of force with which the current of electricity flows. The current amperes, usually referred to as amps, is the quantity of electricity passing through a circuit.

The voltage in a circuit can be looked at diagrammatically as a water tank, this provides the pressure or force. The amp can be likened to the amount of water which flows from a tank, i.e. the bigger the outlet the bigger the flow of water. Therefore the greater the power rating of an appliance the greater the amount of current consumed.

The watt is the amount of power consumed by the circuit. A 1 kw electric fire which is run for one hour will use 1 kw hour of electricity, and this is equal to one unit. The Electricity Board charges each domestic consumer for the amount of units used and, at present, this stands at 3.24p per unit.

The watt or kilo-watt (1000 watts) is the result of the pressure (volts) multiplied by the amount of current (amps). By transposing the formula $W=V\times A$, if two factors are known then the third can be calculated as follows:

$$W=V\times A \qquad A=\frac{W}{V} \qquad V=\frac{W}{A}$$

The ohm is the unit of resistance (R) a circuit has which opposes the current. The resistance ohms can be worked out providing the voltage, current or wattage are known, as follows:

$$A=\frac{V}{R} \quad R=\frac{V}{A} \quad V=R\times A$$

The normal formula symbol for amp is I and therefore it will be quite usual to see the above-mentioned formulae written as:

$$I=\frac{V}{R} \quad R=\frac{V}{I} \quad V=R\times I$$

and hence if the wattage needs to be worked out and the current is not known but both the voltage and the resistance are known, then for

$$W=V\times I \quad \text{substitute} \quad \frac{V}{R} \text{ for } I$$

then

$$W=V\times\frac{V}{R}=\frac{V^2}{R}$$

An ohm meter is a piece of equipment which will measure both resistance and continuity of a circuit; most ohm meters also have the facility for checking voltages and current flow (amperes). These meters are relatively expensive and are not an essential piece of equipment for a householder. If, however, you need to check a piece of faulty electrical equipment such as a heating element from a kettle with an ohm meter, you will find that most electrical retailers will check the equipment free of charge.

2 Entry of Electricity into the House

Electricity normally enters the house along a thick, steel-reinforced, pitch-covered cable from underground. In a few cases the supply is brought to the house by overhead cables, these houses tending to be older types in more rural areas.

This pitch-covered cable then enters a fuse box which is the property of the Electricity Board, and in view of this must not be opened by removal of the lead seal. From this main 60 A fuse two double insulated cables lead to the electricity meter, which again is the property of the Electricity Board and is sealed. Two more cables are taken from the meter to the main switched fuse box or consumer unit.

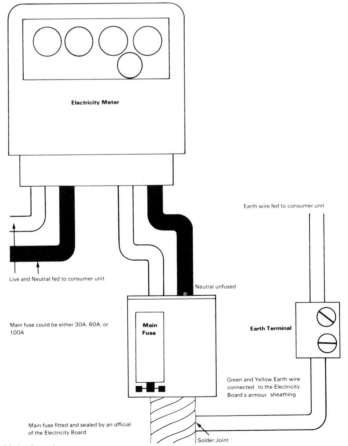

Electricity Meter

Earth wire fed to consumer unit

Live and Neutral fed to consumer unit

Neutral unfused

Main fuse could be either 30A, 60A, or 100A

Main Fuse

Earth Terminal

Green and Yellow Earth wire connected to the Electricity Board's armour sheathing

Main fuse fitted and sealed by an official of the Electricity Board

Solder Joint

Main fuse layout

In modern houses the main fuse and meter are often contained in a covered recess on an outside wall of the house so that the Electricity Board officials can have access to the contents without needing to enter the house.

Under this arrangement the main fuse box or consumer unit is still contained inside the house. This main consumer unit can usually be found:

- In the cellar—in older houses
- In the porch—usually in a cupboard
- Under the staircase
- In the garage—more modern houses

Meter Cupboard

Consumer Unit

Electricity Meter

Main Fuse

Fuse box location

3 Precautions

Electricity cannot be seen, heard or detected by smell, but nevertheless can be extremely dangerous, even resulting in fatality. In view of this it is vital that before starting any work involving electricity certain safety precautions are followed.

In all circumstances the **main switch must be turned off**.

It must be noted that in some cases where additions to the original circuit have been made, there may be more than one main switch. An example of this could be in an older property, where an immersion heater has been installed. Owing to the lack of a spur fuse a new fuse box could have been fitted resulting in two main switches. Once familiar with the electrical layout of the house it would not be essential to switch off all main fuses but **if in doubt do switch off all main switches**.

4 Fuses

A fuse is incorporated into an electrical installation as a safety device to protect the domestic wiring. It consists of a thin piece of wire held in an insulating material. During normal use this allows electrical current to flow uninterrupted. In the event of an overload, a greater flow of current than the circuit was designed for causes the wire in the fuse to heat up and eventually melt. This causes a break in the circuit.

Types of Fuse

In the main consumer unit there are three main types of fuse:

(a) Rewirable fuses   } these are found in the main consumer unit
(b) Circuit breaker

(c) Cartridge fuses—these are found in plugs (and see page 176).

The rewirable types all operate on the same principle and involve the use of fuse wire. This wire is made in a wide range of thicknesses and it is important that the wire appropriate to the fuse is used. Generally, the thicker the wire the greater the current-carrying capacity.

Rewirable Fuses

These are manufactured from an insulating material, usually bakelite or porcelain. The two contact blades (metal pins) are connected by a length of fuse wire, usually held in place by a piece of asbestos.

In the event of an overload the fuse will become blown. The melted fuse will not be in one continuous length and there may be some discoloration of the porcelain or asbestos.

Fuse wire would be broken
There would be signs of burning, and small metal globules of fuse wire contained in the ceramic tube

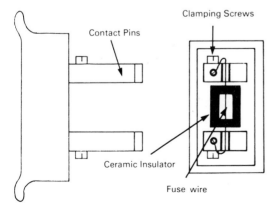

Clamping Screws
Contact Pins
Ceramic Insulator
Fuse wire

Rewirable fuse

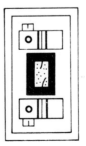

Signs of a blown rewirable fuse

Rewiring a Fuse

1. Switch off main switch.
2. Remove blown fuse from consumer unit.
3. Select correct fuse wire; e.g. for a 30 A fuse use only 30 A fuse wire and likewise for a 5 A fuse use only 5 A fuse wire. The fuse rating is generally marked on the fuse holder.
4. Loosen the screw attached to the contact blades.
5. Remove all traces of previously fitted fuse wire.
6. Loop one end of the fuse wire round one screw and retighten securely.
7. Lay wire across fuse holder in channel provided.
8. Loop the other end round other screw and retighten; *N.B.* do not overtighten screw which may break the fuse wire, or undertighten the screw leaving the fuse wire slack.
9. Cut residual fuse wire close to screw.
10. Replace fuse.
11. Switch on main switch.

If the fuse should blow again there may be a fault in the circuit or in an appliance connected to the circuit and this should then be investigated.

Circuit Breakers

These can be used instead of rewirable fuses and have certain advantages:

1. They break the circuit more quickly.
2. They do not require to be rewired.
3. They last indefinitely.

The biggest advantage in using a circuit breaker is that it does not require rewiring. Should the circuit become broken, the colour-coded button disengages in a push button manner, thus the operation is easily visually identified. Because there is no need to rewire a circuit breaker it is easily reset by simply depressing the button. Should there be a need to isolate the circuit the red button below can be pressed which then disengages the circuit. To complete the circuit the colour-coded button would need to be depressed.

Fuse Ratings

Consumer units can contain up to eight fuse spaces. These can then be fitted with either rewirable fuses or miniature circuit breakers of any value. A typical arrangement could be:

1. Two 30 A upstairs and downstairs power circuits (sockets).
2. Two 5 A lighting circuits upstairs and downstairs.
3. One 30 A or 45 A electric cooker—the 45 A is only required for large cookers.
4. One 15 A or 20 A immersion heater—rating dependent upon type of heater.
5. Two spare spaces for any additions, for example garage, greenhouse, etc.

The rating of fuses and circuit breakers can be easily determined.

In all cases the rating is indicated in the bakelite or porcelain moulded holder. In addition to this, more modern types are colour coded.

45 A	Green
30 A	Red
20 A	Yellow
15 A	Blue
5 A	White

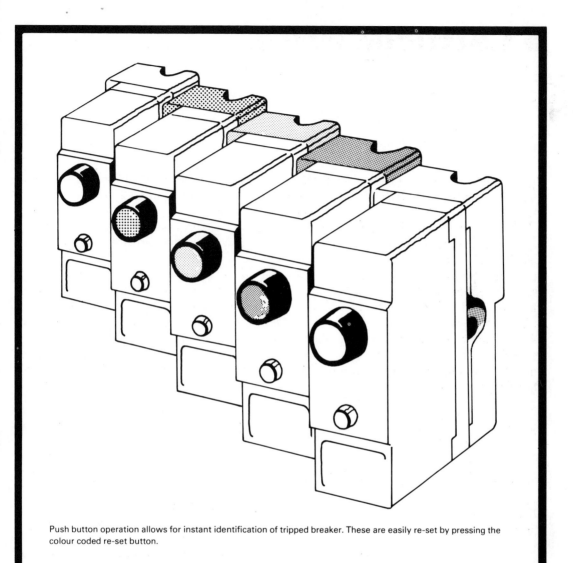

Push button operation allows for instant identification of tripped breaker. These are easily re-set by pressing the colour coded re-set button.

Circuit breakers

5 Cartridge Fuses

This kind of fuse differs from the rewirable type in that it basically consists of a short ceramic cylinder capped at either end in steel.

The fuse wire is positioned in the centre of the cylinder and is connected to the steel cap at either end. This fuse is not rewirable and if it blows it must be discarded.

As the ceramic cylinder is opaque it is impossible to see if the fuse needs replacing. Therefore, a suitable method must be used to determine if a replacement fuse is needed.

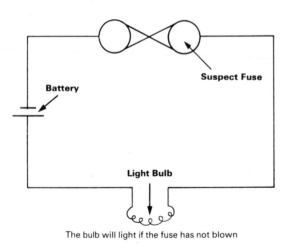

The bulb will light if the fuse has not blown

Fuse-checking circuit

An electrician would use an ohm meter to check fuses, but an alternative method would be to conduct the following simple test:

1. Connect a $1\frac{1}{2}$ V (U.2) battery to a small light bulb such as one used in a torch.
2. Insert the fuse to complete the circuit as shown in the diagram.

If the bulb lights you can be assured the fuse is working. If the bulb does not light the fuse has blown and needs replacing, providing the circuit without the fuse enables the bulb to light.

Cartridge fuses are obtainable in a number of current values to suit varying applications. Typical values are:

1. 13 A—washing machines, electric fires above 1 kw, electric kettles.
2. 5 A—refrigerators, vacuum cleaners, irons, one-bar electric fires.
3. 3 A—electric blankets, hair driers, power drills, sewing machines, food mixers.
4. 1 A—standard lamps, table lamps.

The function of the fuse is to protect the wiring circuit from an overload in the event of an appliance developing a fault and causing an excess current to be drawn.

It is important to check that all manufacturers' recommendations regarding suitable fuse ratings for electrical appliances are complied with.

Calculation of Fuse Rating

To calculate the correct fuse value, a simple calculation is required. The standard voltage obtained from the Electricity Board is 240 V. Each electrical appliance will be rated at a certain wattage.

Using this, one divides the power consumption of the appliance (wattage) by the supply voltage to calculate the current drawn in amps.

for example:

A single-bar (1 kw) electric fire

$$\frac{1000\,W}{240\,V} = 4.16\,A$$

Having calculated the current drawn in amps for an appliance, the fuse with a fuse rating nearest above this value is used.

for example:

A single-bar (1 kw) electric fire

current drawn = 4.16 A
fuse rating = 5 A

The table below is meant to act as a guide only. Any new electrical appliance should have its wattage noted before any calculation of fuse value is made.

Cartridge fuses are colour coded for easy identification:

1 A   Green
3 A   Red
5 A   Black
13 A   Brown.

Typical current consumption of domestic appliances

Appliance	Wattage	Voltage	Current Used	Fuse Value
3-bar electric fire	3000 W	240 V	12.5 A	13 A
single-bar electric fire	1000 W	240 V	4.16 A	5 A
vacuum cleaner	650 W	240 W	2.64 A	3 A
television	260 W	240 V	1.8 A	3 A
food mixer	120 W	240 V	0.5 A	1 A
stereo radio	60 W	240 V	0.25 A	1 A

6 Cables and Flexes

Rewiring of circuits and electrical appliances requires 'wire' but it is important that the correct type of wire is used. For rewiring circuits 'cable' is used whereas for electrical appliances 'flex' is needed.

Both cable and flex consist of copper wire to conduct the electricity and an outer covering of an insulating material, often plastic or rubber.

Types of Cable

Cable is used for the installation of power and lighting circuits.

This consists of two strands of copper each insulated with plastic and, as these are live and neutral conductors, they are colour coded with red and black plastic sheaths. The earth conductor is not insulated and is positioned between the other two conductors, the whole lot then being surrounded by a grey plastic insulation.

The insulation can alternatively be made of rubber although this does tend to crack and perish more readily than plastic.

It is essential that the correct size of cable is used for a particular application. In general, the thicker the conductor the greater the current carrying capacity of the cable.

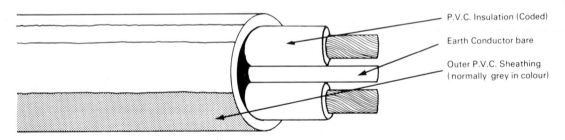

P.V.C. Insulation (Coded)

Earth Conductor bare

Outer P.V.C. Sheathing
(normally grey in colour)

PVC double insulated cable

The measurements in *Figure A* apply to the area of the cut end of the conductor; thus the larger the area of the cut end (cross-sectional area) the greater the diameter of the conductor and so the thicker the wire overall.

All measurements on cables referred to in *Figure A* are metric measurements. Cables other than those recently fitted will not have metric measurements and *Figure B* shows the construction of these.

To identify the type of cable used the copper conductors can be examined to determine whether they are single-stranded or multi-stranded conductors, as shown in the diagrams above.

It is possible to connect up to two types of cable as they have the same current-carrying capacity, e.g. 3/029 cable can be safely connected to 1.5 mm² cable.

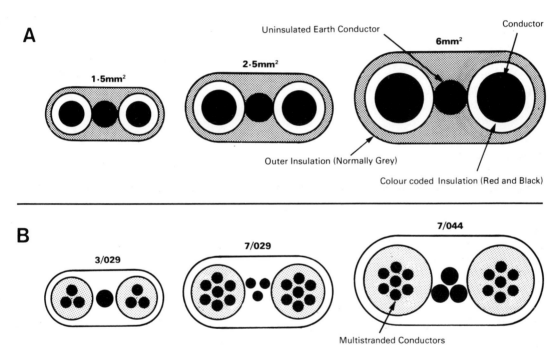

A

1·5mm²

2·5mm²

6mm²

Uninsulated Earth Conductor

Conductor

Outer Insulation (Normally Grey)

Colour coded Insulation (Red and Black)

B

3/029

7/029

7/044

Multistranded Conductors

The prefix number indicated the number of strands

Cross-sectional view of cable sizes

Types of Flex

Flex is used for connecting electrical appliances to the socket outlet.

Two-Core Flex: This can be obtained in various forms:

(a) *Twin-core flat*—two strands of non-insulated wire moulded into a plastic insulator.

Colour code—none. The plastic insulation is manufactured in a range of different colours. There is therefore no significance in the colour of the insulation as there is in the case of the cables already detailed.

(b) *Twin-core insulated*—two separate strands of insulated wire twisted together.

Colour code—none. This again is manufactured in a range of different colours and in this respect is similar to the previous flex.

(c) *Twin-core circular*—two insulated strands surrounded by an outer insulation.

Colour code:
Live conductor   brown
Neutral conductor blue.

On older appliances the flex colour code is:

Live conductor   red
Neutral conductor black

These are surrounded in an outer insulation which can be in a variety of colours.
These two-core flexes are used on

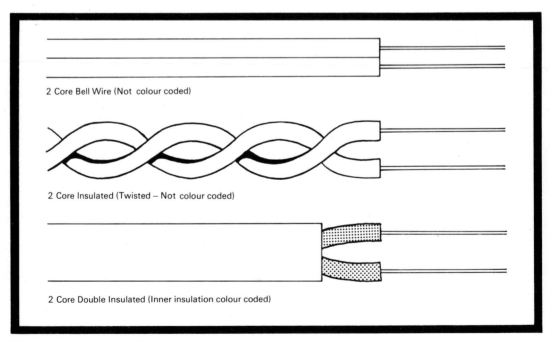

2 Core Bell Wire (Not colour coded)

2 Core Insulated (Twisted – Not colour coded)

2 Core Double Insulated (Inner insulation colour coded)

Two-core current-carrying flexes

low power consumption appliances where no earth wire is required. **On no account** must twin-core flex be used on metallic or part metallic appliances.

Twin-core flex must only be connected to the live and neutral terminals of the plug and **under no circumstances** must the earth terminal be used.

Three-Core Flex: This can be obtained in three forms:

(a) *P.V.C. double insulated*—three multistrand strands of wire each insulated in colour coded plastic or rubber surrounded by an outer plastic or rubber insulation.

(b) *Butyl rubber double insulated*—this is similar in construction to that just described, but differs in that all the insulation is of heat resisting butyl rubber.

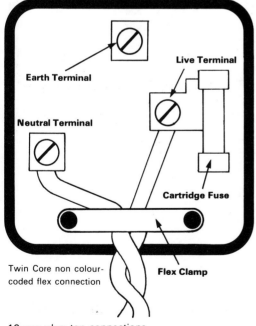

Twin Core non colour-coded flex connection

Earth Terminal

Neutral Terminal

Live Terminal

Cartridge Fuse

Flex Clamp

13 amp plug-top connections

(c) *P.V.C. double insulated* (*non-kink*)—this is similar to the previously described three-core flex but differs in that it contains a layer of separate strands of fibrous material contained inside the outer insulation. This gives the flex a greater rigidity and prevents knotting and tangling.

All three-core flexes are manufactured with the conductors insulated with colour coded plastic and rubber.

Colour code—

Live conductor   brown
Neutral conductor   blue
Earth conductor
        green and yellow striped.

On older appliances the flex colour code is:

Live conductor   red
Neutral conductor   black
Earth conductor   green.

Three-core flex must only be connected with the earth conductor connected to the earth terminal of the plug.

Ratings and Uses

Two-core flex is used only for low current consuming appliances, where no earth connection is required.

The thickness of the flex is determined by the current consumption of the appliance. Therefore, an appliance drawing a large current requires thick cable in comparison to one drawing a small current which requires a thin cable. All types of twin-core flex are available up to 6 A current carrying capacity. Two-core cable with a current rating from 3 to 6 A can be used for:

electric clocks, hair driers, table lamps, standard 'lamps, some portable hand lamps, christmas tree lights and all double insulated domestic appliances where no earth is required.

Three-core flex can be used for all appliances where an earth wire is required. It is also capable of carrying large currents ranging from 3 A to 20 A or even more in certain cases. It is important when connecting an appliance to a socket outlet that the correct current carrying capacity flex is used.

Typical applications are:

Electric kettle   Washing machine
Refrigerator   Electric drill
Vacuum Cleaner   Dish washer

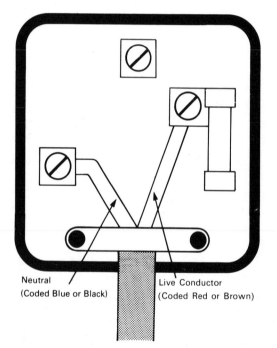

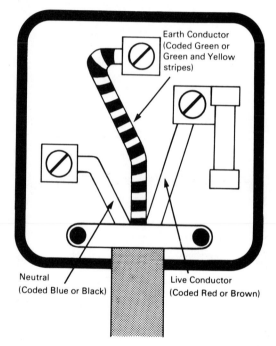

Plug connections for colour-coded two-core and three-core flex

7 Plugs and Sockets

Plugs

There are a variety of different styles of plug but the basic requirements are all the same. Plugs are manufactured to a British standard specification (BS 1363). The most generally used plug is the white bakelite type, the later styles of which have semi-insulated pins that prevent small children accidentally being electrocuted should they ever be allowed to come into contact with them.

At the base of the plug is the cord grip which in all cases must clamp the outer sheathing of the flex; failure to do this could result in the cable becoming detached from the three terminals and a serious short could occur. The three terminals used to clamp the conductors are normally one of two types.

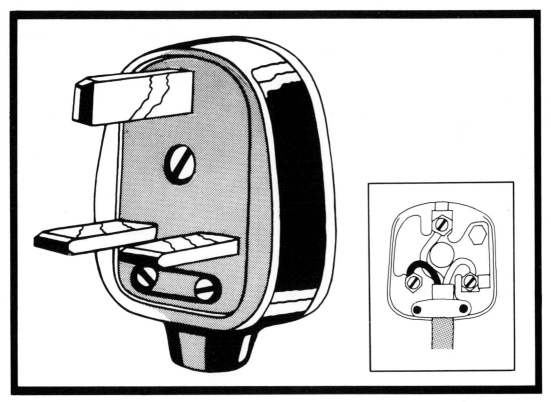

13 amp plug

1. The terminal has a hole in it which the wire passes through and is then clamped securely in place by the locking screw.
2. The wire is clamped to the terminal by a knurled, slotted nut.

There is no particular advantage or disadvantage with either type, but in the case of the latter the cable must be twisted round the threaded terminal in a clockwise direction—failure to do this could result in the cable becoming detached as the screw is tightened. The best method of wiring a plug is:

1. Strip back 50 mm of the outer sheathing of the flex.
2. Pass the flex through the cable clamp until the flex is directly under the clamp.
3. Tighten the clamp securely. In the case of a rubber crush-proof plug the plug top must be slid over the flex before connection to the plug takes place.
4. Connect the live conductor to the fused side of the plug taking care to trim back the flex in order to leave no slack.
5. Connect the neutral conductor in the same manner.
6. Connect the earth conductor.
7. Check fuse rating of the appliance fitted to the plug and fit accordingly.
8. Replace plug top.

Sockets

There are many types of sockets each having a particular application.

Three pin square sockets are used for both domestic ring main circuits and industrial applications. The socket face can be manufactured from either:

- White bakelite (general domestic use)
- Satin stainless steel with white plastic inserts (general domestic use)
- Aluminium painted mild steel with plastic inserts (industrial applications, garages, etc., where appearance is not paramount).

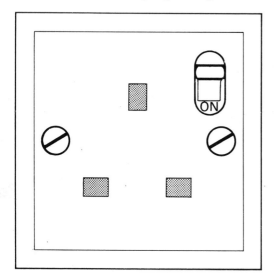

3 pin switched socket

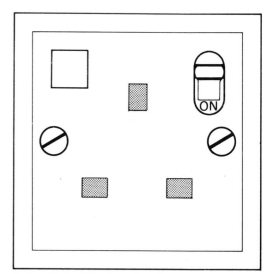

3 pin switched illuminated socket

The socket can be mounted flush to the wall or raised 50 mm from the surface. The two methods of fitting are known as 'flush fixed' and 'surface fixed'. For most industrial applications, e.g. factories and laboratories, sockets are surface fixed, that is to say a steel box is screwed on to the wall and the socket face screwed on to the front of this. The cable is fed to the socket by passing it through conduit tubing.

For domestic purposes plastic boxes are obtainable for surface fixing sockets; these are neater in appearance than the industrial steel type. The cable is 'chased' into the socket, which means that the wall plaster is removed and the cable laid in a channel. The cable is then covered by a plastic cover (capping) to prevent it being accidentally pierced. The channel is then plastered over. An alternative method is to flush-fix the socket. For this a hole needs to be made some 75 mm × 75 mm and approximately 50 mm deep to allow the box to be fitted flush with the wall. The box can either be held in place with screws and plugs or cemented in. The socket face can then be screwed to the box which will fit flush with the wall.

Both single and double sockets are obtainable; these can be either switched or unswitched and in some instances are fitted with a neon light. It is preferable, and far safer, to fit a double socket rather than to fit a single and risk the possibility of overloading it by inserting a two- or three-way adaptor, sometimes called a jack, to increase the number of appliances used from the socket.

Sockets with an inbuilt neon light are ideal where an electric kettle is used so that an immediate visual check can

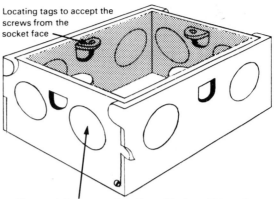

Locating tags to accept the screws from the socket face

The round discs are weak sections of the box which can be nicked out to allow entry for the cable
Wall-depth socket box

be made to see whether it is switched on or off.

Cord outlet fused sockets are available for certain applications. These consist of a plain socket face with the facility for a special fuse carrier to be fitted. Instead of the outlet consisting of three pins into which the plug fits, a piece of flex is fed through a hole in the front and connected internally, this flex in turn being connected to an appliance. Two typical applications for this type of socket face are:

- Central heating boilers
- Night storage heaters

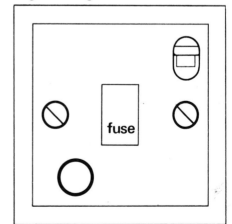

Cord-outlet fused socket

8 Switches

Fitting and Removal

Modern switches are held to the wall by two 2 BA screws and are usually white in colour. Single switches are generally the most common and can be obtained in as many as up to four in a block. Quite often single on/off switches are made with a two-way switch in one unit. A typical application for these is in a hallway where a single-way downstairs light is fitted and an upstairs two-way light is used. This allows for the upstairs light to be switched on from downstairs.

To surface fix a switch to the wall a plastic box must be purchased. This box is similar to the plastic box used for surface mounting a socket but is only some 15 mm deep. The reason for this is that the cable used in lighting circuits (1.5 mm²) is thinner and that therefore it does not take up so much room.

To flush fix a switch a steel box needs to be set into the wall similar to that of the flush-fixed socket. Again this is only some 15 mm deep and usually only requires the plaster to be chipped from the wall to allow it to fit flush with the surface.

To connect a single on/off switch it will be seen that there is one piece of cable (usually 1.5 mm²) entering the box in which there are live, neutral and earth conductors. The earth conductor is connected to a screw usually mounted in the back of the box, whether the box be made of plastic or steel.

To connect the live and neutral conductor, there are two terminals on the back of the actual switch, some have 'live' marked against one terminal and 'switch' against the other. In this case the red conductor should be connected to the 'live' and the black to the 'switch' terminals. It is not essential, however, to do this as some switches are not marked. However, if the wires are changed over, the switch's 'off' position will then be in the normal 'on' position. 'Off' is usually the upward position, 'on' the downward one.

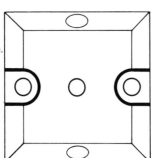

Switch boxes are fitted to plaster depth and can, therefore, be manufactured shallower than for sockets

Plaster-depth switch box and switch plate

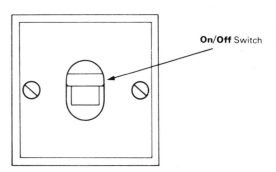

On/Off Switch

Dimmer Switches

Dimmer switches can normally replace any single on/off switch. There are only two connections, similar to those of a normal switch. Dimmer switches are an electronic device used to limit the current and hence produce the effect of dimming the light. It is important when purchasing a dimmer switch that the power handling capabilities (wattage) are noted as these vary from manufacturer to manufacturer.

Some dimmers have an on/off switch fitted to them, the advantage of this is that when the correct brightness has been selected the dimmer can be switched off at this setting. On re-entering the room a level of instant light is obtainable by merely flicking on the switch.

In the other type of dimmer the switch is incorporated in the variable light control knob. These controls therefore require to be switched on and the brilliance increased gradually. Illumination is not as instantaneous as in the other type but the switch does look slightly neater.

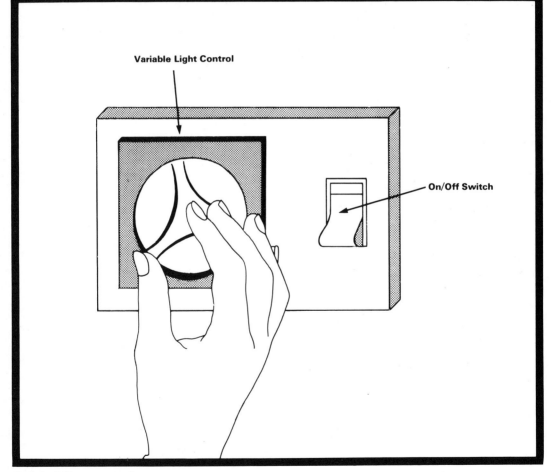

Switched dimmer control

Two-Way Switches

The fitting of one of these is similar to an ordinary one-way switch apart from the fact that there are three terminals on the back of the switch, two of which are marked 'common'.

When fitting a two-way switch a piece of 1.5 mm² twin-core cable with earth must be used to connect the two switches together. A live feed must be fed to one switch and a neutral taken from the other switch to the ceiling rose.

In a great many cases a two-way switch is mounted with a single-way switch as used in a hall. The live conductor can be looped from the live side of the single-way switch to the two-way switch. From the upstairs switch a neutral conductor must be taken to the light rose and the lighting flex must be connected to the two neutral wires.

It must be noted that a two-way switch will not always be 'off' in the downward position or in fact 'on' in the upward position.

An alternative to this is to use a piece of 1.5 mm² three-core cable with earth to connect the switches together. The coding of the cable is red, yellow and blue. The red is connected to common, and the yellow and blue to the other terminals. The red lead from one switch is connected to live, the red lead from the other is connected to the lamp, the other side of the lamp being connected to neutral. All connections are made through a six-way junction box.

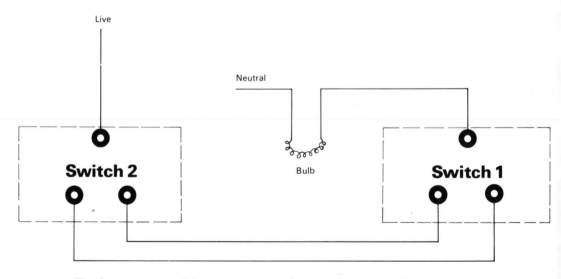

Twin core cable to strap the two switches

Two-way switch wiring circuit

Pull-Cord Switches

These switches are fitted to the ceiling and are operated by a pull cord. It is essential that **in a bathroom this type of switch is always fitted.** A normal wall-mounted switch contravenes the regulations governing electrical installations. Pull cords are often used in bedrooms in a two-way switch configuration which allows one to switch the light off or on whilst in bed.

Some pull-cord switches light up when switched on; these are mainly used in bathrooms where a light/heater is fitted and this gives an indication that the heater is turned on.

The first job in fitting a pull-cord switch is to secure the back plate to the ceiling. This means that the ceiling joist must be found and the plate screwed to it; an alternative to this is to secure a piece of wood between the joists and fix the plate to this.

Once the back plate has been fixed the switch is screwed to it with two 2 BA screws. If one decides to fix to a joist instead of to a piece of wood fitted between the joists, it should be remembered to fit the plate to one side of the joist so as to allow the cable to be fed through to the switch.

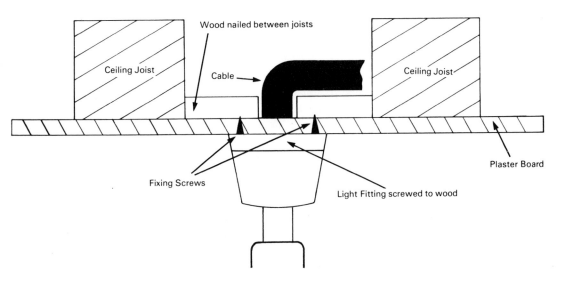

Ceiling rose fixing

9 Bulbs

Types

There are two different types of fittings:

    (i) Bayonet Type
    (ii) Screw Type

(i)   The bayonet type is the more common and is generally found in the everyday household. This consists of a plastic holder with two spring-loaded brass contacts which make the connection with the two lead contacts at the end of the bulb. In order to fit a bayonet bulb it has to be pushed into the bayonet holder and twisted clockwise about 15–20 degrees, the two small lugs on the side of the bulb fitting into the insets of the bayonet holder.

(ii) The screwed type is similar to the bayonet type externally but is fitted with an internal thread into which the bulb is screwed. There is only one contact in the centre of the holder and the brass cap on the end of the bulb serves as the second contact.

Until recently domestic bulbs have been rather unimaginative and were only different from one another in their wattage ratings, i.e. light output. These range from 30 W to 150 W and can still be purchased with either clear or pearl (opaque) glass. During the last few years bulb manufacturers have started to produce more different and unusual colours and types of lights. Bulbs can be designed to give a wide range of colour and different types of beam, i.e. floodlight, diffused beam and spot concentrated beams, and the majority of these can be obtained in either bayonet or screwed types. The more exotic bulbs are usually used with a track lighting set up – this is explained more fully on page 192.

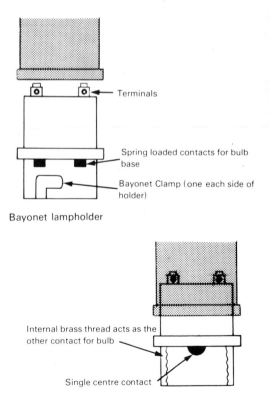

Terminals

Spring loaded contacts for bulb base

Bayonet Clamp (one each side of holder)

Bayonet lampholder

Internal brass thread acts as the other contact for bulb

Single centre contact

Screwed lampholder

Fluorescent Tubes

These tubes are made of glass and fitted with two steel end caps from which protrude two small pins. Fluorescent tubes are bought in length and not wattage rating as in the case of ordinary bulbs. There are, however, different types of light given off from a variety of tubes and an example of this is 'warmlight'. This type of light is the normal one for domestic use. Another type is 'colour match' which gives a light as near as possible to actual daylight. This latter type can, of course, be fitted into any normal fluorescent light but is more generally used where a very natural, harsh light is required, for example in a spray booth where extreme accuracy is needed to match paint.

In addition to normal straight tubes there are also round and U-shaped ones. The round tubes, when suitably concealed behind a shade, make an ideal light for a lounge where a good light is needed. The U tubes can be used where concealed lighting is fitted behind curtains, pelmets, etc.

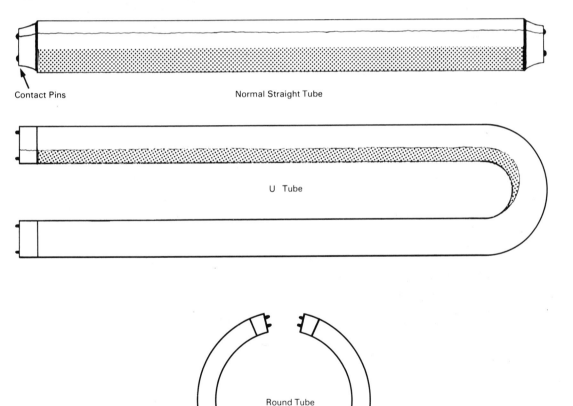

Contact Pins

Normal Straight Tube

U Tube

Round Tube

Fluorescent tubes

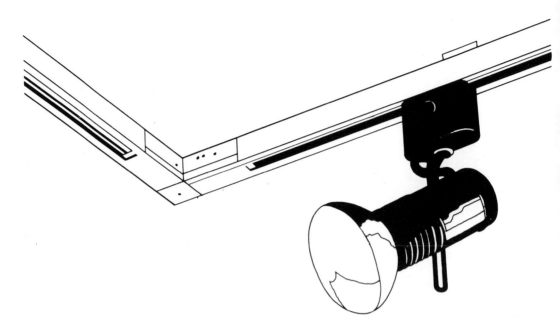

One type of track lighting

Track Lighting

This is a modern concept of lighting and can be installed reasonably easily in a normal home. Some manufacturers give as many as four individual circuits in one track and therefore by arranging the different types of light, i.e. spot, diffused and the varying colours, a good effect can be obtained.

The track can be fitted from an existing ceiling rose if desired, but it must be borne in mind that if this method of connecting is used all the lights on that section of the track would operate simultaneously, but if four separate wires are fed from switches then there can be many permutations of lighting. Electrical appliances with a power rating of less than 500 W can normally also be connected to a track system.

To realise the full versatility of a track system it is probably ideal to consult the literature produced by the various manufacturers before installing a track. It must also be appreciated that each individual manufacturer's specifications differ slightly from the others.

Christmas Tree Lighting

All Christmas tree lighting operates on a two-wire system, that is, no earth wire is connected. Two basic types of system exist:

  (a) Series wired
  (b) Parallel wired

  (a) *Series wired*. This means that if one light bulb is taken out of a socket then the complete light set will be extinguished. If, for example, there were 24 bulbs in a set then the voltage required at each bulb would be 10 V, i.e. 240÷24—this is the most common type of configuration.

(b) *Parallel wired*. This means that if one bulb is omitted from the circuit the other bulbs will still operate and the working voltage of each bulb would be 240 V.

Power source (Normally 240V)

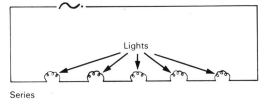

Lights

Series

Power source (Normally 240V)

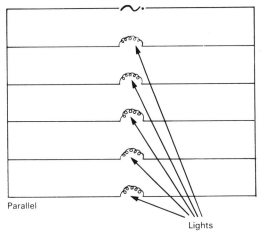

Parallel

Lights

Series and parallel wired circuits

Generally, when Christmas tree lights are brought out of the attic a couple of weeks or so before Christmas they do not always work. If this should be the case the first thing to do is check the plug connections (i.e. live and neutral) and also the fuse and its rating. If these are found to be satisfactory a common complaint is usually that the bulbs are loose in their sockets and therefore are not making a good contact in the bulb holder. If, after checking the bulbs, they still do not light up it could be that in the case of the parallel wired all the bulbs have blown (although this is most unusual) or that the wire has broken somewhere along its length. If this is suspected then each conductor can be checked for continuity by disconnecting from the mains and then using an ohm meter to check continuity, or the bulb and battery method can be used as described on page 176.

In the case of the series connected lights, checking for continuity between each bulb holder can be carried out in the same manner as for the parallel connected ones. However, to check the actual bulbs may be more difficult and ideally the most satisfactory method is to use an ohm meter or, if the coloured glass is not too opaque, a visual check can be made. Failing this, check the bulbs' working voltage and then connect the batteries together to obtain the voltage, following which the bulbs should be checked. A car battery (12 V) is quite often sufficient for this method and in a great many cases is easily obtainable as the majority of householders own a car.

10 Electrical Appliances

Kettles

Electric kettles contain a small electrical heating element in the bottom of the kettle. The live and neutral conductors are encapsulated in a steel sheath containing a white powder which acts as the insulation. Most kettles have a rating of 2.5 to 3 kw which is equal to a three-bar electric fire. These elements sometimes break. The usual cause for this is:

1. Switching the kettle on without ensuring that there is sufficient water in it to cover the element.
2. Insulation breaking down, thus causing a short circuit.
3. In some hard-water areas it will be found that the elements are sometimes attacked by the salts in the water. These salts cause the outer steel sheathing to corrode and ultimately allow water into the insulation, causing a short circuit.

When purchasing a kettle it is important that the appliance conforms to a British Standard Specification. Most of the British manufacturers construct their kettles to conform to this specification and in most cases are better than the specification demands. The normal kettle will require to be switched off once the water has boiled and therefore it could be worth bearing in mind that a 13 A plug which has a red neon light fitted to the plug top might serve as a visual check when the kettle is switched on. Most modern kettle elements have a fail-safe device which ejects the plug connecting the kettle to the flex if the element gets too hot. It will be found, however, that once this device has operated it is not always resettable and may result in a new element having to be fitted.

To fit a new element to a non-automatic cut-out kettle

The element consists of the conductors encapsulated in a steel sheath. The conductors are connected into a plastic termination (A) into which the plug fits to conduct the power to the element. Moulded to this is a steel sleeve which has a thread cut on it (B). The washer (C) is made of a heat-resistant rubber which fits tight against the shoulder (D).

To remove the old element, the locking ring (E) needs to be unscrewed; to do this one hand is required to hold the element inside the kettle whilst the other hand has to turn the locking ring (E) **anti-clockwise.** Try to avoid using a wrench to grip the ring as this will scratch the chrome plating.

After the locking ring has been removed the element can be taken out from the inside of the kettle. It will be noted that the rubber washer will be tight against the shoulder (D)—this forms a water-tight seal to prevent

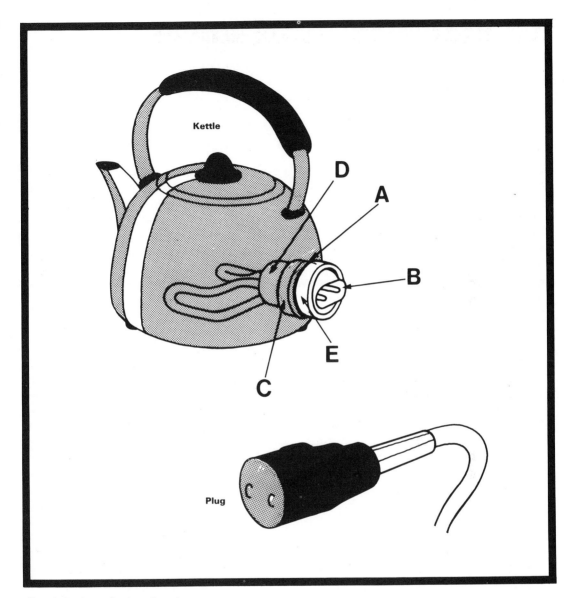

Electric kettle and connecting plug

water from leaking from the kettle. Different brands of kettles tend to make the collar (B) of varying diameters so it is important, when purchasing a new element, to point out to the supplier which brand of kettle you own. Assuming the element is the correct type, place it through the lid of the kettle ensuring that the rubber sealing washer is in place. Insert the threaded collar through the hole in the back of the kettle and screw on the locking collar, applying a firm pressure while holding the element steady in the kettle. Fill the kettle with water and check for leaks before connecting the flex and switching on.

To change an element on an automatic cut-out kettle

There are now a number of kettles on the market which automatically switch off when the water boils. The elements in these kettles tend to be slightly more difficult to change than the ones mentioned previously.

An automatic kettle works on the principle of a metal plate expanding when it heats up due to the steam being generated; this pushes a plunger which in turn breaks the electrical contact.

The element differs from a normal electric kettle inasmuch as there are

three fixing bolts used to hold the element. Two of the bolts are held in place by brass nuts and the third is held by a round slotted nut (a special screwdriver with the centre of the blade missing is needed in order to tighten this screw).

The points which are used to break the electrical contact become pitted after continual use and these sometimes stick, ultimately resulting in the kettle not cutting out. If this is the case the points can be cleaned by using a piece of emery cloth to remove any pitting; if this does not remedy the prob-

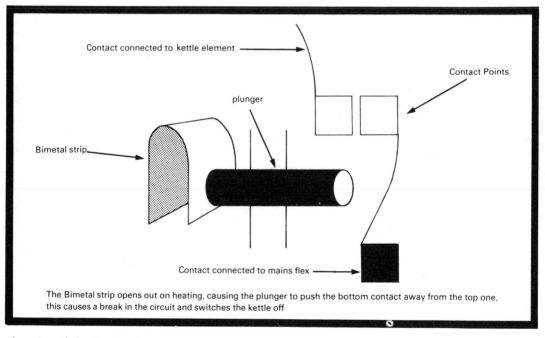

Contact connected to kettle element ⟶

Contact Points

plunger

Bimetal strip

Contact connected to mains flex ⟶

The Bimetal strip opens out on heating, causing the plunger to push the bottom contact away from the top one, this causes a break in the circuit and switches the kettle off

An automatic kettle cut-out

lem a new pair of points can be fitted and in some cases it may be beneficial to fit a complete new cut-out assembly, which is not too expensive and can normally be obtained from an electrical retailer. It will quite easily be seen how to fit this new assembly by comparing the relative holes in the new one with the one already fitted in the kettle; and by simply removing some six screws one is able to fit the new assembly.

One important item to remember when using an automatic kettle is never to leave the house unattended with the kettle switched on. It is a rare occurrence to hear of a kettle malfunctioning but **it can happen** and this will result in the house becoming full of steam. Damage to the kettle element will also occur as in most cases there is no plunger fitted which ejects the plug connection to the kettle, as in the non-automatic cut-out type.

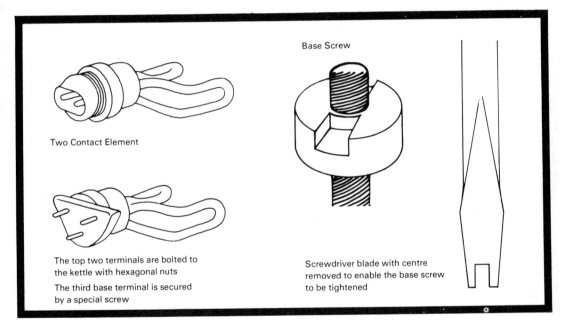

Base Screw

Two Contact Element

The top two terminals are bolted to the kettle with hexagonal nuts

The third base terminal is secured by a special screw

Screwdriver blade with centre removed to enable the base screw to be tightened

Kettle elements, base screw and modified screwdriver

197

Fault Diagnosis

Kettle failing to heat water.

1. Check fuse—if faulty replace. If the new fuse blows there is possibly a short circuit.
2. Check flex to see if the insulation has become worn and shorted the two conductors together; if this is the case **do not repair with insulation tape—replace it**.
3. Check flex to see if there are any breaks in the wire conductors.
4. Check plug which connects the kettle to the flex. Take particular note to see if there are any burn marks, etc.
5. Check element with an ohm meter. If one is not available then quite often an electrical retailer will do this for you. If found to be faulty then replace.

Electric Fires

There are two basic types of fire:

(i) The convector heater which is an electrical heating element with a fan fitted beneath it to help spread the heat into the room.
(ii) Chrome reflector heater in front of which there is either one, two or three elements, usually of 1 kw each (1000 W).

Convector Heaters

These usually have a spring coil element supported on ceramic insulations. A dial is normally found on the front of such an appliance and this regulates the heat output. The fan works continuously while the appliance is switched on. Some heaters have a red light fitted on to them to give a red glow, which does little to the fire's efficiency but gives it a more pleasing appearance when switched on. When fitting a new element it is important to make sure the correct one is purchased for the appliance. To replace an element normally requires only two or three securing screws to be removed together with the connections to the conductors. When the element has to be changed make certain that the screw terminals holding the live and neutral conductors to the elements are securely retightened.

Reflector Heaters

The heater elements consist of a ceramic tube on which is wound manganin wire. Each element normally gives a power output of 1 kw and is mounted between two steel pillars which are connected to the input mains, and these are held firm by brass nuts.

If the fire has only one bar then the element automatically becomes connected when the appliance is plugged in.

With a two-bar fire a switch is fitted to select either one or two bars.

Three-bar fires normally have a three-position switch fitted.

Special types of wall-mounted electric fires can be fitted in a bathroom but these need to have a special type of element fitted. The value of the element is 750 W—i.e. smaller than a normal fire—and this has to be encapsulated in a silica glass envelope to protect the element from steam and water and to prevent a short circuit occurring.

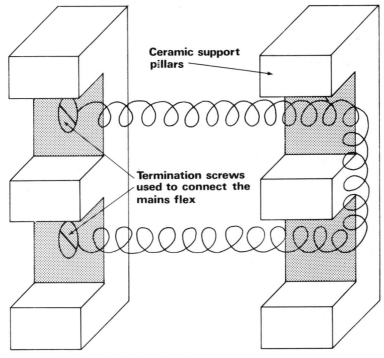

Ceramic support pillars

Termination screws used to connect the mains flex

Open-wound convector heater element

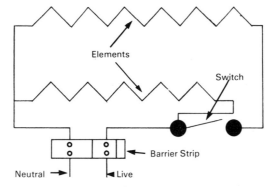

Elements

Switch

Barrier Strip

Neutral → ← Live

Element connections of a two-bar electric fire

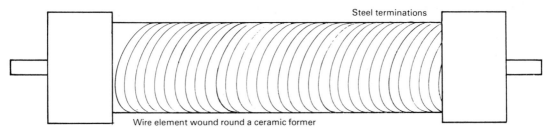

Steel terminations

Wire element wound round a ceramic former

Close-wound reflector heater element

Electric Cookers

How to install an electric cooker

In the majority of kitchens there is an electric point marked 'cooker' which usually incorporates a switched socket, and this can also be used for various other kitchen appliances. The switch on the cooker panel marked 'cooker' will isolate the supply to the cooker. The fuse in the main consumer unit which connects up the cooker panel will be either a 30 or 45 A fuse, depending on the size of cooker to be fitted.

A wire is usually fed from the cooker panel and down the wall, this is chased into the plaster and emerges from the wall just about two feet from floor level. This is normally about the height at which the connecting terminals are mounted on the rear of the cooker. Due to the high current drawn by a cooker (6 to 12 kw) the terminals for the connections are usually in the form of large bolts locked in position by two brass nuts. The live and neutral terminals are usually mounted on ceramic insulators and the earth terminal is connected directly on to the case of the cooker. It is important to ensure that when the cable is connected to the cooker the terminals are tightened securely. Failure to do this could result in arcing and the terminals becoming burnt, giving rise to an ultimate short circuit and causing the fuse or circuit breaker to trip out.

A special terminal plate must be fitted to the cable where it emerges from the wall. This plate locks the cable securely, thus not allowing it to be pulled from beneath the plaster. A safety chain can also be fitted between the cooker and the wall; this needs to be of a shorter length than the connecting cable so as to take the strain should the cooker be pulled away from the wall for cleaning purposes.

How to replace a hot plate ring

Most modern cookers have a lift-up top plate to facilitate ease of cleaning. If this top plate is removed the hot plate and the connections will be seen and a simple change of element can then be effected. In some cases one lead from the hot plate needs to be connected through the on/off regulator switch normally mounted on the front panel. Should this be the case, providing the correct type of element has been purchased for the replacement, the connections will be quite self-evident. It is impossible to list all the numerous types of elements fitted as they vary greatly from manufacturer to manufacturer.

The oven elements will become visible for changing once the side of the oven has been removed, which is usually easily achieved by removing four screws—one at each corner of the plate. It cannot be stressed enough that the correct element must be purchased. **Do not try to fit a substitute, insist on the correct one for your model**. If difficulty is experienced in purchasing an element or hot plate ring consult your local Electricity Board office or write direct to the manufacturers, listing exactly what you require, and the make, serial number and model number of the cooker.

Fault Diagnosis

Cooker fails to heat up:
1. Check main fuse or circuit breaker.
2. Check connections to rear of cooker.
3. Check connections in cooker panel.

Hot Plate or Oven fails to heat up:
1. Remove hot plate and check with an ohm meter.
2. Remove switch and check with ohm meter—replace faulty part.

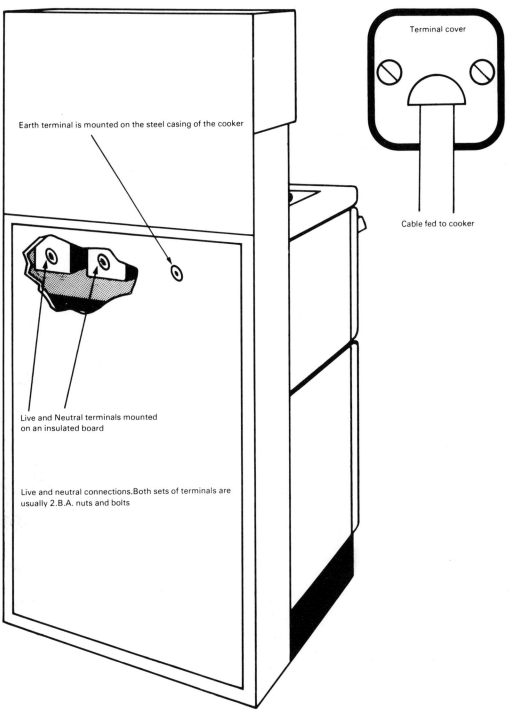

Terminal cover

Earth terminal is mounted on the steel casing of the cooker

Cable fed to cooker

Live and Neutral terminals mounted on an insulated board

Live and neutral connections. Both sets of terminals are usually 2.B.A. nuts and bolts

Cooker terminal plate and rear view of cooker showing location of terminal mounting bolts

Immersion Heaters

Immersion heaters are fitted into the hot water cylinder and provide a means of heating the water in the cylinder. There are two general types of elements used for immersion heaters, long ones and short ones.

The short ones are used mainly for heating just the top of the cylinder quickly and relatively cheaply; the power rating can vary from 1 to 2 kw.

The large ones are used for heating the whole cylinder and range from 2 to 3 kw. These can be expensive to run but will heat, quite efficiently, a 900 × 460 mm hot water cylinder.

A double element heater can now be purchased which incorporates both the long and short elements. This gives the consumer a choice on the amount of water he or she feels requires heating at any one time. It is ideal to use the small one, apart from when baths are required.

The immersion heater fits into the cylinder from the top, and on removal of the insulating jacket the protective plastic cover covering the connecting terminals will be seen. This is generally held in place by a large-headed screw. On removal of this box there will be seen the three terminal connections and a small plastic box some 25 mm square—the thermostat. In the centre of this will be seen a small dial with a central screwdriver slot, and on this is marked a series of temperatures. The thermostat can be set to any desired temperature but ideally this should be around 160° to 180° F, dependent on the outside weather conditions.

If the hot water cylinder is fitted in a bathroom the on/off switch should be fitted elsewhere, an ideal place being just outside the bathroom. The flex connecting the switch should be of butyl rubber three-core flex, preventing any heat damage which could result if ordinary PVC cable or flex were used.

A point worth bearing in mind is that if you fit an illuminated switch you will easily be able to check the state of the heater.

How to replace a faulty Immersion Heater. First turn off the cold water supply to the cold storage tank, usually by means of a stopcock found under the kitchen sink (in the older types of property this may be found in the garden). The upstairs and downstairs cold taps should then be turned off, emptying the cold pipe feeding the tank. The next step is turn on all hot taps in order to empty the water supply, apart from that left in the cylinder. Undo the top copper pipe connection to the cylinder and place a short length of hose into it, then, with the other end, suck the water through the tube. Once the water begins to flow make sure that the end of the hose is at a lower point than the cylinder—i.e. pass it through a window and hang it down outside the house. Only a small amount of water needs to be syphoned off, sufficient to bring the water level below the height of the immersion heater nut. If this syphoning is not carried out then about one to one and a half gallons of water will spill on to the floor once the immersion heater nut is undone.

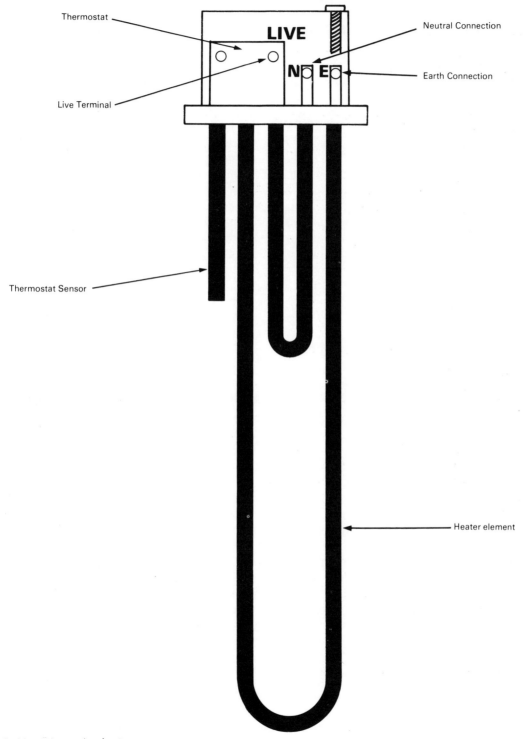

Thermostat

Live Terminal

LIVE

N E

Neutral Connection

Earth Connection

Thermostat Sensor

Heater element

Inside an immersion heater

A very large spanner or a pair of 450 mm stilsons will be required to undo the nut (if you do not possess any then they can usually be hired quite cheaply from a tool hire firm or plumbers' merchants). Take great care when undoing the nut not to distort the cylinder as these cylinders are only made of thin copper sheet and are quite weak. Once the nut is undone the whole immersion heater can be withdrawn. If the element is of the long variety then the shelves, if fitted above the cylinder, will need to be removed in order to extract the element. Once this has been effected the new heater can be fitted. Before fitting the element, however, PTFE tape must be wound around the thread on the nut so as to effect a water-tight seal (this tape can be purchased from most plumbers' merchants). When this has been completed the heater can be fitted and tightened securely. The copper connections at the top of the cylinder can be reconnected once the heater has been fitted. Both hot and cold taps should then be closed and the cold water supply turned on; wait to check that both the disturbed connections are water-tight before leaving the cylinder. Finally, the terminations of the immersion heater can be reconnected and the thermostat set.

If only the thermostat on the immersion heater has broken, and this will be evident if either the water does not heat up at all or if it just boils, it can be removed and replaced by simply disconnecting the wires and withdrawing it. Once removed the thermostat can be checked by connecting this, together with a bulb and battery, into a circuit— it should be possible to switch the bulb on and off providing the thermostat is immersed in a glass of hot water.

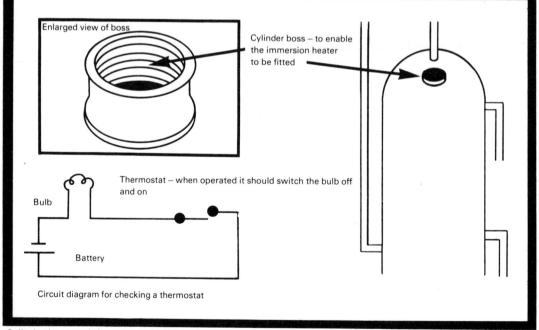

Enlarged view of boss

Cylinder boss — to enable the immersion heater to be fitted

Thermostat — when operated it should switch the bulb off and on

Bulb

Battery

Circuit diagram for checking a thermostat

Cylinder boss and thermostat checking circuit

Table Lamps

Table lamps and standard lamps utilise the same type of fixings and connections.

How to replace the fitting at the top of a lamp. First remove the locking ring (A) to make removal of the shade possible, then separate the two halves of the connector by taking off the serrated locking flange (B). This will then expose the two leads connected into the spring loaded bayonets which in turn supply the current (amps) to the bulb. Once the two wires have been disconnected from the terminals the connector can then be unscrewed from the top of the lamp. The lamp holders can be purchased either with or without an on/off switch. There are only two connections in the lamp holder into which the live and neutral conductors should be connected. On older types of lamps it may be found that a brass connector is fitted; if this is the case it might be beneficial to refit the lamp with a plastic or bakelite one.

Replacement of flex fitted to a standard or table lamp is relatively simple providing that, before removing the old flex, a piece of string or the new flex is tied on to it; this eliminates the problem of trying to feed a piece of flex through what, in the case of a standard lamp, could be a $1\frac{1}{2}$ metre long hole. In some instances a clamping screw is fitted in the base of a lamp, this prevents the cable from accidentally being pulled out of the light fitting when replacing the plug on to the new flex.

Be sure to check that the fuse is of the correct rating.

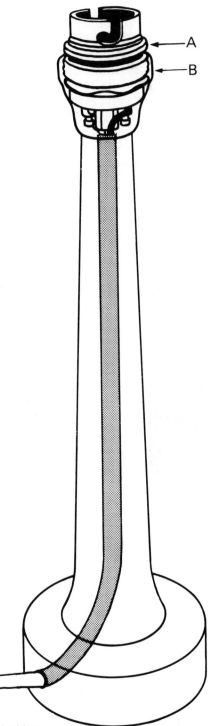

Standard lamp

Door Chimes

There are two types of door chimes:

1. Mains operated
2. Battery operated

Mains operated system. To fit a mains operated type of door chime a live lighting cable has to be found. To do this the floorboards will need to be lifted in a bedroom to find a piece of 3/029 or 1.5 mm² twin with earth cable, on to which will need to be connected a new piece of cable to fit the door chimes.

Removal of the floorboards is a relatively easy task. First go along the edge of both sides of the board with a sharp bolster chisel, removing the tongue from the floor board, then gently prize the board up. If some nails tend to be stubborn and hold the board, continue to exert a firm pressure upwards from under the board whilst hitting the top of it with a hammer. This will generally provide sufficient shock to release the board. Once the board is loose it will need to be cut into two above a joist—**do not saw it in half**

between two joists. Once the board has been removed and the cable found the power must be turned off. The cable must be cut into and a new piece of cable connected on to it. The best method of doing this is to place a sharp knife in the centre of the cable and draw it along; the outer sheathing can then be peeled off for a distance of approximately 150 to 200 mm. The live and neutral conductors will be left exposed but still insulated.

The next step is to screw a 15 A joint box on to the side of a joist and lay the cable across it. Where each conductor rests on a terminal remove the insulation from the live and neutral conductors and place in the terminals, then strip back the insulation on the new piece of cable which is going to feed the door chime and connect this into the joint box. The lid on the box can then be secured.

The reason for stripping the existing cable in the way mentioned is to avoid having to connect three pieces of wire into each terminal, as this sometimes can prove almost impossible.

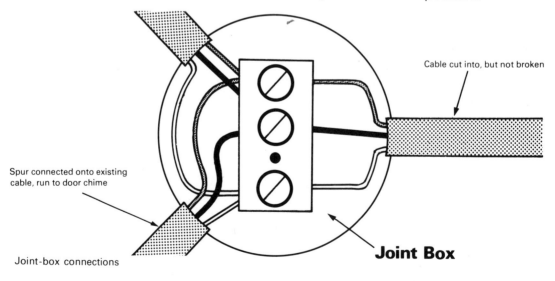

Cable cut into, but not broken

Spur connected onto existing cable, run to door chime

Joint-box connections

Joint Box

The new piece of cable which is to be fitted to the door chimes will be protected by the 5 A fuse in the consumer unit, in the same manner as the lighting circuit from which it was taken. This cable then needs to be connected into the chime transformer. A transformer is a device which can be made to increase the mains voltage from 240 V to, for instance, 500 V or reduce it from 240 V to, say, 6 V.

Transformers used for door chimes are usually built into a plastic box and have six terminals mounted into the plastic. Two of these are for the mains cable to be fitted and will be marked '240 V ac'. There is not normally provision for connecting the earth wire. **If there is no terminal leave the earth wire disconnected**. The other four terminals are used for connecting the single-strand two-core flex to the actual chimes. Normally one of the terminals will be marked 'common' and the other three may have numbers stamped by the side of them, and these numbers will indicate the output voltages between the common and that particular terminal. The normal value of output voltages is 6, 8 and 10 V. You will select the appropriate terminal at the transformer, depending upon the voltage at which the door-chimes work.

In general the transformer is mounted on the side of a joist between the ceiling and floorboards. The twin-core flex then needs to be fed to the push button and the chimes. Ideally, the floorboards that were lifted to install the transformer should be as near as possible above the door where the push button and chimes are to be fitted.

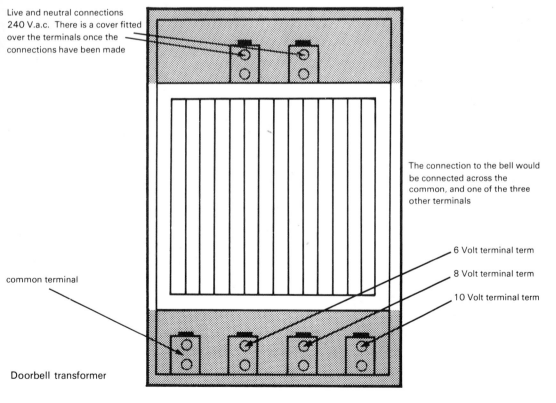

Live and neutral connections 240 V.a.c. There is a cover fitted over the terminals once the connections have been made

The connection to the bell would be connected across the common, and one of the three other terminals

6 Volt terminal term

8 Volt terminal term

10 Volt terminal term

common terminal

Doorbell transformer

To fit the actual box containing the chimes a masonry drill will be required in order to drill and plug the wall to provide a firm fixing. The twin-core flex must then be fed from the joist space down the wall to the chime box. To avoid damage occurring to decorations this cable can be surface-clipped to the wall and then chased into the plaster at a future date when redecorating is carried out. A wire must also be fed from the chime box to the push button switch which will be mounted on the outside of the door pillar. **Do not mount the switch on to the door** as continual opening and shutting will cause the flex to crack and ultimately break. With the transformer-operated door chimes an illuminated push button switch can be fitted which is useful in dark conditions, as it helps one to select the correct door keys, etc. This is not to be recommended for battery operated systems as the continual illumination of the light would flatten the batteries in a very short time.

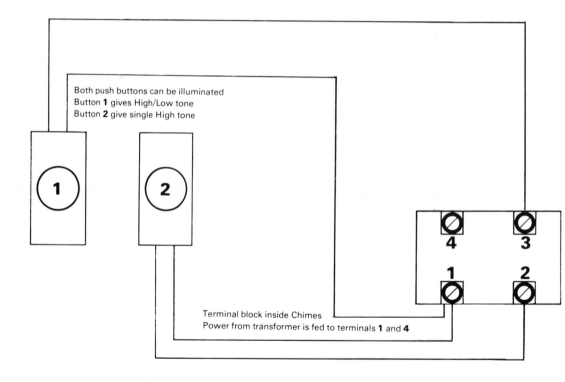

Both push buttons can be illuminated
Button **1** gives High/Low tone
Button **2** give single High tone

4   3

1   2

Terminal block inside Chimes
Power from transformer is fed to terminals **1** and **4**

Doorbell connections for one- and two-button operation

Battery operated systems. The fitting for this type of system is exactly the same as for the mains operated system, apart from the fact that there are no connections into the mains supply and batteries are fitted into the chime box. Under normal conditions the batteries will last up to twelve months.

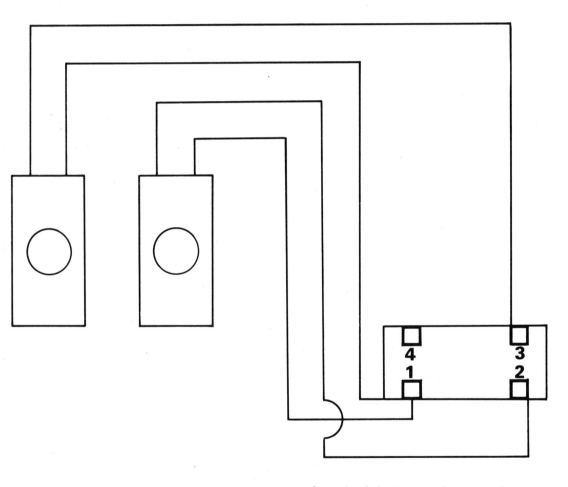

Connections for battery operated systems are the same as for a transformer one, with the exception of batteries fitted into the door chime case

Battery-operated doorbell system

Shaver Points

A shaver point can be fitted into a bathroom. It is the only type of socket that can and **under no circumstances must an ordinary 13 A socket be fitted**. Shaver points are only two-pin sockets and require no earthing through to the appliance, as electric shavers are double insulated and therefore require no earthing themselves.

To fit a shaver point. First of all the lighting cable must be located. If the bathroom is upstairs, which is normally the case, finding the lighting cable is relatively simple. If one enters the loft the lighting cable will be seen running in a continuous loop from light rose to light rose and ultimately back down the wall to the consumer unit. The shaver point can then be fitted as a spur to the lighting main or can be included into the ring main and form an integral part of the circuit.

When fitting a shaver point as a spur the ceiling rose cover in the bathroom must first be removed, and this will expose the cables feeding the light. In modern houses a 'three-plate rose' is used, which allows for a live and neutral conductor to be fed into the light rose and for a live and neutral conductor to be fed out of the rose and ultimately to the next rose in the circuit, or back to the consumer unit if that particular rose happens to be the last one on the circuit. Also fed from the light rose are a live and neutral which connect the rose to—in the case of the bathroom—a pull-cord switch. The live conductor of this cable is connected to the two other live conductors. The neutral is connected into the third terminal in the rose on its own. The flex which feeds the light is connected between the neutral conductor and the other terminal, which has connected to it two neutral conductors.

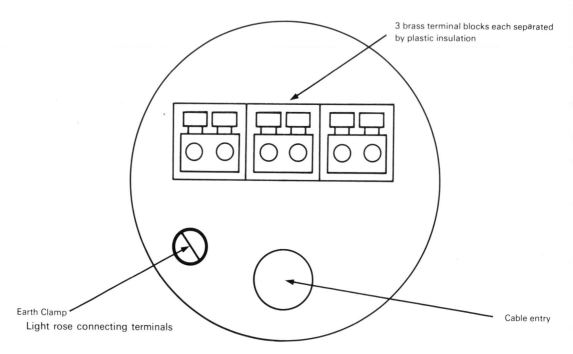

3 brass terminal blocks each separated by plastic insulation

Earth Clamp

Light rose connecting terminals

Cable entry

To fit the shaver point as a spur a live and neutral conductor must be connected into the rose on to the two live and neutral terminals. This cable is then fed to the position at which the shaver point is to be fitted. One point which must be noted is that, although there has been no mention of the earth terminal, it must be connected and in all lighting fittings, i.e. roses, switch boxes etc., a small brass terminal will be found. This brass terminal is for the connection of the earth lead. The purpose for this earth terminal is so that a continual earth loop is fed round the house, and should, for instance, a steel light fitting be fitted, it would automatically be earthed.

Shaver points usually incorporate a strip light and are best fitted above a mirror. The light can be one of two types—incandescent or fluorescent. The fluorescent ones probably give a better shadow-free, brighter light but in some cases they can tend to make a buzzing noise. The incandescent type are made in the same way as a normal light bulb but are encapsulated in a long cylindrical glass envelope, instead of the normal pear shape. A point in favour of this latter type is that it lights instantaneously, whereas the fluorescent ones can take seconds to ignite. The shaver point is normally mounted in the end of the light fitting.

To fit the shaver point into the ring main to make it an integral part of the circuit, one of the cables feeding a light rose must be removed and fed down to the position where the shaver point is to be fitted. If the cable is not long enough then a 15 A joint box must be fitted and another piece of cable connected on to it. When this has been fed to the light a return piece of cable must be fitted and fed back into the light rose to the same point from which the other piece was removed. This method is the one to be preferred as it does mean that the ring is continuous and that a spur has not been fitted. However, this method tends to be more expensive than the one mentioned previously.

Another method of connecting an appliance or fitting into a ring main is to cut one piece of 3/029 or 1.5 mm² cable and on to each end connect a 15 amp joint box, and then from each joint box two separate cables should be run down to the shaver point. Remember to connect the earth terminals.

Actual maintenance of a shaver point is not necessary. The only thing that could possibly occur is for the lighting

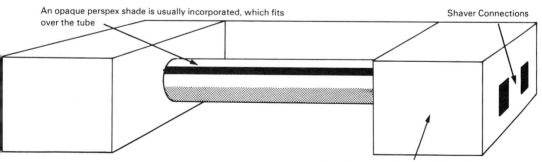

An opaque perspex shade is usually incorporated, which fits over the tube

Shaver Connections

The end caps can be removed to enable the tube to be replaced

Illuminated shaver point

tube to blow or the terminals, which connect the shaver, to become coated in verdigris. The latter would really only occur in extremely damp or steamy bathrooms, and then could take some considerable time to do so. If this should happen the light fitting should be removed and the terminal cleaned with a mild abrasive (emery cloth) or, in less severe cases, metal polish should be sufficient.

Bathroom Heaters

There are basically two types of heater:

1. Circular type fitted in place of the bathroom light (this type of heater usually incorporates a light also).
2. Strip wall heater.

Circular heater. To fit this type of heater the light rose must first be removed to expose the two cables forming the feed in and out of the rose and a further piece of cable which connects the switch to the rose. If the circular heater and light do not have a three-plate fixing inside (see previous section

on shaver points) connections must be made using a barrier strip connector.

The next step is to connect the live, neutral and earth conductors into the barrier strip and then connect the switch wire between the live terminal and a spare terminal in the barrier strip. The wires from both the neutral terminals are then connected and these should be fed to the heater. The heater element is generally only a 750 W element, unlike normal electric fire elements, and is encapsulated in a silica glass tube. This is to prevent steam from coming into contact with the element which could cause a short circuit. The heater would normally be switched on by a pull-cord hanging from the heater.

Strip wall heater. This type of heater can either be fitted into the ring or run from a spur, and the method of connecting this type of heater is as described under shaver points (see page 210).

The wall-mounted type of heaters do not have a light incorporated in them. If the element should fail to heat up, in

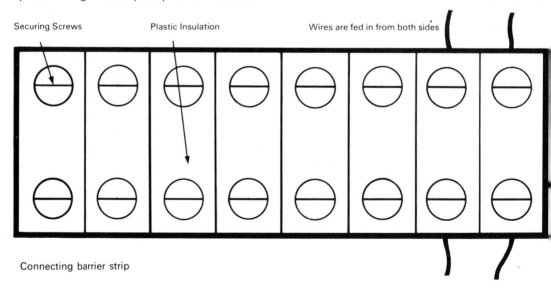

Securing Screws   Plastic Insulation   Wires are fed in from both sides

Connecting barrier strip

either case, this can easily be removed by undoing the two securing bolts at either end of the element in order to check it with an ohm meter.

Electric Irons

An electric iron basically consists of an electrical heating element encapsulated in a steel or aluminium plate forming the base of the iron. The temperature of the iron is governed by a thermostat which is adjusted by the knob on the top of the iron. The knob is usually graduated by the words nylon, rayon, cotton, etc. Generally, electric irons will work satisfactorily for a great many years, but should they malfunction the common faults are either a faulty thermostat or a broken element.

If the iron breaks down, the element and the thermostat should be checked. This is achieved by first removing the heat control knob which will allow the thin steel plate immediately under the knob to be pulled off. This will expose a large hexagon-headed nut—this nut must also be removed. The heel (back) of the iron then has to have its back plate removed so as to expose two terminals, these are live and neutral. The terminal screws have to be disconnected so as to allow the element and thermostat to be removed from the casing. The live terminal will be found to run to the thermostat and then on to the element, whilst the neutral is connected directly to the element. The thermostat can easily be detached by undoing the one securing screw. If the contact points are badly pitted it is advisable to replace the thermostat. The element will need to be checked on an ohm meter and should you not possess one then most electrical retailers will check the element for you free of charge. If the

element is found to be faulty then, of course, this must be replaced. Assembly of the new element and thermostat is exactly the reverse procedure of the disassembly.

Vacuum Cleaners

A vacuum cleaner consists of an electric motor to which is connected a fan. This fan causes a vacuum resulting in a sucking action which pulls the dirt and dust from the carpet and into a disposable paper bag (in the older models this is a non-disposable canvas bag).

There are two types of vacuum cleaner:

1. *The upright type*—these have fitted to them a revolving brush and beater which it is claimed helps remove the dirt and lift the pile.
2. *The cylinder type*—these have a long hose attached to them on to which are connected the various cleaning tools.

Both types of cleaner work on almost the same principle and that is of a vacuum being caused by an electrically powered fan. Therefore, the only electrical fault that is likely to occur is a motor failure, apart from obvious cable fractures or loose terminals.

There are two carbon brushes fitted to the motor and should the motor fail it is generally due to the brushes becoming worn. If the motor is visually examined two plastic serrated caps approximately 15 mm high by 15 mm diameter will be seen. If these are unscrewed they will spring away from the motor as under these plastic caps are fitted springs on to which are connected the carbon brushes. These brushes transmit the power from the mains input on to the commutator (the revolving part of the motor). If after replacing the two carbon brushes the motor still fails to run the fault will either be in the commutator section or the outer set of windings in the case of the motor. If the latter is the case then the windings will need to be checked on a special, rather expensive, piece of equipment, by a firm specialising in motor rewinds.

Hair Driers

Hair driers consist of a heater element and an electric motor which drives a fan. The heating element is usually made in the form of a loose wound spring which is wrapped round a former, the former being made of a heat-resisting insulating material, usually ceramic. The heater element is normally fitted with a thermostat to protect the element from overheating. The thermostat, which is not adjustable and is set by the manufacturers to cut out at a predetermined temperature, forms an integral part of the heating element. The fan is driven by an electric motor which is generally a synchronous motor that requires no brushes and virtually no maintenance.

If a fault occurs in the hair drier, the fault can be isolated to either a motor failure or a heater failure. If the motor is found to be faulty then the probable cause of this will be a burnt winding. This can sometimes be seen but, if the windings are burnt on the inside, then no visible signs will show. The only remedy for this type of fault is either to replace the motor or to take it to a motor rewind firm in order to get the winding rewound. It must be pointed out, however, that the latter method could prove to be more expensive than replacement of the complete motor.

If the heater element or themostat are faulty then these also must be replaced. When purchasing a new heating element it may be quicker to write direct to the manufacturers and order a replacement direct from them. To expose the element and thermostat it will be found that if the five or six case securing screws located in the side of the case are removed, the case will split into two leaving all the electrical parts easily accessible.

The element will have a live and neutral wire connected to it. The two screws retaining the live and neutral conductors must be undone. If there are any screws securing the element to one side of the case, these must also be removed to allow the element to be withdrawn and the replacement fitted.

In the case of the motor, it will be found that there are two conductors, one live and one neutral, feeding the motor. These must be disconnected and any securing screws holding the motor in place must also be removed to allow the motor to be withdrawn and the replacement fitted.

How to Change a Central Heating Pump

A great majority of houses have some form of central heating system fitted. At least 70 per cent of these systems rely on radiator heating and this method requires a pump to circulate the hot water round the system. The pump is mounted in a steel casing which incorporates the motor armature. Fitted to this armature is an impeller which is a steel disc with raised veins which, when turned, circulates the water round the system. This part of the pump is similar to a water pump fitted in a motor car.

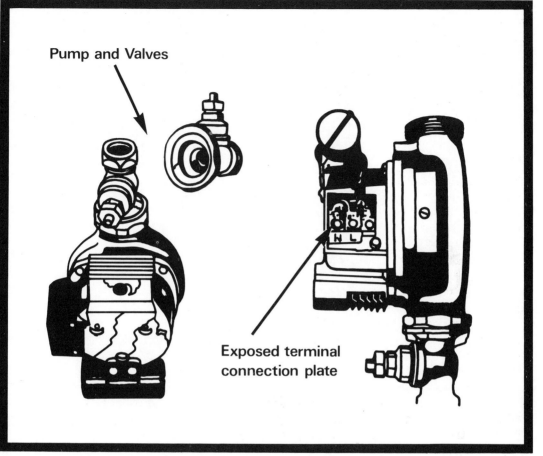

Pump and Valves

Exposed terminal connection plate

The isolating valves and terminal connecting plate of a central heating pump

Central heating pumps are usually fitted with a variable speed switch, normally graduated by the numbers one to five. If fitted in a two-storey house the pump will only need to be set on numbers two or three but, if installed in a three-storey house, then the pump may require to be set as high as number five. However, should the pump be set too high it will pump the water with such a force that the water will be ejected from the expansion pipe into the heating supply tank fitted beneath. This tank is usually located in the loft space.

Should the pump malfunction in any way, such as seizing or making a noise due to worn bearings, then it will need to be changed. To change the pump, two valves, which will be found one on either side of the pump, have to be turned off in a clockwise direction; this will isolate the water to the pump. Two large nuts connecting the pump to the copper tube then have to be undone and this will allow the pump to be withdrawn from the piping. Once this has been carried out the electrical connections can then be removed in one of two ways. The most common method is simply to withdraw the plug from the pump thus enabling it to be

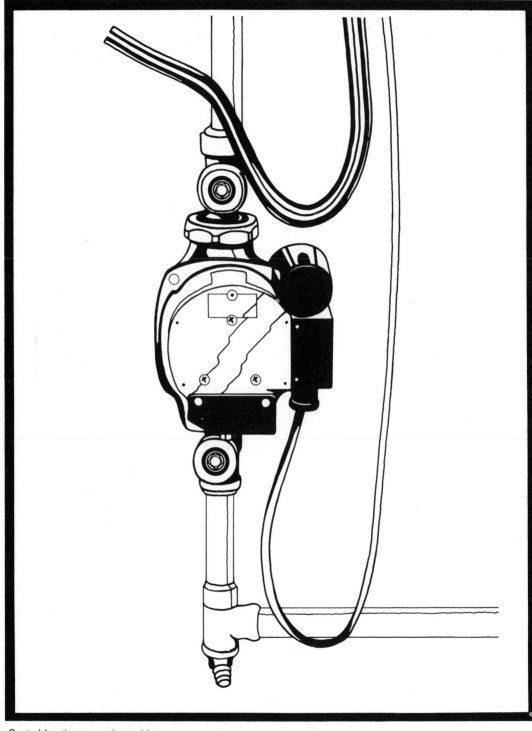

Central heating pump in position

completely removed. In older types of systems it may be necessary to remove an inspection cover and disconnect the input conductors from the motor terminals.

Replacement of the new pump is exactly the reverse process of the disconnection.

To ensure that the valves are completely watertight foliac pipe compound or PTFE pipe tape can be added to the joints before reassembly. The isolating valves should be reopened and any air that may be in the pump impeller will then be allowed to flow into one of the radiators, which will then necessitate the bleeding of each radiator. Following this the electrical section must then be replugged in or the terminations connected on to their respective terminals in the pump.

Once the pump has been replaced and the electrical and plumbing connections have been satisfactorily completed, then the new pump must be set to its correct setting. To do this a screwdriver will need to be inserted into the screw slot, pressed inwards and then turned to the correct setting.

Generally, central heating pumps can be purchased on an exchange basis, and therefore when buying a new pump it is advisable to enquire if an allowance will be made on the old pump should it be returned once the new one has been installed.

11 Rewiring and Extending Existing Ring Mains

Wiring a Cooker Panel

To wire a cooker point from the mains input to the actual cooker the first item to check is the type of cooker to be installed and whether it will require a 30 A or 45 A fuse. Most cookers will only require a 30 A fuse. The consumer unit should be checked to see if there is a spare fuse space. If there is, the cable can be connected into it but, if not, then a new fuse box must be purchased. A single-way type would be satisfactory but it is advisable to fit a two- or three-way, thus leaving one or two spare fuse spaces should other extensions or additions be required in the future.

If a new fuse box has to be fitted then the live feed to the new consumer unit

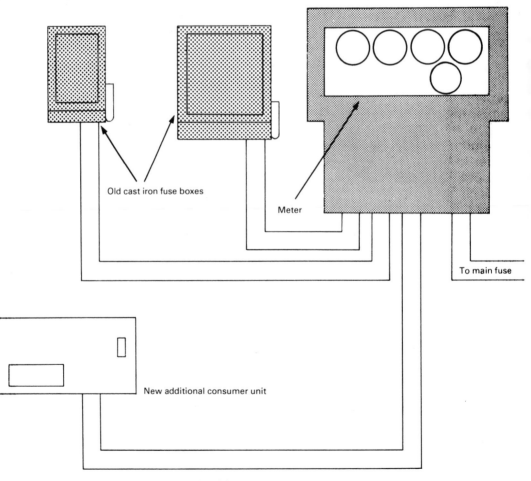

Old cast iron fuse boxes

Meter

To main fuse

New additional consumer unit

Old and new consumer units connected to electricity meter

must be fed from the meter. To do this the Electricity Board **must** be notified of what you intend to do in order that they can make arrangements to check the completed work. The lead seals can then be removed from both the electricity meter and the main 60 A or 100 A input fuse,* and then this fuse can be removed.* This will isolate the complete electrical installation in the house including the meter and the consumer unit already fitted. The front cap of the meter can next be removed and connected to a new piece of cable* (meter tails), which has to be 16 mm² double insulated cable, and this then has to be fitted into the new consumer unit. Following this the meter cover can be refitted* and the main fuse replaced.* Power to the house will now be reconnected and a live and neutral feed will be made to the new consumer unit.

In the new unit there will be found a large brass terminal block for the earth connections, from this terminal a piece of single insulated green and yellow striped insulated 6 mm² cable should be bonded (connected) to both the gas and water pipes, notably on the supply side of the stop valve and gas valve. Another piece of this cable should then be connected to the steel casing of the mains input cable. If, however, a termi-

nal is not fitted to this cable the Electricity Board will, if notified, fit one **for** a small fee.

The new consumer unit is now ready to receive any new appliance which is going to be connected to it.

If a number of small fuse boxes **are** already fitted it may be preferable to scrap these and fit a new, larger consumer unit to replace them, and this **will** also provide the required number of new fuse spaces for the intended additions to the circuit. Whichever method is adopted it must be realised that in order to render the consumer unit terminals and the meter dead (switched off) **the main sealed Electricity Board's fuse must be removed in order to render the circuit safe.*** Do not attempt to connect a new consumer unit without first switching off the power—people have been known to do this in order to avoid calling in the Electricity Board to check the work once it has been completed. Once the new consumer unit has been fitted work can commence on fitting the new cooker panel.

There are a number of different cable sizes which can be used, depending on the size of the cooker and the distance between the cooker panel and the consumer unit, but 6 mm² double insulated

*These operations should only be carried out by an Electricity Board operative.

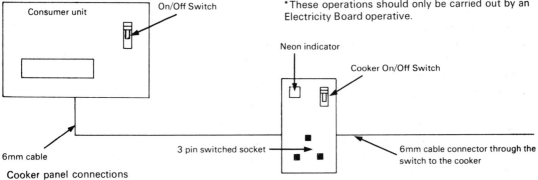

Cooker panel connections

219

cable with earth will be of sufficient capability to run all types of domestic cookers.

If the house is fitted with wooden floorboards it is probably best to run the cable under the floor to the kitchen, or wherever the cooker panel is required. If the floors are made of concrete then the cable will need to be routed up the wall, under the upstairs floorboards and back down to where the cooker panel is to be fitted. It must be noted, however, that in fitting a cooker panel, unlike a normal socket, it does not have to be on a ring, i.e. there does not have to be a return wire fed back to the consumer unit.

The cooker panel usually incorporates a 13 A socket and can be made with small neon lights to give an immediate visual check to see whether it is switched on or off. When actually mounting the cooker panel on to the wall be sure that the terminals are extremely well tightened as the cable will be carrying a load of anything up to 7–10 kw.

From the cooker panel a piece of cable must be fed to the cooker. Normally this is chased into the wall below the plaster and emerges from the wall at approximately the same level as the terminals on the cooker. At this point a terminal plate must be fitted to prevent the cooker from being pulled away from the wall which would ultimately pull the cable out of the plaster.

Installing an Immersion Heater

Again, the first step to be taken is to see if there is the facility for connecting a spare fuse in the consumer unit; if there is not a new fuse box and consumer unit must be fitted. An alternative to this is to replace the old consumer unit(s) with a larger new consumer unit, capable of accommodating the existing fuses and having sufficient space left to fit more as and when required. You must remember to use 16 mm² double insulated cable for the meter tails when connecting the consumer unit to the electricity meter. In most cases the immersion heater will need a 15 A fuse but, in a small number of cases, a 20 A fuse may be required. In order to check if a 15 A fuse is sufficient the wattage rating of the heating element must be found (this is usually stamped on the top of the element). The fuse value can be calculated by working out the following formula

$$A = \frac{W}{V}$$

An example of using this formula can be found on page 177.

The cable will need to be of 2.5 mm² twin with earth. Only one piece of cable will need to be fed to the immersion heater and no return will be necessary. It may take some considerable time to feed the cable from the consumer unit to the copper cylinder, as it may mean it traversing from ground to upstairs level and also from one side of the house to the other.

It is important to remember when chasing cables into plaster that they should always be run vertically. You will then be able to guess where the cable runs and avoid it if ever you need to drive nails or picture hooks into the wall.

When running the cable between the joist space it will be necessary either to drill holes in the joist or to cut small chases in the top of the joists. If holes are to be drilled then they should be 50 mm from the top of the joist, this

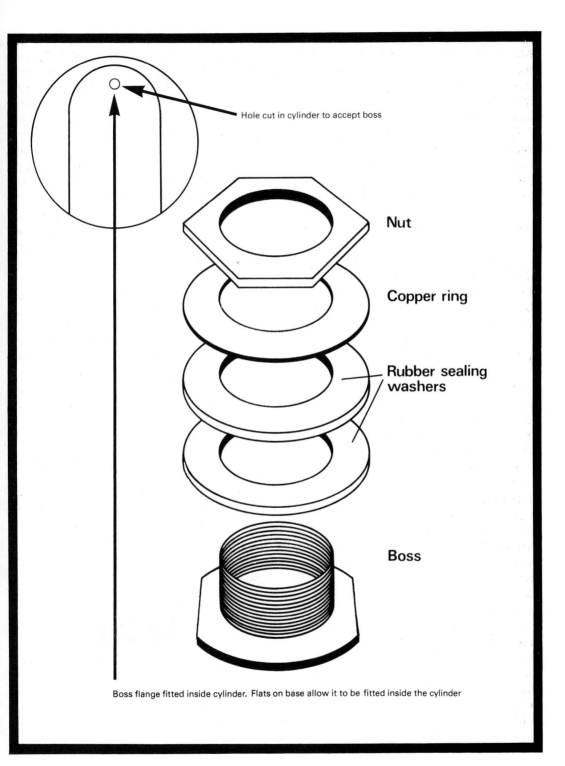

Hole cut in cylinder to accept boss

Nut

Copper ring

Rubber sealing washers

Boss

Boss flange fitted inside cylinder. Flats on base allow it to be fitted inside the cylinder

Exposed view of cylinder flange

again will prevent the cables from inadvertently becoming nailed. If chases are to be cut then they should be in the centre of the joist in order to avoid the cable being damaged when the floorboards are renailed.

Once the cable has been fed through to the cylinder, which is normally in the bathroom, a switch must be fitted. If the cylinder is in the bathroom then the switch must be fitted outside the room to eliminate the possibility of steam causing a short circuit in the switch. From the switch another piece of cable must be run to the cylinder. It is advisable to use butyl rubber 3-core flex for this purpose as it is heat-resistant and will endure the continual heat applied to it from the cylinder.

If the cylinder has an immersion heater boss (usually a 75 mm diameter hole with an internal thread) this is normally blanked off with a large brass nut. Once the cylinder has been drained (as mentioned on page 202) then the boss can be removed and the immersion heater fitted. If, however, the cylinder has not got a boss, or if the cylinder is fitted close to the ceiling, thus making it impossible to fit the element into the cylinder, then a special adapting thread ring must be fitted. The adapting ring can be purchased from a plumbers' merchants. To fit the adapting ring a hole will have to be cut in the cylinder, which can easily be achieved by drilling a series of holes close together in a circle of 75 mm diameter. Once the holes have been drilled they can be cut into one large hole by using a pair of tin snips, taking great care not to let the waste copper drop into the bottom of the cylinder. With a half-round file the hole can be filed out until the boss, when tried upside down,

will fit tightly into the hole. It will be noted that the boss will have a flange approximately 20 mm wide round the base. This is circular with the exception of two flats filed on it—these two flats allow for the boss to be fitted through the hole in the cylinder.

Once the hole has been adjusted and PTFE tape wrapped round the threads of the boss, the boss can be fitted. In order to do this the boss must be placed on its side and fed into the cylinder, then by carefully tipping the boss in a horizontal position it can be pulled upwards into the hole. With great care remove one hand at a time so that the locking nut can be placed on to the top of the thread bush. With one hand hold the boss and with the other hand hold the nut and turn until it is tightened. Finish this off securely with a spanner or pair of stilsons. Once this work is completed the immersion heater can be fitted (as described on pages 202-4).

Lighting Circuits

If an extension to a lighting circuit is required, it must be decided how many extra lighting points are going to be needed. If it is only two or three then the existing lighting ring can be con-

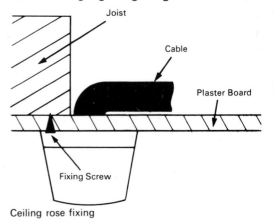

Ceiling rose fixing

nected into, provided no greater than eight lighting points in all are connected. Connecting into the ring can be achieved in two ways, as described on pages 210-12, but probably the easiest method is to locate a piece of 1.5 mm² cable, cut it in two and connect two 15 A joint boxes—one to either end. From one joint box a new piece of 1.5 mm² cable must be run to the position where the first light is to be fitted. The light rose can then be fitted to the ceiling, preferably on to a joist. When fitting the rose to the joist it should be put to one side of the joist, which will allow the cable to be run down the side of the joist and into the rose.

Another piece of cable then has to be taken to the newly installed light rose, and this should be run to the next position where a light is required. Repeat this process until all the new positions have been fed with an input cable and an output cable. From the last lighting rose in the new additions feed the outgoing cable back to the second of the two 15 A joint boxes; this will ensure that all the lighting roses are on the ring. The two pieces of cable protruding from each light rose can then be connected. The two live conductors have to be connected to one of the terminal blocks and to one other terminal block the neutral conductors. This will leave one spare block of terminals.

Once the above work has been completed the switch wire will need to be connected. First decide where the switches are to be fitted and fix a plaster-depth steel box into the plaster, securing it either by cement or, preferably, a wall plug and screw. If, as normal, the light switch is near to a door the cable can be fed up the wall behind the architrave on the door casing. Normally there is a reasonable gap suitable to feed the cable in once the architrave has been removed. This will conceal the switch wire up to the height of the door. From this point on it is a matter of personal choice whether to surface fix the cable (clip to the surface of the wall) or to chase a groove in the plaster and bury it. The latter results in a more professional looking job, but some people tend to surface fix until they next redecorate the room and then chase in the cable at that stage. The switch must be fed to the light rose, and the live and neutral conductors must then be connected. The live has to be fitted into the same block of connectors as the other two live conductors. The neutral is connected into the third, as yet, unused terminal block. The lighting flex then has to be run from the two neutral conductors to the lamp-holder. The final connection and probably, from the safety factor, the most important is to connect the three single-strand earth wires to the small terminal in the light rose. The reason for wiring in this fashion is to eliminate having a live wire permanently connected to the lamp-holder, this method of connection being known as a 'switched live'. In some older types of houses the neutral wire was the one which was 'switched', resulting in a permanent live terminal at the lamp-holder.

If more than three extra lights are required it may be more advantageous to fit a new consumer unit or use, if available, a spare fuse in the original consumer unit. If a new lighting ring is installed it is important to ensure that the cable is fed from the consumer unit to the lighting points and then back to the consumer unit. The amount of lights permitted on a ring is not clearly defined. There have been cases where only 1.0 mm² cable has been used and one ring has had all the upstairs and downstairs lights connected to it, but I would suggest that 1.5 mm² is always used for lighting and not more than eight lights are run from one particular ring.

Normally it is better to have one lighting circuit for upstairs and one for downstairs. Wall lights, if fitted, can be fitted on a separate fuse. In the event of a power failure of the lighting circuit, by fitting the wall lights on a separate fuse, it will at least ensure that a light of some description is available whilst the other ones are being repaired.

If a garage light is required and the garage is an integral part of the house, then this light can be included in the downstairs circuit. If, however, the garage is some distance from the house then a special fuse must be added in order to run a cable from the consumer unit to the garage (this problem is dealt with on page 227).

One advantage of fitting a new consumer unit and completely new circuit is that the installer knows, for future reference, exactly where the circuit runs and what is connected to it. If, however, there are a multitude of differing types of consumer units then it is preferable to disconnect the lot completely and purchase a new consumer unit large enough to take all the existing circuits plus any new additions and, if possible, leaving one or two spaces for any additions that might be required in the future.

Power Circuits

13 A power circuits can be fitted anywhere throughout the house and an un-limited amount of sockets can be fitted if the floor space is less than 100 square metres (1000 square feet), which covers most normal three and four bedroomed houses. In general, although there is no limit to the number of sockets that can be fitted into a ring, it is preferable to fit one ring upstairs and one downstairs. From a 13 A ring main one spur is allowed and not more than two sockets can be fitted on to this spur or one permanent corded outlet device (e.g. oil-filled electric radiator, central heating boiler point). It is possible to connect on to the existing power circuit by using the method mentioned previously for lighting, with the exception that the joint boxes must be 30 A rating and **not** 15 A. If a number of sockets are to be added then it may prove more economical to run a new circuit.

To run a new power circuit is a relatively simple process. First a new consumer unit large enough to run the circuit from must be fitted or, alternatively, a consumer unit fitted large enough to accommodate all the original points as well. Then, equipped with a bolster chisel, flat chisel and lump hammer, cut into the brickwork to a depth of 50 mm where the sockets are to be fitted. At this point it is perhaps advisable to cut holes large enough to fit double sockets rather than single ones. The hole in this case needs to be 175 mm wide by 50 mm high.

If the floor is made of wood the socket holes should be cut near to the skirting board, and in this way only a small amount of plaster will need to be removed between the hole and the top of the skirting board. If a very thin chisel is used it is possible to force this down behind the skirting board, thus removing the plaster. Considerable force will then be needed to force the chisel through the piece of floorboard. Once this has been completed the cable can be fed from under the floorboards, behind the skirting board and up to the socket hole. This makes for a far neater job than if the skirting board were to be removed or, indeed, if the cable was fed over the skirting board and into the socket. This latter method not only looks ugly and unfinished, but may also be dangerous as the socket can easily be caught by persons walking past or by a vacuum cleaner being pushed hard against the cable which could cut or chafe the insulation.

If the downstairs floors are solid then, unfortunately, the cable must be fed between the joist space and ultimatedly down the wall, either on the surface or chased into the wall, and protected by capping. If this is the case it would be beneficial to mount the sockets level with the appliances to be fitted into them, and an ideal height seems to be between 300 and 600 mm from the floor.

The socket boxes can be fitted either by pushing out the circular disc which is meant for the cable entry and then bedded in cement (this will hold them quite firmly) or, alternatively, they can be secured by a wall plug and screw.

If the cement method is used, the boxes will need to be left for a couple of days to allow the cement to set hard. If difficulty is encountered when bedding the cable under the floorboards due to it getting caught in the joist stringers (small pieces of wood used to keep the joists vertical and parallel) a piece of oval-shaped capping which is extremely flexible can be fed from one end of it. If the 2.5 mm² cable is folded into two it can be forced down the end of the capping; on withdrawing the capping the cable will also come with it. The capping is made in 3-metre lengths, therefore this method only reads good for runs of up to 3 metres, runs of a greater length will need another floorboard removing to provide a halfway point.

If the new power points are to be added to an existing ring main then all the socket faces can be connected. A good guide to the amount of cable that should be left for connection is to place the socket face under the box and at 90° to it (i.e. sticking out from the wall), the cable should be 15 mm longer than the end of the socket. The outer sheathing then has to be stripped back exposing the live and neutral conductors, both insulated, and the non-insulated earth wire. Following this strip back the insulation on the live and neutral conductors for approximately 15 mm (at this point care must be taken not to cut into the actual conductors), these can then be connected into the live and neutral terminals in the back of the socket. The earth wire which is insulated must be sleeved with PVC green sleeving to prevent it from accidentally touching one of the other two terminals which would result in a short circuit, and then connected to the earth terminal. When this has been done the socket face can be screwed on to the box, but care must be exercised to feed the cable gently into the box making sure not to trap any between the socket face and the edge of the box. As the socket face is slightly larger than the box it is a good idea to cut a hole carefully into the brickwork; once the socket has been fitted it will hide the coarse edge of the brickwork.

Once all the sockets have been connected the power should be switched off and the two pieces of cable forming the start and finish of the new circuit should be connected into the two 30 A joint boxes. Following this the power can again be switched on and the new sockets will be an integral part of the ring.

If a new ring is to be fitted then the method would be the same as just mentioned, except that the two ends of

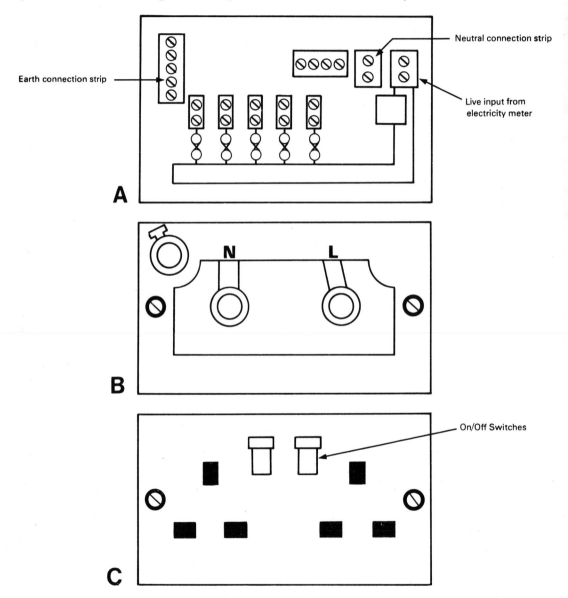

Earth connection strip

Neutral connection strip

Live input from electricity meter

A

N   L

B

On/Off Switches

C

(A) Consumer connecting plates; (B) Rear of socket showing terminal connections; (C) Front of 13 amp double switched socket

the cable would be fed into the consumer unit and ultimately a 30 A fuse.

If a garage is built on to the house a socket can be fitted into the garage as part of the ring but, as mentioned previously in the lighting section, if the garage is some distance away from the house then a special circuit must be fitted.

Wiring a Garage for Lighting and Power

As with all additions to the existing wiring circuit, a new consumer unit must be fitted to accommodate the fuses needed to supply the garage. The cable or cables, whichever the case may be, can be either fed underground or supported on insulated pillars and strung from the side wall of the house to the garage.

To run the cable underground one must dig a trench of at least 2 spade depths deep from the point of emergence from the house to the garage. 2.5 mm² cable can be used but this will need to be protected from both the weather and any insects or even rodents. To protect the cable either galvanised steel conduit piping or the more modern type of conduit which is made of plastic can be used. Both types consist of a tube made of metal or plastic and can be obtained in sizes ranging from 15 mm to 50 mm diameter.

The steel type has screw threads cut on either end and a series of connectors which are steel tubes 30 mm long with a thread cut on the inside used for joining two lengths of pipe together. Square bends can also be purchased in order to allow the pipe to be run in any desired direction. The steel pipe can be bent but this requires a special pipe bender and a large capital outlay would

be required to purchase one. Hiring this bender could prove as expensive as engaging an electrician to do the work for you. It is, therefore, far simpler and more straightforward to use galvanised piping. Plastic tubing utilises the same principles as the steel but is cheaper and probably easier to work with. Although not to be encouraged, it can be bent, if it is slightly heated and bent gradually and with extreme caution. If, however, the plastic is heated too much it will be found that on trying to bend it it will collapse. The best method of heating the pipe is to hold it over a gas ring or a small blowlamp.

An alternative to the method of threading normal 2.5 mm² cable through the conduit is to use a special rodent-proof underground cable. The outer sheathing is made of special heavy gauge PVC to help protect it from the minerals in the earth and from rodents and pests. The heavy gauge PVC does offer some resistance if at any time someone should inadvertently dig deep and come into contact with the cable. An idea to mark the presence of such a cable is to sprinkle a coating of fine gravel over the cable before replacing the soil. This will give a visual check of its presence.

Another method of feeding a cable is to use mineral-insulated PVC coated cable; this is an expensive type of cable and requires specialist tools to seal the termination ends. This cable basically consists of three single strands of copper wire encapsulated in a white insulating powder which are all encapsulated in a circular copper sheath. The copper sheath is then coated in PVC for added protection. As stated, this cable is expensive and does require specialist tools in order to fit it, but I mention it

227

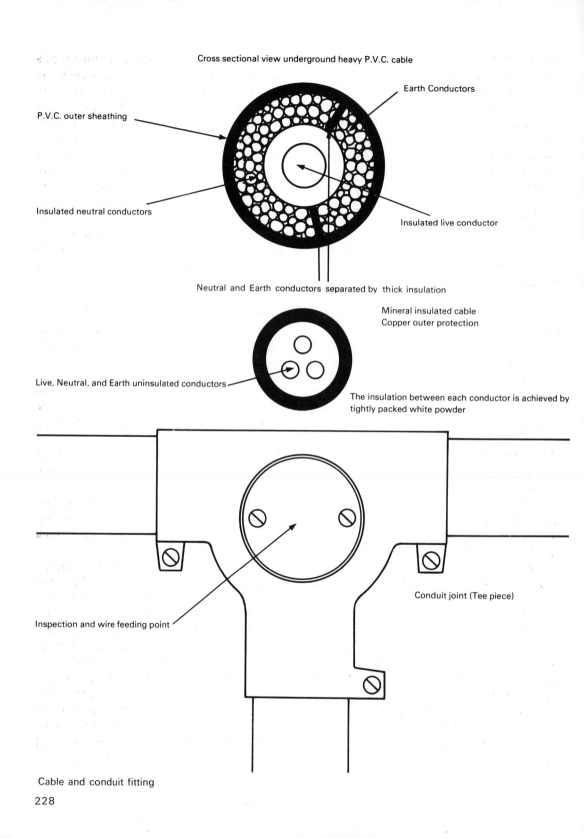

Cross sectional view underground heavy P.V.C. cable

Earth Conductors

P.V.C. outer sheathing

Insulated neutral conductors

Insulated live conductor

Neutral and Earth conductors separated by thick insulation

Mineral insulated cable
Copper outer protection

Live, Neutral, and Earth uninsulated conductors

The insulation between each conductor is achieved by tightly packed white powder

Conduit joint (Tee piece)

Inspection and wire feeding point

Cable and conduit fitting

as an alternative should anyone have easy access to such tools.

If the cable is run overhead from the house wall to the garage this cable, normally 2.5 mm² PVC, needs to be supported by a piece of heavy gauge wire, similar to the old type of wire clothes line. At the emergence of the cable from the house an insulated support must be mounted on the wall and the cable should be securely wrapped around the support. The supporting cable should be fitted to the wall and run to the garage wall and supported there; the cable should then be taped to this at not greater distances than 450 mm. Finally the cable is wrapped round the insulator mounted on the garage wall and fed through the wall into the garage.

Of the two types of cable feeding, the underground method, although involving more work, is to be preferred as it makes for a much neater appearance when completed.

Having now discussed the methods of feeding the cable to the garage it must be decided how many power points and/or lighting points are needed. If lighting and power are required in the garage then ideally two cables will need to be run to the garage, 1.5 mm² for lighting and 2.5 mm² for power. If, however, only one socket and one light is required then a simple circuit can be used. For this a piece of cable should be run from the power main (see the previous section on power circuits—one spur with two points connected to it). One single piece of cable can be run to the garage and into the power socket. From the socket a piece of 2.5 mm² must be run to a cord outlet spur box (see section on sockets) and from the cord outlet spur box a piece of 1.5 mm² can be fed to the light rose required—**make sure the fuse in the cord outlet spur box is 5 A.**

Once the electricity has been connected to the light rose it only requires a switch and switch wire to be fitted to the rose to complete the circuit. It must be emphasised that under no circumstances can this circuit be added on to as it conforms only to the minimum of requirements and, although basically acceptable, it is not the most preferred system.

It is possible that the garage will need two or three lights plus two or three sockets, in which case a separate ring main for both lighting and the power circuit will be required. Two spare fuse spaces should be available in the consumer unit; if not then a new two fuse unit should be installed to enable two separate ring circuits to be run to the garage and back again. Remember, the lighting circuit should have no greater than eight lighting points on that circuit, but the ring power main can have as many sockets as one wishes providing that the floor area does not total more than 100 square metres (1000 square feet). This is the best method in which to feed a garage with both lighting and power sockets, as the circuits can be extended to include a greenhouse, if desired, by cutting into the ring and using joint boxes (as described on pages 210-12).

12 Earthing

Earthing is probably the most important part of any electrical installation. The main purpose of the earth is to prevent overloading in a circuit and help eliminate the possibility of a person being electrocuted. The current will, if allowed, find the easiest path to earth in the event of a fault occurring in the circuit.

The continual earth wire which connects all the sockets or light fittings in one continuous loop is ultimately fed into the consumer unit and from there to the earth tag on the Electricity Board's armour sheathing on the input cable. The resistance of this wire is something in the order of less than 1.5 ohms. Maintaining the resistance at this low level will ensure that any stray current will flow along this wire to earth. The resistance of a human body can vary from between $10\,k\Omega$ (10,000 ohms) to $100\,k\Omega$ (100,000 ohms). It can therefore be seen that the presence of the earth wire, which is something in the region of 20,000 times lower resistance than in a human, does ensure that a shock will not affect a human being. Should no earth wire be fitted in the circuit, then the only path available for the stray current would be through the human; this would at the least result in a very nasty shock and at worst in fatality.

Earthing regulations up until 1973 were such that the lighting and power circuits had to have a continually uninterrupted earth loop on all circuits. The lighting circuit earth wire, which is fitted into both the light rose and the light switch, is mainly for the prevention of an accident occurring should a steel light fitting be used. Should a short occur in a steel light fitting, then the omission of an earth wire would mean that when one went to change the bulb the circuit would be taken down to earth and a nasty shock, which again could be fatal, would result.

The earth loop fitted to the power main has provision made for its connection into the circuit by producing the 13 A socket faces with three terminals, one for each—live, neutral and earth. Lighting circuits are somewhat different inasmuch as the lighting switches have no facility for the earth conductor to be actually connected to the switch. However, there is a terminal fitted in the switch box which is mounted on the wall. Ceiling light roses have an earth terminal mounted in the back plate of the rose which is separate from the other three sets of terminals used for connecting the live and neutral conductors; this layout does provide a continuous earth loop round the lighting circuits. Both earth terminations are ultimately connected on to a common earth terminal in the consumer unit.

The connection of the earth terminals from the consumer unit to the earth tag or stake can be carried out in three or four different ways, and these are best dealt with separately in detail, as follows.

1. Using the Electricity Board's Armour Outer Sheathing

If the property was built approximately before 1973 the earth connections must be made in the following manner. First of all the earth on both the lighting and power circuits must have a continuous earth wire which is fed into the consumer unit. All the earth wires are connected on to the same common terminal and from this common terminal a piece of 6 mm² single cable—colour coded yellow and green—must be fed to the input side of the gas meter should one be fitted, and another to the input side of the mains water pipe. If, however, the input water main is made from alkathene pipe (plastic) then an earth connection to it would not provide a good conductive connection as the piping material is an insulator; the earth wire is therefore connected on to the copper pipe just before the main input stopcock. This will provide a good conductive connection and the water inside the copper pipe will then conduct the current along the alkathene pipe and ultimately into the main water pipe situated somewhere in the road. This water pipe is made of cast iron, again another good conductor of electricity, and will therefore take the stray current directly to earth. A third wire, again 6 mm², must be fed to the earth tag

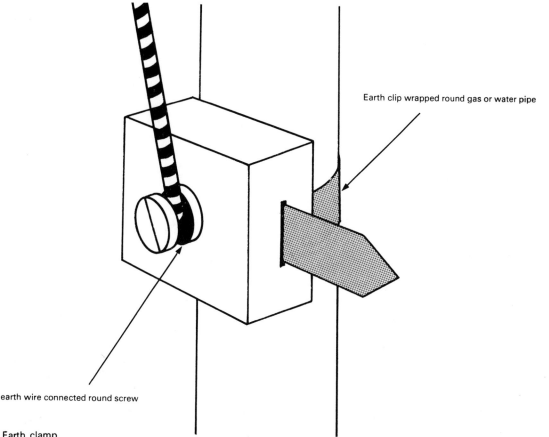

Earth clip wrapped round gas or water pipe

earth wire connected round screw

Earth clamp

soldered on to the Electricity Board's armour-protected sheathing. By connecting the earth leads to three sources, which ultimately go to earth, there is multiple protection against the risk of an overload. The clamps used to connect the earth wires to the various pipes must be of a recognisable standard, and any electrical factors will assist in the purchase of these.

2. Protective Multiple Earth

Houses which were built in 1973 and after will have a protective multiple earth system fitted. This is similar to the previous method inasmuch as the gas and water pipes must be earthed, but in addition to this the sink top which is made of either stainless steel or enamelled steel must also be earthed. Most modern sink tops are fitted with a short strip of steel which has a number of holes drilled in it to which the earth wire can be bolted. As the water stopcock is nearly always situated under the sink, bonding the sink top does not pose any considerable difficulty or inconvenience. If, however, the stopcock is fitted in, for example, a cloakroom, then a separate wire must be fed to the sink top. The old idea of bonding all the taps and wastes to the bath leg can be omitted as this no longer constitutes a requirement, since most modern properties are now fitted with plastic waste pipes.

The Electricity Board, instead of providing an earth tag on their armour cable, have produced a new type of main fuse. In old properties the live and neutral wires were fed into the main fuse which was of either 30 A or 60 A (nowadays a 100 A fuse is used) and then on to the meter, the live conductor having the fuse in the circuit and the neutral being fed straight through. Under this old system it meant that the voltage measured between the live and neutral was 240 V, but in some instances it was possible to produce a voltage between neutral and earth, although this was probably only something in the region of 3 or 4 V. In the interests of safety, the Electricity Board have now fitted a main fuse which has the facility for the live to be connected to the main fuse while the neutral and earth terminals are internally linked, which ultimately puts the neutral and earth at the same potential. This type of earthing is known as multiple protective earthing and most electricity authorities will provide a pamphlet dealing solely with this type of earthing.

It should be noted that when protective multiple earthing is used the instructions and recommendations given in the leaflets must be rigidly adhered to, and that the installations should be thoroughly checked by the Electricity Board before any attempt to connect the circuit to the supply is made.

3. Earth Leakage Trips

If the main input cable is fed into the house by overhead means, which is still common practice in some rural areas, then there is no provision for an earth, as an earth fitted from a pylon would not be suitable to take any stray current down to earth and ultimately to safety.

In the case of overhead power systems, the normal domestic wiring has its continual earth run uninterrupted round the circuit and is fed into the consumer unit in the normal manner. From the consumer unit there must be an earth wire connected to both the gas and water pipes and another earth wire must be fed to an earth leakage trip.

The earth leakage trip is an appliance which will trip out and render the circuit safe if an overload or current is present in the earth wire. These trips have four main terminals and into these the live and neutrals are fed from the Electricity Board's main fuse and then out of the earth leakage trip to the main consumer unit. There are also two terminals marked 'F' and 'E'; in the case of overhead wiring the 'E' terminal is used. An earth wire is run from the consumer unit to terminal 'E' and subsequently to a copper stake which must be hammered into the ground, a complete circuit then being formed via the earth leakage trip to earth. A small current flowing along the earth wire does suggest a fault in the circuit and therefore the trip will trip out, cutting the live and neutral to the consumer unit. Sometimes, however, a minor fault will occur in an appliance such as an electric kettle and the trip will trip out indicating a faulty circuit when, in fact, it is the appliance at fault. When an electric element becomes old the insulation in the element sometimes loses some of its insulation properties and a small current flow is then set up between neutral and earth resulting in the trip tripping out. If this is found to be the case then the only thing to do is to keep re-setting the trip until the appliance becomes so bad that it persistently trips the circuit. When this occurs then it will be necessary to replace the element.

Earth leakage trips have been known to trip out due to vibration, and people living at the side of a busy trunk road have found this to be a positive nuisance.

Earth leakage trips can also be used in houses where the cold water system has been installed in plastic pipes, thus allowing no facility for an earth wire to be connected on to it. If, however, the mains input cable is fed from overhead and the water pipe is plastic then both the 'E' and 'F' terminals of the earth trip need to be used. Two wires are fitted from the consumer unit, one to terminal 'E' and one to terminal 'F'. These two wires are fitted to two copper stakes which must be placed at least two metres apart thus providing two separate earth paths for any stray electrical current.

Should the reader be in any doubt as to what system is employed in the property in which he finds himself working, then the earthing regulations can be obtained from any regional office of the Electricity Board. However, these regulations have not been drawn up in order to make life difficult but have been produced with one fact in mind, and that is to provide a safe and efficient multiple path for any stray electrical current to pass directly to earth thus safeguarding anyone from becoming electrocuted. So remember, never flaunt the rules by trying to be clever and leaving out any of the requirements stipulated to effect a safe and reliable earth system.

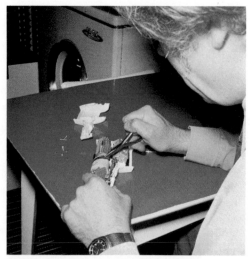

Fig. 20. Mending a hair dryer (p. 214)

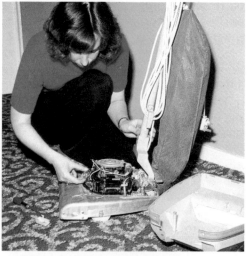

Fig. 22. The motor of a vacuum cleaner (p. 213)

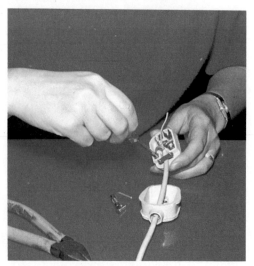

Fig. 21. Wiring a plug (p. 184)

Fig. 23. Fitting a new light switch (p. 186)

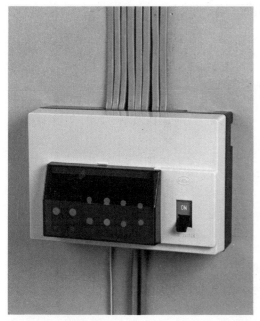

Fig. 24. A modern domestic fuse box mounted on the wall (pp. 173-175)

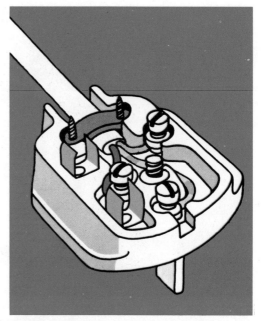

Fig. 25. This diagram shows the correct way to wire a plug (see p. 184)

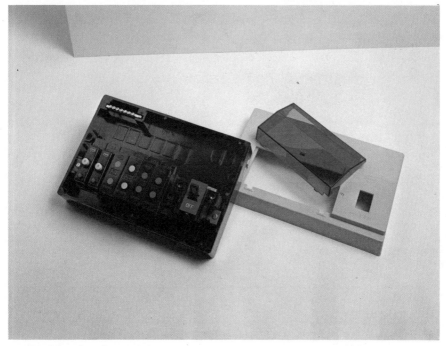

Fig. 26. A fuse box dismantled

Fig. 27. A pipe bending machine

Fig. 28. Plastic laminates make hygienic, easy to clean surfaces for toilets and bathrooms

Fig. 29. A pipe wrench

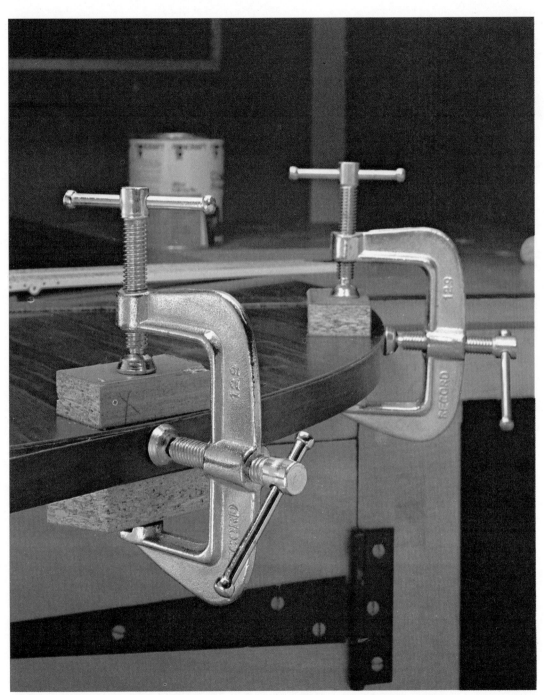

Fig. 30. Attaching a plastic laminate edging strip to a curved edge using special edging cramps

Fig. 31. Bathrooms need not be cheerless, functional places. This luxurious 'Sepia' suite teams up with unusual furnishings and accessories to produce a very striking effect

Fig. 32. The warm tones of natural wood give this bathroom a welcoming appearance

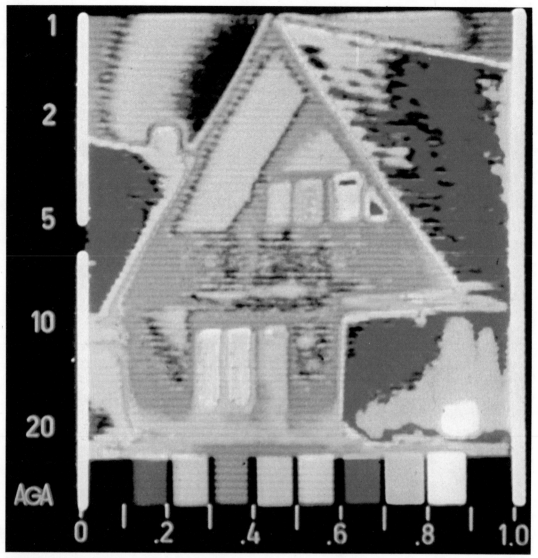

Fig. 33 This is a thermogram, or heat map. It shows the heat loss from different parts of the building. A special camera records the different temperatures and represents each half degree centigrade as a different colour. The lowest heat loss is shown as dark blue, increasing losses are light blue, dark green, light green, violet, magenta, red, orange and yellow, and white shows the area of greatest loss

DOUBLE GLAZING

Fig. 34. Replacement double windows

Fig. 35. A secondary window

Fig. 36. Patio doors

Fig. 37. 20% of the heat loss from an uninsulated house escapes through the roof. This picture shows glassfibre insulating material being installed in a loft (see p. 334)

Fig. 39. Cavity walls being injected with foam insulation (see p. 322) ▶

Fig. 38. An unlagged hot water tank can constitute the biggest single heat loss in a house (see p. 361) ▼

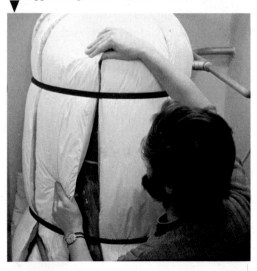

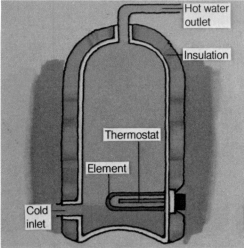

Fig. 40. Section through a lagged tank

Hot water outlet

Insulation

Thermostat

Element

Cold inlet

INVEST IN LIVING

Part IV

PLUMBING

by

Tom Pettit

Introduction

The installation of a complete bathroom suite, including all the necessary plumbing and the fitting of a fireback boiler in a house previously without a bathroom is within the author's experience. Many enterprising householders must have undertaken this project successfully just as many others have installed their own hot-water central heating systems. Although such achievements are not uncommon, they do necessitate considerable preplanning. Research is required to ensure the efficiency of the completed work; care taken to avoid breaching local authority requirements; knowledge of the structure of the building because it is inevitable that walls will have to be drilled and floors taken up; the craft skill and confidence necessary to carry this out, coupled with a considerable financial outlay.

However, these are rather ambitious projects and somewhat outside the brief of this book which is aimed at the householder who wishes to be self-sufficient regarding what can be considered as minor domestic plumbing, thereby avoiding the need to seek professional help for all but major tasks.

In the belief that basic knowledge is of fundamental importance, the opening chapters discuss the domestic water supply in general indicating how water is provided by the local water authority, the usual arrangement of the average domestic plumbing system and the few common tools necessary to cope with simple repairs and modifications to it. Up to the 1920s most domestic plumbing was carried out entirely in lead piping which was heavy, unsightly, vulnerable as lead is such a soft metal, and in some circumstances a health hazard. Copper, and more recently plastic pipes have almost entirely replaced lead, but have necessitated the development of new techniques with which to work them. These are included within the text, as are the techniques required for the maintenance of taps and waste pipes. The book also discusses the possibilities of replacing damaged or outdated components, and the installation of the modern shower unit.

Although drainage is normally considered to be the province of the builder, the author is of the opinion that as it is such an integral part of the water system of a house it is proper to include it within the book, and some basic details of care and maintenance are given.

As the conditions, and the degree of skill by which any suggested work is carried out, are beyond the control of the publishers or the author, results cannot be guaranteed. However, every effort has been made to ensure that information provided is correct and that within the space available procedures are sufficiently detailed.

If any modifications to the existing plumbing installation are being considered, either to the pipework, or by the addition of other fitments there could well be regulations which you must observe. To avoid infringement of your regional water authority requirements you are advised to make the necessary enquiries.

About the Author

Tom Pettit has also written the section on Maintenance and Outdoor Repairs (see p. 19).

1 The Supply of Domestic Water by Local Authorities

The oceans of the world contain nearly 90 per cent of all the water on earth, the remaining 10 per cent being in rivers, underground in the pores and fissures of rocks and as moisture in the atmosphere. All this makes up what is a fixed volume of water which circulates by natural climatic processes in the so-called hydrological cycle. Water evaporates from the oceans mainly due to the heat of the sun, the resulting water vapour forming clouds which are blown over the land. When conditions are suitable rainfall is precipitated from them, finally making its way back to the sea again in streams and rivers. This is surface water, or it may percolate through the underlying rock strata seeping back to the sea as underground water. Water vapour is also transpired into the atmosphere by plants and trees. Fortunately, since water is essential to our lives, the water authorities have the necessary technical knowledge to utilise this continuous natural cycle to meet our ever-increasing demands. It is estimated that a total of 22 million litres (approximately 5 million gallons) per day is required to meet the domestic, industrial and agricultural needs of a population area of 100,000 people. Approximately 20 per cent of the population lives in the area north and west of a line joining the Severn Estuary to the Wash, the remaining 80 per cent being in the south and east. Geologically the ground to the north and west is mountainous and consists of older and harder rocks than the flatter south and east. Rainfall is therefore higher in the north and west, approximately 1,800 mm (70 in) per year as opposed to 500mm (18 in) in the south east, because our prevailing winds are moisture ladened south-westerlies from the Atlantic Ocean which precipitate heavy rain over the high ground. *(Fig. 1.)*

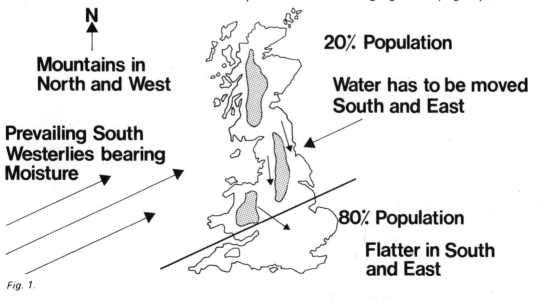

N

Mountains in North and West

Prevailing South Westerlies bearing Moisture

20% Population

Water has to be moved South and East

80% Population

Flatter in South and East

Fig. 1.

At present all water supplies depend upon rainfall, although fresh water can be distilled from sea water by a very expensive process. The deep valleys between the mountains of the west and north are suitable for storing the run-off rainfall by constructing dams across them to create reservoirs. In the flatter south east rivers are utilised and underground resources are tapped with boreholes. (Fig. 2.)

There is usually a vast natural store of underground water so that a regular supply can be pumped from wells and boreholes, whereas the run-off from streams and rivers can be variable—heavy in winter and light in summer. Because of this there is the need to build impounding reservoirs in which to store the water. An alternative surface supply may be from a river, the water being pumped to a nearby reservoir. Reservoirs at or near the source of water are generally for long-term storage, while service reservoirs are near to where the water is to be used and are short term.

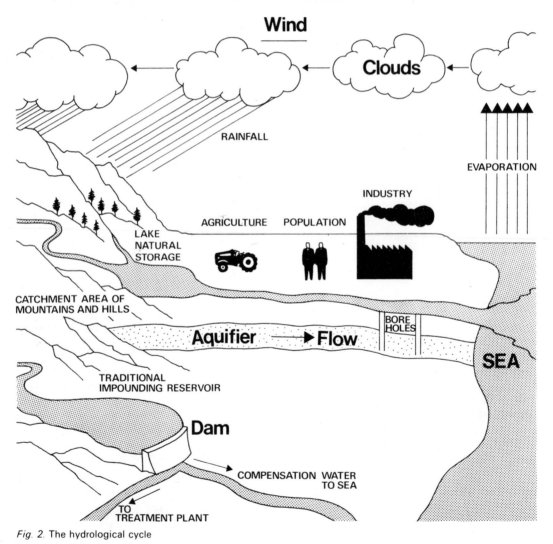

Fig. 2. The hydrological cycle

By Act of Parliament the consumer is entitled to a wholesome potable water which can be defined as being: clear, colourless, tasteless, and odourless, free from sediment, free from living creatures, free from bacteria, free from toxic substances and not corrosive to metals, especially lead. This means that the water must be suitably treated before it is supplied to the customer.

Large pipelines or aqueducts convey water from the works at its source. The water may be gravity fed from a high level to a lower one, or it may be pumped if there is not sufficient 'fall'. Depending upon the geological formation of the area which the water is to serve it is fed into service reservoirs at ground level, or into raised water towers, from where the water mains distribute it to the customer. *(Fig. 3.)*

The water is made potable at the water-treatment works by screening, straining, sedimentation, filtration and sterilisation. Floating matter and some suspended particles are removed by screens, very fine residues sometimes being removed by microstrainers. Both horizontal flow and vertical flow sedimentation tanks are used to settle out further suspended matter followed by filtration. This is sometimes assisted by chemically coagulating the suspended matter. Any remaining impurities and most of the bacteria are removed in sand filters operated by gravity or under pressure. The water is finally sterilised with chlorine to ensure that all bacteria have been killed.

So called 'hard waters', which on account of their mineral composition do not lather easily, may be 'softened' at the works by the addition of lime or soda. Alternatively, softening may be by 'ion exchange' either at the works or by a domestic water-softener. It is interesting to note that synthetic detergents are equally effective in hard or soft water, as these are not dependent on a lather for cleaning.

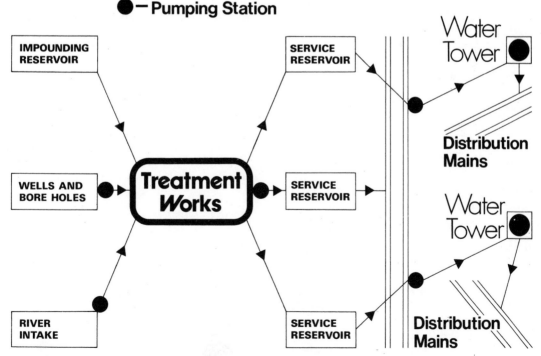

Fig. 3. Water sources, treatment and distribution

2 The Domestic Plumbing System

The average household uses about 450 litres (100 gallons) of water per day for personal drinking, washing and bathing, washing clothes, domestic utensils and the car. It is also used for washing floors and paintwork, the preparation of food, flushing toilets and at times watering the garden. Before any maintenance to the plumbing system is considered it is important to know how it works.

Your plumbing system begins at the point where the water leaves the water authority's stopcock. This is usually near to the boundary of the property, and near to the authority's water main in the road. Its purpose is to shut off the supply when repairs are to be carried out, and as a precaution against frost is usually about 760 mm below ground. A turn key (see Chapter 3) is generally required to turn it on account of its depth. Access to the stopcock is by a hinged lid on an iron surface box, the lid having a small recess on the edge opposite the hinges where a lever can be inserted with which to lift it. The supply to a number of houses may be controlled by one stopcock if the property is old and this should be checked or neighbours may be inconvenienced! Where the service pipe enters the house there should be a second stopcock (often under the sink), or in a block of flats one to each, so that the system can be isolated. If the water pressure in a particular area is low the service pipe may be 22 mm, but it is more usual to be 15 mm for domestic buildings where there is average water pressure. The stopcock works in just the same way as a tap (see Chapter 7) to control the flow, but is designed to be plumbed into a pipeline having either capillary or compression connections at each end. An arrow on the body shows the direction of flow and this must be observed. If fitted wrongly the water pressure will simply hold the washer down, cutting off the supply. Water authority regulations require that the jumper must be of the loose type so that if the mains supply fails the jumper and washer fall into place (see Chapter 7). This acts as a non-return valve preventing a backflow of water into the mains with the additional possibility of contamination.

The advantage of the second stopcock within the property is in being readily available in an emergency. Imagine the sort of problem you might have on a dark night with the only stopcock outside under several metres of snow and ice!

Once the supply passes the second stopcock it is known as the 'rising main' and then becomes part of a 'direct' or 'indirect' system. Whichever system it feeds, however, water authorities require that a supply point must be taken from it where water is required for cooking and drinking; this is generally in the kitchen so it is usual for the mains supply to enter the building just under the kitchen sink.

Direct System

Direct systems are more usual in older properties, all cold draw-off taps being fed directly from the rising main. (Fig. 1.) There are advantages and disadvantages to this system.

Advantages
- Potable water can be had from any cold tap.

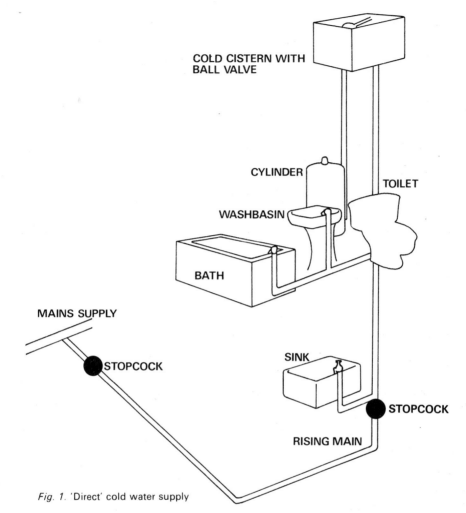

COLD CISTERN WITH
BALL VALVE

CYLINDER

TOILET

WASHBASIN

BATH

MAINS SUPPLY

STOPCOCK

SINK

STOPCOCK

RISING MAIN

Fig. 1. 'Direct' cold water supply

- The cold cistern to supply the hot-water cylinder is at a lower level, usually in the airing cupboard, and so is not subjected to freezing.
- Being in the airing cupboard dirt is less likely to fall into it.

Disadvantages

- All taps and ball valves are at mains pressure which is quite high and are therefore subjected to more wear.
- High pressure ball valves on cisterns and toilets are more noisy, although many have silencer tubes fitted (see Chapter 7).

- There is more chance of noise in the pipes due to 'water hammer'. This is often due to the ball valve bouncing before it finally cuts off, because of the greater pressure. The noise can be transmitted throughout the system.

- Because it is possible to draw off cold water directly in this way from several points at once it leads to greater demands being made upon the mains supply.

- Increased danger from 'back siphon-age' if mains pressure falls.

Indirect System

It is more usual in modern properties to employ the indirect system (*Fig. 2.*) where there are no direct cold draw-off points other than the one in the kitchen. The rising main then feeds a large capacity storage cistern in the underdrawing or roof space, a suitable size being 320 to 360 litres (70 to 79 gallons) approximately. This cistern then supplies cold water to all other parts of the system. It is placed as high as can be to give as big a head of pressure as possible at each draw-off point as they are now only gravity fed.

Because of this, indirect supplies to the bath at least require to be run in a 22 mm pipe to obtain an adequate flow, although 15 mm to washbasins is usually satisfactory.

Advantages
- A quieter system as the supply cistern is in the roof space and other cisterns and cold taps are fed from it at a lower pressure.
- The large cistern provides a reserve store of water for other than drinking purposes should the mains supply fail.
- The lower pressures under which the system operates produce less wear and tear on the pipes and fittings.

Disadvantages
- There is only one point in the building where really potable water is available – the kitchen.
- The supply cistern, sited as it is in the roof space, may collect dirt if it is open at the top.
- It is also exposed to possible frost damage particularly in view of ceilings being insulated. The cistern must therefore be adequately lagged (see Chapter 14.).

With either system it is usual for 'instantaneous water heaters' – geysers – to be supplied from the rising main since the hot water they supply may be used

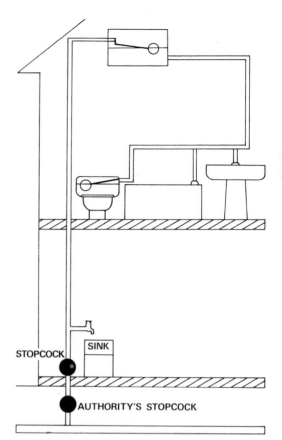

Fig. 2. 'Indirect' cold water supply

in the preparation of food and drinks, and for washing up, among other things.

Larger amounts of hot water may be produced from a number of different energy sources – the electrically powered immersion heater, the traditional fireback boiler, or a variety of solid fuel, gas or oil-fired independent boilers. Very often these also provide hot water for central heating, a pump being placed in the circuit to ensure rapid and even circulation. Domestic hot water from each system is gravity fed and therefore at a comparatively low pressure so 22 mm pipe is used to ensure an adequate flow to baths where large quantities of hot water are required quickly.

Again, there are two systems, the 'direct'

and 'indirect'. In each case the hot water is collected in a copper storage cylinder below the cold-water cistern in an airing cupboard. Cold water is fed from the cistern to the bottom of the cylinder through a 22 mm pipe which in the direct system feeds the boiler. Hot water from the boiler then rises and collects in the top of the storage cylinder. This can be drawn off at the hot taps, sufficient 'head of water' being provided by the cold-water cistern through the cold feed pipe and the pressure of the expanded hot water. As this hot water is drawn off it is replaced by the cold water flowing in at the bottom, and by circulation between the cylinder and boiler, further hot water collects at the 'crown' of the cylinder. *(Fig. 3.)* This system provides domestic hot water only.

In districts where the water is hard (see Chapter 1) and may lead to scale or 'fur' being deposited in the boiler and pipes, an 'indirect' cylinder should be used. This separates the 'primary' water, i.e. the water circulating through the boiler, from the 'secondary' which is drawn off for domestic use. The primary water heats the secondary by transmitting heat through the walls of the inner cylinder, copper being a good conductor of heat. In this way the primary water circulates continuously and as it is not drawn off there is only a small initial deposit of scale with little further increase. A small cold-water feed cistern is necessary to maintain the supply of water in the primary, making

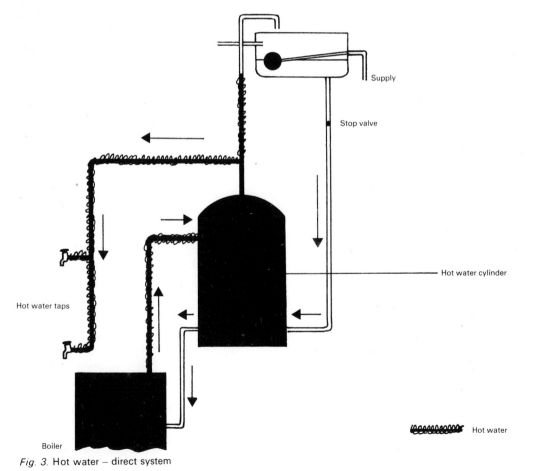

Supply

Stop valve

Hot water cylinder

Hot water taps

Hot water

Boiler

Fig. 3. Hot water – direct system

good any loss because of evaporation, or from steam caused by boiling. Direct and indirect systems require expansion pipes from the top of the cylinder reaching over the edge of the cold-water cistern(s). Any surge of expanding hot water is then contained. The end of the expansion pipe must not touch the surface of the cold water or water may circulate between the cistern and cylinder.

Radiators for central heating can also be on this scale-free circuit, the water not being able to contaminate the domestic supply. A cylinder with a calorifier, i.e. a coiled copper tube, which replaces the indirect cylinder may be used as an alternative. *(Fig. 4.)*

Heat from the hot water passes to the metal radiator, and by radiation and convection heats the air which circulates in the room. Recommended temperatures are 16°C (60°F) for bedrooms and 21°C (70°F) for other rooms. Adequate radiators must also be positioned in halls and staircases to prevent a heat loss from the rooms.

Radiators may be of cast iron or pressed steel, the amount of heat they radiate depending on their surface area and the temperature of the water. At one time, particularly in public buildings, radiators were always matt black, it being generally acknowledged as the best radiating surface, this is now ignored in favour of modern colour schemes. Radiators are so designed to have the maximum surface area, either in the form of elliptical pipes or ribbed panels.

Heated towel rails are usually plumbed into the domestic hot-water system rather than into the central heating system since they are required to be in continuous use.

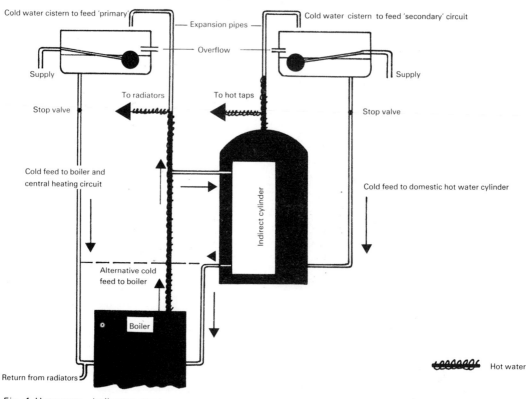

Cold water cistern to feed 'primary'

Expansion pipes

Overflow

Cold water cistern to feed 'secondary' circuit

Supply

Supply

To radiators

To hot taps

Stop valve

Stop valve

Cold feed to boiler and central heating circuit

Indirect cylinder

Cold feed to domestic hot water cylinder

Alternative cold feed to boiler

Boiler

Hot water

Return from radiators

Fig. 4. Hot water – indirect system

3 Plumbing Tools and Sundries

Several of the tools used for plumbing are of the general purpose variety, being necessary items of equipment for other aspects of home maintenance. Naturally there are many others designed specifically for plumbing to ensure the efficient manipulation of pipework and the installation of fittings. The skilled plumber, as any other skilled craftsman, knows the tools of his trade and is thoroughly conversant with their use, knowing that without them the work cannot be carried out effectively. This more than holds good for the enthusiastic amateur, as it would be folly to embark upon even the simplest of plumbing projects without adequate tools. He or she should study the proposed work carefully, making sure that the requisite tools are available and if necessary practise with them on surplus materials beforehand. Most modern domestic plumbing installations are run in copper pipe, or a combination of copper and plastic. Plastic is suitable for waste-water pipes, and may also be used for the cold-water supply (see Chapter 4). It is sound advice to trace the pipework in your home, so that being familiar with it you have the tools available to deal with any emergency which may occur. Probably the most elementary of plumbing repairs is the renewing of a tap washer for which only the minimum of basic tools are required, but with experience more ambitious repairs and modifications may be undertaken for which specialist tools will be necessary.

With this probability in mind the following list is suggested. They will allow simple work to be carried out with ease, and also be the foundation of a tool kit by which the majority of domestic plumbing work can be accomplished.

1. Screwdrivers – general purpose for slotted screws x 100, 150 and 250 mm.
2. Posidriv screwdrivers – many modern fittings employ screws with heads of this type. No. 2 fits screw gauges 5 to 10 and is suitable for most household tasks. Both types being generally shockproof will withstand considerable rough use and have plastic handles which are impervious to water.
3. Pliers – combination type x 175 mm – those with insulated handles are much more comfortable to grip, but care must be taken to avoid melting the plastic cover if working with a blow torch. Will cut wire and grip small tubes, thin sheet metal and small nuts.
4. Pliers – gas – the jaws are designed to grip and turn pipes, and other cylindrical work, but the teeth are coarse and will cause marking if undue force is used. One handle has a screwdriver end which can be used as a screwdriver or a lever; the end of the other handle is conical and can be used for flaring the ends of small-bore pipes.
5. Pliers – universal gland nut – slim and adjustable to several positions. The jaws are serrated, the teeth so formed for gripping cylindrical shapes firmly. As with all pliers there is the danger of marking the work, so if this is a matter of some concern, e.g., chromium plated or stainless steel fittings, they must be protected by a cloth or heavy self-adhesive tape.

There are many adjustable wrenches, and the following are some of the different types used in plumbing:

6. Wrench — mole (from the original advert, 'your third hand') — the advantage is that they may be clamped onto the work and will stay in position until released, leaving both hands free to do other work. The capacity of the jaws is adjusted by the knurled screw at the end of the handle and the tool can then be locked in position by pulling the handles together.

7. Wrench — adjustable open-ended (often referred to as an adjustable spanner) — these are used on hexagonal or square nuts, and the mechanisms of taps and valves. Their size is measured by length, for general purposes 310 mm is adequate, 205 mm for smaller work. The larger size has a bigger capacity. Note how the wrench is fitted to the nut so that the applied force is towards the moving jaw. The nut should be as far into the jaws as possible which in turn should be adjusted to fit firmly round it. Used in this way the jaw will not open accidentally, resulting in the wrench slipping off with possible damage to the work and hands.

8. Wrench — monkey — used for the same kind of work as the adjustable open-ended wrench, but as it is somewhat thicker is not quite so convenient if space is limited. Care should be taken how the wrench is fitted to the work and in which direction the force is applied — see *Fig. 8*. Similar sizes as for the open-ended wrench are suitable.

9. Wrench — 'Footprint' — adjustable pipe — basically for pipework only, the turning force applied locks the wrench firmly to the work.

10. Wrench — 'Stillson' — pipe — used for heavier work on iron pipes on which the hardened steel jaws bite and grip. The movable jaw is pivoted so that as leverage is applied to the back of the handle the wrench grips the pipe. Often two wrenches are required on a job, one to hold the pipe and one to turn the fitting. As they work only in one direction, they must be placed in opposing positions. They are most efficient if the jaws are so adjusted that they bite on the work at their centre point. These are tools which are much too heavy for work on brass nuts or light tubing, particularly if it is polished or with a chromium-plated finish. The teeth would certainly leave marks and there would be the danger of collapsing the tube.

11. Wrench — strap — for coping with the light work (referred to above) — light tubes in copper, brass or plastic, or soft lead pipes can be handled without damage to them. The strap is looped round the pipe in the opposite way to the direction of rotation, the end slipped through the slot below the handle and drawn tight. Pulling the handle further tightens the strap so the pipe is gripped and turned. The strap wrench is also ideal for removing the 'easyclean' cover from taps if they prove to be very tight (see Chapter 7.) The chain wrench operates in a similar way, being for really heavy use on large-diameter iron drain or steam pipes.

12. Wrench — basin — specially designed to fit the backnut below washbasin taps where because of curvature of the basin and its proximity to the wall there is very limited space.

Other essential tools are as follows:

13. Plumber's vice — special vices are available, designed specifically to grip pipes. This has a very limited application however, and the new multipurpose 'Lockjaw' vice is so designed that it will meet all the forseeable needs related to domestic plumbing, and many more besides. Irregular work can be held firmly

without damage in self-adjusting jaws. These are interchangeable with optional rubber-faced jaws which will grip polished work without scratching or deforming it.

14. Steel tape — flexible steel tape of at least 2 m length is necessary even if only the most modest work is proposed. It is invaluable for checking the position of fittings and measuring pipe lengths. The tape should be fitted with a 'true zero hook' so that accurate 'hook over' or 'end on' measurements are possible.

15. Hacksaw — junior — ideal for light work and cutting small-bore pipes, as it can be used in one hand leaving the other free.

16. Hacksaw — 250 mm length — for heavier work. Fine-toothed blades should be used for sawing pipework to ensure smooth cutting. By the use of a simple jig, pipes may be cut squarely to length (see Chapter 5).

17. Saw — general purpose — the hardened teeth make the saw suitable for cutting wood, metal or plastic. Ideal for rough sawing in wood where nails or plaster work may be present.

18 Pipe cutter — an alternative to the hacksaw. Clamps onto the pipe which it cuts accurately as the pressure is increased. The pipe cutter illustrated can be fitted with a reamer attachment for removing burrs from the bore of the pipe.

19. Bending springs — these are used to maintain the round section of copper tube and are about 600 mm long. Internal and external types are available, the former being most common, and are tapered with a loop at the end to which a wire can be attached for easy withdrawal. With the spring in place, the tube can be bent over the knee.

20. Files — assorted — the 150 and 250 mm sizes as illustrated will be adequate for most work. The woodwork rasp is useful for the quick roughing down of wood at corners round which pipes are to be run.

21. Hammer — general purpose — the engineer's ball-pein hammer will be found satisfactory. The flat pein can be used for heavy work, the ball for lighter use and for tapping up bursts in pipes — particularly lead — before repairs are made. The head is forged and hardened by heat treatment, the shaft made of ash or hickory which is weatherproofed by the manufacturers. 455g is ideal for general use, but for heavier work on brick or stone use 905g.

22. Chisels — Plumber's wood — these are specially designed and as they are made entirely of metal can be used with the hammer, a mallet being unnecessary. Recommended sizes are from 12–32 mm.

23. Chisels — cold — a wide range of widths and lengths are available, 150 x 13, 230 x 19, and 255 x 25 mm are recommended. The one illustrated is of hexagonal section steel and can be file-sharpened.

24. Rawldrill — toolholder — for use with the hammer — a number of 'Rawldrills' are made to fit. They will be required when walls have to be plugged to carry fitments, pipe clips, etc.

25. Rawlplugs — plastic ones are recommended as they are impervious to water and decay; the plug must be set below the level of the plaster so that its full length is in the brickwork.

26. Brace — 150 mm sweep. The small radius sweep is advisable because holes for pipes have often to be drilled in areas where space is limited. It should also be a ratchet brace for the same reason.

27. 'Jennings' type auger bits — sizes 13, 19 and 25 mm. These bits will drill accurate holes through timber in any direction.

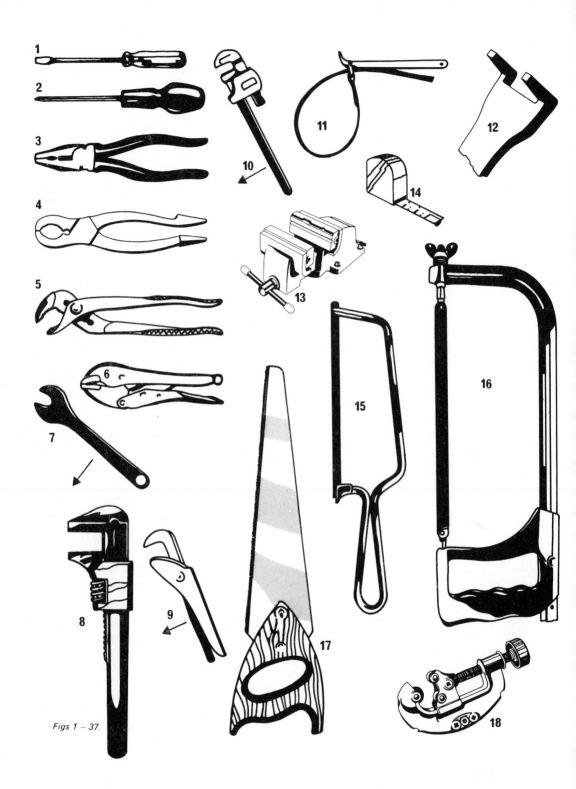

1

2

3

4

5

6

7

8

9

10

11

12

13

14

15

16

17

18

Figs 1 – 37.

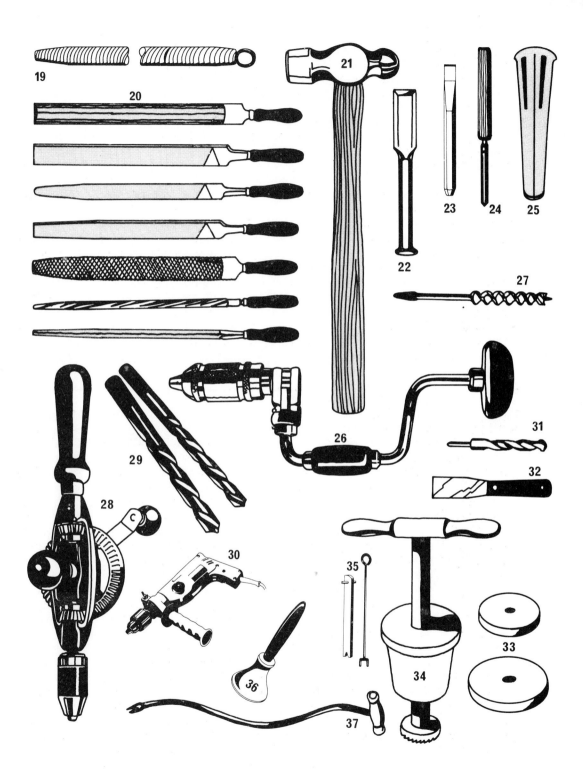

19

20

21

22

23

24

25

26

27

28

29

30

31

32

33

34

35

36

37

28. Hand drill — capacity 8 mm for use with metalworking twist drills, and possibly masonry drills. Light drilling in metal and wood, heavier work in brick for rawlplugs.

29. Metalworking twist drills — for general purpose use in wood or metal — diameters 3, 5, 6 and 8 mm.

30. Rotary percussion drill — heavy duty work in concrete, brick and stone. The hammer action makes the drilling of holes in these materials very much easier. The drill illustrated is two-speed with maximum capacity of 13 mm in concrete, 19 mm in masonry, 13 mm in steel or 38 mm with hole saw, and 22 mm in hardwood. It can also be used as a plain drill by disengaging the percussive action.

31. Masonry and percussive drill bits — these have tungsten steel tips for cutting into walls and floors of concrete, etc. Once the cutting action has been established the hole should be completed as quickly as possible to prevent overheating of the bit. It should be withdrawn from time to time to clear waste from the hole.

32. Putty knife — this is useful for applying putty, e.g. to bed a washbasin, and dressing off the surplus. A stout pocket knife with a strong pointed blade is also useful for cutting tape or string and, at times, removing washers.

33. Washers — for draw-off taps and stopcocks; modern hard rubber composition washers are best. Use 19 mm diameter for 15 mm sink and basin taps, and 25 mm diameter for 19 mm bath taps; 10 mm or 13 mm diameter washers are necessary for ball valves depending upon their size and type.

34. Tap reseating tool. The washer seat in the body of the tap should be smooth and free from any defects; this can be checked by visual inspection or by running a finger round its edge. If faulty it can be corrected with a seat-dressing tool of which there are several types all working in much the same way. The tool fits into the body of the tap and the T-handle on the stem is rotated, turning the fluted cutter which trues up the seat.

35. Stop tap turn key — these may be of metal or wood, and are essential for turning off the water at the authority's stop tap should this be necessary. The taps are placed approximately 760 mm below ground as a precaution against frost.

36. Force cup — for clearing lavatory pans when obstructed. The tool is held vertically in the bottom of the pan and the handle worked vigorously up and down.

37. Drain auger or snake — a flexible tool, made of spring steel or coiled wire with a small metal handle. Used for removing particularly difficult objects from waste or drainage pipes.

Miscellaneous Items

Modern blowlamps — operated from small butane gas cartridges or larger cylinders are widely available (Fig. 38.). Neat and powerful they have largely replaced those which burn petrol or paraffin. They are easy to ignite, some being fitted with piezo electric automatic lighting for fine flame and plumber's work; they can be conveniently turned on or off during jobs to save gas. Accessory kits are usually available with these lamps making them easily adaptable to other kinds of work, such as paint stripping and hard soldering. The Camping Gaz Cercotub concentrates the heat, the insulating element protecting the immediate surroundings from the direct heat of the flame.

Glasspaper — medium grade $1\frac{1}{2}$ and fine grade 0 — for cleaning copper and brass prior to making a soldered joint. Used in preference to emery cloth, which may be oily, or steel wool — particles of which may find their way into the joint and by rusting ultimately degrade the solder.

Flux — a non-corrosive paste is recommended for copper and brass work, whereas tallow is required for wiping joints in lead (see Chapter 6).

Soft solder — for use on copper and brass, Tinman's solder 50 per cent tin, 50 per cent lead. For use on lead pipe, Plumber's solder 30 per cent tin, 70 per cent lead.

Graphite impregnated string — for repair of glands; as an alternative use soft white string and tallow.

Plumbers hemp or PTFE (polytetrafluoroethylene) — this is tape for winding round the thread of screwed unions before they are tightened up, thus making them completely watertight.

Jointing compound — such as Boss White — used in conjunction with plumber's hemp and also occasionally on the olives of compression joints (see Chapter 6). The reader is also referred to the tool list provided in *Home Maintenance and Outdoor Repairs* in this series. Many of these tools will be found useful by the home plumber particularly where brickwork has to be made good.

Fig. 38.

4 Pipes for Plumbing

Some metal pipes and fittings may be corroded by the supplied water which is then termed 'aggressive', but other waters may deposit a protective coating preventing corrosion. Local bye-laws will prohibit the use of pipes and fittings made from materials known to be unsuitable for that particular area. With this in mind, piping may be of lead, galvanised steel, stainless steel, copper or plastic. If it is known that the water is 'plumbosolvent', i.e. of a type which can take lead into solution, then lead pipe would be prohibited for health reasons. Similarly, galvanised steel pipe would be prohibited where the water causes severe corrosion. If any brass pipe fittings are to be used enquiries should be made as to their suitability, as some waters cause heavy corrosion of brass called 'dezincification' (brass is an alloy of zinc and copper). Polythene pipe is not suitable for hot-water supply lines because it becomes soft with constant heat, resulting in leaking joints and sagging pipes.

Modern pipework is however almost invariably of copper or plastic. Both are used for interior and exterior plumbing: copper is used almost exclusively for domestic central heating, whereas plastic piping is only suitable for cold-water supply, waste-water and soil pipe systems.

Copper tube should be made from non-arsenical copper to BS 1172 (C106) and manufactured to the standards required by BS 2871. It is available as 'drawn tube' in Half Hard Temper Table X ($\frac{1}{2}$ H) or Hard

Old imperial bore size	Metric outside diameter	Wall thickness			Lengths in m	Recommended bending spring size	
		$\frac{1}{2}$H Table X	O Table Y	H Table Z		$\frac{1}{2}$H	O
	6 mm	0·6	0·8	—	6		
	8 mm	0·6	0·8	—	6		
$\frac{3}{8}$ in	12 mm	0·6	0·8	—	3 6	10·62	10·18
$\frac{1}{2}$ in	15 mm	0·7	1·0	0·5	3 6	13·40	12·74
$\frac{3}{4}$ in	22 mm	0·9	1·2	0·6	3 6	19·97	19·37
1 in	28 mm	0·9	1·2	0·6	3 6		
$1\frac{1}{4}$ in	35 mm	1·2	1·5	0·7	6		
$1\frac{1}{2}$ in	42 mm	1·2	1·5	0·8	6		
2 in	54 mm	1·2	2·0	0·9	6		
	67 mm	1·2	2·0	1·0	6		
	76·1 mm	1·5	2·0	1·2	6		
	108 mm	1·5	2·5	1·2	6		
	133 mm	1·5	—	—	6		
	159 mm	2·0	—	—	6		

Table Z (H) as indicated. Tube from 6 mm to 54 mm is also made in 20 m coils and is fully annealed – Table Y (O). All are suitable for hot and cold-water services, gas and sanitation installations, grade O being particularly recommended for underground supplies and radiant heat systems.

Soft copper tube for 'minibore' central heating systems is also manufactured.

Outside diameter	Wall thickness	Coil lengths
6 mm	0·6 mm	10, 25, 50 m
8 mm	0·6 mm	10, 25, 50 m
10 mm	0·7 mm	10, 25 m
12 mm	0·8 mm	10, 25 m

You will observe that the soft annealed pipe O has thicker walls than the others. H is light gauge, gaining strength from its hardness. Being hard it is non-manipulative and is intended for use in straight runs only. All three grades may be jointed with capillary fittings, care being particularly necessary with soft temper tube where it is essential to re-round the ends with a former after cutting and before jointing. Similarly, all grades may be jointed with compression fittings (see Chapter 5), but it is necessary to use type A (non-manipulative) on H, and type B (manipulative) on O. Grades $\frac{1}{2}$H and O in diameters up to 12 mm may be hand-formed as indicated in *Fig. 1;* taking care not to collapse the tube. Tubes being bent on the knee or former without internal support should be eased round gradually and uniformly to the following recommended minimum centre line radii.

Tube	Radius
15 mm	130–180mm
22 mm	250–300 mm
28 mm	300–350 mm

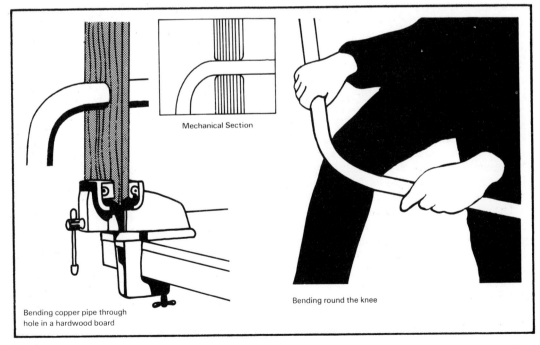

Mechanical Section

Bending copper pipe through hole in a hardwood board

Bending round the knee

Fig. 1.

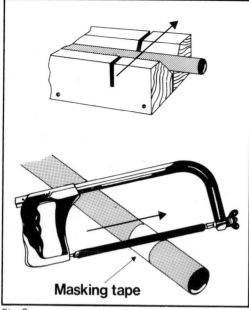

Masking tape

Fig. 2.

The 15, 22 and 28 mm tube should always be supported internally by an appropriate spring when bending. For larger sizes of tube it is necessary to use a bending machine; this can be hired. The tube is held in a groove as it is being bent, so preventing flattening. *Fig. 2.* shows alternative ways by which tubes may be sawn square if a pipe cutter is not available. Any burrs so formed should always be removed with a fine file.

Copper tube, in $\frac{1}{2}$H and O grades, sheathed in seamless polythene and suitable for gas or water service pipes in most corrosive/aggressive situations is available. The colour code for gas is yellow ochre, and green for potable water.

The introduction of plastic piping for plumbing has in many cases made the job for the amateur much simpler, as the materials are lighter and generally more durable. Those in common use are as follows:

Polythene – low density

Very flexible and strong – long pipe runs above or below ground. Does not rot or corrode and is resistant to acids and alkalis. Resists freezing and has good insulating properties. If the water it carries does freeze, because of its elasticity the pipe will expand and then recover as the ice melts. Diameters above 50 mm must not be used below ground as they would be crushed.

The following maximum pressure ratings are based on water at 20°C (68°F):

Low density polythene pipes to BS 1972/67

Class B/Red Mark 6·1 kgf/cm^2 (0·60 MN/m^2: 200 ft.hd: 86·6 lbf/in^2).

Class C/Blue Mark 9·14 kgf/cm^2 (0·90 MN/m^2; 300 ft.hd:130 lbf/in^2).

Class D/Green Mark 12·2 kgf/cm^2 (1·20 MN/m^2: 400 ft.hd: 173·3 lbf/in^2).

High density pipe has greater tensile strength and being more rigid is more suited to withstand higher pressures in large bore pipes, Class C and D.

1 lbf = 4·448 22N

Polyvinyl chloride – PVC

The unplasticised form is generally used for soil and drainpipes. Also domestic cold-water supply systems.

Acrylonitrile butadiene styrene (Abs) and polypropylene

This is used for hot-water waste systems because of its relatively high softening point.

Polythene piping is available in coils up to 150 m in length, pipes for waste-water and overflow systems are usually in lengths of 3 m in the following diameters:

	Mean outside diameter	Nominal inside diameter
Push-fit waste system	34·6 mm	32 mm
	41·0 mm	38 mm
	54·0 mm	50 mm
Solvent-weld waste system	36·3 mm	32 mm
	43·00 mm	38 mm
	56·00 mm	50 mm
Push-fit overflow system	21·5 mm	19 mm

Recommended bores for plastic pipes are: washbasin 32 mm, bath and sink 38 mm and WC 75 mm or 102 mm.

Bends can be made in plastic pipes as follows:

Polythene – low density

Cold bending – mean radius not less than eight times external diameter. Hold with pipe clips at each end of the bend or it will straighten.

Hot bending – insert bending spring, heat in boiling water or fan gently with blowlamp.

Caution – overheating will melt the pipe.

Polythene – high density

As above – mean radius for cold bend ten times external diameter. Hot – with blowlamp, six times external diameter.

In each case allow hot bends to cool before removing spring.

Polyvinyl chloride (PVC) and acrylonitrile butadiene styrene (Abs)

Heat with blowlamp, avoiding the end of the pipe to prevent distortions. With care this can be done without use of bending spring.

If a bend is needed near the end of a pipe, form it well back from the end of a long length and saw off the surplus. Connectors and fittings with solvent welded cold-water supply lines are similar to those for use with the solvent weld waste system. Use a fine-toothed hacksaw for cutting all plastic pipes, and glasspaper, file or even pocket knife for removing burrs.

For any work being undertaken in galvanised piping a pair of Stillson wrenches will be required and possibly dies with which to thread the ends of the pipe, which in turn requires a pipe vice. Common steel pipe sizes are shown in the table below.

Pipe bore	Length of thread screwed into fitting at each end
12 mm	12 mm
18 mm	12 mm
25 mm	15 mm
32 mm	15 mm
38 mm	15 mm
50 mm	18 mm

Measuring pipe lengths for cutting must be done accurately and a steel tape is most convenient as it can be used to measure bends. Where these are in the run of the pipe add 50 mm to allow for any loss in the overall length because of the bend being formed. Whatever type of pipe is being used, try to set out the position of connectors or fittings, measure between their end faces and then add the amount to be entered into the fitting at each end; in the case of copper or solvent welded plastic, this is usually the same as the pipe diameter. With push-fit plastic the pipe must be cut a little shorter according to the manufacturer's instructions to allow for expansion (see Chapters 5, 6 and 10).

5 Pipe Fittings and Sundries

In order to fulfil its function a pipe may have to follow a very devious route, making many turns and changes of direction. An array of fittings is available to make this possible. The range is much too numerous to illustrate or describe fully within the limits of this book but all have one thing in common – they are ordered by the size and type of pipe which they will accommodate, e.g. for copper a 15 mm tee will join two 15 mm pipes to a third at 90 degrees; 22 mm elbows, 90 degrees, or obtuse at 45 degrees, will take a 22 mm pipe at each end, whereas a reducing coupling 22 mm x 15 mm will accept a 22 mm pipe at one end and a 15 mm pipe at the other. A limited selection of capillary fittings is illustrated in *Fig. 1.*

An equally extensive range of compression fittings is available for use with either $\frac{1}{2}$H or H grade copper (non-manipulative fittings) (see Chapter 6) or $\frac{1}{2}$H and 0 grade (manipulative fittings).

Manipulative fittings require the ends of tubes to be flared out and it is common practice to use non-manipulative fittings with adaptors as in *Fig. 2.* Capillary and compression fittings are made to adapt from 'imperial' copper tube to metric sizes (see *Fig. 1.* and Chapter 4).

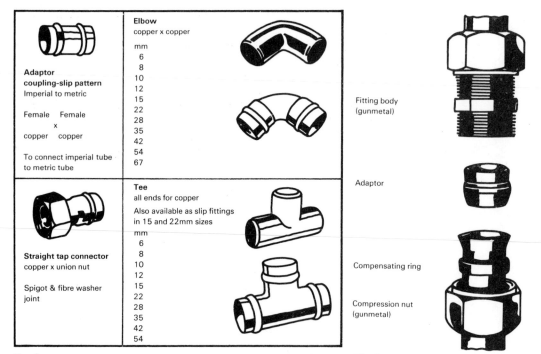

Adaptor
coupling-slip pattern
Imperial to metric

Female   Female
x
copper   copper

To connect imperial tube to metric tube

Elbow
copper x copper

mm
6
8
10
12
15
22
28
35
42
54
67

Straight tap connector
copper x union nut

Spigot & fibre washer joint

Tee
all ends for copper

Also available as slip fittings in 15 and 22mm sizes

mm
6
8
10
12
15
22
28
35
42
54

Fig. 1.

Fitting body
(gunmetal)

Adaptor

Compensating ring

Compression nut
(gunmetal)

Fig. 2.

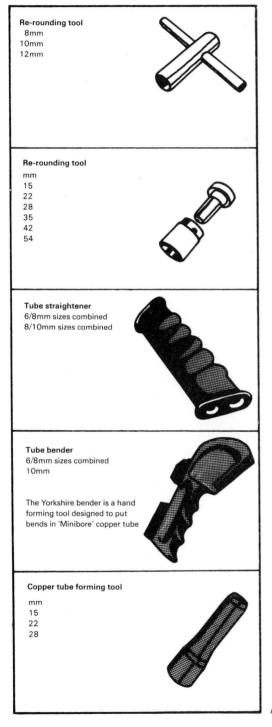

Re-rounding tool
8mm
10mm
12mm

Re-rounding tool
mm
15
22
28
35
42
54

Tube straightener
6/8mm sizes combined
8/10mm sizes combined

Tube bender
6/8mm sizes combined
10mm

The Yorkshire bender is a hand
forming tool designed to put
bends in 'Minibore' copper tube

Copper tube forming tool
mm
15
22
28

Fig. 3.

The tools used for flaring are simply punches bevelled at the appropriate angle. Soft copper tube is easily deformed by cutting, but is also equally easily reshaped with a simple re-rounding tool.

Small-bore tube supplied in coils is straightened with a tube straightener. A little lubricating oil is applied and the tool pulled along the tube. An equally simple tool is also used for bending. *(Fig. 3.)*

Both capillary and compression fittings are available threaded male or female to adapt from copper to BSP. These are British Standard Pipe Threads of the type used on plumbing fitments, and galvanised pipework. The threads are often referred to as 'iron' — MI indicating male thread and FI female; *Fig. 4.* illustrates two examples.

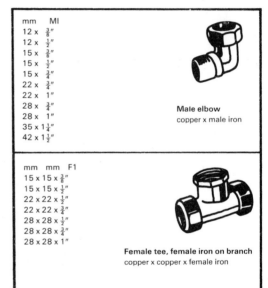

mm   MI
12 x $\frac{3}{8}''$
12 x $\frac{1}{2}''$
15 x $\frac{3}{8}''$
15 x $\frac{1}{2}''$
15 x $\frac{3}{4}''$
22 x $\frac{3}{4}''$
22 x $1''$
28 x $\frac{3}{4}''$
28 x $1''$
35 x $1\frac{1}{4}''$
42 x $1\frac{1}{2}''$

Male elbow
copper x male iron

mm   mm   F1
15 x 15 x $\frac{3}{8}''$
15 x 15 x $\frac{1}{2}''$
22 x 22 x $\frac{1}{2}''$
22 x 22 x $\frac{3}{4}''$
28 x 28 x $\frac{1}{2}''$
28 x 28 x $\frac{3}{4}''$
28 x 28 x $1''$

Female tee, female iron on branch
copper x copper x female iron

Fig. 4.

'Nevastops' are small in-line isolating valves designed for inlet supplies to appliances. They make it possible to service the appliance without turning off the supply elsewhere and being small are not unsightly. They can also be used to restrict the flow rate of water to taps if this is found to be excessive. Four types are available from Deltaflow, as shown in *Fig. 5.*

A similar range of compression fittings to those used for copper is also available for polythene piping. Suitable 'liners', which are colour coded according to the density and working pressure of the piping, must be used (see Chapters 4 and 6); they are class B-red, C-blue and D-green.

As stated earlier galvanised pipework is jointed by fittings threaded BSP *(Fig. 6.).* Traditionally these joints were painted and wound with plumber's hemp before being made, but threaded joints in general are now made quite watertight by the use of PTFE plastic tape.

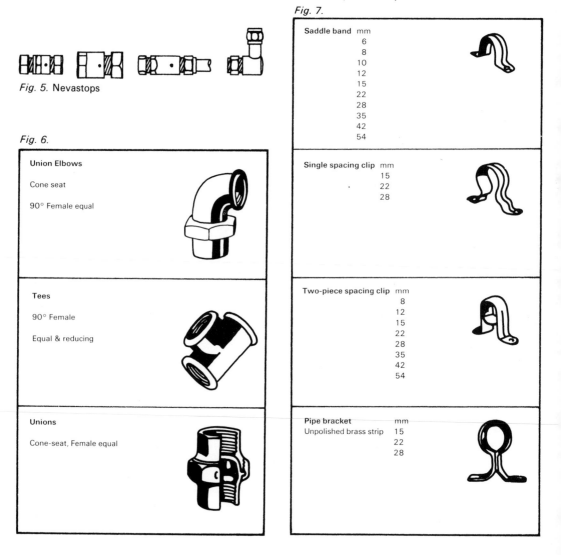

Fig. 5. Nevastops

Fig. 6.

Union Elbows
Cone seat
90° Female equal

Tees
90° Female
Equal & reducing

Unions
Cone-seat, Female equal

Fig. 7.

Saddle band	mm
	6
	8
	10
	12
	15
	22
	28
	35
	42
	54

Single spacing clip	mm
	15
	22
	28

Two-piece spacing clip	mm
	8
	12
	15
	22
	28
	35
	42
	54

Pipe bracket	mm
Unpolished brass strip	15
	22
	28

Fig. 7. indicates a few of the many clips used for supporting runs of pipe, and Fig. 8. shows recommended solder and flux.

Solder wire

In tins
Small
(75 grammes)
Medium
(500 grammes)
Large
(3.36 kilogrammes)

Fig. 8.

'Yorkshire' flux
Made specially for 'Yorkshire' fittings

BRITISH STANDARD PIPE THREADS
Dimensions in inches

Nominal bore of tube		App. outside dia. of tube		Outside dia. of thread	Depth of thread	Core diameter	No. of threads per inch
$\frac{1}{8}$		$\frac{13}{32}$		·383	·0230	·337	28
	$\frac{1}{4}$		$\frac{17}{32}$	·518	·0335	·451	19
$\frac{3}{8}$		$\frac{11}{16}$		·656	·0335	·589	19
	$\frac{1}{2}$		$\frac{27}{32}$	·825	·0455	·734	14
$\frac{5}{8}$		$\frac{15}{16}$		·902	·0455	·811	14
	$\frac{3}{4}$		$1\frac{1}{16}$	1·041	·0455	·950	14
$\frac{7}{8}$		$1\frac{7}{32}$		1·189	·0455	1·098	14
	1		$1\frac{11}{32}$	1·309	·0580	1·193	11
$1\frac{1}{4}$		$1\frac{11}{16}$		1·650	·0580	1·534	11
	$1\frac{1}{2}$		$1\frac{29}{32}$	1·882	·0580	1·766	11
$1\frac{3}{4}$		$2\frac{5}{32}$		2·116	·0580	2·000	11
	2		$2\frac{3}{8}$	2·347	·0580	2·231	11
$2\frac{1}{4}$		$2\frac{5}{8}$		2·587	·0580	2·471	11
	$2\frac{1}{2}$		3	2·960	·0580	2·844	11
$2\frac{3}{4}$		$3\frac{1}{4}$		3·210	·0580	3·094	11
	3		$3\frac{1}{2}$	3·460	·0580	3·344	11
$3\frac{1}{4}$		$3\frac{3}{4}$		3·700	·0580	3·584	11
	$3\frac{1}{2}$		4	3·950	·0580	3·834	11
$3\frac{3}{4}$		$4\frac{1}{4}$		4·200	·0580	4·084	11
	4		$4\frac{1}{2}$	4·450	·0580	4·334	11
$4\frac{1}{2}$		5		4·950	·0580	4·834	11
	5		$5\frac{1}{2}$	5·450	·0580	5·334	11
$5\frac{1}{2}$		6		5·950	·0580	5·834	11
	6		$6\frac{1}{2}$	6·450	·0580	6·334	11
7		$7\frac{1}{2}$		7·450	·0640	7·322	10
	8		$8\frac{1}{2}$	8·450	·0640	8·322	10
9		$9\frac{1}{2}$		9·450	·0640	9·322	10
	10		$10\frac{1}{2}$	10·450	·0640	10·322	10
11		$11\frac{1}{2}$		11·450	·0800	11·290	8
	12		$12\frac{1}{2}$	12·450	·0800	12·290	8
13		$13\frac{3}{4}$		13·680	·0800	13·520	8
	14		$14\frac{3}{4}$	14·680	·0800	14·520	8
15		$15\frac{3}{4}$		15·680	·0800	15·520	8
	16		$16\frac{3}{4}$	16·680	·0800	16·520	8
17		$17\frac{3}{4}$		17·680	·0800	17·520	8
	18		$18\frac{3}{4}$	18·680	·0800	18·520	8

Angles of thread 55°. Threads rounded at crests and roots leaving depth of thread=0·64 pitch app. Taper screws coned $\frac{1}{16}$inch (measured on diameter) per inch length.

267

6 Making Joints in Pipework

Depending upon the age and locality of the property the householder may find his water systems (cold, domestic hot, wastewater and central heating) run in a combination of galvanised steel pipe, lead, copper or plastic. The purpose of this chapter is to explain how joints in these pipes can be made.

It would be unusual now to run interior supplies in steel piping but should this exist, if repairs or extensions are being considered it is advisable to change to copper. Mains supplies may be of steel, and water for agricultural purposes is often run in steel piping as it is tough and durable. However, this too is being superseded by plastic piping which is flexible, less susceptible to bursts and even more economical.

Steel pipework is screwed together using fittings threaded with BSP (British Standard Pipe Thread). Unions may be purchased which are already threaded, but lengths of pipe need to have their ends threaded once they have been sawn to length. This necessitates having a pipe vice and suitable dies and die stock, or ordering the pipe cut to the required lengths and threaded by the merchant. Pipes *in situ* will have rusted and considerable pressure, using a pair of Stillson wrenches, will be required to loosen them. Heating with the blowtorch will help, one Stillson gripping the pipe/or union and the other turning in the opposite direction. The most simple joint is that using a coupling, connecting pipes of the same size which are not expected to be disconnected again in the forseeable future. All the threads should be smeared with jointing compound and those on the pipes then wound tightly with a few strands of plumber's hemp starting about one thread away from the end of the pipe. Grip one pipe with one Stillson, engage the coupling with the pipe thread which is made easier by not having the hemp right to the end, and using the other Stillson screw up tightly. Now change the position of the Stillsons so that the coupling is gripped firmly and screw in the second length of piping. Pull off surplus hemp from the joint and with a cloth smooth off the jointing compound round the coupling. *(Fig. 1.)*

PTFE tape (see Chapter 3) can be used as an alternative to hemp and compound — two thicknesses are bound clockwise round the thread.

Fittings are available for adaption from steel pipe to copper. They are threaded internally (FI) to receive the steel pipe and are hexagonal at that end, so that a spanner can be used to tighten them. Again hemp and compound or PTFE tape should be used to make the joint. The other end will have either capillary or compression fittings to join it to the copper.

The traditional 'wiped' joint is used to connect two sections of lead piping together, or to join brass or copper adaptors or spigots to it, so from that point the system can be run in copper. The end of one piece of the lead piping must be flared slightly; this can be done with a tapered hardwood boss which is hammered into it. The other pipe is then bevelled off with a rasp or knife, so that the two fit snugly together with the bores in line. Paint a ring of plumber's black round each pipe about 30 mm from the end and from this scrape each one bright with a knife or shavehook. The complete joint should be approxi-

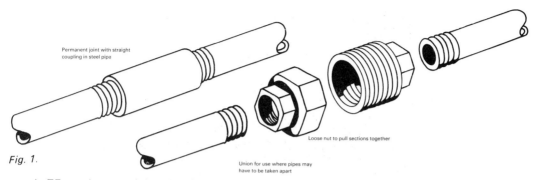

Fig. 1.

Permanent joint with straight coupling in steel pipe

Loose nut to pull sections together

Union for use where pipes may have to be taken apart

mately 75 mm long and the plumber's black restricts the solder between these limits. If adapting to copper, the tail of the adaptor, or alternatively a short piece of pipe to which a capillary or compression fitting can later be added, should be cleaned with glasspaper and tinned (i.e. coated with plumber's solder) — plastic range 183°C to 262°C (70 per cent lead, 30 per cent tin with a little antimony in some qualities).

The tube must be smeared with a non-corrosive flux and the end heated with the blowtorch, so that as it is rubbed with the plumber's solder sufficient melts off to cover it with a thin coating.

The joint must now be held together making sure that each part is in line, if necessary by using some form of clamp, and the whole area of the joint heated evenly, tallow being smeared over it to facilitate the spread of the solder. The stick of solder has to be heated at the same time, so that as it melts solder runs onto the joint. Only apply sufficient heat to keep the solder in a plastic condition, it is essential to pack the rim of the flared end to capacity.

You now require a plumber's moleskin, which is a specially woven cloth pad used for wiping the solder round the joint. It too should be heated and coated with hot tallow to assist the spread of the solder. With the moleskin supported by all four fingers, the semi-molten solder is spread firmly over the joint. Adjusting the pressure, tapers it off towards the ends. Apply further solder as required taking

care that the joint is not allowed to cool until it is finally complete. If necessary keep the solder workable by the application of further heat. Once sufficient solder has been applied to produce the typical rounded mass over the joint, it should be given a final wipe round to produce a smooth finish. *(Fig. 2.)*

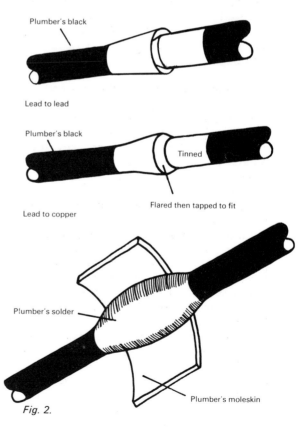

Plumber's black

Lead to lead

Plumber's black

Tinned

Flared then tapped to fit

Lead to copper

Plumber's solder

Plumber's moleskin

Fig. 2.

269

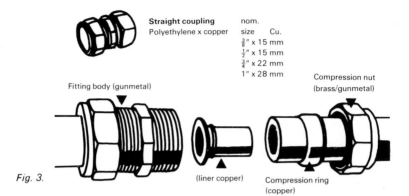

Straight coupling
Polyethylene x copper

nom. size	Cu.
$\frac{3}{8}$"	x 15 mm
$\frac{1}{2}$"	x 15 mm
$\frac{3}{4}$"	x 22 mm
1"	x 28 mm

Fitting body (gunmetal)

Compression nut (brass/gunmetal)

Fig. 3.

(liner copper)

Compression ring (copper)

If sheet metal is tinned, it can be 'sweated' together. The two pieces should be cleaned thoroughly, if necessary by scraping or filing, then glasspapered and fluxed. The purpose of the flux is to prevent oxidisation of the metal as it is heated and to assist the flow of the solder. Solder is then applied either by rubbing it on to the heated metal or with a soldering iron. Both are again fluxed, and brought together under heat until both layers of solder fuse together. In sheet metal-working this has many applications and is the method suggested for the repair to the ball valve in Chapter 7.

It should be remembered that pipes full of water are heavy and that lead, copper and plastic will sag if not properly supported by the appropriate fittings as recommended by the manufacturer (see Chapter 10).

Compression fittings for plastic piping are similar to those for use with copper, but a flanged inset must be placed in the pipe to prevent distortion of the flexible plastic. If necessary the end of the pipe can be softened by gentle heating, so that the insert can be fitted easily. *(Fig. 3.)*

The recommended procedure is as follows:

1. Use correct type, class and size of polythene pipe for the situation (see Chapter 4).
2. Make sure pipe is round, ends squared and burrs removed.
3. Slip compression nut and compression ring over pipe.
4. Insert correct liner (see Chapter 5) into pipe until flange touches pipe end.
5. Push pipe end into body of fitting up to the shoulder or stop in the bore.
6. Hand-tighten compression nut.
7. Make a further one and a half turns with a spanner to complete the joint from the point at which the compression ring begins to grip the polythene pipe. An arrow head on the coupling nut is a useful guide. When correctly tightened the pipe cannot be twisted within the fitting.
8. For large fittings in particular, remove all traces of dirt or grit from the thread of the body and nut, and apply a few drops of light oil to facilitate tightening. Spanners of at least 600 mm length should be used because of the amount of torque necessary to tighten the compression nut.

Capillary fittings make the neatest joints in copper tube *(Fig. 4.)*, but compression joints are simpler. For either type the ends of the tube must be cut square with a hacksaw or pipecutter. A piece of masking tape wrapped round the tube provides an edge to cut to, ensuring squareness. Pipe cutters are rather like G-clamps and are fitted to the tube and rotated, the pressure being gradually increased until the cutting wheel severs the tube. Both methods raise burrs which must be removed from inside and outside the pipe by filing. If end-feed capillary fittings are being used,

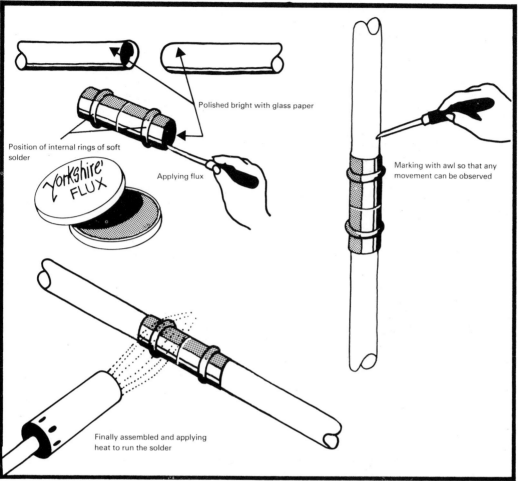

Polished bright with glass paper

Position of internal rings of soft solder

'Yorkshire' FLUX

Applying flux

Marking with awl so that any movement can be observed

Finally assembled and applying heat to run the solder

Fig. 4.

solder must be applied at the fitting mouth as the joint is being made.

Presoldered joints have a sunken ring of solder inside and are much easier to use. The inside of the fitting and the ends of the tube must be cleaned with fine glasspaper and pressed together up to the stop inside the fitting, mark the length of pipe entered with a scratch. The pipes are then withdrawn from the union, a non-corrosive flux applied to each and the joint reassembled. The scratch will indicate correct fitting and heat is then applied by a gas blowlamp to the union and the pipe. Heating should be overall and the solder will melt and creep between the tube and union by capillary attraction until a bright ring of solder appears all round the joint. A ceramic tile behind the joint will reduce the fire risk. When cool, surplus flux should be wiped off. When necessary, joints may be taken apart by reheating, and then withdrawing the tube. It can be remade by fluxing the tinned end and reheating until it can be pushed fully home once more, adding extra solder if required. New pieces of tube must be tinned before use in such a situation.

Compression joints do not rely upon solder, so no heat is required. To assemble,

271

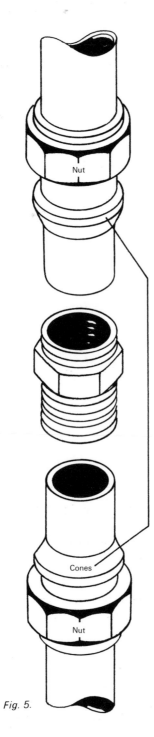

Nut

Cones

Nut

Fig. 5.

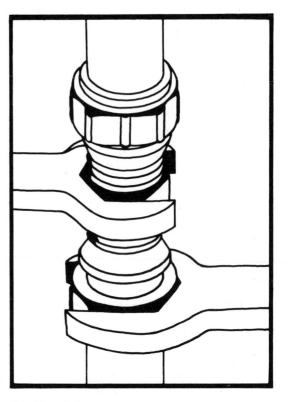

Assembling using two spanners

slide the nut onto each pipe followed by the cone (other names are olive or compression ring). If this has a long chamfer, this should be towards the end of the pipe. The pipes should then be pressed in up to the stop and the union assembled finger-tight, then the pipes marked as before, so that any tendency to creep out, as the nuts are tightened with spanners, can be observed and checked. A second spanner should hold the fitting as each nut is tightened, three turns are usually sufficient. Overtightening may result in damage to the threads or cone resulting in an unsatisfactory joint. *(Fig. 5)* Manufacturers do not recommend the use of a jointing compound preferring the metal to metal connection of the accurately machined fitting.

Three types of joints are also employed for plastic pipework. They are by compression nut, solvent cement welding or push-fit joints sealed by rubber 'O' rings located in a moulded housing and retained by a snap-in clip as in the Bartol System. *(Fig. 6.)*. Cement welding may be used for both cold-water supply systems and waste-water pipes, whereas the push-fit system is for waste water only, as this is not under pressure. To make the cement welded joints:

1. Ensure that the pipe end is cut square and remove burrs with a coarse file. Apply solvent cleaner to both areas to be joined.
2. Apply Bartol solvent cement to both clean surfaces to be joined.
3. Insert the pipe into the socket with a slight twist. Clean off surplus cement. The joint can be handled with care in less than five minutes. Wash out the

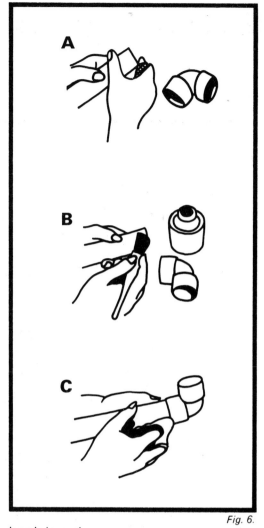

Fig. 6.

brush in a cleaner.

The jointing sequence for push-fit pipework is illustrated in *Fig. 7*. The parts are lubricated with soft soap before assembling.

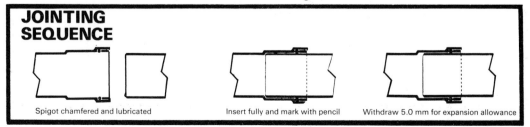

JOINTING SEQUENCE

Spigot chamfered and lubricated   Insert fully and mark with pencil   Withdraw 5.0 mm for expansion allowance

Fig. 7.

7 Renewing Washers

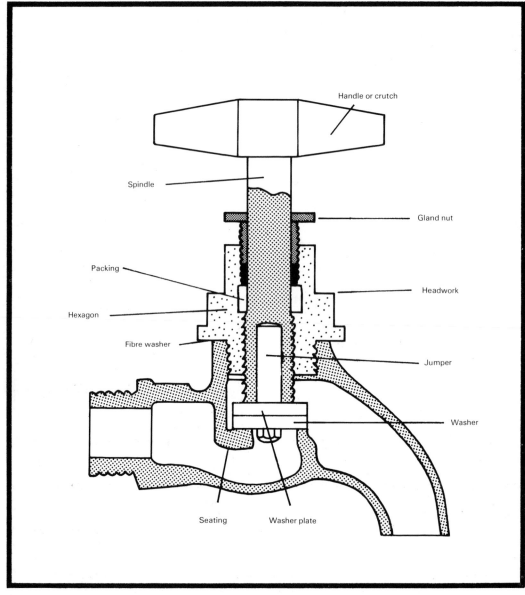

Fig. 1. Section through a tap

Water should cease to flow or drip from a tap which is closed without undue turning force having to be applied to the crutch or handwheel. As these are rotated the spindle is turned applying pressure to, or relieving pressure on, the washer. A mechanical device such as a tap is necessary to regulate the flow of water from the domestic system because of the water pressure. *(Fig. 1.)* Water is supplied by the authorities to the consumer at pressures of between 30 lb/sq in and 80 lb/sq in, in accordance with the 1945 Water Act. These will raise the water from a minimum height of 21·329m (70ft) to a maximum of 54·846m (180ft) respectively, depending upon requirements; to convert to metric pressures — 14·05lb/sq in = 1 bar. In older direct systems this is the pressure at each cold tap or ball valve. The more modern indirect system (see Chapter 2) results in a lower pressure at both cold and hot taps. By this method, both are gravity fed and the pressure depends upon the height of the cold-water cistern above the tap. The greater the difference in levels the bigger the pressure and flow rate.

The tap washer is located on the underside of the jumper or washer plate and is held in place by a small nut. *(Fig. 2.)* The spigot of the jumper fits into a hole in the bottom of the spindle, which in some taps is held in and in others is quite loose. In either case it is a sliding fit being free to turn. Therefore as the spindle presses the washer onto its seating it stops turning, thus preventing wear. In stop taps, and cold-water taps in direct systems, the jumper is quite loose, so should there be a drop in mains pressure when the tap is open, the washer will drop on to its seating preventing a back-syphonage of water into the mains and causing possible contamination. Taps used on indirect systems are designed to lift the washer from its seating as the tap is opened because of the lower water pressure (see Chapter 2). If a tap drips after being closed, or makes odd noises when open it is an indication

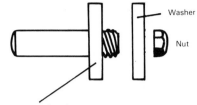

Jumper or washer plate
Fig. 2.

that the washer should be renewed. A washbasin or bath may be badly stained by water which is constantly dripping. The author can remember being called to advise on such a stain in a bath. A considerable area below the tap was green, obviously arising from the copper pipework and a solvent in the water. It was not until the washer was replaced, and after several weeks of regular application of a cleaner, that the stain was finally removed. It should also be remembered that a dripping tap is a potential source of trouble in frosty weather if the stackpipe is external as the trickle of water will freeze rapidly in the hopper head. In these days of energy conservation it should be remembered that if it is a hot-water tap, fuel is also being wasted. A few years ago it was customary to fit hot taps with red fibre or hard rubber washers, and cold-water taps with leather or soft rubber. It is now common practice to use synthetic rubber washers which are suitable for both hot and cold water. Be sure to have the correct diameter washer available for the size of tap. Tap sizes are measured by the bore of the pipe to which they are fitted.

The steps taken to renew the washer are as follows:
1. For cold taps on a direct supply, turn off at the consumer stop tap. Where the system is indirect, turn off at the consumer stop tap if the faulty tap is at the sink, or at the appropriate wheel valve nearest to the tap. Such wheel valves are often situated in the hot-water cylinder cupboard, but if they have not been provided, the water may be cut off at the cold-water cistern.

This is done with string, tying the arm of the ball valve tightly to a piece of wood placed across the edges of the cistern to keep the valve closed as water is drained off. *(Fig. 3.)*

2. When the necessary steps have been taken, the faulty tap should be opened and all water allowed to drain from it.

3. Unscrew the bell-shaped shield which is designed for easy cleaning. (Stop taps and those designed for outdoor use do not have these fitted.) The shield should only be finger-tight, but some do have flats around their bottom edge to which an adjustable spanner can be applied. Failing this, if a mole wrench, or Stillson, has to be used, protect the chromium plating with a rag, or heavy duty adhesive tape, but a strap wrench (see *Fig. 11.,* Chapter 3) is the ideal tool.

4. When the cover is lifted up to the underside of the crutch, a large nut is exposed, which is part of the spindle casing or tap headgear. This must be unscrewed using a plain spanner of a suitable size across the flats, or an adjustable spanner. While this is being done, the tap should be supported firmly by hand, or with a suitably padded wrench to avoid undue strain

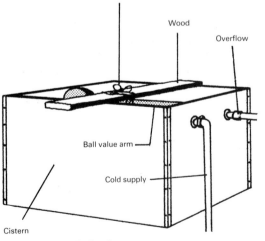

Fig. 3. Tying up ball valve arm

being put on it, or its connection with the washbasin, bath or pipe. If, because of age, this casing is difficult to unscrew, a smart blow with a hammer at the far end of the spanner will usually free it.

5. Once unscrewed, this spindle assembly, or headgear, may now be lifted clear of the tap.

6. Lift out the jumper from the body of the tap, if it is of the loose variety, and unscrew the small retaining nut on the underside. If a fixed jumper, it will have been lifted out with the head. The spigot or the washer plate of the jumper may have to be held in a wrench or with pliers, while a small spanner is applied to the nut.

7. Twist off the old washer and fit the new one.

8. Now replace the retaining nut and tighten up. If it bites a little way into the washer, this helps to lock the nut.

9. You will have found a thin red fibre washer between the spindle assembly and the body of the tap. If this happens to be damaged it should be renewed, but in the author's experience these washers are not always easily obtained, so care is advisable.

10. Examine the washer seating within the body of the tap to ensure that it is not damaged. Abrasions may be seen, or felt with the finger. If there is damage to the seating this should be made good with a reseating tool (see *Fig. 34.,* Chapter 4). This is the simplest pattern. More complex types are available for use on both tap and ball valves. Your local tool hire firm should be able to help with this.

11. Replace the jumper in the spindle if it was loose.

12. Screw in the assembled head complete with fibre washer and tighten down with a spanner. As previously, support the body of the tap to avoid strain.

13. By hand, screw down the shield.

14. Close the tap.

15. Turn on the supply once more and/or release the ball valve.
16. Open the tap slowly so that air is expelled from the system, then check that the tap is working efficiently.

One modern version of the pillar tap (see Chapter 9) has its nozzle and hand-wheel combined to point down at the sink. With this pattern there is no need to turn off the supply when renewing a washer. As the head is removed a valve in the tap body closes cutting off the water.

Stop taps are heavy duty and are designed to give exceptionally good service over many years, seldom giving much trouble. Consumer stop taps can be re-washered in the same way as any other tap if they fail to shut off the supply, providing there is a company stop tap by which they can be isolated. Be prepared for water draining back out of the system once the tap headgear is removed.

If the water authority's stop tap proves to be inefficient then the authority should be notified.

Ball Valves

A ball valve *(Fig. 4.)* will control the flow of water into your cold-water cistern or header tanks for the hot-water system or central heating. It is also the common method controlling the supply to WC cisterns. The level of water is governed by the rise and fall of the floating ball. When water is drawn off, the ball is lowered and the valve allows water to enter the tank. As the cistern refills the water is cut off once more as the ball rises. Should the cistern overfill, water will drip or trickle from the overflow pipe, which extends to the outside of the building. Occasionally ball valves will stick causing this to happen, but it is usually an indication that the washers should be renewed. It is

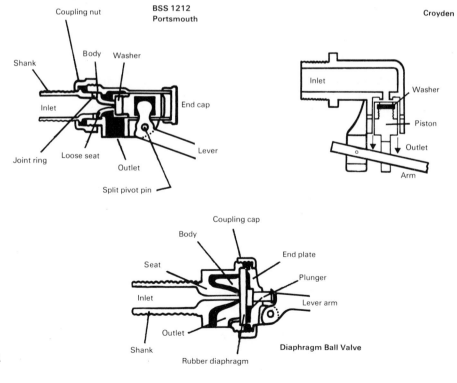

Fig. 4.

just possible, however, that the lever arm connecting the ball and valve is slightly bent upwards so that the water is not cut off soon enough. If you suspect that this is the case, bend the arm carefully downwards, then drain off some of the water, checking that the water level stops about 25mm below the overflow when it refills. The cistern may also overfill if the ball leaks, allowing it to become heavy with water. Should this be the case, tie up the lever arm as indicated earlier, and unscrew the ball from the end. If it is made of copper it may be possible to drain out the water, warm it gently to dry it thoroughly, clean with glasspaper, and sweat on a thin copper patch with soft solder (see Chapter 6). Failing this, or if the ball is made of plastic, it is wiser to renew it completely. The ball valve will be high pressure (HP) or low pressure (LP) depending on whether or not it is part of a direct or indirect system. HP or LP will be stamped on it, and should it be necessary to replace it completely be sure to obtain the correct type.

To replace the valve washer follow this procedure:
1. Turn off the supply at the stop tap and partially drain off the cistern.
2. Slip a piece of string through the eye of the split pin and secure to a convenient point. This is to avoid losing the pin in the cistern if it is dropped. Nip the open ends together with pliers and withdraw the pin.
3. Lift out the ball and arm on to an old cloth or newspaper as it will be wet, and withdraw the piston.
4. Place a screwdriver in the piston slot to give leverage and with combination pliers or a mole wrench unscrew the piston end.
5. Fit the new washer to the end and screw back. Smooth off any burrs which may have been raised.
6. Replace the piston with its slot in the correct position to receive the arm once more and replace the split pin. Open the ends with a screwdriver just sufficiently enough to prevent it from withdrawing accidentally.
7. Test that the arm and piston move freely by raising and lowering the arm manually, then turn on the supply again at the stop tap.
8. Make a final check that the water level is 25mm below the overflow when the valve cuts off. The incoming water from the valve may be directed downwards into the cistern by a short plastic tube which restricts noise. Check that this is screwed firmly into its socket.

Corrosion and residual dirt in cisterns are sometimes a problem – this is dealt with in Chapter 16.

8 Repairing Leaking Glands in Taps

The reader is referred to *Fig. 1.* in Chapter 7, which shows the section through a tap illustrating the usual arrangement of the various parts. It will be appreciated that as the tap is opened the water is directed upwards around the screw threads at the base of the spindle. This is because of the pressure of the water which causes considerable turbulence around the washer before the water is controlled and directed outwards by the nozzle of the tap. The more often a tap is used the more wear there is on the screw threads around the spindle and the greater the tendency for water to escape upwards. Any which does so is contained by the packing and the gland nut. The possibility of water being driven upwards in this way is increased if, by the attachment of some other domestic equipment, the flow from the nozzle is restricted. Water escaping through the packing will ooze out above the gland nut and trickle down the headgear. If an easy-clean shield is fitted this will gradually fill with water and after a time there will be an accumulation of dirt within it which becomes unhygienic, and which in turn leaks out around the spindle.

In older taps the packing consists of graphite impregnated string, but in newer ones a plastic sleeve may be used. Constant use of the tap results in the packing becoming less tightly fitted around the spindle, but by tightening down the gland nut it can be further compressed so taking up the wear. This is easily done on those taps not fitted with a shield so that the headgear is exposed. However, if a shield is fitted the crutch must be removed (or the handwheel) to give access to the gland nut. The crutch fits onto a square section at the top of the spindle, and by the removal of a small screw it can be lifted, or gently tapped off. Take care not to lose this small screw down the waste pipe — put the plug in place! Once the crutch has been taken off, lift the shield and tighten down the gland nut as indicated previously.

Should this prove to be ineffective the packing should be renewed completely, the easiest way generally being to cut off the water and strip down the headgear, so that the old packing can be easily removed from the 'stuffing box'. The new impregnated string, or soft white string charged with tallow, must be compressed into the stuffing box with the spindle in place, and the gland nut then tightened down. The rotation of the spindle should now be tested by replacing the headgear into the body of the tap and turning with the crutch. The packing should fit firmly round the spindle under the pressure of the gland nut, and at the same time it should be possible to rotate the spindle without undue force being necessary. It will be possible to feel the friction between the spindle and the packing and assess its efficiency.

This can then be tested by turning on the water and if necessary making further adjustments to the gland nut. Once this is found to be satisfactory, any remaining dirt should be cleared from the headgear. Finally, screw down the shield finger-tight and refit the crutch.

Obviously it is sensible to check the packing at the same time as a washer is being renewed, or vice versa.

9 Fitting Taps, Modern Tap Tops, Mixer Taps

Until quite recently taps were manufactured to BS 1010 which for twenty-five years or so specified the dimensions to which they should be made for use with sinks, washbasins and baths. Their overall sizes were dependent upon whether they were for use with $\frac{1}{2}$in bore pipes (sinks and washbasins) or $\frac{3}{4}$in bore (baths).

Three common types were made *(Fig. 1.)*, many of which are still in use.

a. Bib tap — kitchen use with sinks.
b. Pillar tap — standard fitting for washbasins and baths.
c. Globe tap — fitted to baths depending upon their design.

Maintenance of these taps is outlined in Chapters 7 and 8.

The new British Standard BS 5412 represents a fundamental change in permitted water fittings being concerned with the performance in use, adequate flow rates, reliability and durability. This has allowed manufacturers to develop individual designs. One such design is illustrated in *Fig. 2.*, its main features are:

- A lubricated spindle chamber from which water is excluded.
- Closing friction which is eliminated by a PTFE thrust washer.
- Washer arrangement and seating which reduces noise in the supply pipes.
- Reduction of tap water washer wear.
- Elimination of weeping glands.
- General ease of operation.

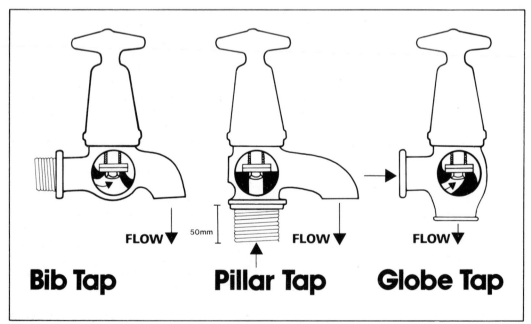

Bib Tap **Pillar Tap** **Globe Tap**

FLOW 50mm FLOW FLOW

Fig. 1.

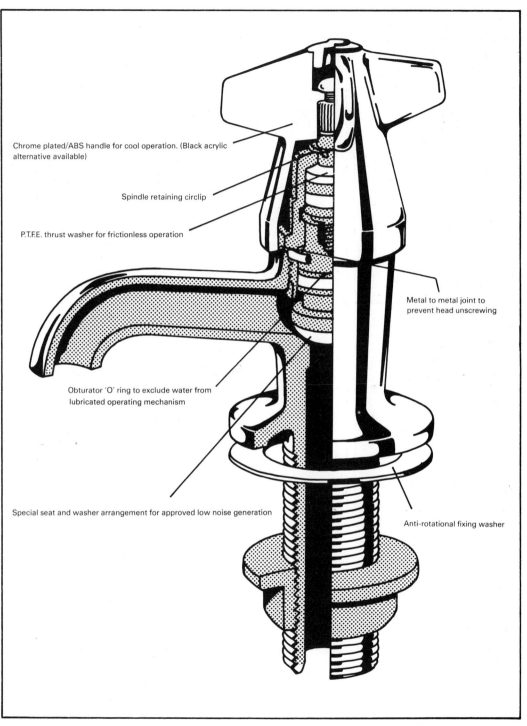

Chrome plated/ABS handle for cool operation. (Black acrylic alternative available)

Spindle retaining circlip

P.T.F.E. thrust washer for frictionless operation

Metal to metal joint to prevent head unscrewing

Obturator 'O' ring to exclude water from lubricated operating mechanism

Special seat and washer arrangement for approved low noise generation

Anti-rotational fixing washer

Fig. 2.

The new British Standard has enabled manufacturers to demonstrate that taps do not have to be ordinary to be functional or because they must be economical they will be inelegant. Modern taps are meticulously engineered and attractively designed. *Fig. 3.* indicates the range of taps available in one such design.

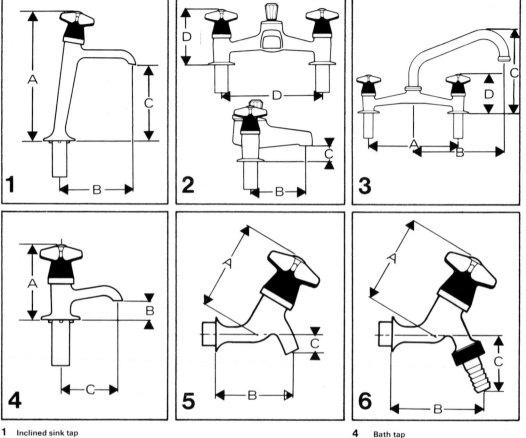

1 Inclined sink tap
½" BSP sink pillar
A: 172 mm
B: 100 mm
C: 100 mm

2 Pillar bath mixer
¾" BSP. Complete with diverter. Suitable for exposed shower units.
A: 180 mm
B: 100 mm
C: 26 mm
D: 93 mm

3 Dual flow sink combination unit
½" BSP pillar fitting.
Dual flow outlet
A: 180 mm
B: 180 mm
C: 163 mm
D: 75 mm

4 Bath tap
¾" BSP bath pillar
A: 92 mm
B: 82 mm
C: 25 mm

5 Bibcock
½" BSP bicock
A: 73 mm
B: 66 mm
C: 15 mm

6 Bibcock with hose union
½" BSP bicock fitted with hose union
A: 73mm
B: 79 mm
C: 43 mm

Fig. 3.

Existing taps can be given a modern styling by exchanging the crutch and shield with a new handle and 'headwork assembly'. *(Fig. 4.)* Kits are available for $\frac{1}{2}$in and $\frac{3}{4}$in taps, the method being as follows:

1. Shut off the hot and cold water supplies, open the taps and leave to drain.
2. Expose the hexagon. If your tap has a crutch or capstan handle with easy-clean shield, then open the tap fully. Unscrew the shield and hold it as high as possible under the handle, exposing the hexagon.
3. Put a spanner on the hexagon and turn anti-clockwise until the headwork assembly detaches. When removing old headworks jerk treatment is more effective than a strong pull. Support the body of the tap (c) to prevent damage to the bath or basin. Before fitting your new top, take a look inside the tap body. Clean out any scale or solids, but in particular, inspect the seat (d). It should be perfectly smooth. If it is in any way pitted or ridged, it can be recut, using a standard $\frac{1}{2}$in or $\frac{3}{4}$in BSS 1010 reseating tool, which can be hired. Alternatively, a qualified plumber can do the job quickly and inexpensively. This is important because a bad seating will cause a continuous leak. You are now ready to insert your new top.
4. Screw the spindle of the new top into the fully open position, so that the washer is raised.
5. Separate the handle from the headwork assembly simply by lifting out the press-fit indice (e) and undoing the retaining screw (f).
6. Fit the head washer (g). Then fit the headwork into the tap body, tightening the hexagon (b) with your spanner.
7. Finally, push the domed handle (a) firmly on to the spindle, tighten the retaining screw, insert the indice, close the tap and turn on the water supply.

Rather than give your taps a facelift you may decide to replace them, in which case here are a few practical points. As previously, turn off the water, drain the taps and disconnect the union with the pipe. Support the tap at all times to avoid strain on the fitment, particularly if it is of vitreous china as are most washbasins. Undo the backnut with the basin wrench and carefully withdraw the whole tap which, if bedded in putty, may be quite solid. Old putty may have to be picked out from behind or below. Once the old tap is released clean up the fitment thoroughly, then proceed as follows:

1. The tap must discharge cleanly into the fitment. Check dimensions.
2. Be sure that indices are correctly positioned — H to hot and C to cold.
3. Fit the taps symmetrically using the anti-rotational washer.
4. It is no longer recommended practice to set the tap in a hard-setting compound such as putty — use a modern non-setting type.
5. Secure with backnut, tightening down onto the thick plastic washer which is now normally supplied with a new tap.
6. Remake the union with the supply pipe, smearing it and the threads with pipe-jointing compound, or use PTFE tape. Formerly taps had 'tails' $2\frac{1}{2}$in long. The new British Standard is 50 mm, so if the supply pipe is rigid you may need an adaptor to make up the difference. These are available for $\frac{1}{2}$in and $\frac{3}{4}$in taps.
7. Turn on the supply — check for leaks. Note that the tap should shut off with light pressure only.

After use if hard screwing down is necessary it is an indication that the washer should be replaced.

Many modern styles of tap now incorporate a handwheel moulded in acrylic, the advantages being both a sparkling appearance and, as it is a good insulator,

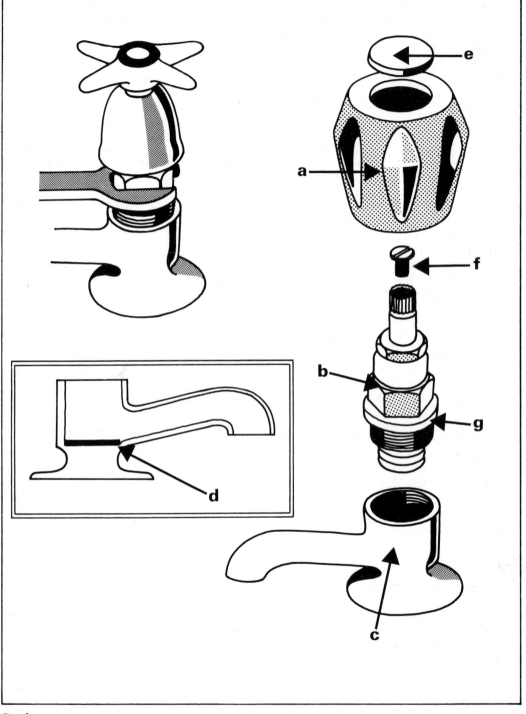

Fig. 4.

284

remaining cool even when the tap is discharging very hot water. For luxury water fittings, solid semi-precious onyx hand wheels are increasingly popular because of the beautiful grain displayed.

The 'Supatap' introduced by Deltaflow was and still is unquestionably unique. The design has found favour on innumerable occasions being an inspired piece of simplicity and restraint. Supatap maintenance can be carried out without shutting off the water supply because of its built-in automatic valve which cuts off by water pressure when the nozzle is removed. *(Fig. 5.)*

All taps and other fittings should be connected to conform with the regulations of the local water authority. The flow rate per tap as recommended in the BS Code of Practice (rate in litres per minute) is as follows:

Bath — 18 l/min
Washbasin — 9 l/min
Sink — 11 l/min
Shower — 7 l/min

Combination fittings should discharge almost double these volumes. In this context combination fittings are mixers into which hot and cold water are fed, being discharged from a common outlet. They are used for washbasins, baths and to a lesser extent for sinks. The fitting mostly used for sinks is a combination unit with dual flow, which is not a true mixer.

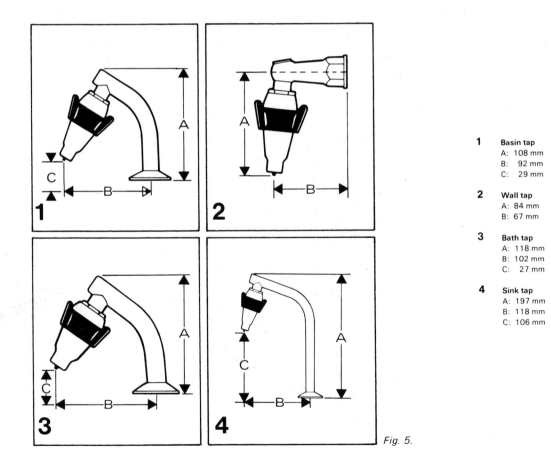

1 Basin tap
A: 108 mm
B: 92 mm
C: 29 mm

2 Wall tap
A: 84 mm
B: 67 mm

3 Bath tap
A: 118 mm
B: 102 mm
C: 27 mm

4 Sink tap
A: 197 mm
B: 118 mm
C: 106 mm

Fig. 5.

285

10 Traps, Waste Pipes and Overflow Pipes

Until comparatively recently it was common practice to take the pipes carrying waste water from toilets, baths, washbasins and kitchen sinks through the outer wall of the building to discharge into the underground drainage system. Waste from the toilet in such a system was flushed into a vertical soil pipe connected to the foul-water sewer often near to an inspection chamber (see Chapter 15). This vertical soil pipe was extended as a vent pipe beyond the point at which waste water entered, its highest point then being above any windows usually a little above the eaves. *(Fig. 1.)* Foul air can then escape without being objectionable. Other waste

water from baths etc., was then discharged into a rainwater head in the down pipe from the gutters which in turn ran into the drains via a gully at ground level. External waste-water systems such as this are very vulnerable to frost in severe weather. The modern practice is the single-stack system where all waste water from sanitary appliances is discharged into just one internal pipe which in turn is connected to the underground drain. *(Fig. 2.)* In this way no waste pipes are exposed outside the house with the exception of that carrying rainwater. This too is sometimes run down the inside of walls particularly in newer public buildings.

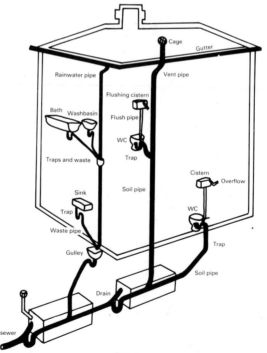

Fig. 1.

Any odours associated with waste water from toilets, bidets, baths, washbasins and sinks are prevented from passing back into the building by water-sealed traps. These may be P- or S-traps depending upon their shape, those for toilets being an integral part of the fitment, others being installed in the pipework. In older property these will invariably be of lead, but nowadays are more often of copper or plastic; the principle being that a small quantity of water will remain in the U-bend to form the seal. It should be emphasised that nothing which may cause the trap to become blocked should

be discharged with the waste water from baths, washbasins, sinks etc. Any solid object accidentally allowed to do so will rapidly build up a blockage of small pieces of debris around it, which would otherwise have passed through the trap.

The different ways in which blockages may be removed without dismantling the trap are dealt with in Chapter 16, but should these be unsuccessful lead and copper traps have brass cleaning eyes set into them. These are at the bottom of the U-bend, usually at the sides of P-traps, and underneath S-traps. The plug(s) can be unscrewed with a wrench or may

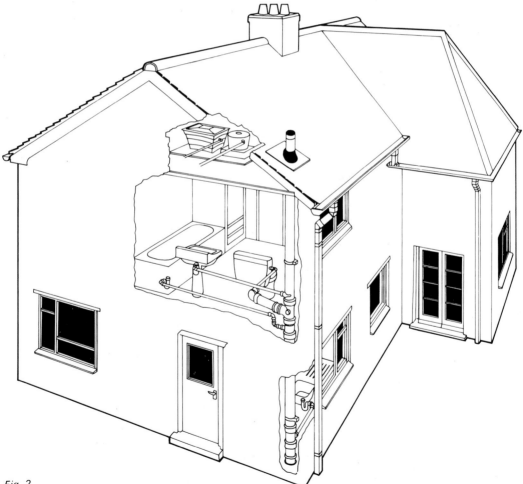

Fig. 2.

have slots in which a lever can be applied. Care must be taken to replace the hard rubber or fibre sealing ring and to give the pipework adequate support as the plug is removed or replaced.

Modern plastic pipework for waste water is specially formulated to withstand hot water and to resist the acids and detergents associated with domestic waste. *(Fig. 3.)* The traps designed for this system are swivel-necked to give maximum adjustment when being installed. The connection of the waste pipe is simplified because the direction of the outlet from the trap can be adjusted through 270 degrees to almost any desired position. In confined spaces such as those behind washbasins, pedestals or under sinks this is particularly useful. These plastic traps have excellent flow and self-cleaning properties, but when necessary the centre joint does provide easy access for the removal of blockages; BS 2494 part 2 specifies the high quality of the rubber seals required for plastic traps and pipework. The outlets of plastic traps are

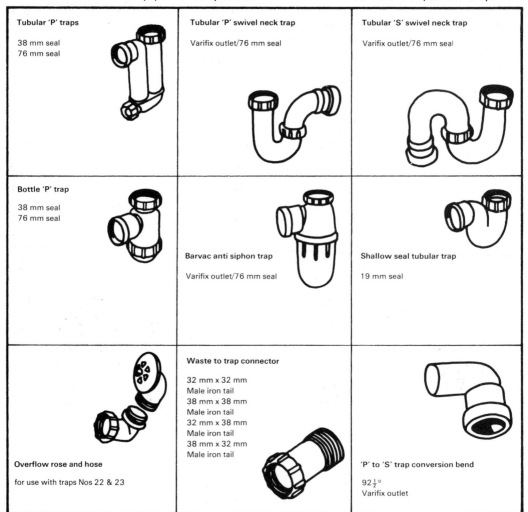

Tubular 'P' traps

38 mm seal
76 mm seal

Tubular 'P' swivel neck trap

Varifix outlet/76 mm seal

Tubular 'S' swivel neck trap

Varifix outlet/76 mm seal

Bottle 'P' trap

38 mm seal
76 mm seal

Barvac anti siphon trap

Varifix outlet/76 mm seal

Shallow seal tubular trap

19 mm seal

Overflow rose and hose

for use with traps Nos 22 & 23

Waste to trap connector

32 mm x 32 mm
Male iron tail
38 mm x 38 mm
Male iron tail
32 mm x 38 mm
Male iron tail
38 mm x 32 mm
Male iron tail

'P' to 'S' trap conversion bend

$92\frac{1}{2}°$
Varifix outlet

Fig. 3. Traps and fittings. 32 and 38 mm bore

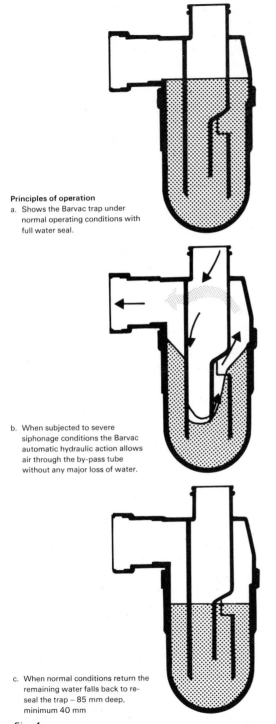

Principles of operation

a. Shows the Barvac trap under normal operating conditions with full water seal.

b. When subjected to severe siphonage conditions the Barvac automatic hydraulic action allows air through the by-pass tube without any major loss of water.

c. When normal conditions return the remaining water falls back to re-seal the trap — 85 mm deep, minimum 40 mm

Fig. 4.

usually designed to accept imperial and metric copper tube, push-fit and solvent-welded plastic pipework.

The water seal in traps can be broken under certain circumstances, e.g. if a washbasin empties with such rapidity that all water is drawn away with it, or exceptionally strong winds suck out the water from the trap where the outlet is outside the building. The introduction of the single-stack system created further problems when it was found that in order to preserve the water seal any 32 mm installation, e.g. a washbasin, or 38 mm, e.g. baths and sinks, had to be no more than 1·675 m and 2·286 m respectively from the stack even though special deepseal traps were used. Failure to observe these distances resulted in loss of seal, but the problem has now been overcome by the development of the anti-siphon bottle trap. This allows the architect or plumber to position fitments wherever they are required within a building with no risk of siphoning off the water seal. *(Fig. 4.)*

The traps for WCs are an integral part of the fitment, the U-shape being formed in the pan and the water it holds forming the seal. The outlet then connects with the soil pipe. The majority of WCs are wash-down types, and when flushed water from the cistern is discharged down the flush pipe. This runs inside the rim of the pan and flows over the inner surface. When a sufficient head of water has been built up the contents of the pan are displaced, being flushed through the soil pipe forward to the drains. This leaves the pan clean and the trap recharged with water, the waste matter being cleared by the volume and velocity of the water. Other WCs work by siphonic action and the pans can be single trap or double trap. The outlet of the single trap is so formed to impede the flow until the bend above is full of water when the siphonic action begins. In the double-trap type an air pipe connects the space between the two traps. Air is sucked out through this pipe as the water rushes down the flush pipe assisting the siphonic action *(Fig. 5.)*

Extreme care must be taken to avoid allowing anything to fall into the pan of a WC which could cause a blockage. This is particularly important with the siphonic types.

To replace an outdated lavatory pan is not too difficult, remembering that as well as being of different kinds, they are available with different spigots, i.e. the drain end which connects to the soil pipe. Both washdown and siphonic pans may be

Wash down WC

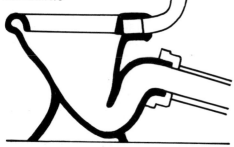

Siphonic WC, single trap type

Siphonic WC double trap

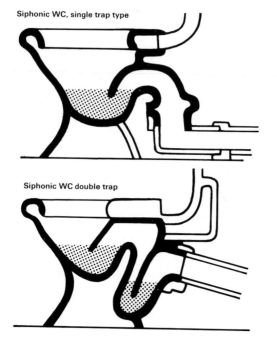

Fig. 5.

obtained with the spigot so inclined to connect with soil pipes passing through the wall or down through the floor. Check to get the right type, matching the measurements of the new as closely as you can with the old, paying particular attention to the fitting of the spigot to the soil pipe. The outlet of modern P-type pans is standard, the centre being 190 mm from the floor. If a low-level cistern is being fitted instead of a high one, the pan may need to be further from the wall, necessitating the use of extension pipes. Your plumber's merchant will advise on what is available. Failing this, slim cisterns are made which protrude only 100 mm or so from the wall. However, in order to contain the amount of water necessary to flush the toilet, these are of a larger area and take up more wall space.

Modern low-level cisterns are screwed to the wall and are so designed that the brackets which support them are hidden. It may also be necessary to make a hole through the wall for a new overflow pipe. The procedure to adopt in renewing a WC is as follows, with some possible minor amendments for individual cases:

1. Flush the pan clean, turn off water at stopcock and empty the cistern by flushing again. Mop out the trap with rags.
2. Take out the screws holding the pan to the floor; these should be of brass to avoid corrosion.
3. Disconnect the flush pipe – this may be a simple finned rubber seal, or a clamped rubber seal wrapped round a rubber sleeve.
4. The ideal is to release the pan so that it can be removed without damaging the soil pipe. It is at this stage where most care is required, much depends upon how the joint has been made. Most difficulty is likely to be experienced where the WC has been mounted on a concrete floor, the soil pipe cemented in vertically and the joint between the

two made with cement. In this case, to avoid damage to the socket of the soil pipe, the pan spigot may have to be shattered with a hammer. Binding first with a strong adhesive tape will prevent broken pieces falling down the soil pipe. Once the pan can be lifted clear, the soil pipe should be stuffed tightly with a rag to prevent other pieces falling in as the socket is cleared. The rag also blocks off unpleasant odours.

5. A small, sharp cold chisel and light hammer should be used to chip out remaining waste, working inwards and away from the soil pipe — damage to which must be avoided at all costs.

This joint will most likely have been made with paint and putty if the WC was mounted on a wooden floor, so that it is resilient to allow for movement of the timber (this could be due to expansion or contraction of the wood, or slight flexing of the boards as the floor is walked on). If the floor is solid concrete, then the joint may have been made with a mortar of one part cement to three parts of sand, but in each case the joint will first have been packed with hemp before being pointed off with putty or mortar. As an alternative to these methods the new pan may be joined to the soil pipe by means of a patent connector such as Bartol's 'Polyflex'. Basically these are flexible sleeves which allow for up to five degrees of misalignment and where necessary will mould themselves to misshapen spigots. The actual connection is a simple push-fit. Because of the different outside diameters of pan spigots, a range of connectors is made.

6. If the cistern is being replaced, this should now be screwed to the wall on its brackets. The height is important so that the flush pipe reaches down to its connection on the pan.

7. Try the new pan in position, check the fitting of the flush pipe and mark for the fixing screws. In a wooden floor, a pilot hole for each screw can be made with a bradawl, but a concrete floor must be drilled and plugged. A rotary percussion drill such as a Wolf 3548 (see *Home Maintenance and Outdoor Repairs* in this series) is ideal for this purpose, the holes being drilled to accept fibre or plastic plugs. Remember to use brass screws of a suitable length and avoid overtightening which may crack the pan. A pan which is slightly too low to meet the soil pipe can be lifted a little on a board cut to the profile of the base, but keep this to a minimum since the height of the pan is designed to suit persons of average build. Pans being set on concrete should be bedded on a mortar of one part cement to four parts sand, pointing it off neatly round the base.

8. Now connect the flush pipe — the fittings with which to do this will have been supplied by the manufacturers (see Chapter 12).

9. Make off the joint between spigot and soil pipe — first pack with hemp and ram down firmly, then fill with mortar or putty, depending upon requirements (also see *5.* above). This should be pressed well in to seal the joint and pointed off to a neat bevel. A putty joint should be allowed to stand several days and be painted to prevent it from crumbling.

10. Reconnect the cold supply and overflow pipes to the cistern using suitable washers and jointing compound. Turn on the supply once more at the stopcock, flush the pan and check for leaks.

Waste from WCs is discharged into the soil and vent system of pipework. These are now almost invariably of plastic with push-fit joints facilitating easy on-site

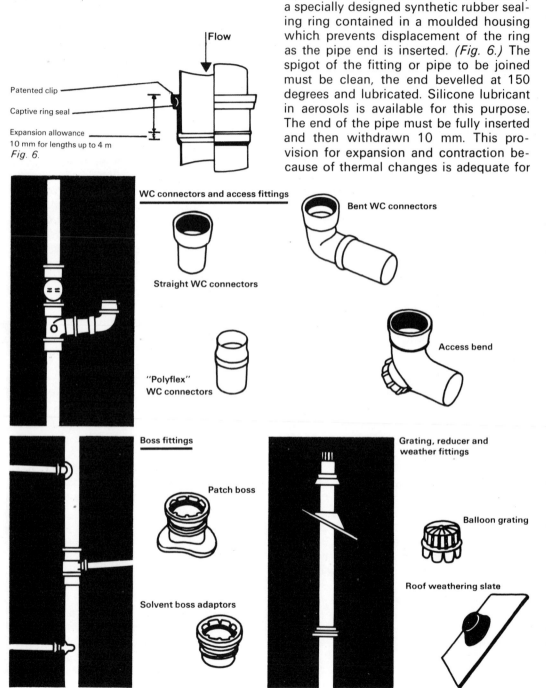

Flow

Patented clip

Captive ring seal

Expansion allowance
10 mm for lengths up to 4 m

Fig. 6.

assembly. The joints are made efficient by a specially designed synthetic rubber sealing ring contained in a moulded housing which prevents displacement of the ring as the pipe end is inserted. *(Fig. 6.)* The spigot of the fitting or pipe to be joined must be clean, the end bevelled at 150 degrees and lubricated. Silicone lubricant in aerosols is available for this purpose. The end of the pipe must be fully inserted and then withdrawn 10 mm. This provision for expansion and contraction because of thermal changes is adequate for

WC connectors and access fittings

Bent WC connectors

Straight WC connectors

"Polyflex" WC connectors

Access bend

Boss fittings

Patch boss

Solvent boss adaptors

Grating, reducer and weather fittings

Balloon grating

Roof weathering slate

Fig. 7a.

lengths up to 4 m and must be maintained by fixing the pipe at its upper end with a socket bracket. Provision for expansion must also be made at the foot of the stack by using a drain connector, the top of which must always be above finished floor level so that there is free movement in the expansion socket. Connectors are available to adapt to clay drains or cast iron.

Where the vent pipe passes through the roof a multipitch weathering slate is used. These are in three slate sizes and are suitable for roof pitches from 10 degrees to 55 degrees. A rubber cone fits snugly round the pipe, and the malleable aluminium base can be dressed easily to the profile of the slates. A balloon grating prevents birds from getting into the pipe.

Other waste pipes can be run into the soil pipe by means of a range of solvent-welded bossed fittings which incorporate a similar push-fit principle. Suitable holes are drilled with a hole cutter and the boss fitted with gap filling solvent cement. *(Figs. 7 a and b.)*

These waste pipes are mainly from

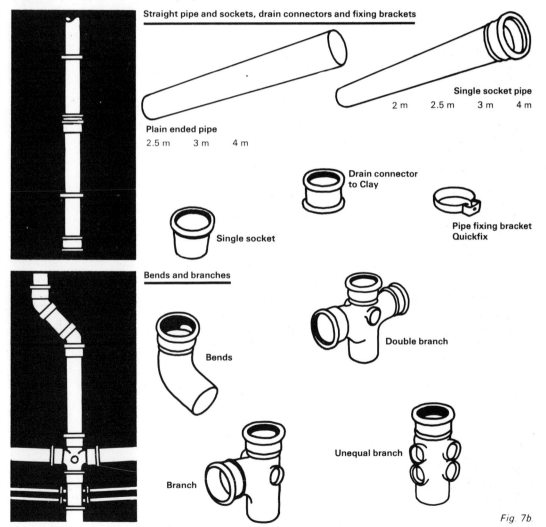

Straight pipe and sockets, drain connectors and fixing brackets

Single socket pipe
2 m   2.5 m   3 m   4 m

Plain ended pipe
2.5 m   3 m   4 m

Drain connector to Clay

Single socket

Pipe fixing bracket Quickfix

Bends and branches

Bends

Double branch

Branch

Unequal branch

Fig. 7b.

293

washbasins and baths and are 32 mm, 38 mm and 50 mm bore with pipe-wall thicknesses of 1·8 mm, 1·9 mm and 2 mm respectively, each supplied in 3 m lengths. *(Fig. 8.)* They may be a push-fit system as are soil pipes, or solvent-welded (Chapter 6). The plastics from which they are made are not affected by boiling water and are resistant to those acids and detergents in domestic use. Installation is simple, only a small toothed saw is required to cut the pipe and a file or pocket knife to bevel the

Fig. 8. Push-fit waste systems. 32, 38 and 50 mm bore

Plain ended pipe   3 m long

Bend   135°

Knuckle bend   90°

Straight connector

Waste coupling   Spigot tail

Swept bend   92½°

Socket reducers   34.6 to 21.5 mm
41 to 21.5 mm
41 to 34.6 mm
54 to 34.6 mm
54 to 41 mm

Swivel elbow
92½°/waste to soil connector, varifix outlet

Swept tee   92½°/equal ends

Tank connector   with back nut

Pipe clip

Waste coupling   Push-fit socket/equal ends

Bend   150°/waste to soil connector

Access plug   with screw cap

end.

Expansion is allowed for in the sockets of the push-fit system, whereas expansion connectors must be used at intervals in the solvent-welded system to provide for thermal movement. Where it is desirable to prefabricate waste pipes prior to installation the solvent cement method of jointing is particularly suitable. *(Fig. 9.)* The joining of traps to waste outlets is by compression nut and washer; the nut should not be overtightened.

Fig. 9. Solvent-weld waste systems. 32, 38 and 50 mm bore

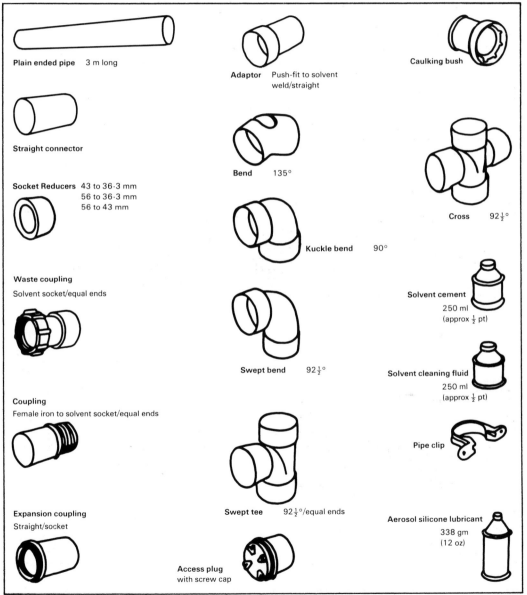

Plain ended pipe   3 m long

Straight connector

Socket Reducers   43 to 36·3 mm
56 to 36·3 mm
56 to 43 mm

Waste coupling
Solvent socket/equal ends

Coupling
Female iron to solvent socket/equal ends

Expansion coupling
Straight/socket

Adaptor   Push-fit to solvent weld/straight

Bend   135°

Kuckle bend   90°

Swept bend   92½°

Swept tee   92½°/equal ends

Access plug
with screw cap

Caulking bush

Cross   92½°

Solvent cement
250 ml
(approx ½ pt)

Solvent cleaning fluid
250 ml
(approx ½ pt)

Pipe clip

Aerosol silicone lubricant
338 gm
(12 oz)

Cisterns fitted with ball valves must have overflow pipes connected which discharge outside the building. Push-fit systems with 19 mm bore are ideal for this purpose, the connections to cisterns and terminal fittings being with compression nuts. *(Fig. 10.)*

Support brackets	Maximum distance between centres		
	Bore	Horizontal	Vertical
Soil and Vent Waste, Push-fit and Solvent-welded	75, 100 mm 32, 38, 50 mm	1·00 m 0·76 m	2·00 m 1·22 m
Overflow	19 mm	0·76 m	1·22 m

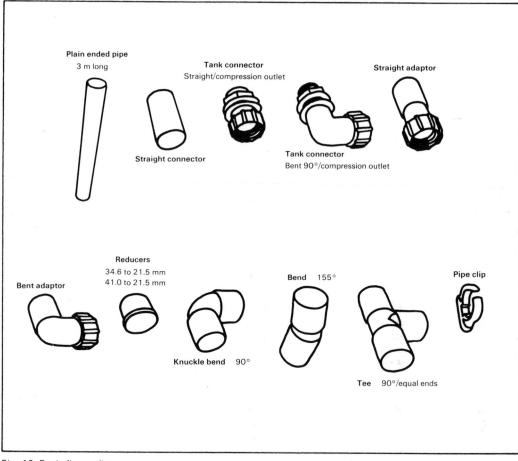

Fig. 10. Push-fit overflow system

11 Modern Cisterns

Cisterns are those plumbing fitments designed for the storage of cold water. Within the domestic system they are confined to the cold-water supply to baths and washbasins, expansion tanks for central heating systems and the means by which WCs are flushed. Over the centuries cisterns have been constructed from many materials, including stone and slate. For many years those for bathroom and central heating systems were of galvanised steel. It is now usual to install modern plastic ones which have the advantages of being free from corrosion, light in weight and robust in use. Good quality polypropylene cisterns as those manufactured by Bartol Ltd., are manufactured to BS 4123 and approved by the National Water Council. A variety of shapes and sizes are made *(Fig. 1.)*, with capacities from 18 litres to 227 litres. These are injection moulded from polypropylene and as they are unaffected by discharges of hot water may also be used as expansion tanks. A further range of circular cisterns, with capacities of 114 litres and 227 litres, are made for cold-water storage only. *(Fig. 2.)* Matching lids are available for all of these to form a safe dustproof seal.

Recommended fixing instructions are as follows:

1. Ensure that the cistern is received free from damage.
2. Drilling
a. A hole saw should be used to produce a perfectly circular hole.
b. The cistern wall must be supported while drilling, i.e. with a piece of timber held behind it.
c. Heated metal tubing is not recommended.

Fig. 1   Cold water storage and expansion cisterns

Fig. 2   Circular cold water storage cistern

3. Positioning.

d. A level, firm support must be provided for the whole of the base.

e. It should not be positioned close to electric light bulbs or any source of concentrated heat.

4. Assembling

f. Pipework must enter at 90 degrees to the cistern wall being so aligned to avoid distortion.

g. All pipes must be firmly fixed and supported independently of the cistern.

h. Do not overtighten backnuts.

i. Do not use jointing compounds. For sealing the connector use PTFE tape and polyethylene washers between the cistern wall and the flanges of the tank connectors.

j. The ball-valve plate, which is supplied loose, must be fitted to the outside of the cistern with the lock nut. The centre for this hole should be 38 mm from the rim of the cistern.

k. If the cistern has to be distorted in order to pass it into the loft do not drill until this has been done. The hole would create a weak point at which splits may occur. For the same reason care must be taken to avoid deep scratches.

Cisterns for toilets may be of vitreous china or plastic and may be low-level or close-coupled. (Fig. 3.) They are designed to hold 9·1 litres of water and may be of conventional dimensions or 'Fineline'. These are used where limited space requires the cistern to project the minimum amount from the wall, usually about 110 mm. However, because of the necessary capacity they are therefore larger in area. WC cisterns must conform to BS 1125 (1973) and be suitable for use with WCs to BS 1213 (1945). They should have easily cleaned surfaces and a minimum of joints or mouldings where dirt can collect; they may be fixed by screwing to the wall, or supported on concealed brackets, or by a combination of both.

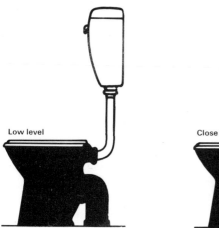
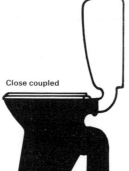
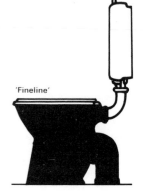

Low level   Close coupled   'Fineline'

Fig. 3.

12 The Modern Bathroom Suite

As it became customary for each house to have a bathroom, the fitments were often very austere and limited in number, often only a bath and washbasin with a separate WC. Depending upon the available space it is now not uncommon to have a bath, one or perhaps two washbasins, a WC and more recently a bidet. Of late, the shower cubicle (Chapter 13) has become a further addition as its value becomes increasingly appreciated, although it may not necessarily be sited in the bathroom. All too often the bathroom tended to be a somewhat cold, bleak room with a rather clinical atmosphere, and with little in the way of comfort. Modern materials and approach to design have brought about a revolutionary change, now making it possible for the bathroom to be one of the most stylish, pleasant and enjoyable rooms in the home. Whether you are planning a new bathroom, or giving an old one a facelift, you should consult the many manufacturer's brochures which are readily available. There is a quite bewildering array of styles and colours requiring careful consideration so that finally the right choice is made. For guidance, Table 1 gives an indication of the approximate amount of space occupied by a fitment and the necessary amount of space around it to permit easy movement. However, since it is unlikely that every fitment will be in use at the same time, these access areas may overlap to some extent. It is assumed that each fitment stands against a wall, and the distance it protrudes is then its 'projection'. All dimensions are in mm.

With these measurements as a guide, if you cut out rectangles of paper in proportion they can be fitted onto a plan of the room. This must, of course, be drawn to the same scale and the pieces, which should be labelled, or of different colours, moved around on it until the most suitable positions are found. You must, naturally, take into account the position of existing features such as doors, windows, cylinder cupboard, radiators, etc.

Probably the most significant factor in bathroom modernisation is the successful use of acrylic plastic from which to make baths, outdating the traditional cast iron or pressed steel. Both were cold, vulnerable to rust and the enamel chipped all too easily.

The advantages of acrylic fitments are numerous:
- Warm to the touch.
- Light in weight.
- Meet hot and cold service conditions favourably.

Table 1

Fitment	Average length against wall	Projection	Access area length width
Bath	1500–1800	690–790	1200 X 750
Washbasin	650	500	650 X 600
WC	450–500	700	500 X 600
Bidet	360–400	600	600 X 600
Shower	775	770	775 X 700

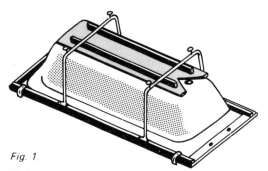

Fig. 1.

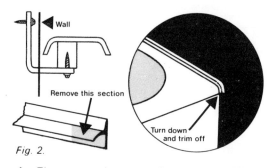

Fig. 2.

- Impact strength conforms to BS 4305 (1972).
- Resistant to most common household chemicals (paint-stripper, nail varnish and some dry-cleaning agents are exceptions).
- Surface has natural anti-slip properties when wet.
- Tough, resilient and durable.
- Easily cleaned by rinsing with soapy water immediately after use.

The material is readily moulded enabling many alternative designs to be manufactured, all of which ensure comfort in use. Baths are formed from acrylic sheet 8 mm thick, or, depending upon their design, from 3 mm sheet with a bonded fibreglass (GRP) backing for strength. Accidental scratches can be removed with a fine abrasive, e.g. wire wool, followed by repolishing with metal polish. Scorching from cigarettes can also be remedied in the same way. This can be done without loss of colour.

Being a resilient material acrylic baths are delivered bonded to a cradle or with a supporting framework to which metal legs and feet are attached. *Fig. 1.* illustrates the method employed for the Chloride-Shires Symphony (see cover picture) and *Fig. 2.* the means by which it is anchored to the wall.

Installation is as follows:

1. Push tubular legs in to sockets on edge battens.
2. Fix legs in to notches on baseboard with screws.
3. Screw on wall brackets at required positions.

4. Fit taps and waste pipes; use resilient washers between nuts and bath, with sealing compound under waste flange; apply only moderate pressure when tightening nuts.
5. Place in position and level at a height of 500 mm using adjusting feet; lock the feet and screw to floor.
6. Screw fixing brackets to wall.
7. Seal between bath and wall with sealing strip supplied; fix with contact adhesive. *(Fig. 2.)*

Washbasins, WCs and bidets are generally of matching vitreous china because of the need for rigidity, and the use of household cleaners for hygiene, although some washbasins are of acrylic when used in vanity units. Many washbasins are screw-fixed to the wall and supported on a pedestal. They can be fixed on wall brackets in place of the pedestal if this is desirable, but the advantage of the pedestal is to conceal the pipework. Washbasins are usually moulded with anti-splash front rims, soap recesses and slotted overflows at the rear. Holes are provided for standard $\frac{1}{2}$ in taps or in some models for mixer taps.

WCs may be washdown or syphonic, low-level or close-coupled (Chapter 11). The pans are screw-fixed to the floor, close-coupled cisterns being supported by and bolted to the pan.

Bidets too are screw-fixed to the floor, with 'rim-supply' and 'pop-up' waste plug, and are ideal for full personal hygiene.

Vitreous china fitments should conform to BS 3402 (1969), the surface being resistant to most household chemicals and cleaning agents.

13 The Shower Unit

Whereas a short time ago a shower may have been considered as a luxury item in addition to the bath, people have been quick to appreciate its advantages. It is hygienic; the installation is comparatively simple and it is economical in use. A shower may be had using approximately one-sixth of the water needed for a bath, conserving both water and energy. A minimum flow rate of 3 to a maximum of 9 l/min are considered adequate; 4 to 7 l/min being a good working average. The efficiency of these flow rates is dependent on the discharge rose being well designed. A bewildering array of types of shower are available, ranging from a simple moulded rubber hose which connects to the bath taps — the correct mix being obtained by adjusting the hot and cold taps, to the modern, sophisticated thermostatic shower. This has two controls, one to select the flow-rate and the other the required temperature. It is the old story of paying your money and getting what you pay for. More satisfactory than the moulded rubber attachment are the 'panel bath mixer', the 'pillar bath mixer' and 'deck bath mixer' with diverters for shower fitments. *(Fig. 1.)* To taps such as these shower units similar to those in *Fig. 2.* may be attached. These are exposed units as opposed to the shower arm *(Fig. 3.)*, the supply pipe to which is concealed in the wall. The efficiency of cistern-fed shower units such as these depends upon the bottom of the cold-water cistern being not less than 1 m above the shower rose. *(Fig. 4.)* In order to achieve this it may be necessary to raise the level of the cistern in the loft on extra battens or trestles. If this is not possible then it may be necessary to install a pump into the system between the mixer and shower head.

With showers that are virtually an integral part of the bath, the water has to be contained, so that it is discharged down the bath-water system. Any walls against which the bath is set must be tiled, using a waterproofed grout. Open sides to the bath must be fitted with a plastic curtain or panels to direct the water down into the bath.

A number of kits are available, suitable for installation over a bath or in a separate shower cubicle. The latter immediately doubles the bathing facilities of the house, being particularly advantageous in that it need not be installed in the bathroom, but simply where there is sufficient space available and that all necessary connections may be made to it.

Water of an even, comfortable temperature can be obtained by the 'blended valve' principle, precise quantities of hot and cold water being drawn into the mixing chamber from where the blend of water required is dispensed. The valve, which may be concealed within the wall *(Fig. 5.)* or be surface mounted *(Fig. 6.)* may be fitted with shower arrangements similar to those in *Figs 2.* and *3.* This type of shower mixer is, however, non-thermostatic and is therefore only suitable for use where pressures are nominally equal.

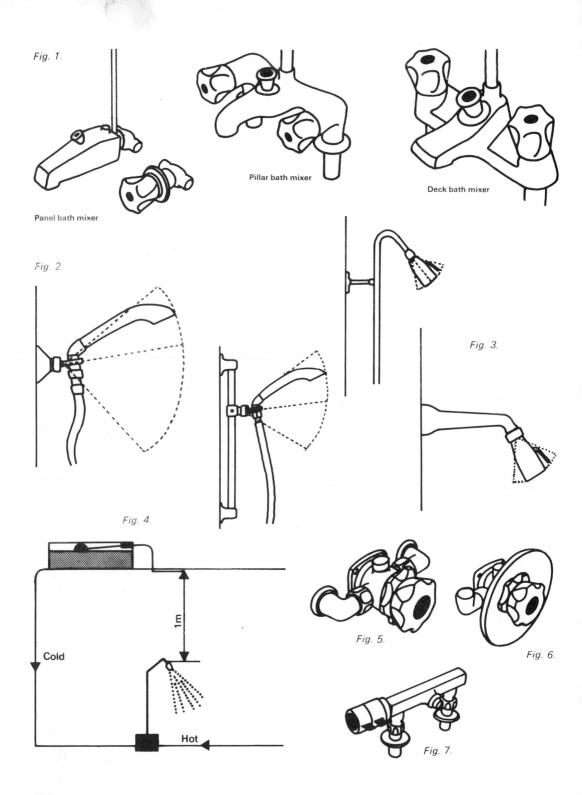

Fig. 1.

Panel bath mixer

Pillar bath mixer

Deck bath mixer

Fig. 2.

Fig. 3.

Fig. 4.

1m

Cold

Hot

Fig. 5.

Fig. 6.

Fig. 7.

The addition of a thermostat is a further refinement *(Fig. 7.)*; the unit has two controls, one selecting the flow of water, the other the required temperature. The temperature is monitored and for safety, should the cold-water supply fail, an anti-scald device operates.

Whereas the previous kits rely on the plumbing system for their hot-water supply, packs are available which operate independently. Being so they may be sited at almost any desired part of the house. They operate from the cold-water supply, the unit's thermal element heating only the water which passes through as you take a shower *(Fig. 8.)* The saving of hot water is immediately obvious.

Complete kits are now available to enable you to build shower cubicles such as the Shires Osprey *(Fig. 9.)* fitted with an instantaneous water heater as above. This eliminates much extensive replumbing, thus reducing installation costs, as the only connections necessary are those to the cold supply and the electrical circuit. A waste outlet, usually in plastic, must also be run to dispose of the waste water. Cubicles require about 1 sq m of floor space, and once the position has been chosen, pipes for supply and waste should be run, finally moving the cubicle into place to make the final connections, the cubicle tray usually being supported on steel-framed cradles screwed to the floor. Access panels are provided to facilitate easy connections to the pipework and the heater has, of course, to be connected to the electrical supply. These same access panels also provide for easy maintenance (see also Chapter 10, and other chapters which cover the fitting of supply and waste water pipes).

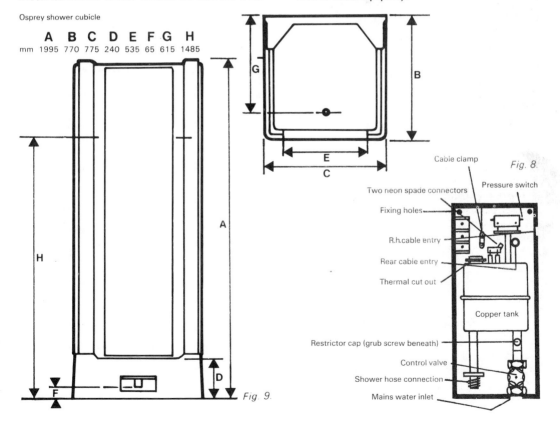

Osprey shower cubicle

A	B	C	D	E	F	G	H
mm 1995	770	775	240	535	65	615	1485

Fig. 8.

Cable clamp
Two neon spade connectors
Pressure switch
Fixing holes
R.h.cable entry
Rear cable entry
Thermal cut out
Copper tank
Restrictor cap (grub screw beneath)
Control valve
Shower hose connection
Mains water inlet

Fig. 9.

14 Insulation of the Plumbing System and Frost Precautions

Conservation of energy in any form is acknowledged to be of world-wide importance. Conservation of heat in the domestic situation is economic common-sense, and assists in overall conservation. Insulation of the house is dealt with in more detail in other books of this series, whereas here we are basically concerned with plumbing. Suffice to say that lofts should be insulated with granular vermiculite or fibreglass between the joists. Both hot and cold-water pipes in basements, and ventilation areas under floors or unheated areas such as roof spaces should be lagged. So too should the hot-water cylinder; several patterns of cylinder jackets are available. Failing this the author has found that two or three layers of corrugated card fitted carefully round the cylinder and tied with string are very effective. Efficient insulation of the system not only conserves heat, but also guards against frost which can cause great inconvenience and expense. The volume of water increases by about one-tenth when it freezes, exerting great pressure, and this causes damage to, or bursting of pipes. Freezing obviously begins at the coldest point and depending upon its severity gradually extends along the pipe. Service pipes should not therefore be fixed to the inside of external walls, but be brought into the building at sufficient depth below ground until they can be brought up on an internal wall. Freezing will stop the flow of water and cut off the supply, but also if the pipes burst the escaping water may cause considerable damage to the structure of the building and its decor as the ice melts.

The cold-water cistern in the roof space must be lagged and this can be done by placing a loosely fitting box around it and filling the cavity with vermiculite or fitting slabs of expanded polystyrene round it. They can be held in place with string or a suitable industrial self-adhesive tape. As an alternative, fibreglass bonded mat may be used. A slab of polystyrene placed over the cistern will insulate the top and keep out dirt, but if any expansion pipes discharge into it provision must be made for this by leaving a suitable gap.

Some danger points for pipes have already been mentioned, but in addition pipes in outbuildings or garages, near air-bricks and ventilators or where cold draughts may occur should be lagged. Depending upon their situation this may be with pre-formed plastic foam, or pre-formed fibreglass both of which are normally supplied split to clip around the pipe. *(Fig. 1.)* Alternatively, thermal insulating material can be obtained in rolls to be wrapped around the pipe as a bandage. Different types are made of hair felt, polypropylene-backed jute mixture and fibreglass. *(Fig. 2.).* The recommended thickness for thermal insulation is 25 – 65 mm for pipes depending upon their diameter and situation, and 13 to 38 mm for cisterns. Insulation will delay heat loss and retard freezing, but if the temperature remains below freezing, further precautions may be necessary, such as placing a small electric or paraffin heater at vulnerable points. Electric heaters with porcelain enclosed elements, or 'black-heat' elements are best. If a paraffin heater is used it should be of a safety type with gauze round the flame.

Taps and overflows should not be

allowed to drip or waste pipes may freeze up. Because of this it is advisable to leave plugs in washbasins and baths during severe frost.

If any pipe is found to be frozen, place a small heater or even the electric iron near it, or cover it with a thick pad of cloth soaked in hot water on which further hot water can be poured from time to time until the pipe is thawed. Should the pipe be burst temporary repairs can be carried out by gently tapping the pipe back to shape then binding with plastic self-adhesive tape held in place with closely-wound strong string.

No attempt should ever be made to thaw pipes with a blowlamp, nor if the hot-water system is frozen should the

boiler be fired, or in the case of a back boiler the fire lit in the hearth. A severe explosion could be the result in either case.

If the house is to be unoccupied for more than twenty-four hours in frosty weather and cannot be heated, the whole of the water system should be drained off. This means closing the service stopcock and opening all the draw-off taps, including drain taps for heating systems. Also, salt or anti-freeze solution should be added to the traps of WCs, baths and washbasins.

To refill the system, drain taps must be closed, the stopcock opened and finally all the taps closed once the water is flowing freely and all air has been driven out.

Preformed pipe insulation

For hot and cold water pipes. Self-extinguishing, lightweight and flexible. Operating temperature maximum 105°C (220°F), minimum minus 40°C (minus 40°F).

Supplied split for easy fixing but can be supplied unsplit in 2 m nominal lengths. Wall thickness 9 mm ($\frac{3}{8}$ in).

For 15 mm copper tube
For 22 mm copper tube or $\frac{1}{2}$ in ferrous pipe
For 28 mm copper tube
For 35 mm copper tube or 1 in ferrous pipe
For 42 mm copper tube
For 54 mm copper tube
        Tape 2 in x $\frac{1}{8}$ in In 100 ft rolls
        Adhesive 500 ml tin.

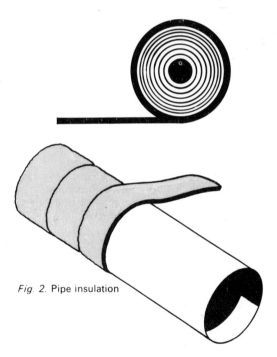

Fig. 2. Pipe insulation

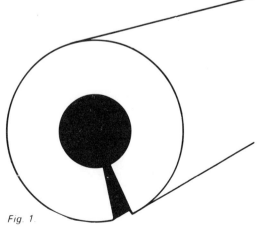

Fig. 1.

15 Drainage Information

Domestic drainage systems consist of above-ground work from gutters, sinks, baths and toilets connected to the below-ground system of drains. It is essential to know just how this is done for any particular house before considering maintenance or repair work. Whenever drainage is discharged into the system, foul air is prevented from escaping into the house by means of traps or water seals, the most common being the U-bend. *Fig. 1.* indicates the above-ground arrangement of external cast iron pipework typical of older property.

The so-called soil pipe carrying waste from the WC is extended above the eaves, or the level of any dormer windows as a vent for foul air. Surface water from gutters may also discharge into the foul-water sewer depending upon the requirements of the local authorities. If excess water of this nature might result in the local sewage works being overloaded, it may have its own sewer running into a stream or river. Should this not be convenient it may run into a soakaway situated quite near to the house providing the subsoil is sufficiently absorbent. Above-ground pipework for

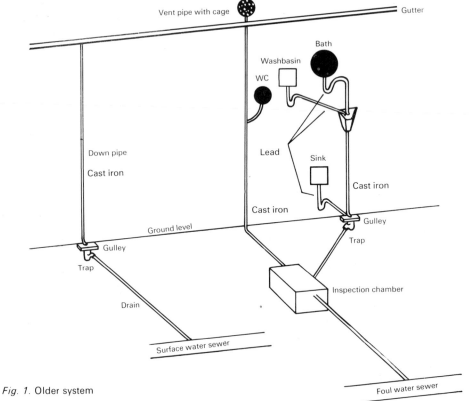

Vent pipe with cage

Gutter

Bath

Washbasin

WC

Down pipe

Cast iron

Lead

Sink

Cast iron

Cast iron

Gulley

Ground level

Trap

Gulley

Trap

Inspection chamber

Drain

Surface water sewer

Foul water sewer

Fig. 1. Older system

such a system is invariably attached to the outside of the building; it is liable to freeze, requires costly maintenance and is aesthetically undesirable. This has led to the now compulsory modern system where a common soil and waste-water pipe (see *Fig. 2.*, Chapter 10) is constructed inside the walls of the house. In both cases, of course, rainwater is carried to the drains or soakaway by its own system of pipework. The soakaway should be fitted with a lid or concrete cover and consists of a pit with porous walls, the cavity being open or filled with rubble.

Underground drainage pipes must 'fall' away from the building, so that water and waste matter run away freely. There will be manholes within the system at convenient points. These are to allow for inspection and for 'rodding' should blockages occur.

Gullies have a U-bend which forms a permanent water seal and are frequently used where waste-water pipes join the main drainage system. Modern gullies are designed so that the waste pipes enter either through the grid or below it by a side or back entry. In this way waste matter does not lodge on top of the grid, a cause of frequent overflowing. *(Fig. 2.)*

Underground drainage pipes were traditionally of glazed earthenware or cast iron, more recently of pitchfibre, and are now often of plastic. Where rainwater pipes connect to a combined drain a gulley must

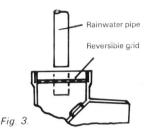

Fig. 3.

be used. The Plastidrain access gulley is ideal for this purpose since the connection is roddable from the gulley and avoids the need for an inspection chamber.

Where separate stormwater drains are provided a Plastidrain access gulley may still be used for the rainwater pipe connection in order to filter leaves from roof drainage in wooded districts or deal with surface water run-off from paved areas. *(Fig. 3.)* Otherwise, for connections to separate storm-water drains Plastidrain adaptors provide push-fit connections. The hole in the top face of the adaptor is offset to allow for the variations in distance between the down pipe and the building. *(Fig. 4.)*

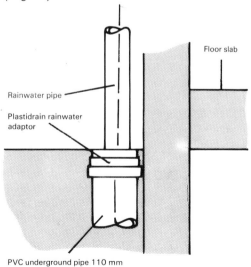

Fig. 4.

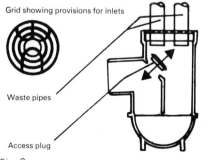

Fig. 2.

The inspection chamber is probably the most expensive part of traditional house drainage since it is normal to find all drains from the house connected to the sewer or collector drain via manholes which are generally 1·5 – 2·5 m deep. The high costs of excavating and constructing manholes, as well as the cost of site concrete in deep excavations near to foundations, can be avoided by the use of shallow Plastidrain glass reinforced plastic inspection chambers positioned off the main run of drain. *(Fig. 5.)*

An inspection chamber should be installed in the closest location permitted by the pipework connections and consistent with rodding accessibility. Placed this way, the chamber will usually need to be 610 mm deep, as will all the drains from the house. *(Fig. 6.)* In more complex designs the last chamber before the collection drain should be no deeper than 910 mm.

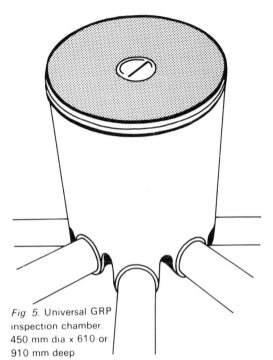

Fig. 5. Universal GRP inspection chamber. 450 mm dia x 610 or 910 mm deep

Fig. 6.

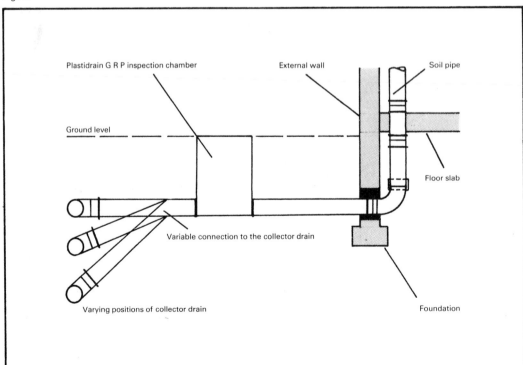

Plastidrain G R P inspection chamber

External wall

Soil pipe

Ground level

Floor slab

Variable connection to the collector drain

Varying positions of collector drain

Foundation

So that the cost of inspection chambers at the head of small branch drains may be saved, Building Regulations permit the use of Plastidrain rodding eye terminals.

Blockages

Blockages are the most common drainage faults and within the house occur most frequently in the trap below bathroom and kitchen fitments. They can often be cleared with a rubber plunger, the fitment being half filled with water, the plunger placed evenly over the drainage hole and worked vigorously up and down (see Chapters 3 and 6). If this is unsuccessful, the drain plug must be removed, care being taken to support the pipework adequately as it is unscrewed. Place a suitable container below the drain plug to catch the waste water.

Should the blockage occur in a drain it will be obvious by overflowing at the gulley, or at a rodding eye, or at the inspection chamber depending upon its situation. Modern gullies are provided with an access plug *(see Fig. 2.)* through which flexible drainage rods may be inserted. Older earthenware gullies do not have this facility and cleaning round the trap is more difficult. In either case sludge should be removed from them periodically with a scoop *(Fig. 7.)* and the grid kept clear of waste. Blockages within the inspection chamber can usually be cleared with a stick, care being taken not to damage the pipework or in the case of bricked chambers the 'benching' around the open pipes in the bottom. Blockages at some distance along the pipe can only be

Fig. 7. Tools for cleaning out gullies

Stick to which tin is nailed

Scoop

freed with the aid of drainage rods and fittings, which are often available on hire.

The location of such a blockage may be determined by examining the inspection chamber(s). If there is only one and it is clear, then the blockage must be between it and the house, but if it is overflowing then the blockage may be at its outlet or beyond. Where there is more than one chamber the blockage will be above the first chamber to be found empty.

Before rodding the drain, the outflow pipe should have a piece of wire netting placed across it to catch the solids which are released, allowing the water to pass. Rodding should then begin from the chamber above using the rubber plunger head. This should be screwed to the end of the first rod and inserted into the pipe. As the rod is pushed in, further sections must be screwed on until the obstruction is reached. *At no time should the rods be turned anti-clockwise or they may become unscrewed.* Once the head of the rod touches the blockage it should be pressed firmly against it until it is released. Should this fail an alternative head should be tried — a hook, a scraper and a screwhead are usually included. The screw is designed to screw into blockages of rag or paper so that they may be withdrawn, again — *do not turn anti-clockwise.* Once a blockage has been released the system should be thoroughly flushed out and where necessary disinfected. If all attempts fail to free the obstruction, replacing the blocked section must be considered. Its location can be traced by laying the length of rods on the ground above the run. It is then necessary to dig out a trench taking care not to disturb any other services which have been laid underground. Debris from the trench should be thrown sufficiently clear to avoid running back. It must be possible to work in the trench, which if necessary, because of depth or soft soil, may have to be shored with timber. Any infilling from around the pipe should be placed separately for replacement.

Replacing a Pipe

The replacement of a pipe may also be necessary if it is fractured, and tracing a leak is rather more difficult. An expanding drain stopper is required *(Fig. 8.)*, so that the point furthest from the house may be plugged and the system completely filled with water, any trapped air being allowed to escape through breather tubes inserted round the bend of gullies, or by removing the access plug in modern plastic ones. A leak would be indicated if there is an appreciable fall in the water level after about an hour. Actually finding the leak may require extensive digging and inspection particularly if the drain runs under paths etc. There may be obvious points to inspect first, such as where it is clear that there has been recent subsidence, or where heavy traffic has crossed the line of the drain.

Once the fault has been located, be it a blockage or fracture, if possible the system should be plugged temporarily above this point, so that it is not flooded by the accidental discharge of waste water, and the pipe broken out taking care not to damage the ends of those pipes to which it is connected.

Earthenware pipes are easily broken up with a hammer; pitchfibre or plastic may have to be sawn. Once laid, clay pipes are rigidly joined at the socket with mortar, a tarred hemp gasket being first rammed into the joint to align the pipes and prevent mortar escaping into the bore. Alternatively they may be purchased with a plastic coating so that the joint is sealed with a rubber ring as the spigot and socket are pushed together. *(Fig. 9.)* This leaves the system flexible and less likely to fracture.

Because of the slack fitting of the joint in plain clay pipes, they are often used to repair faults as they can be eased into place *(Fig. 10.)*, the joints then being made up with gasket and mortar (one part cement to two or three of sand). It is advisable to test the system once a repair

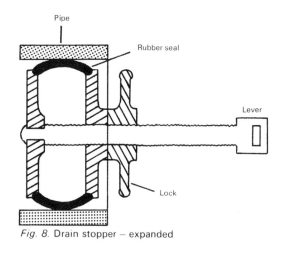

Fig. 8. Drain stopper — expanded

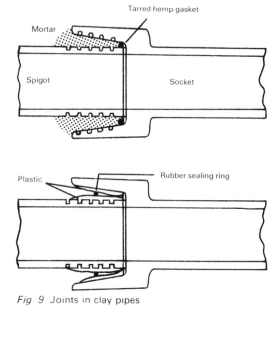

Fig. 9. Joints in clay pipes

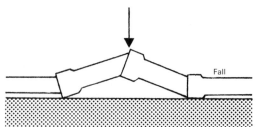

Fig. 10. Inserting new pipes

has been made before filling in the trench. Once this has been done, the infilling should be carefully packed around the pipes, and the soil then replaced in layers each being trodden down as the work progresses.

As indicated previously pitchfibre and plastic pipes may be sawn to length; if clay ones have to be cut they should be placed on soft soil and nicked round and round very carefully with a sharp cold chisel and hammer until they part. Both pitchfibre and plastic pipes may have push-fit joints sealed with a rubber ring, or plastic ones may be solvent-welded (see Chapter 11). Adaptors are also available for joining plastic pipes to clay or cast-iron systems.

16 General Care and Maintenance

Your plumbing system gives a lot of useful service generally with the minimum of trouble. This can be prolonged by taking a few simple precautions and giving the system a little thoughtful care. More than one member of the family should be familiar with its functioning, and it is sound practice to label important features, such as stopcocks and wheel valves and the supply which they control.

Blockages of traps and overflows in sinks, washbasins and baths resulting from an accumulation of grease and sediment are commonplace. The former can often be cleared with the force cup (see Chapter 3). The fitment should be partially filled with water, the cup placed over the waste pipe and the handle worked vigorously up and down. Should this fail, place a bucket below the trap and unscrew its plug, taking care to avoid damage to, or loss of the sealing washer. Then clear out each side of the trap with a flexible wire. A simple coil made by winding the wire round a length of thin dowel is ideal; this will pull out the blockage and the trap

should then be flushed with hot water before the plug is replaced. Finally run more water through the trap to check that it is really clear and to remake the seal. Now ensure that the plug is not leaking and dispose of the waste water down the drain. Flexible expanding curtain wire is ideal for clearing overflows if they are found to be blocked. Simple blockages of this nature can often be avoided by regular use of cleaning fluids applied to sinks and washbasins. Similarly, cleaning fluid should be applied regularly to the WC since all pipes which discharge waste water are unhygienic. Wear rubber gloves when working on them and then wash gloves and hands thoroughly when the job is completed.

Take care not to drop bottles or jars from the bathroom cabinet into the washbasin. Those of vitreous china chip or crack too easily. Similarly avoid the use of abrasive cleaners on baths, washbasins and plated taps or other metal fittings. Hot water and household liquid cleaners are preferable.

Traces of corrosion on metal fittings can be removed with a fine abrasive cleaner, and buffing with a wax-based polish will delay further spread.

A fine slurry will often accumulate in cold-water cisterns. The opportunity to mop this out with a cloth should be taken when the water is turned off at any time, and the cistern drained. It is not advisable to scrape galvanised cisterns or holes may develop because of more rapid corrosion.

Minor leaks in threaded unions can usually be stopped by giving the nut a further half turn, ensuring adequate support is given to the rest of the pipework or fitment. Failing this, turn off the supply, drain the pipe and remake the joint with PTFE tape. Take at least two turns of tape clockwise round the male thread, pulling taut so that the tape moulds itself to the shape of the thread.

Temporary repairs to small pinhole leaks which occasionally occur in pipes can be made by binding the pipe with self-adhesive plastic tape and clamping with a small jubilee clip until the defective tube can be cut out and replaced.

Make sure that the outdoor stop tap is always accessible. Clean deposits of dirt from round the lid which covers it, and in periods of frost apply salt to prevent it from freezing fast.

It is becoming increasingly advisable to be economical in the use of water. It is a commodity for which there is a growing demand — on average 150 litres per person per day.

Avoid dripping taps and waste from overflows. It has been calculated that one drip per second wastes 1,416 litres per year.

Finally, remember that all water authorities have bye-laws relating to contamination, misuse and waste of water. These bye-laws also define the kinds of pipes and fittings which may be used in their particular area. They are regulations with which your plumbing system, and any modifications to it, must conform.

INVEST IN LIVING

Part V

ENERGY SAVING

by

Roger Broadie and David Simpson

Introduction

Since the 'energy crisis' has spotlighted the need to conserve energy, much work has been done by individuals and Government legislation towards saving the energy resources we have.

As the cost of energy increases, it becomes not only worthwhile but necessary to insulate buildings properly and to conserve fuel as far as possible.

This book is about the practical methods of saving energy, and therefore money, in your home. Most of the methods employed can be undertaken by anyone with a little practical experience and the emphasis throughout is placed on things you can do yourself.

Insulation and the economical use of fuel can give you benefits which you use in one of two ways: you can keep your house at the same temperature as before and save money by using less fuel; or you can take the benefits as increased comforts in a warmer house but for the same amount of money as you pay now.

About the Authors

David Simpson is a graduate biologist, presently working as Head of a School Science Department.

Roger Broadie graduated in engineering and now works as a teacher of physics.

The authors met while at the same school and have combined their separate skills to cover the important topic of Energy Saving.

In writing the book, Roger Broadie has concentrated on the theoretical aspects, whilst David Simpson used his wide experience to write the practical sections.

Each has lived in and worked on four houses as well as helping friends with their insulation problems. Whilst the authors do not pretend to be first-rate craftsmen, they have first-hand experience of the techniques described and therefore know the methods to be workable, economic and feasible for any moderately competent handy person to undertake.

1 The Principles Involved in Energy Saving

What do we Mean by Energy?

Energy itself is intangible, and very few people really understand what it is. The most direct way we experience it is when it warms us as heat, but it can can also exist in many other different forms. Light and radio waves are energy. Oil, coal and gas contain energy locked into their structure. Water stored in a dam has energy because, if channelled, it can run downhill and turn a turbine. In fact anything that is moving has energy, even down to the electrons moving in wires that we call electrical energy. It is possible to store energy temporarily in such things as night storage heaters and hot water bottles, but most of the time energy just goes where it wants to, and this is our problem.

When we say we use energy, we mean that energy is in the right form to do what we want it to — as heat if we want to get warm, light if we want to see and so on. We can never destroy energy, we can only change it to a different form. In burning a fuel we change chemical energy to heat. Some of the energy that was locked inside the fuel comes out, and it leaves a substance, as ash or smoke, that contains less energy locked in. Eventually all energy ends up as heat. The food you eat contains chemical energy (calories); this allows you to move, so you have movement energy, but your movement makes you warm, thus the energy still ends up as heat.

Your house has a heat balance. You bring in energy mainly as heat from the fuel that you burn, but you also get heat from food, from light and from radios, televisions and all other electrical appliances. Your house radiates heat to the air outside at the same rate that you bring the energy in. If you wish to save energy, you insulate the house. The better the insulation, the slower the escape of energy so the less you have to bring in in the first place. This book is concerned mainly with energy used for heating. The amounts of energy involved in lighting and in running appliances do matter, but their total is only about one-quarter of that used for heating a house.

How does Heat Move?

Heat will always move of its own accord to a cooler place. All we can do is slow the movement down (insulate), but we can never completely stop it. There are three methods by which heat moves. It uses the easiest method, which can be any one or more of the three, depending on the conditions.

Radiation

The heat is carried through the air as a wave of electromagnetic energy. When the heat of the sun is felt directly, then the heat is caused by radiation but remember that warm objects still radiate, even if they do not appear to glow (see the front cover).

Radiation becomes much more important as the temperature goes up. A kettle holding boiling water at 100°C is radiating heat about fifty times faster than it is when at 50°C − only half the temperature.

Conduction

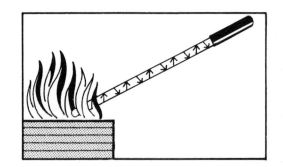

Heat makes the molecules inside a substance move. The movement is transmitted along the substance rather as the movement of an engine is transmitted along a line of shunted railway wagons. This movement is felt as heat. The faster the molecules vibrate, the hotter the object is. Some substances pass heat by conduction much more easily than others. Most metals, for instance, are very good conductors. An *insulator* is a material which is very bad at conducting heat, and one of the best insulators available is still air.

Convection

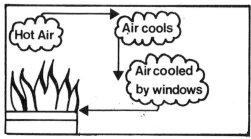

Water and air expand and rise when heated. Watch what happens to the smoke from a cigarette; the smoke is carried by the upward-moving air, and as the hot air is moved away upwards, air is dragged in to fill the space it left. This air will be cooler. The cool air is now next to the heater and it too will be heated. It will rise, dragging in more cool air to be heated, and as this process continues a convection current is set up. This is by far the most important method of heat movement in water and air, and it is the method by which rooms are heated and by which energy starts to be lost.

Slowing and Helping Heat Movement

For each of these methods of heat movement we can help the heat along, or we can slow it down, by doing various things.

Radiation

■ To help it — rough, dark and dull (matt) surfaces are good at radiating heat. They are also good at absorbing radiated heat that falls on them.

■ To slow it down — Heat falling on silvery and polished surfaces is reflected, and these surfaces are poor at giving heat out (radiating) if they themselves are warm. *For example:* a silver teapot really will keep the tea warmer than the traditional dark brown pot, and cricketers wear white to reflect the sun.

Conduction

■ To help it — we use metals which are good conductors to give us fast heat movement. *For example:* a pan is made of metal so the heat can easily reach the food inside.

■ To slow it down — we use a bad conductor (an insulator). *For example:* a pan handle is made of wood or plastic to stop you burning your hand.

Convection

■ To help it — (a) large spaces allow good convection currents to be set up. In big rooms most of the heat will be up near the ceiling where it is doing no good; (b) heating the air or water at the bottom gives it room to rise. For this reason radiators are always placed near the floor.

■ To slow it down — (a) block up the air or water into small spaces to break down the circulation. *For example:* most house insulation materials are of cellular construction and contain many small pockets of trapped air; (b) if all the air or water in a space is at the same temperature, convection cannot happen, so prevent local cooling from draughts and windows in a room.

Insulating Materials and Values

Manufacturers quote the insulating properties of their materials in a variety of ways. Here we have only used metric units; you can find all the equivalent imperial units and their conversions in Appendix 6.

The 'K' Value

This is the thermal conductivity of a material. It is a measure of how good a material is at conducting heat from one side to the other. The lower the 'K' value, the better the insulating material. It is expressed as how much heat can get through a 1m thick piece of material over an area of 1 m^2.

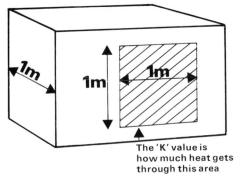

The 'K' value is how much heat gets through this area

The units used are watts/metres, degrees centigrade (W/m,°C); for example, the 'K' value of (unplastered) brick is 45·4.

The 'K' value is unwieldy once the material is made up into different thicknesses for construction, so you will find the following two values more useful.

The 'U' Value

This is the thermal conductance, and it is the unit we concentrate on in this book. It says much the same as the 'K' value, but it is expressed for a particular wall or a type of insulating material in the form in which you can buy it. It gives a direct measure of the amount of heat let through over an area of 1 m^2. It is expressed as the heat lost through each m^2 of the material for a certain temperature difference between the inside and the outside; the lower the

'U' value, the better the insulator.

The units used are watts/square metres, degrees centigrade (W/m^2,°C); for example, the 'U' value of a sheltered wall of single unplastered brick 114 mm ($4\frac{1}{2}$ in.) thick is 2·9.

The 'R' Value

This is the thermal resistance. While the 'U' value says how much heat is let through, the 'R' value says how hard it is for the heat to get through. The higher the 'R' value, the better the insulator. It is really just the reverse of the 'U' value. The units used are square metres, degrees centigrade/watt (m^2, °C/W). The 'R' value can be found from the 'U' value and vice versa.

'R' value $= 1 \div$ 'U' value; and
'U' value $= 1 \div$ 'R' value

The greater the difference in temperature between the inside of a house and the outside, the faster the heat goes from one to the other. This is stating the obvious fact that a house loses more heat in the winter. However, the insulating properties of materials also depend on the temperature difference, and different manufacturers may quote similar materials for a different temperature drop. For example, the same material could be quoted as:

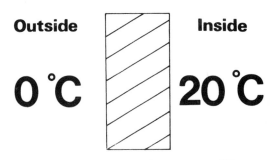

'U' $= 0·5$ watts/m^2 for a 20 °C temperature difference

Or:

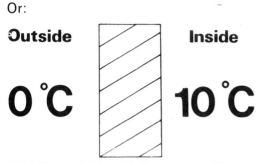

Outside   **Inside**

0 °C   10 °C

'U'=0·25 watts/m² for a 10 °C temperature difference

These are the same, the second saying that if there is only half the temperature difference, then only half as much heat is lost.

Manufacturers often quote 'K', 'U' and 'R' values for their materials.

Condensation

This is when small drops of water form on a cold surface; it is when the windows 'mist up'. It is an important problem, because in a house severe condensation can ruin paintwork and wall decoration. Therefore it must be reduced as much as possible. It happens because warm air nearly always contains a lot more water vapour than cold air can. If you cool the warm air down it can no longer hold the water vapour, and it condenses out. In a room the warm air is cooled by the cold glass of the windows, and the excess water vapour forms into tiny drops or 'mist'. This can also happen inside walls if they are porous and air is allowed to seep through, and it can lead to damp walls.

While extra insulation in a house can reduce condensation on the inside of rooms and windows, it can also increase the amount of damp inside walls unless precautions are taken to prevent this. These are considered in each section where relevant.

2 Preventing Major Heat Loss

For most people the biggest energy (and therefore cash) loss is when air which has been warmed to make a room comfortable leaks or transfers its heat away through cold walls and ceilings. In effect you can be warming up the cold air outside — think how much that costs!

In a house where no attention has been given to preventing heat loss, as much as 75 per cent of the heat can be lost. In other words, for every £100 you pay for fuel, you get only £25 benefit.

You can see from the diagram where the greatest heat losses are likely to be, and it is sensible to deal with the greatest loss as a priority. This will mean treating the walls of most houses. However, as dealing with wall insulation costs much more in time and

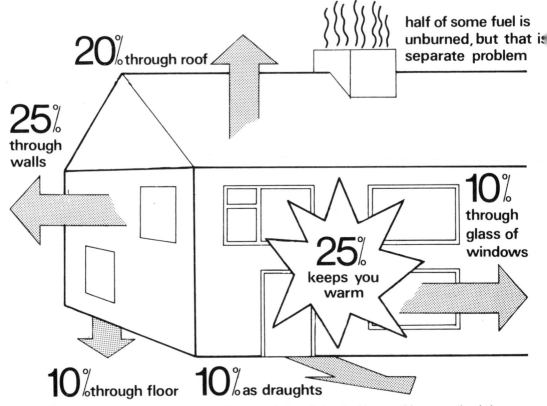

half of some fuel is unburned, but that is separate problem

20% through roof

25% through walls

10% through glass of windows

25% keeps you warm

10% through floor   10% as draughts

This diagram shows where the heat losses are from a typical semi-detached house with no extra insulation. Terrace houses will lose less heat through wall and detached houses will lose more; bungalows will lose more heat through the roof.

money than, say, curing draughts, the cost of each operation and the time it takes has to be considered as well as the potential saving in fuel. We suggest that you *aim* to cure the big problem first, but if you cannot afford the big jobs for some time, then make sure at least that you tackle the small ones.

By now you should realise that you can save so much heat on proper insulation that you can get back the cost of the material on reduced fuel bills in a short time. You may for example recover the cost of draughtproofing in less than a year. So the lesson is that you can save money by wise spending on insulation!

Comfort and Health

A warm house is not only a comfortable house, it is also a healthy one. With warm walls and draughtproofing more of each room can be used, and indeed more of the whole house is available for comfortable use even in the winter. Condensation can be reduced, and as it is the cold wet patches that cause structural damage and increase the need for decorating this is a further saving.

Putting Heat Loss in Perspective

The following chapters are set out to deal with each area of heat loss in turn, dealing with the various methods of reducing loss and looking at likely savings.

As the costs both of fuels and insulating materials continue to rise, we have not placed much emphasis on actual cash but on relative costs and percentage savings. It is helpful to know that cavity wall insulation costs, for a certain type of house, half as much as double-glazing yet can save over three times as much heat. The cash terms for these figures will vary with time and in different areas. Also you will need to make your own up-to-date estimates to suit your particular house. To help you to go into this in more detail, Appendix 2 deals with 'Cost Calculations'.

3 Preventing Heat Loss through the Walls

As far as heat loss through walls is concerned, the warmest houses to live in are either the middle flats in a block or back-to-back terrace houses. In these places all adjacent houses share heat and your neighbour's heat loss is your gain. However, semi-detached houses have three walls exposed and detached houses have, depending on their shape, at least four. Within the house the rooms with the greatest number of outside walls tend to be the coldest. Aspect and exposure also have a part to play in heat loss; north-facing and wind-exposed walls are colder than those on the sheltered sunny side of a house, and constantly wet walls will lose more heat than regularly dry ones.

Building methods have improved over the years and modern houses lose much less heat than older ones. However, in any house the greatest heat loss is usually through the walls; even in a post-war house 25 per cent of your heat can go out this way. With proper insulation this may be cut to 10 per cent or less.

Since about 1930, houses have been built with a 50 mm (2 in.) cavity between two leaves of brick. In recent years the inner leaf has been constructed of lightweight blocks rather than brick. The purpose of the cavity is to prevent damp from passing from the weather-exposed outside into the house. It does improve insulation to some extent and can be used to advantage for cavity wall insulation.

Insulating Cavity Walls

The 'U' value of a cavity wall with a plastered inner surface is about 1·9 (see chapter 1). This value will be higher (worse) in a brick-brick wall than in a brick-lightweight block wall. It will also be higher in wind-exposed, north-facing or rainsoaked walls. So people in houses in the wetter north-west of the country and in higher or coastal areas will get less insulation from their walls.

Under the new building regulations, houses built since 1975 should have walls with a 'U' value of 1·0.

Insulating cavity walls is most often done by filling the cavity with a material which traps air, making an internal 50 mm (2 in.) insulating layer. The insulation is achieved by blowing in treated mineral fibres, or by pumping in urea-formaldehyde foam which hardens to a bubble-filled plastic.

The foam is more widely used as it is slightly cheaper, but the fibres are rather better in wet areas. This point will be explained later, page 324. Both materials are injected into the cavity through holes drilled in the outside brickwork and both methods have to be done professionally with special equipment. The holes are filled up and pointed at the end of the process.

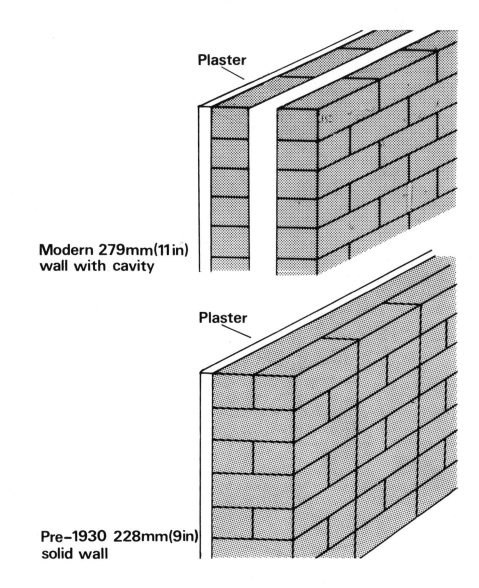

Plaster

**Modern 279mm(11in)
wall with cavity**

Plaster

**Pre–1930 228mm(9in)
solid wall**

This diagram shows the two common methods of constructing brick walls. An examination of the outside of a house may show the construction type.

The work should only take a day and there will be plenty of choice in the Yellow Pages of the Telephone Directory under 'Insulation Contractors'. You should be able to get a free quote.

If you have a partly boarded house or a wood-faced dormer, where the wood forms the outside leaf of the house and is not fastened over an existing cavity wall, then the only way of insulating this part of the house is to have the wood taken off and a layer of fibreglass matting fixed behind the wood. Check that this operation is included in the quote. The contractor will investigate the wall behind the wood and tell you what needs to be done.

Problems with Cavity-wall Insulation

Filling a cavity with insulating material breaks the Building Regulations which state that the cavity must be left clear. However, most local authorities allow the operation if the contractor has an Agrément Certificate*. In a very low per cent of houses cavity filling has created damp patches. This is usually because although the material is water repellent it can crack and may also funnel damp along mortar droppings in the cavity. Many firms will give a guarantee – if possible get a *written* guarantee that says that the work was carried out satisfactorily *and* that the walls were in a suitable condition for the work to be carried out. Then even if you are among the unlucky few the firm will repair the damage.

Mineral wool fibres seem to have less of this type of problem than the foam.

If your house is in a position exposed to driving rain, it may be wise to spend a little extra on this type of filling.

If you choose a firm which has no certificate, you may need to make a formal application for planning permission to your local authority. The firm should be able to advise you on the particular requirements of your area. In this case read the guarantee particularly carefully!

Costing Cavity-wall Insulation

Because this method of insulation provides such good savings, potential purchasers of your house will be keen to know that it has been done. It is therefore a good investment in this sense.

An accurate price cannot be put on the work because it varies from area to area and of course with the type and size of house, but a reasonable estimate is a few hundred pounds.

A cavity wall, uninsulated, will have a 'U' value of about 1·9 for houses built before 1975. Filling the cavity with foam will change the value to about 0·7. This will reduce the heat loss through the walls by 60 to 66 per cent. The total heat loss from the whole house would be reduced by almost 20 per cent, so by this method of insulation alone you could save up to 20 per cent of your annual fuel bill.

Mineral fibre insulation may give a slightly better 'U' value – about 0·6 – but as this represents an extra saving of only about 1 per cent on the total fuel bill, it is probably not worth the

*The Agrément Board is a government-sponsored body set up to check on building materials and methods.

extra cost — unless you live in the type of wet exposed area mentioned above.

Houses with double-brick walls will get a better saving than those with brick and blocks. Older houses with double-brick walls may save over 20 per cent per annum. This is because the brick-brick walls have a higher (worse) 'U' value than the brick-block constructions and so are better subjects for treatment.

All houses built since 1975 are required to have outside walls with a 'U' value of 1·0 or better. This is achieved by building the inner leaf of special lightweight insulating blocks. Filling these walls may change the 'U' value to 0·4 or less. In this case the annual reduction on the fuel bill will be about 5 per cent. This is obviously a much longer-term investment.

If you can save 20 per cent on your total fuel bill each year, it is easy to calculate the amount of time in which you will get your money back. Simply find 20 per cent of the total amount spent on all fuel each year, divide this into the cost of the insulation and the answer is the approximate length of time it takes to get your money back.

For example, with a fuel bill of £150 and an insulation cost of £200:

$$20 \text{ per cent of } £150 = \frac{150 \times 20}{100} =$$

£30 saved per year

$$\frac{£200 \text{ insulation}}{£30} = 6 \cdot 6 \text{ years, which is}$$

roughly **7 years**

So in this case it would take 7 years to repay the investment you made in buying the insulation. After this you are making a profit, and of course the bigger the fuel bill in the first place, the less time it takes to 'pay off' the cost.

Insulating Solid Walls

The insulation of walls with no cavity is a much longer job than undertaking cavity insulation. Nevertheless it is something that you can do yourself and it can be done in stages, taking the coldest part of the house first and working through the rest of the house as convenient. Usually it is only economical to insulate the outside walls. However, you may consider insulating the inner walls of a group of rooms in a large cold house, creating a cosy house within a house. This would also apply to a flat.

Insulated Area

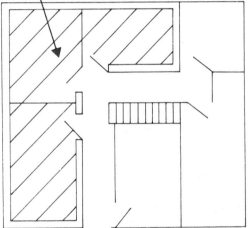

Diagram to show how a section of a large house may be isolated by insulation from the rest

There is a variety of materials and methods available, but the common problem is that the walls are lined and and so made thicker. The extra has to be coped with around door and window frames, light switches and plugs. The work can be done in three stages:

1. Check the Existing Walls

If the walls are damp, knock off some plaster and drill or chip a brick to see if the bricks are damp also. Damp bricks mean that water is getting in from the outside and some treatment will be required before the insulation is applied*

If the plaster alone is damp, this can be due to it taking up water from the air, in which case it will be necessary to remove all of the old plaster. This is not a difficult job, but it is messy — wear a dust mask, use a wide chisel and completely empty the room before you begin.

2. Choose a Suitable Material and Method

You can either fix insulating material directly onto the wall, or by making a framework of wooden battens you can line the wall and leave a cavity behind the material. Further insulation can be achieved by filling this small cavity.

Where the wall is fairly flat, direct fixing is often satisfactory; an uneven wall is given a better finish over a batten framework. However, remember that it is easier and cheaper to fix direct to the wall, but a batten framework gives better insulation, particularly when filled.

It is not worth fixing soft materials to the walls; fibreboard and expanded polystyrene are better avoided as they are so easily damaged.

A visit to your local builders' merchant will show the variety of materials available. Commonly used are sheets of plasterboard with a backing of polystyrene foam, plasterboard with aluminium foil, or plasterboard on its own over battens with glassfibre in the cavity. The plasterboard in each case

faces outwards and can be decorated by a skim of plaster or with a heavy wallpaper.

3. Arrange a Vapour Barrier

If the material you choose does not have a dampproof layer incorporated into it, then it will be necessary to include a vapour barrier in your construction. This can be a sheet of heavy-grade polythene, but heavy aluminium foil is perhaps better as it is waterproof and reflects radiated heat, thus improving the insulation. The barrier goes behind the wall lining and over any glassfibre. Check whether it is required for the material you choose.

Insulation Fixed Directly on to a Solid Wall

Once you have chosen a suitable material, ask the supplier what the recommended fixing method is. If a suitable adhesive is available use it in preference to masonry pins, which, though they give a good strong fix, damage the outer surface of the boards. If you have to use masonry pins check on the packet that they are a suitable length for the thickness of material to be fixed. Use a punch to knock them home and avoid too much marking of the board surface.

Handle the boards carefully and cut them with a sharp knife against a straight-edge. Where the exposed edges show around the windows, cover them with plastic moulding glued on. Irregularities where the board meets an uneven wall can be filled with board-finish or any wall filler.

Cavities in the original wall can be ignored if they are small, but if a large part of the wall is out of true, or if there are a few deep cavities, pads of cloth

*See Tom Pettit's book in this series *Home Maintenance and Outdoor Repairs* for details of dampproofing walls.

can be folded to the correct thickness and soaked in adhesive to take up the space. Alternatively blocks of wood can be cut to fit and used with adhesive on each side.

Calculate the depth to be filled by putting a long straight piece of wood across the wall, measure and mark the places where packing is needed.

Some bumps can be dealt with by chipping off the protruding plaster, but walls seriously out of line or out of true are best dealt with by fixing battens under the insulating lining.

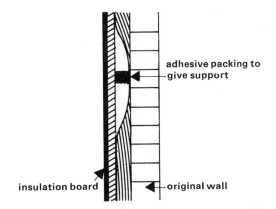

adhesive packing to give support

insulation board

original wall

Diagram to show how packing can be used to provide support and bridge minor gaps

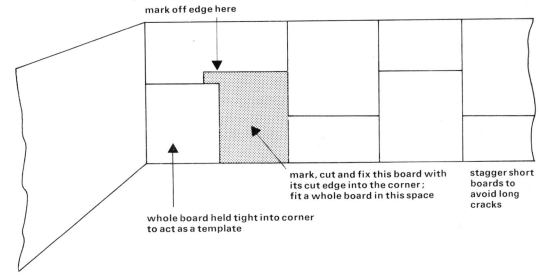

mark off edge here

mark, cut and fix this board with its cut edge into the corner; fit a whole board in this space

stagger short boards to avoid long cracks

whole board held tight into corner to act as a template

This diagram shows how to mark off boards to fit neatly into a corner. The cut edges should be fitted into corners where they can be touched up with plaster if necessary; switches and sockets should be repositioned on top of the the insulation board. In many cases it will be possible to do this using the same fitting fixed into place with longer screws.

Insulation Fixed on to a Batten Framework over a Solid Wall

This method can be used to cover uneven walls and as it creates a space behind the wall-lining material, it gives better insulation — particularly if this space is filled with glassfibre. However, because of the wooden frame-work used to support the insulating panels, it is a much more costly and time-consuming method. Also as the battens give an extra thickness to the walls, it causes some problems with door and window surrounds and with electrical switches and sockets.

1. Materials

If the cavity between the battens is to be insulated with glassfibre or expanded polystyrene sheet, then the new wall can be tongue and groove timber (knotty pine is popular) decorative panelboard, plasterboard or hardboard. If you do not intend to fill the cavity, then plasterboard with a polystyrene backing should be used.

To prevent condensation you must have the usual vapour barrier behind the decorative wall lining and over the insulation. A suitable material is heavy-grade polythene obtainable in large sheets from a builders' merchant or ironmonger. Aluminium foil is good as it both acts as a barrier and reflects radiated heat, thus providing extra insulation. Whatever you use, be careful not to tear it, and fasten up the joins with carpet tape. Do not use a cheap sticky tape for the joins as this will harden and shrink in time, opening gaps and ruining the barrier.

2. Fixing the insulation and battens

If you intend to fasten shelves or heavy objects to the new wall, plan this before you start and fix battens to the wall with plugs and screws under the point where the load will fall.

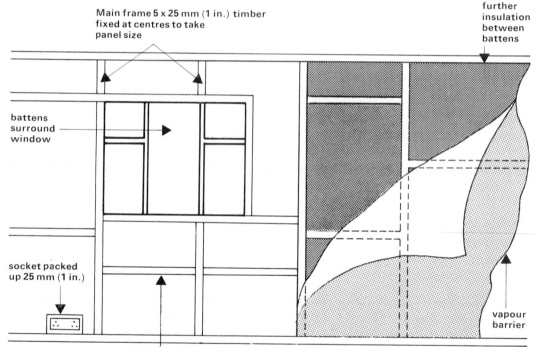

Main frame 5 x 25 mm (1 in.) timber fixed at centres to take panel size

further insulation between battens

battens surround window

socket packed up 25 mm (1 in.)

vapour barrier

subsidiary members of 25 x 25 mm timber to give a maximum unsupported gap of 1 m (3.2 feet) or less if specified for the insulation board you choose

Set up the framework as shown in the diagram. Use 5×25 mm (2×1 in.) timber for main supports and 25×25 mm (1×1 in.) timber for subsidiary supports

Fasten the battens to the wall with masonry nails (25 mm – 1 in. battens require 75 mm – 3 in. nails) or better still with 65 mm (2½ in.) screws plugged in at 450 mm (18 in.) centres. If the wall is very uneven it is necessary to construct the batten frame so that it holds together as a single unit, nailing or screwing the cross pieces to the upright so that large uneven areas can be spanned.

Make sure that the uprights and crosspieces are placed so that the edges of all insulating panels can be fixed to the wood. Plan the whole job out on paper before you begin. Remember to deal with the light switches, power sockets and the skirting board. When you have finished erecting the supporting frame, paint it with a colourless preservative and allow it to dry thoroughly before applying the lining.

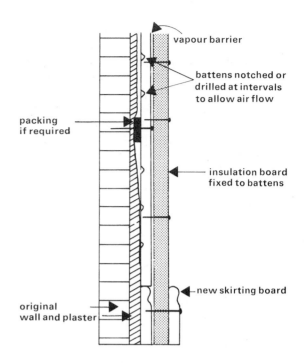

Fix the insulating material using the method recommended by the manufacturer. See the section on fixing insulation boards direct to the wall for further details. On wall corners and around doors and windows where the insulating material has exposed edges, plastic moulding can be used to advantage to give protection to the corners.

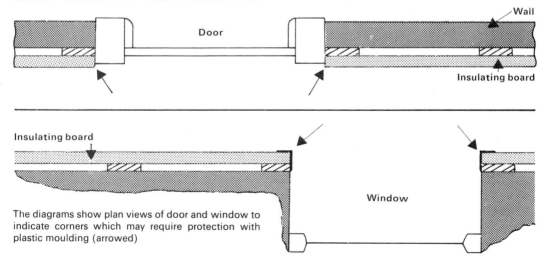

The diagrams show plan views of door and window to indicate corners which may require protection with plastic moulding (arrowed)

Costing the Insulation of Solid Walls

Insulating solid walls in the way we have described may improve them from an original 'U' value of about 2·1 to about 'U'=1·2. This would reduce the heat loss from the rooms insulated to the outside by about 40 to 45 per cent. Insulating all of the outside walls on all floors would reduce your total fuel bill by about 10 to 12 per cent. Insulating with plasterboard and polystyrene over battens and glassfibre may give you a better saving; less effective insulation, or fewer rooms insulated, would reduce the percentage saving.

If you do not wish to go to the trouble of insulating all rooms, the most sensible ones to do are those used most often, and remember it is the outside walls that lose the greatest amount of heat.

You will need to do a detailed costing of all the materials you are likely to use, perhaps costing several alternatives. For instance, assume you are going to insulate the downstairs rooms only: let us say in this case you may save 9 per cent of your total annual fuel bill.

With a total fuel bill of £150:

9 per cent of £150 is $\dfrac{£150 \times 9}{100} =$ **£13·50**

So you would save £13·50 each year. If you spend £160 on materials then it would take $\dfrac{£160}{£13·50} = 11·8$ years, which is approximately twelve years to repay the outlay.

4 Preventing Heat Loss through the Roof

Of the heat lost from an uninsulated house 20 per cent goes out through the roof. Preventing this loss is often one of the easiest and most profitable jobs in house insulation. If you look at the roof of a house after snow or frost you can see how well insulated it is. The frost should stay on all of the roof except the area close to the chimney stack. If the frost on your roof vanishes before that on the roof of your neighbour's house, then you had better see to your loft insulation.

As warm air rises in a house, the ceilings in the upstairs rooms are warmed and a ceiling with poor insulating properties (high 'U' value) becomes a liability. In a two-storey house with a 25 mm (1 in.) insulation blanket in the loft (as specified by the 1965 Building Regulations), 20 per cent of the total heat produced in the house will leak away through the bedroom ceiling and into the roof. If you have no loft insulation at all, or if you live in a bungalow or in a house with the living accommodation directly under the roof, then obviously much more heat will be wasted. The basic principle is, the larger the surface area and the greater the temperature difference on either side of the surface, the greater the heat loss will be.

Materials to Use

The first point to consider is that materials must not be flammable. Proprietary insulating materials should satisfy the Fire Regulations, but do not be tempted to do the job cheaply by filling the loft with shavings or other flammable waste.

Most of the insulating materials for this purpose are 'high void', that is they contain large amounts of air trapped in pockets and acting as an insulator against the conducted heat which accounts for most of the loss.

Aluminium Foil

This is the exception to the 'high void' rule. It only stops radiated heat which is not the major loss through ceilings. It is easily damaged in position (as people tend to store things in lofts) and once dusty or dirty its radiation resistance falls.

Vermiculite

This is a fairly expensive expanded mineral. It is bought by the sackful and used as a loose fill. If you use it buy the insulating variety which is proofed against pests and fungus. The horticultural version is not suitable!

Loose Expanded Polystyrene

This is bought and used like vermiculite, but is usually much cheaper and has a better 'U' value. You can also get slabs of polystyrene but we do not recommend you to use them for this job as it is difficult to fit them exactly in the roof.

Glassfibre

This the material which is most commonly used. It is bought in rolls and laid as a blanket. If possible buy the rolls split to the width of your joists. This material is commonly sold in thicknesses of 80 mm (3¼ in.) or 100 mm (4 in.). As the rolls contain the same quantity of fibre, the 100 mm type will roll out to give a shorter length. Some firms make this material into mats faced with oiled paper.

Mineral Wool

This is bought and used like glassfibre, but it is more expensive.

Insulation Boards

Most of the materials mentioned in the previous chapter on wall insulation (see page 16) can be used for suspended ceilings.

Aluminium foil is not good to use on its own, and as the other materials have similar 'U' values, the choice is restricted to the thickness of the material, its suitability for the job and its cost. Glassfibre must be recommended where possible as it is cheap, easy to lay, has good insulating properties and is not easily disturbed by draughts. It is however most unpleasant to handle.

Thickness of Materials

The diagram below shows the 'U' values for a variety of thicknesses of glassfibre laid above a ceiling.

You will see that over 25 mm (1 in.) there is not a large drop (improvement) in 'U' value as the thickness of the insulation is increased. At the time of writing 80 mm (3.4 in.) is the most economical. Over this thickness you will not get your money back in saved fuel. However, fuel prices will continue to rise and thinking of roof insulation as a long-term investment, 100 mm (4 in.) may be an economical safeguard against future high fuel prices. Certainly if your loft already has an old 25 mm (1 in.) quilt, put an 80 mm (3.4 in.) layer over it.

You can lay loose-fill material to whatever depth you like. By putting down several layers of glassfibre you can do the same with this material.

Thickness

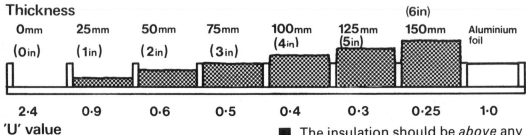

0mm	25mm	50mm	75mm	100mm	125mm	150mm	Aluminium
(0in)	(1in)	(2in)	(3in)	(4in)	(5in)	(6in)	foil
2·4	0·9	0·6	0·5	0·4	0·3	0·25	1·0

'U' value

Laying the Insulation

In this section we discuss the insulation of a variety of roofs. From this information most people should be able to adapt the methods to suit their own circumstances.

Remember the basic principles:

■ The insulation should be *above* any regularly used living area;

■ the insulation should be around and over (never below) the cold-water tank;

■ you must lag any water pipes which are above the finished insulation;

■ do not make the loft completely draughtproof.

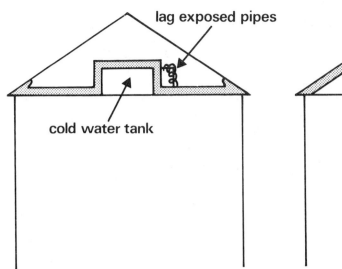

1. Loft vacant or used for storage. Insulation above ceiling and over water tank. Exposed water pipes lagged.

2. Loft in use. Insulation is between rafters faced with plaster board. Partition wall backed with polystyrene slab.

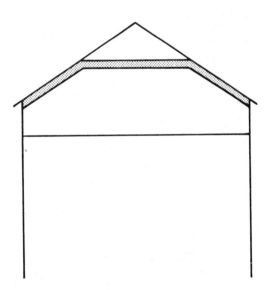

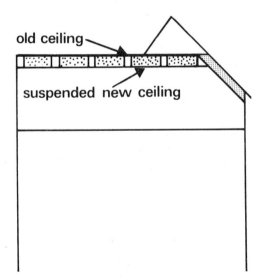

3. Where it is not possible to get above an existing ceiling, a new suspended ceiling is installed with insulation applied between the new battens. Or the old ceiling can be knocked down and replaced after insulating between the existing joists.

4. In this case insulation is pushed carefully down from the loft space into the inaccessible cavity above the sloping ceiling.

Insulating above the Ceiling

Insulating the type of loft shown in diagram 1 on page 333 is relatively easy, and for most householders this will be the job they have to tackle.

You will need an extension lamp, two firm boards to stand on, wide enough to span the joists (do not risk falling through the ceiling!), and we suggest you wear overalls, gloves and a dust-mask if you are handling glass-fibre or mineral wool. You can make a dust-mask by holding a handkerchief over your nose and mouth with a scarf tied round your head. Chemists and ironmongers sell cheap disposable dust-masks which are useful for all sorts of other jobs and we suggest that you buy these if possible. The glass and mineral fibres are very irritating to your skin and can be most distressing when inhaled, so take care to protect yourself.

Laying glassfibre or mineral wool

Start at one side of the loft and roll the quilt out. Turn the quilt up at the eaves but leave one space at either side of the loft where some air can blow through, thus preventing condensation.

The materials are easily cut with scissors or a sharp knife. Do not pack the insulation down, it works best by being loose. However, it must fill all the odd corners, and small pieces can be used for this purpose. If you have a lot of small, odd spaces to fill, you might consider buying. a bag of loose expanded polystyrene for this purpose.

RIGHT

Fill in up and down between the joists *not across them*

WRONG

Draughts blow through the spaces next to the joists and spoil the effect of the insulation

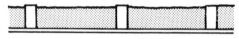

If you wish to build up a deep quilt, you can lay the second layer across the joists

Insulating the Cold Tank

Leave the space underneath the cold tank without insulation to allow some heat to rise and prevent it from freezing.

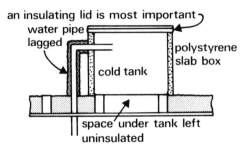

an insulating lid is most important
water pipe lagged
polystyrene slab box
cold tank
space under tank left uninsulated

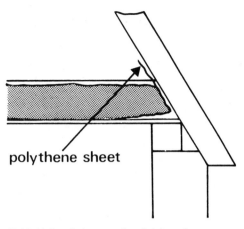

polythene sheet

Fold thick polythene and tuck it into the eaves to stop the granules falling through the spaces there.

Glassfibre can be used to insulate the tank, but it tends to fall apart when used in this way. It is better to make, or buy readymade, a box of expanded polystyrene slabs. Where possible water-pipes should be covered by the quilt, otherwise wrap them with a pipe-lagging material. Nail or glue glassfibre or a piece of expanded polystyrene onto the back of the loft trapdoor. If it is a bad fit, draughtproof the edges.

Using Vermiculite or Loose Polystyrene

Loose-fill insulation materials can be spread straight from the sack and levelled to the depth required with a template cut from scrap wood.

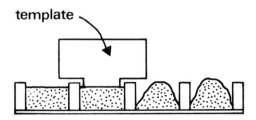

template

Some Other Points

Once installed, these types of insulation should last a lifetime providing that the material is not disturbed or packed down. Avoid storing things standing on the loft insulation. If you use the loft for storage, consider putting down chipboard for a floor over the joists. This will further improve insulation.

As loft insulation hides most of the pipes and wires up there, mark the surface of the insulating·material with sticky tape or paint to show the position of pipes, wires and particularly ceiling lights.

Insulating under a Ceiling

To insulate ceilings where the loft space is not accessible, or the ceiling of a flat, for instance, it is necessary to suspend the insulation below the existing ceiling (see diagram 3, page 333). We give the methods most commonly used. These can also be modified to insulate the rafters of a loft space that is used for living in.

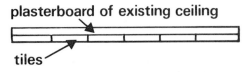

plasterboard of existing ceiling

tiles

12.5 mm ($\frac{1}{2}$ in.) polystyrene tiles can be stuck onto the ceiling. The insulation they provide is not particularly good, but this is a cheap and easy method. Make sure they are self-extinguishing in case of fire.

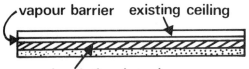

vapour barrier   existing ceiling

new insulation board

(polystyrene faced with plaster)

Plasterboard with a polystyrene backing can be pinned to the ceiling joists over a vapour barrier of aluminium foil. Push a spike through the old ceiling to mark accurately the position of the joists. See the section on insulating walls for further details of handling this material and use pins that will not rust. If you are to have the ceiling plastered, then galvanised nails are most suitable.

Further Methods of Insulation

Though the previous methods are quite satisfactory, better insulation and soundproofing is obtained by using the following systems:

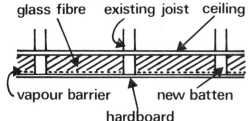

glass fibre   existing joist   ceiling

vapour barrier   new batten

hardboard

1. Fix new battens over the existing joists, using 40 x 40 mm (approx 1$\frac{1}{2}$ x 1$\frac{1}{2}$ in.) timber. Fill the spaces between the battens with a thin glassfibre quilt or polystyrene slabs, and cover the whole lot with a vapour barrier and hardboard (see the section on floor insulation for the method of treating hardboard). However careful you are the hardboard will tend to bulge and this scheme is not recommended for rooms where you are concerned about having an absolutely flat ceiling.

2. The most effective method, but also the most expensive, is as follows:

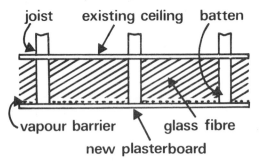

joist   existing ceiling   batten

vapour barrier   glass fibre

new plasterboard

Fix 75 x 50 mm (3 in. x 2 in.) battens under the existing joists and fill in with 75 mm glassfibre held above an aluminium or polythene vapour barrier and finished with plasterboard.

3. For increased sound insulation against aircraft or impact noise from above, pin egg-cartons above a thinner glassfibre quilt.

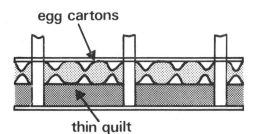

egg cartons

thin quilt

4. You could also replace the plasterboard with cellular construction wall partition board, though by now the work will be uneconomical in terms of energy saving.

Insulating between Feature Beams

If you have rafters or beams which you wish to preserve as a feature of the room, it is sometimes possible to insulate between them.

Fix 25 x 40 mm (1 x $1\frac{1}{2}$ in.) battens to the side of the beams and suspend cut hardboard or plasterboard as shown in the diagram. This method is time consuming and wasteful of materials, but does preserve some of the character of a room. You have to work out how much rafter or beam you want to show, bearing in mind the thickness of the insulation (see page 332), and come to a suitable compromise.

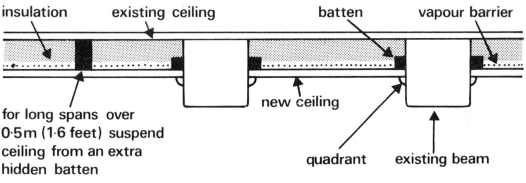

insulation   existing ceiling   batten   vapour barrier

new ceiling

for long spans over 0·5m (1·6 feet) suspend ceiling from an extra hidden batten

quadrant   existing beam

Costing Roof Insulation

Because of the variety of materials you could use, it is impossible to give accurate figures. As with solid wall insulation we advise you to cost several alternatives.

Remember that with a suspended ceiling containing 75 mm (3 in.) of glassfibre you can reduce heat loss through the roof by about 80 per cent. You can save a similar figure with an 80 mm (3.4 in.) quilt above the ceiling. In the case of suspended ceilings, the big expense is wood and plasterboard.

As more than 20 per cent of your heat is lost through the roof, insulating in this way can reduce your total fuel bills by about 15 per cent. (This would not apply to insulation by polystyrene tiles which would give a much lower saving although costing much less than other methods).

With a fuel bill of £150, 15 per cent is

$$\frac{£150 \times 15}{100} = \textbf{£22.50} \text{ saved each}$$

year. If you spend £50 on a glassfibre quilt, you could get your money back in

$$\frac{£50}{22.50} = \text{about two years.}$$

After that you would make a profit.

Find 15 per cent of your annual fuel bill:

$$\frac{\text{fuel bill}}{100} \times 15 = \text{annual saving;}$$

cost a few alternatives and divide the cost by your annual saving to see how many years it takes to get your money back:

$$\frac{\text{cost of insulation}}{\text{annual saving}} = \frac{\text{number of years}}{\text{to repay outlay}}$$

The final decision is then up to you.

5 Preventing Heat Loss through Floors

Very little attention is ever given to insulating floors, yet they are responsible for 10 per cent of lost heat.

If you are having a new house built on a concrete raft, it will be worthwhile to consult the architect or builder about having a 75 mm (3 in.) layer of lightweight blocks, foamed PVC or other suitable high-void material under the final floor screed.

Insulating Existing Solid Floors

A 100 mm (4 in.) thick solid floor may have a 'U' value as high as 3.0. A carpet with a good thick underlay or foam back is probably the most economical way of preventing heat loss. However if you have a floor in bad condition and you wish to resurface it, then it is probably worthwhile to include insulation as part of the work. If the floor is damp, include a dampproof membrane (DPM) of builder's polythene or bitumen paint.

On a floor with minor irregularities lay large expanded polystyrene sheets over the DPM and cover with tongue-and-grooved chipboard.

Do not allow the joins in the polystyrene to coincide with those in the chipboard. Turn the DPM up and fasten it behind the skirting board — which will have to be raised. If you use polythene, handle it with care and check that there are no nails or sharp pieces of grit on the floor. If punctured it loses its usefulness. Fasten the chipboard with wood glue at the tongue and groove, otherwise it is not fastened to anything else. It is held in place by its own weight and the overlapping skirting board.

If the original floor is very uneven it will be necessary to give it an initial screed of concrete to flatten it before laying the DPM and insulation. Cork tiles can be used on a flat dry floor to give both good insulation and a good decorative effect. Whatever materials you use, you will need to cut the bottom from doors opening into the room, to allow for the increase in floor height.

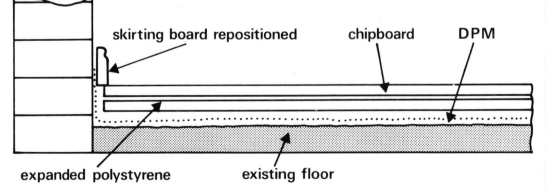

skirting board repositioned   chipboard   DPM

expanded polystyrene   existing floor

338

Insulating over the Floor

A bare timber floor on joists has a 'U' value of about 1.9. This figure can be improved on by either laying insulation over, or suspending it under, the floorboards. Do not forget that floors, particularly around the edges, can be draughty. See to the draughts as part of your floor insulation programme.

Insulating Suspended Floors

Soft Insulating Fibreboard

This is useful over a rough floor as it takes up the irregularities. It has good insulating properties, but being soft it needs protecting with a strong floor covering, and heavy furniture tends to sink into it. The skirting boards will need to be raised and doors trimmed to accommodate the thickness of the sheet.

Before laying, spread the sheets out on the floor of the room where they are to be laid, or stack them on end separated by pieces of wood. This allows air to circulate around each sheet and they adjust to the moisture content of the room. Leave them like this for at least two days before fixing into place.

Cut the material with a trimming knife and nail it to the floor. Stagger the joints and avoid butting the boards over a floorboard joint if at all possible.

Lay the boards like this:

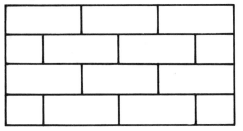

In view of the expense and difficulty of this method we would only recommend it for a really cold floor where you cannot get underneath to suspend insulation.

Hardboard

This can stop draughts through gaps in floorboards and it is a useful base upon which to lay tiles or vinyl flooring.

Buy the sheets as large as you can manage to handle. As hardboard swells when wet, avoid uneven floors by wetting the rough side of the boards with water, about $\frac{1}{4}$ litre per m^2 ($\frac{1}{2}$ pint per square yard approximately) applied with a watering can. Stack the boards flat on top of each other and use after two days. After this time they will have swollen to their full size and when nailed down they will shrink and become taut. Lay hardboard as fibreboard, but cut with a fine-toothed tenon or panelsaw.

The insulation value of hardboard is not very good and again it is better to get under the floor if you can.

Aluminium Foil

This is probably the easiest and cheapest means of stopping draughts and radiated heat. However, if you have a very cold floor that is cold to the touch, it will not be much improved by this method.

Use the strengthened foil which is available from builders' merchants and ironmongers in wide rolls. *Kitchen foil is no use!* Make sure the floor is clean and free from protruding nails. Roll the foil out, turning it 25 mm (1 in.) up the skirting-board. Overlap adjacent lengths and fix with carpet tape.

Pin 12.5 mm ($\frac{1}{2}$ in.) quadrant in the angle between the floor and skirting board to trap the foil and stop floor-edge draughts. Re-lay the carpet with care.

This is a very effective method for most floors as, unlike roofs, 70 per cent of the heat lost here is by radiation.

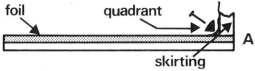

foil   quadrant   A

skirting

Insulating under the Floor

If you can get under the floor, then insulating here saves a great deal of upheaval in the rooms you insulate. It can, however, be a most unpleasant job. Go down and have a look before deciding on the method you are to use.

Aluminium Foil

Buy it as described above, pin it under the joists with drawing pins, overlapping the lengths.

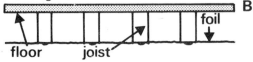

B

foil

floor   joist

Polystyrene

Unless you can get the slabs under the floor easily, do not consider this method.

Fasten 12.5 mm ($\frac{1}{2}$ in.) battens to the joists. Cut the slabs to size with a trimming knife and manoeuvre it into place to sit on the battens.

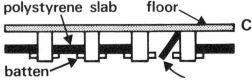

polystyrene slab   floor   C

batten

Glassfibre

Protect yourself and handle the material as described on page 334. Pin the quilt onto the joists with battens.

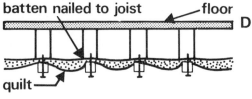

batten nailed to joist   floor   D

quilt

Costing Floor Insulation

Of the whole heat loss from a house, 10 per cent is through the floor, 7 per cent by radiation and 3 per cent by conduction and draughts.

Aluminium foil under or over the floor can improve the 'U' value of a suspended wooden floor from 1.9 to 0.7. This is a reduction of 37 per cent of the heat lost through the floor, and 3.7 per cent of the heat lost from the whole house. 50 mm (2 in.) of glassfibre under the joists reduces the 'U' value from 1.9 to 1.6, a reduction of 13 per cent of heat lost and 1.3 per cent of the heat lost from the whole house.

Unless you have a floor which is very cold to touch we would recommend that you use aluminium foil. You can decide whether it is to go under or on top of the floorboards, as this is just a matter of convenience. With aluminium foil you should get back about 3.7 per cent of your fuel bill each year. With an annual fuel bill of £150: 3.7 per cent of £150 is: $\frac{£150}{100} \times 3.7 = £5.55$.

If you spend £10 on the foil then you get your money back after about two years.

In the case of a floor which is cold to touch, glassfibre from below or insulation board from above may solve the problem. However, with a saving of only 1.3 per cent per year, the return on this outlay will be very slow. You may be better off with a new carpet over aluminium foil.

In the case of a solid floor, a good carpet is as useful as anything unless you happen to be doing structural alterations anyway.

6 Preventing Heat Loss through Draughts

If you leave doors and windows open in winter, then you can lose almost 100 per cent of your heat through draughts! However, most people are sensible about leaving doors and windows closed when rooms are being heated and so on average only 10 per cent of heat is lost through draughts.

Draughts are worth treating as they often cause a great deal of personal discomfort and are relatively easy and cheap to cure. They are most noticeable in houses with open fireplaces, and in fact a large old house with a lot of open fireplaces can lose up to 25 per cent of its heat up the chimney with the draught.

Remember that still air is an excellent insulator, so treat the inside doors as well as external doors and windows. The object is not to produce an airtight house, however, as some air flow is needed to prevent condensation. Also boilers and fires which use air from the room are dangerous unless the room is adequately ventilated. It is illegal to use gas appliances without proper ventilation — your Gas Board office or showroom will advise you on this.

So the idea is not to remove all draughts, but to reduce them to an acceptable level and to redistribute them so that they are not noticeable, a few small leaks being better than one howling gale from under the door.

To give you some idea of the amount of air flow required we have included this table:

Room	Recommended temperature		Air changes per hour
	(°C)	(°F)	
Kitchen	15	(60)	3
Hall	15	(60)	2
Bathroom	18	(65)	2
Dining-room	20	(68)	1–1½
Lounge	20	(68)	1–1½
Bedroom	12	(54)	1–1½

You can see that in each room all of the air should be replaced fairly frequently.

Draughts are most noticeable in winter, but do not wait until then to cure them as this is one of the least pleasant jobs on a winter's evening. Check for draughts on a windy day around doors and windows with a wet finger, by blowing smoke, or with a candle or lighter flame. Note the draughty areas.

Draughts are caused by a poor seal between two surfaces, usually the opening part of doors and windows, but occasionally a poor fit between the wooden frame and the plaster of the wall can allow air to flow from the cavity of the wall, or even from outside. In the case of cracks around frames, they are easily filled with a wall-filler or plaster.

Draughts from Floors

We have dealt with this problem in a previous section. However if you are treating draughtproofing as a minor job and do not wish to get involved in the major upheaval of reflooring, a simple way of dealing with draughts from around the skirting board is as follows: Make papier-mâché from newspapers and wallpaper paste — use the heavy duty type with a fungicide — roll back the edge of the carpet and stuff this mixture into the cracks with a putty knife or old kitchen knife. Let it dry and refasten the carpet.

Draughts from Windows

One cure for window draughts is to double-glaze over the entire window (see the section on page 349 on double-glazing) but easier and cheaper solutions are to be found. You can see from the diagram below where draughts are likely to occur.

draughts from cavity　　　**draughts from ill–fitting woodwork**

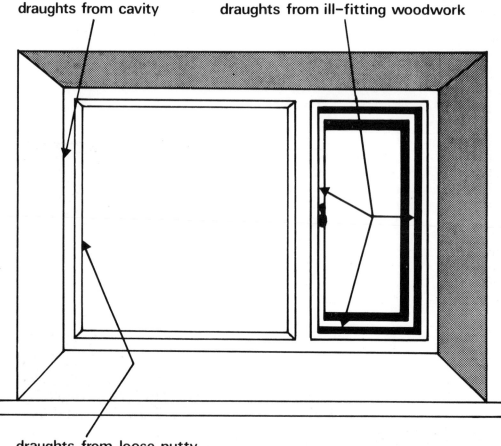

draughts from loose putty

Draughts from the Cavity

These can be cured by filling the crack with a wall filler such as Polyfilla.

Draughts from the Glass Edge

This will be caused by old loose putty. Remove and replace the putty giving it a coat of gloss paint for protection.*

Draughts from ill-fitting Woodwork

Look at the size of the gaps and choose a material that will allow you to close the window properly. You may need two different types or sizes of insulation if the window is badly warped. The following are effective:

- Plastic foam strip
- Weatherstrip
- Plastic tubing.

Plastic foam strip is cheap and effective. It is sold in rolls, and one side of the strip is self-adhesive. Make sure the woodwork is clean and dry before you apply the strip. Do not stick the strip into non-existent gaps, or you will not be able to close the window.

This type of insulation requires replacing every few years, particularly as it tends to accumulate dirt and as it yellows with age. However, it is very cheap and easy to apply so the replacement is not a problem. It is also the only type of draughtproofing that is easily applied to metal frames.

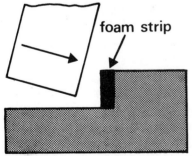

Stick the strip so that the window closes against the foam.

*Full details of reglazing are given in Tom Pettit's book in this series, *Home Maintenance and Outdoor Repairs.*

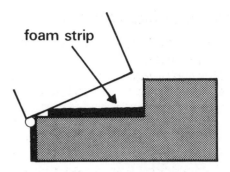

On the hinge side stick the strip here.

Weatherstrip is a plastic or metal strip which is nailed to the frame edge. Make sure that it is positioned so that the strip is against the window when it is closed.

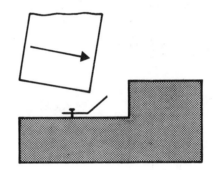

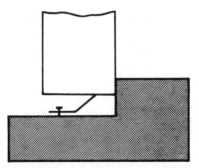

This material will need replacing at intervals; the metal strip lasts longest (up to eight years) but is much more expensive than the plastic strip.

An alternative type is fixed like this:

There are two types of plastic tubing, both noticeable, particularly from the outside of the window.

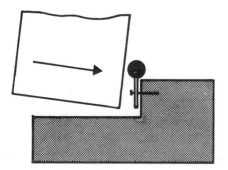

This type is relatively cheap, being made entirely of plastic.

This type, having an aluminium fastening, is expensive.

On the whole we have found the foam strip a useful draught-excluder. Particularly in view of its ease of application and low price we would recommend its use where possible. There are various thicknesses and qualities; the more expensive types are denser and discolour less easily.

Sash Windows

These can be a problem because the surfaces slide over one another. At the moment the proprietary cures are so expensive that you might consider overglazing the window (see the next section). However, you could experiment with one of the methods described above and try to draughtproof the horizontal rails where the material would be compressed. Once closed, the window can be wedged back with a small wooden wedge. The vertical edges, being interlocked, will provide a reasonable seal of their own.

Other Cures for Draughty Windows

If you do not need to open the window, then mastic or putty applied to the window frame and trapped by closing the window gives a near-perfect seal. Trim off the excess so that it is not noticeable. In the spring the window can be opened and cleaned up. Alternatively, it can be left permanently fastened and painted over.

Masking tape stuck over the cracks is a good draughtproofing; it looks unsightly but may be useful for attics and garages. It too can be pulled off when the warm weather requires the window to be opened.

Remember that whatever else you do, a good thick pair of closed curtains stops both draughts and radiation losses through windows.

Draughts from Doors

Minor gaps around doors can be dealt with in exactly the same way as windows.

Excessive gaps caused by warping can be dealt with by cutting a long sliver of wood which is glued into the gap. Be careful not to cut the piece too thick as this will make the situation worse. Once you have the door closing up to wood all around the frame, then you can use the normal draughtproofing materials.

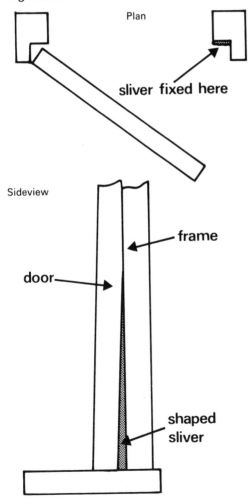

Plan

sliver fixed here

Sideview

frame

door

shaped sliver

Another or an additional cure is to fit a bolt to *pull* in the door to the frame. Fit the bolt so that when the bolt is home, the warped part of the door is pulled tight to the frame. This is useful on doors which are not often used, but as the bolt will obviously be a very tight fit, it is not the most effective method to use on the main door of the house.

Curtains hung over doors, particularly those with glass in them are effective and it is possible to buy curtain rails that open with the door.

The worst draughts come from under doors, in particular those which have been inaccurately cut down to ride over a carpet. Traditionally a 'dog' or sausage of material is used to exclude the draught, but it needs adjusting every time the door is opened.

Interior Doors
There is a variety of ready-made excluders which work effectively.

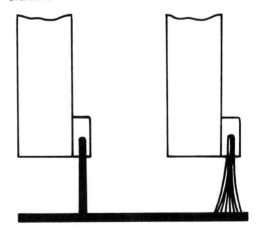

■ Draught strips
These are plastic, rubber or bristles fastened in a strip which sticks or nails to the door. The draughtproofing material hangs down and brushes the floor.

They are efficient and unobtrusive. The stiffer versions tend to wear the carpet near the door. Bristles are better if used over a smooth floor. Make sure that you buy the strip long enough for the door; the longer ones can be trimmed to length. The strips will wear out after a time and require replacing every few years. For sliding doors special wool or bristle excluders are obtainable.

■ Interior threshold excluders
These fasten to the floor and have a strip of foam rubber which seals the gap when the door is closed over it. They are rather more obtrusive than the draught strips and wear rapidly with heavy traffic over them. The bottom of the door may need to be cut, or added to, to accommodate them.

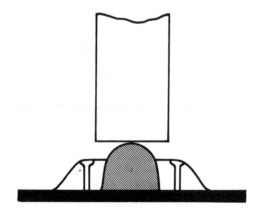

Exterior Doors
Excluders for these doors need to be of heavier construction than those used for internal doors.

■ Draught strip
This can be fitted in the same manner as for internal doors; however, because of the extra grit around outside doors, they wear away very quickly.

■ Hinged excluders
These work on the principle of the plain draught strip, but are hinged. They lift away from the floor when the door is open, thus reducing wear. When the door closes the strip is forced down by a striker plate to make a good seal. This excluder is more expensive than the plain strip, but lasts much longer. It should be good for five to six years.

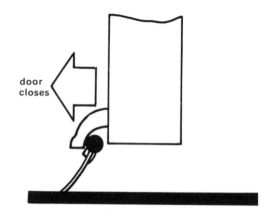

■ Threshold excluders
To fit these you have to remove the wooden threshold bar. If you saw through it in two places it can be levered up with a chisel. The replacement is a strong aluminium threshold incorporating a rubber strip.

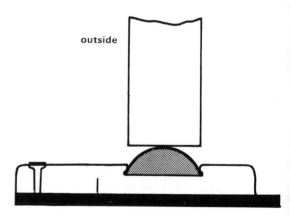

It is easy to screw one of these to a wooden floor, but on a concrete or stone threshold you will have to drill and plug first. Once in place the threshold should be no more of an obstacle than the bar it replaces; however, the door may require removal, trimming and rehanging. Saw or plane the required amount from the bottom of the door, giving a slight bevel towards the outside. Do not be tempted to cut too much off the door at one time. It is better to have several attempts rather than to finish up with a bigger gap than before.

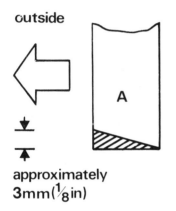

outside

approximately 3mm($\frac{1}{8}$in)

If the door has too large a gap, then nail and glue a strip of wood to the bottom. Treat it with preservative before rehanging. If you need to plane down the new strip, punch down the nails first. We suggest nails and glue rather than glue alone, as most people will wish to rehang the door as soon as possible and the excluder would dislodge a glued strip.

When you have finished, the bottom of the door should make a firm seal with the excluder; but it should not be so tight that you have difficulty in in opening and closing the door.

■ Combination excluders
These are the most hardwearing, but they probably present the greatest obstacle to your feet.

There are various patterns working on the principle of a metal strip on the door contacting a metal seal on the floor. The floor seal replaces the normal threshold. When fitting this type of excluder, fit the floor strip exactly under where the door closes; then with the door closed, screw the door-fitting strip into place. Ensure a firm fit without jamming.

In the case of a very badly warped or rotten door, it may be advisable to start again with a new door.[*]

Costing Draughtproofing

This is the one type of insulation that gives instant rewards; you will immediately notice the difference when effective draughtproofing is installed. Although the savings are not as large as you may imagine from the improvement you feel, in view of the relative cheapness of the insulation, it is a worthwhile investment.

[*]See *Home Maintenance and Outdoor Repairs* by Tom Pettit.

347

If 10 per cent of your total heat is lost through draughts, you may well reduce this figure to 3 per cent with draught-proofing. So if you save 7 per cent of your fuel bill each year, with a bill of £150: $\frac{£150}{100} \times 7 =$ **£10.50** saved each year.

Unless your house is very draughty, it is not likely to cost you much more than £10 to £15 for the work, so you will quickly recover the cost. Older draughty houses will cost more to draughtproof, but as up to 25 per cent of the heat loss in these places may be through draughts, it is still worthwhile to spend the money on the work.

7 Preventing Heat Loss through Glass

About 10 per cent of your total heat is lost through the glass and frames of windows by radiation and conduction (this does not include heat loss through draughts). Half of this heat is lost through radiation, half through conduction.

Double-glazing

Double-glazing is usually thought of as the answer to this problem. It works on the principle of trapping a layer of still air between two windows.

While double-glazing can cut down conduction, it cannot prevent radiation losses. It can lessen condensation on windows, and some types can prevent draughts, but assuming for the moment that you have cheaply cured your draughts with foam strip, then double-glazing will only save you about 5 per cent of your heat, and it is the most expensive form of insulation. Its main advantages are in a house with a large area of glass, or as a selling point because it has a certain prestige value. It also has some advantages in sound-proofing, though the principles of soundproofing and insulation are not altogether compatible.

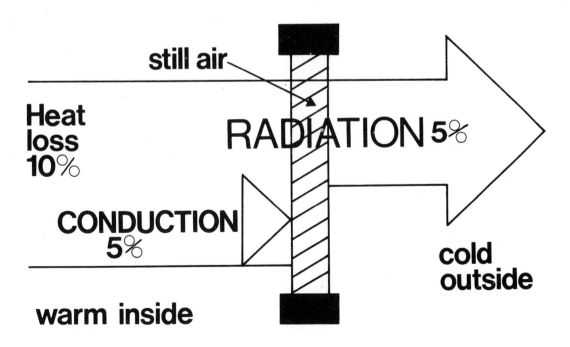

still air

Heat loss 10%

RADIATION 5%

CONDUCTION 5%

warm inside

cold outside

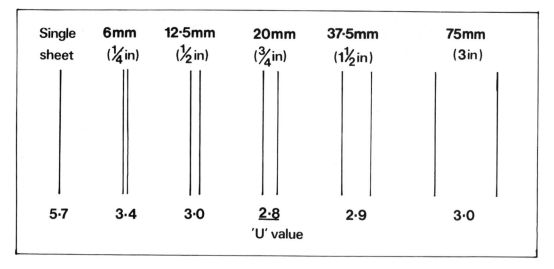

Single sheet	6mm (¼in)	12·5mm (½in)	20mm (¾in)	37·5mm (1½in)	75mm (3in)
5·7	3·4	3·0	<u>2·8</u>	2·9	3·0

'U' value

The diagram above shows the 'U' values for double-glazing with various gaps between the panes.

You will see by the underlined figure above that the optimum gap for insulating purposes is about 20 mm ($\frac{3}{4}$ in.). Below this conduction takes place across the gap and the insulation value is affected. Above this the space is large enough for convection currents to be set up transferring heat from one surface to another and though this is not as serious a problem as with a small gap, it does reduce the insulation value.

With a gap of 75 mm (3 in.) you have the optimum size for sound insulation, but as we have said it is rather too large for useful thermal insulation.

There are many different types of double-glazing; you do not necessarily have to use the same type throughout the whole house. Look at each window and judge its requirements.

Sealed units are inconspicuous and can replace large single windows or the individual panes of smaller windows.

You could probably install the type below yourself.

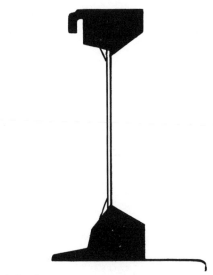

Sealed unit

Secondary windows can be bought or made. They fix inside or outside the existing frame. They can separately cover each pane, but if constructed to cover the whole window it would also act as a draughtproofing measure.

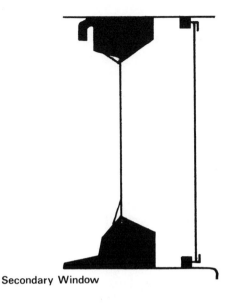

Secondary Window

In the case of secondary windows, it is advisable to have the extra glass removable by sliding, or have it mounted on hinges for cleaning or summer ventilation.

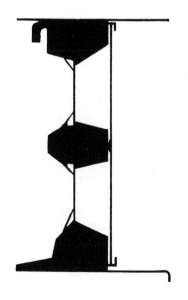

The cheapest common form of double-glazing is a sheet of glass held in place by plastic screw-on channel. Each pane is covered separately so it does not stop draughts. The more expensive systems include elaborate slides in aluminium frames.

Even cheaper than the glass in plastic channel is a sheet of plastic stretched over the window and held on double-sided adhesive tape. It is only useful for one winter and is unsightly, but you may consider it for little-used rooms.

Costing Double-glazing

We have not devoted much space to the large subject of double-glazing because within our terms of reference we do not consider it economical. If you wish to invest in this form of insulation consider the cost carefully, select particular windows and choose the cheapest type which suits your requirements.

You can save 5 per cent of your annual fuel bill if you double-glaze the entire house, perhaps 8 per cent if the system cures draughty windows; 5 per cent of an annual fuel bill of £150 is $\frac{£150}{100} \times 5 =$ **£7.50**. If the double glazing cost £300 then it would repay its costs in $\frac{£300}{£7.50} = 40$ years.

The cheapest form of double-glazing is a sheet of glass held in place by a plastic screw-on channel

8 Saving on Fuels and Heating

Of the energy you use, about 80 per cent is used for heating the house and supplying hot water. The remaining 20 per cent is used for lighting, cooking and so on. This chapter compares the various fuels available, as used for heating, and looks at their relative advantages and disadvantages in both cost and ease of use. How we keep the heat in the house once we have got it from the fuel has been dealt with in the previous chapters.

The advice here will be of most use to those buying a house or installing a new heating system, but for those with existing heating it will give a good idea of the heating costs.

The Advantages and Disadvantages of Fuels

Electricity
Electricity is pure energy. It is convenient and comes straight along the wires with no effort on your part. Practically every house already has it installed, so there are few extra costs when installing electric heating. It is indispensable for lighting etc., but it does not lend itself to central heating very well. However, it will always be available, even when other fuels are scarce. The relative costs of these fuels are dealt with later in this chapter.

Gas
You may be unlucky and have a house that does not have a gas supply. Gas is not always put into new houses, and if it is not already there it can be awkward and expensive to get it there. However, once piped in it is as convenient and clean as electricity. Many people swear by it for cooking and it is effective both for room fires and for central heating. It is not quite so flexible as electricity in that you cannot carry a gas fire from room to room as you can an electric fire, but gas fires do look and feel considerably more like the real thing.

Oil
Oil is a fuel for central heating only. It cannot provide heat for individual rooms. It requires a large storage tank which can be an eyesore and take up much-needed space. You are dependent upon deliveries of oil which you have to remember to order, and you will find with many oil central heating systems that the oil tank is only slightly bigger than the minimum load of oil that you can get delivered. This means that you have to run yourself nearly completely out of oil before a full load will fit into the tank. If you find that you need more oil when there is a shortage, you could find yourself without for several days, usually at the coldest time of the year. Oil is in increasingly short supply worldwide, and as it is needed for so many other things the price could well go up again.

Paraffin

Paraffin is a fairly cheap fuel but it is one with great disadvantages. It must be fetched and carried and stored. It smells strongly and so do paraffin heaters if not properly cleaned and adjusted. When burnt it creates a great deal of water, and so leads to condensation unless you leave windows open for ventilation, which in cold weather can seriously reduce the effect of the heating. Lastly, it can be dangerous, particularly if there are young children or large dogs in the house who could knock a stove over.

Solid Fuels, Coal and Wood

The merits of these depend much on whether you use an open-grate fire, a closed fire or a boiler. In general, though, these fuels require fetching and carrying, often from an outside storage, which is particularly annoying on cold wet days. They can bring a lot of dirt into a house, grates need cleaning and the ashes need taking out, which is also very time-consuming. On the positive side there is nothing more pleasant than a good roaring coal fire on a cold winter's day, even if it is using energy at twice the rate it should.

Coal is in fairly plentiful supply and is likely to remain so, though smokeless fuels occasionally become hard to get. Wood is the only renewable fuel resource available to us, and from that point of view we should use more wood and less of the other fuels, but there is just not enough space to grow that much timber. There are a few areas in the country where it would be possible to consider wood as a main heating fuel, and there are stoves made which

will burn it economically, but that is not for the majority of us.

Comparing the Costs of Different Fuels

It is not possible to simply compare the amounts of energy available from the different fuels, because they require different devices to burn them and liberate the energy from them. These have different efficiencies, that is to say some kinds of fire lose more heat than other kinds. With an open fire or a gas boiler some of the heat is lost up the chimney, whereas with electricity you get all of the energy available. This does not necessarily make electricity cheaper. The Electricity Board had to burn oil or coal in order to make the electricity for you, and the energy that they lost up the chimney is reflected in the price. A comparison, then, has to take account of all these things.

This costing information may be useful for two reasons. Firstly, if you are thinking of installing a new heating system then you will wish to compare the losses inherent in each system, and secondly, it will give you an average fuel consumption figure against which to compare your own fuel consumption.

The amount of energy that a particular system uses to heat a house is not likely to change much, whereas the cost of the energy and of fires and boilers *is* going to change, the cost of the energy taking an ever-increasing share as it becomes scarcer. For this reason, all that we have listed here are the approximate amounts of a fuel needed taking account of the losses involved.

A cost comparison depends upon the present cost of fuel, and this can only be worked out by using up-to-date prices. Empty spaces have been left in the tables below, and the section on cost calculation gives all the information for you to fill in individually. Do not forget maintenance costs.

The figures given below are typical of a house in the South of England. If you live in the Midlands you will use about one-tenth more fuel and if you live in Scotland add one-fifth to these quantities. Similarly if you live in an exposed place, you might need as much as a further one-fifth. We have used three particular examples here, and we hope that you will be able to refer this information to your own home.

1. Heating One Room				
Annual fuel consumption for each type of heater	Current cost of each unit of fuel	Maintenance costs per year	Total cost per year to run	Cost of heater and installation
Paraffin stove—340 litres (75 gallons)/year				
Open grate fire—1·25 tonnes (25 cwt) of coal, or 1 tonne (20 cwt) smokeless fuel				
Closed grate fire— 0·75 tonnes (15 cwt) smokeless fuel				
Gas fire – 200 therms				
Electric storage heater— 3500 units (white meter rate)				
Electric fire—3000 units at day rate				

2. Providing a separate hot water supply				
Annual fuel consumption for each type of heater	Current cost of each unit of fuel	Maintenance cost per year	Total cost per year to run	Cost of heater and installation
Smokeless fuel independent water heater— 0·7 tonnes (14 cwt) of anthracite				
Gas water heater— 235 therms				
Electric immersion heater on white meter tariff – 4000 units on night rate and 600 units on day rate				
Electric immersion heater on general domestic tariff—4600 units on day rate				

3. Full central heating including hot water

Annual fuel consumption for each type of system	Current cost of each unit of fuel	Maintenance cost per year	Total cost per year to run	Cost of installing the system
Oil fired boiler—2272 litres (500 gallons) of standard burning oil				
Gas fired boiler— 800 therms of gas				
Smokeless fuel; gravity-fed room heater with a back boiler —55 cwt anthracite beans				
Electric storage radiators on white meter tariff. 5 radiators and an immersion heater. 18000 units on night rate; 2000 units on *day* rate				

The Advantages and Disadvantages of Different Types of Heating Unit

The primary aim of a fire type of heating unit is obviously to heat a room or a house, but traditionally the fire has served as the focal point of a room, with the furniture arranged so that people can gather round the fire. When planning your home the aim must be to make it look warm and comforting, as well as to actually keep it warm. For some people this can only be done by having a fire with real flames; the sort of person who really enjoys standing with their back to a fire will probably not listen in an unbiased way to arguments about relative fuel consumption and waste of energy.

However, the look of warmth can also be created in other ways. Small rooms look warmer than larger rooms, as do rooms with carpets as opposed to bare boards.

Rooms decorated in warm colours and containing soft furnishings also create the illusion of warmth. Even the lighting can help if you arrange to have several small lights each with their own pool of light, instead of a single central light for the whole room. All this is applied psychology, but it will definitely help you to refrain from lighting a fire or turning the central heating up.

Electric Fires

There are two basic types of electric fire, the radiant type that glows red hot and reflects the heat straight out into the room, and the convector or fan-heater type, which heats the air of the room but does not glow red hot. If you require a fire that looks like a fire then the convector type will not be of any use to you, but both types are just as effective for heating the room. Most electric fires are portable, and this increases their usefulness. They are also fairly controllable and they can be switched on and off with ease, so they can be turned off if you leave the room; energy will not be lost that way. There is no energy wasted in turning the electricity into heat, but this is reflected in the price, because the Electricity Board lost some energy when they converted the oil or coal into electricity.

The only disadvantage of all electric heating is that it tends to make the air in the house very dry. Fan heaters are particularly drying because they make the air circulate around the room faster than it would normally. Fan heaters can also be annoying in that some varieties make a considerable amount of noise.

Electric Night Storage Heaters

The idea behind these is that they use electricity when nobody else is using it — at night. As the Electricity Board have to keep their generators running at night anyway, and they need to supply a certain amount of electricity to run the generators efficiently, it is in their interests to encourage people to use it at night. They therefore offer it at a cheaper rate. This is known as the white meter tariff, and the Electricity Board have to install a second electricity meter if you wish to use it. This and the additional wiring necessary will add to the installation costs of these heaters.

The heaters themselves are simply large boxes which contain bricks.

These are heated up during the night and then allowed to cool during the day, thus giving up their heat to the room. The comments about electricity as a fuel made above also apply here but there are some additional points. Night storage heaters are not portable, they are very heavy, so you must have them precisely where they will be needed, and they cannot be moved out off, but they cannot be turned up and down, so that they do not possess the flexibility of an ordinary electric fire. In fact the time clock which controls the period during which they heat up, and hence the amount of energy they use, can only be adjusted by the Electricity Board.

Because they only heat up at night and sometimes for a brief period during the middle of the day, they tend to become too cool to be effective at certain times particularly in the evening when most people need the warmth most. You will therefore need another fire to keep up the heat in the room at these times.

This and the fact that you cannot turn them up to cater for a particularly cold day makes them unsuitable as a sole source of heat. They do, though, have a use as a type of central heating. If you have this kind of heater they are best used to provide a low background heat to keep the chill off the house, with other fires to bring the temperature of rooms up to a comfortable level. If you do this you will be able to make best use of the white meter tariff, possibly dispensing with the period of heating during the day, and therefore giving you electricity at the cheapest possible rate.

Fires with Flames — Solid Fuel Fires in Open and Closed Grates

These have the distinction of requiring a chimney. The chimney is needed for two reasons, firstly because all these fires produce smoke and dangerous fumes, and secondly to provide an updraught. This pulls air into the fire so that the burning can continue. If a fire is not getting enough air it will smoulder rather than burn, needing somebody to get to work with bellows to get it going. This updraught has to get its air from somewhere, so it pulls air under doors and from around window frames. In the case of a large roaring fire this draught can amount to a small gale, making all those not close to the fire very cold indeed.

If you have a grate that you never use, and that you do not intend ever to use, then the opening can be blocked off more completely, but you must always allow some air to circulate in a chimney to stop damp.

A chimney provides an avenue by which heat can be lost from the room. This will happen whether the fire is lit or not. When you are not using the fire it can be blocked off or the chimney can be closed with a proper throat block; just remember to remove it before you light the fire!

When the fire is lit the only way to stop excess heat escaping is to make sure that the chimney is exactly the right size for the fire. If it is bigger than it need be then air will be pulled round the side of the flames along with the air needed for combustion. This matter of chimney size depends not only on the fire but also on the size of the room and the sort of chimney it is.

It is a matter on which you should take professional advice when you buy a fire. Do not be tempted to partially block a chimney yourself; a build-up of fumes in the room could cause a death.

An advantage that all these fires have is that real flames look very warming, and it is possible to get very close to them and keep warm, even if the rest of the room is rather colder.

Open fires are very expensive in energy terms, a great deal of the heat being lost up the chimney. Even when the fire is glowing well and is radiating a lot of heat into the room, a lot is still going up the chimney, and if you extinguish this glow by putting on more fuel, then most of the heat goes up the chimney. They therefore need constant attention; there should be a 75 to 100 mm (3 or 4 in.) layer of fuel in the grate and it should be banked to be higher at the rear of the grate. Only a little extra fuel should be added at a time. The aim of both these points is to keep the fire glowing and radiating heat out into the room. This also depends upon the grate. If the fire fills the grate and the sides are hot, then these too will radiate the heat out and they will help by reflecting a little. If the grate is too large for the size of fire that you require then you can make it smaller by putting fire bricks around the sides.

Closed grates are rather better. They burn the fuel more efficiently and completely. They can be controlled by opening and closing the dampers as well as in the way you add fuel, and the chimney is not open to the room. The free-standing type of stove, or one that juts out into the room is particularly good, because the casing of these fires gets hot, and heat is convected and radiates well from its usually black surface. The chimney for these often goes up inside the room rather than in the wall, and this too radiates heat. These fires can be kept going at a very low ebb and will still produce heat efficiently.

Gas Fires

Gas has many of the advantages of electricity, in that it is available at the turn of a switch. It is clean and easily controllable and gives you real flames. The fires are not as cheap to install as electric fires, particularly if the gas pipes have to be run from a distance and of course they need a chimney. In this case though it can be very carefully adjusted to be the right size, little heat will be lost from the room whether the fire is on or off. Lastly, gas fires are a 'damp' fire. Burning gas makes water, and this can lead to condensation if a room is kept closed up for a long time with the fire going, but many people find a room heated by gas a lot more comfortable than the dry air produced by electricity.

Central Heating Systems

These can be run from a central boiler or from a back boiler behind a fire. There are also electric radiators on the market, which can be considered as electric fires, and electric night storage heaters have been considered on page 49. The decision between a central boiler and a back boiler will depend in part on the number of radiators you wish to have; bigger systems tend to need central boilers.

The fuel can be gas, oil or solid fuel, and the separate advantages of these have been considered under the section on fuels. Gas and oil are easier to control and require less attention from you, and the choice between them is nothing to do with the actual system of radiators; it is identical for them both.

Having got central heating there is the necessity to run it economically. The time-clock needs setting accurately. It takes about half an hour for a house to heat up or cool down, so the boiler should be set to come on half an hour before you come in from work, and it should be set to go off half an hour before you go to bed. Set it in a similar way for the morning. There is an optimum temperature at which to run the boiler. This is between 55°C and 82°C (77°C in the summer). Running it at less than 55°C will stop the system operating properly, as the water will not circulate properly, and running it at a temperature higher than 82°C will cause excessive heat loss. If there is no separate thermostat on the hot water tank, then it would be wise to keep the water temperature down to about 60°C. Water that is too hot can be dangerous.

Make sure that the room thermostat for the system is in the correct place. It should be somewhere that maintains a steady temperature, not in a room that you often keep hotter than the rest of the house, or next to the boiler or a radiator. It should be away from draughts and not in a position where the sun could shine directly upon it. The air of the room must be able to circulate round it freely. Set it as low as you can without making the house uncomfortable. If you keep the house just 1°C hotter than it need be, then you

are paying about 5 per cent more than you need for fuel; you can always put on another jersey. Take care though if you have very young, old or sick people in the house, because they need higher temperatures than most of us.

Radiators
Radiators spread heat into a room by radiating it into the air just around the radiator. This air then convects the heat around the room. Most houses have the radiators underneath the windows. This will make the heat transfer between radiator and air quite fast because of the great temperature difference, but it will not help the heat spread around the room. This happens by convection and needs a temperature difference from one side of the room to the other. It is possible that if the radiator is by the window then the areas away from the window may not receive the benefit of it. A better spread of heat would be achieved by having the radiator on the opposite wall to the window. We suspect that radiators are put by windows because these are traditionally the coldest parts of the room, but if they are properly draughtproofed this should not be a problem.

The efficiency of radiators can be improved in several ways. For the best radiation they should be painted a dark, matt colour. Aluminium foil can be glued on the wall behind the radiator, to reflect the heat back and to stop it entering the brickwork where it will soon be lost to the outside air. If the radiators are by the windows, then the curtains must be arranged to draw behind them, not in front of them. If you have floor-length curtains then the radiator should be turned off when you draw them; the heat will only be wasted if it goes up behind them. Radiators in rooms not often used can also be turned off, and the doors can be kept shut.

The valves of all the radiators should be carefully adjusted to make the flow even to all the radiators; or better still, thermostat valves can be fitted, which will do the job for you. Often there is a tendency for the hot water to circulate round the downstairs radiators at the expense of those upstairs. By restricting the flow in rooms which are very warm and are taking more than their fair share of the heating, the water can be made to flow to the upstairs rooms.

A lot of heat is lost from the pipe runs, because builders rarely lag these pipes unless specifically told to do so. If you have a cat, notice where it chooses to sleep. This will often be a patch of floor directly over a pipe run. The floor will be quite warm, showing that much heat is being given out where it is of no use to you. To elimi-

nate the problem, lag the pipes, particularly any which run in the void under the house where it is cold.

Lastly, make sure that all the air is bled from the system regularly. If the water gets below a certain level in the radiators, it drastically reduces the circulation in the radiator, and hence the efficiency.

Hot Water

It is more economical to heat your water with a central heating system and to store it hot, than it is to heat it as you need it. If the hot water tank is properly insulated it takes little energy to keep the water at a usable temperature. This can be the biggest single heat loss in a house. An unlagged tank can be costing you upwards of a pound every week, and with cylinder jackets costing only five times this amount, you will get a very quick return on your investment. Two three-hour heating periods are all that is needed to keep up

**Water to correct level
Circulation possible**

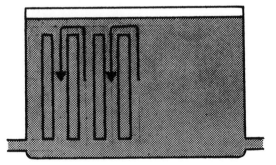

**Water too low
Circulation not possible**

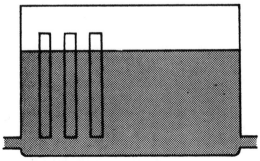

the temperature of the water, and most people run their heating systems for longer than this except in the summer. You can save on the amount of water you have to heat by lagging the pipe runs to and from the tank, and if you are installing a new tank, try to make these runs as short as possible. In some houses you have to run well over 4 litres (1 gallon) of water from the hot tap before it runs hot. When you turn the tap off this amount of water is left in pipes to go cold.

Obviously, the more cautious you are with the way you use hot water, the more energy you save. Never wash your hands or pots under a running tap; always use a bowl as you will use less water. Conversely, a shower uses less water than a bath, unless you stand under it for a long time. Your washing machine is best filled with hot water, rather than letting it heat its own water, and do not use it until you have a full load. If you wash by hand then rinse in cold or just tepid water. Incidentally, tumble-driers are very wasteful of energy indeed; a washing line is much cheaper.

9 Saving on Lighting

Most people do not use very much energy for lighting, but there is room for some saving in this area in most homes. To save on lighting you need to take care on two points:

- Do not allow lights to be left on, and
- Do not use more, or more powerful lamps than you need.

The first point is obvious, and it only needs to be stressed that if you left all the lights on in the average-size house, then this could be the equivalent of wasting the energy needed to run two electric fires. Even leaving just a few lights on, the waste could be many poundsworth in a year. It requires a conscious effort to remember to turn lights off whenever you leave a room, and if it proves impossible to train your family in this way, then it is possible to get time switches for the hall and stair lights, these being the ones most often left on.

As well as remembering to turn off lights when you leave the room, you can also save by turning off general room lights, and using small reading lights instead, of which more later.

The amount of light that you need varies considerably, depending upon what you are doing and where. The Society of Illuminating Engineers have researched this point, and have produced a 'code for interior lighting'. This gives the recommended minimum level of light for different areas in a house,

and for the different activities that are carried out in a home. These are listed below. Provided that you do not get glare (reflection of the light into your eyes), then the more light the better. Sunlight gives you a thousand times more light than you would normally have in an artificially lit living room, but the eye can accommodate well and does not need this amount of light in order for you to see clearly and comfortably. Too little light will strain your eyes and could result in accidents, so it is best not to reduce lighting levels below those recommended.

Light is measured in 'lumens'. This depends not only on the power of the light bulb (the number of 'watts'), but also on how efficiently it converts this electrical energy into light. The ordinary tungsten filament bulb changes most of the energy into heat, with only perhaps 10 per cent of the energy coming out as light. Fluorescent lights are considerably more efficient, and it is possible to work out how much light you are getting if you know the efficiency of the bulb, which will be quoted in 'lumens per watt' (see Appendix 1 for examples of these calculations and also for a guide to the size of light bulb needed). Light falling on a surface is measured in 'lux', which is the number of lumens falling on each m^2 of the surface. This depends on what area a light is covering, as well as on the power of the light.

The recommended light levels are as follows;

Living rooms	50 lux
Kitchens	300 lux
Stairs and halls	150 lux
Bedrooms (general light)	50 lux
Bedrooms (reading light)	150 lux
For casual reading etc.	150 lux
For close work (sewing, prolonged reading etc.)	300 lux

To get these light levels you need not only the right size bulb the right distance away, but it must also be in the right place. If the light is behind you, causing you to cast a shadow over your work, then you are seriously cutting down the light level. For general lighting the light should be far enough away so as not to cast definite, deep shadows, and this can be helped by having the walls painted light colours to reflect the light. In fact we depend upon light reflected in this way most of the time, and dark-painted rooms will need half as much light again as light rooms, in order to achieve the same light level. Lampshades need a mention here, because they too can block much of the light.

Of course the best way of all to save energy on lighting is to use daylight. In days gone by no tailor would dream of having a shop that did not face into the light, preferably to the south, and his workbench would be in the window to make best use of this light. Now that we no longer use candles we have become forgetful, and we arrange rooms with scant regard to natural light, knowing that we can always turn on an artificial one. Arrange your rooms so that you too can work next to a window; daylight is much kinder on the eyes as well as being cheaper.

Types of Lighting

There are two basic kinds of light. Tungsten filament bulbs (the ordinary light bulb) produce light by heating a very thin piece of tungsten wire until it glows white hot. Fluorescent lights make light by passing electricity through a gas, which makes it glow. Most tungsten bulbs give out about 10 to 15 lumens for each watt of electricity that they use, whereas fluorescent tubes give between 35 to 55 lumens per watt. Fluorescent tubes, being much more efficient, will use less energy, but they have disadvantages. Tubes give a rather blue light, which feels 'cold'; even tubes designed to give a 'warm-white' light are still a lot 'colder' than tungsten bulbs. (The warmer colour tubes are the least efficient, the 'daylight' colour tubes the most efficient.) For living rooms most people prefer the 'warmer' tungsten light even at the expense of a little more energy. Tubes also require a more expensive light fitting, and they sometimes flicker in a disturbing way. For areas where you need a high overall light level, such as in a kitchen, fluorescent tubes are ideal. In other rooms high light levels are usually only required over small specific areas, so the inefficiency of tungsten bulbs can be overcome by having individual lights close to your work. Nowadays there are a great many types of light bulb available, and you can choose the one that best meets your requirements. Internally silvered lamps are useful for strong well-directed light, crown-silvered lamps, together with a suitable reflector, can give a soft general light without strong shadows. And have you thought of using a strong directed light to warm you as well as light you while you wash in the cold early morning? The possibilities are endless; a visit to a good lighting shop can be very thought-provoking.

You will probably wish to consider the amount of money you can save, as well as the amount of energy. A lot of firms are starting to produce 'long-life' bulbs. A normal light bulb lasts on average 1000 hours. Long-life bulbs last for 2000 hours, so you only need to buy half as many bulbs. The two kinds of bulbs cost roughly the same, so it would *seem* that you save in more than just convenience with the long-life bulbs. However, these bulbs are made to last longer by making the tungsten filament thicker, and this makes the bulb less efficient; you will need a bigger bulb and it will use more electricity to give the same light. Unless the cost of light bulbs goes down considerably, or the cost of energy increases a great deal, then there is little to choose between the two.

10 Saving on Cooking

Throughout any attempt to save energy, the old maxim holds true that if you look after the pennies, the pounds will look after themselves. This is particularly so with cooking; you need to be careful all the time.

When you cook, you are breaking down the tissues in the food, to make it softer and therefore easier to chew and digest. So any method of softening the food before cooking will help. From an energy viewpoint, the faster food is cooked, the better, because less heat is lost to the surroundings. A pressure cooker helps here; the high pressure increases the temperature of the boiling water inside to over 110°C, and the hotter the food is, the faster the tissues break down.

Ways of softening food before cooking depend obviously on what you are cooking, but various things can be done. Any dried foods need soaking overnight, and many other things benefit from being marinated for various lengths of time. Meat always used to be hung for several days, as pheasant and other game fowls still are, but it can also be beaten with a steak mallet, even if it is only a cheap cut of meat destined for the stewpot. A last general point is to remember always to defrost frozen food thoroughly.

Boiling Food

A lot of cooking involves heating water. This takes a great deal of energy; kg for kg, it takes about eight times as much heat to heat up water than it does to heat up the pan holding the water. It also takes seven times as much heat to actually boil water into steam than it does to get that water up to just below boiling point. The moral is not to use too much water, and never to boil it, unless you are actually steaming the food. We only boil water so that we know that we have raised its temperature to about 100°C, and the trick is to keep the water as close to 100°C as possible without actually letting it boil. This is what simmering means, and on many stoves it requires very careful adjustment; the 'simmering' position provided is always too high.

In addition to the above: always put a lid on; do not allow flames to lick around the side of the pan as the heat will go straight up and not into the pan; if potatoes are to be mashed, then cut them into small pieces before boiling as they will cook quicker; keep the outsides of your pan shiny and clean – a pan with dirty and dull sides loses much more heat to its surroundings by radiation . . . there are probably several tips of your own that you could add to this list. You could even make a haybox.

Frying Food

Grandmother would never use an aluminium frying pan. She preferred the old heavy black cast-iron pan, and she produced the results to justify her preference. It certainly stands to reason that a black pan should fry more evenly, for food that is not touching the bottom of the pan will be heated by the radiant heat that hot black surfaces give off so well. Frying is a fairly energy-wasteful process, because a lot of the heat escapes upwards. However, it is no-where near so expensive as grilling.

Grilling Food

Next to spit-roasting your food in front of an open fire, grilling must be the most energy-expensive way of cooking. A grill tries to make heat go downwards whereas its natural tendency is to rise. Therefore a great amount of the heat is lost even before it gets to the food and, in addition, most grills are designed with open sides and an open front, thus allowing the area around the food to cool rapidly as well.

The only way that heat will go downwards is as radiant heat, and for this to be effective the surface of the grill must be red hot, which uses a lot of energy. There is no way round this problem; about the only things you can do is to look carefully at the design of the grill if you buy a new cooker, and to get the food as close to the grill as you can while still getting even cooking. It will help slightly to have a reflective surface under the food, such as a piece of aluminium foil, but you still lose most of the heat. Always do your toast in a toaster if you have the choice as the heat is much better controlled there.

Roasting Food

Roasting, baking, or any cooking done in the oven is about as efficient as cooking in a pan. An oven is usually on longer than the heat under a pan, so more heat will be lost because of this, but it is insulated whereas a pan is not – provided you do not open the door too often. Using the oven also gives you the opportunity to do several things at once. When roasting a joint of meat you could also prepare a casserole for the following day and warm up a stockpot to make soup. If you wish to do some baking, you can arrange to do it either before or after you use the oven for something else, thus saving the heating-up time.

Buying a Stove

Some stoves are cheaper to run than others. Gas stoves are easier to control; the heat is more quickly variable, and there is no energy lost while a hotplate heats up or cools down after the pan is removed. If you use small pans a lot a gas stove will probably be better for you, as the burners are smaller, though some electric cookers now have dual rings to allow for this. A disadvantage with gas stoves is the pilot lights. Stoves vary in the amount of energy the pilot lights consume, but if it has several then it could be costing you over £5 per year. The alternative is electric ignition either from the mains supply or from a piezo-electric crystal. This latter costs nothing at all to run.

Appendix 5 on fuel consumption tariffs will help you interpret the ratings of burners as given by the manufacturers. Remember, though, when looking at this, that the values given are maximum values. It is rare to have a burner on full for long, and ovens are thermostatically controlled, so they will use less than the maximum. It does however give a guide to the possible costs and savings.

11 Saving on Cooling

As well as using energy to give us heat, a lot of people nowadays use it in refrigerators and freezers. From the strict energy-saving point of view, all fridges and freezers are unnecessary. You cannot manage without heat, but we managed for thousands of years without freezers.

The only real justification for a freezer or fridge is that of convenience. You would have to make do without ice for your drinks, but the old methods of preserving food still work, and can be used fairly easily. The best place to find advice on food storage is in such books as Mrs Beeton's *Book of Household Management* and Cobbett's *Cottage Economy*, but most of it is simply applied commonsense.

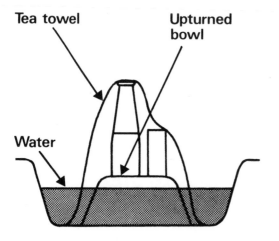

Tea towel

Upturned bowl

Water

Always keep food in naturally cool places such as cellars and garages; buy food when you need it not before, and resist the desire for out-of-season crops. Butter and milk can be kept cool by using a bowl of water and a tea-towel as shown. As the water evaporates from the towel it cools the milk and butter underneath it. There is great scope in this area for your own inventiveness.

The Careful Use of Fridges and Freezers

If you decide that a fridge or a freezer is necessary, then you can economise on the energy it uses by taking care over several points.

All of these devices are really heat-pumps. That is to say that they pump heat from the inside to the outside, leaving the air inside cooler. As well as being a cooling device, a fridge is also a low-power heater for the room in which it is kept, the heat coming from the inside of the fridge and the energy used in the pump and compressor motors.

The colder you require the inside of your fridge, the more energy you are using. You therefore need to experiment with the controls to find the minimum setting that will keep your food fresh. Be careful though; the colder food is, the longer it will keep, and it would be dangerous to try to save energy by keeping your freezer not cold enough. You could easily get food poisoning.

The amount of energy used also depends upon the temperature outside the fridge. If you keep it in the kitchen next to the stove, it will use much more energy than if you•keep it in the cellar or in the garage. When considering where to put it though, do not forget that the heat it gives out can be useful. A freezer in the cellar or kitchen will add slightly to the warmth of the house, while a freezer in the garage could provide just enough heat to stop the car freezing up in the winter. Every little bit counts.

Having placed it in the best position, use it wisely. Every time you open a fridge the air inside warms up, and the fridge has to use energy to make it cold again. This is why chest freezers are more economical than upright freezers. Cold air sinks, so it will quickly come out of an open door, whereas it cannot get up and out of an open lid.

Obviously, the fewer times you open the door or lid, the less energy is used, so decide on everything that you need before you open it, and close it again quickly. Similarly, do not be forever opening the fridge to take out the milk. Take out what you need for the day; if you keep it out of direct sunlight it will stay fresh.

The last point is that a freezer that is full of food uses less energy than an empty one, because there is less air inside to warm up when the door is open. The food itself takes a long time to warm up.

An average-size fridge uses between 150 and 300 units of electricity in a year if it is kept in a cool kitchen. In a warm kitchen it could use up to twice as much. A freezer uses between 700 and 1000 units per year.

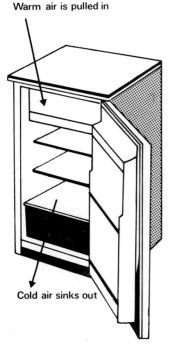

Warm air is pulled in

Cold air sinks out

12 Getting Extra Energy

When you have done all that you can to save energy and to use it economically, the next question is from where can you get cheaper energy. This is what is meant by the search for 'alternative energy'. Not only might this be cheaper energy, but it might be the only kind of energy available when the coal and oil run out. It is a subject about which a whole book can be written; all that we can do here is to outline the possibilities.

There is a large amount of research being done, a lot of it by amateurs and enthusiasts, but also now by the government, into ways of harnessing the sun and wind and rain. Designs for home-built systems are becoming easily available, and a few manufacturers are starting to produce ready-made installations.

The sorts of projects that can now be contemplated are:

■ Solar panels and roofs, which can be made by almost anybody, and can make a useful contribution to your house's supply of hot water.

■ Windmills are being used to generate the electricity to supply remote farms, and as a result manufacturers are researching into smaller and more efficient mills.

■ Heat-pumps are the most efficient heaters possible. You get not only the heat from the energy that you use, but in addition you can pump heat from outside into your house — even if it is cold outside.

Such things as water power or the making of methane gas from household waste may soon also join this list of possibilities.

Appendices

1. Calculating Light Levels

As a 'rule of thumb' guide, the following wattages of light are needed to give a level of 300 lux. The figures are the number of watts you need per square metre of floor area in the room.

	for a bright painted room	for a dark painted room
tungsten filament lamp	40·35	59·2
'warm' fluorescent tube	10·75	16·15
'daylight' fluorescent tube	6·5	10·75

So if you wanted to light a room 3 metres square with a warm fluorescent tube, and the walls were painted a dark colour, then you would multiply the floor area of 9m² by 16·15, which tells you that you will need a 150 watt fluorescent tube.

These figures are for a normal modern house. If you have a house with very high rooms, then you would need to hang the lights well below the ceiling.

If you wish to calculate the number of lux accurately, then you need the following formula.

If the intensity of the light beam is given in candelas, then the number of lux is found from:

lux=candelas÷(distance of the light to the surface in metres)²

For example, a 60 watt tungsten bulb has an intensity of about 125 candelas in a reflective shade. If this is hanging 2 m (6·5 feet) above the floor of a room, then the light level on the floor will be

125 ÷ 2 m²

which is 125÷4=31·25 lux—too little even for a bedroom.

If the light output is given in lumens, then you need to calculate the total area lit by the light, and use the formula given earlier:

lux = lumens − area lit (in metres)

Lights give out a widening beam of light as shown on page 64, which depends on the shade as well as the light bulb. The area lit is given by the complicated formula:

area =

π × (tangent of the × distance of
        beam angle   light, to surface

Manufacturers often give charts to show what lux you can expect from their light fittings at various distances.

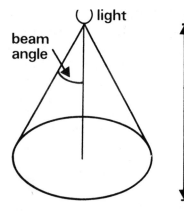

beam angle

light

distance of light to surface

2. Cost Calculations

Working Out Heat Saved

We have used the 'U' value of materials whenever we could in this book because a change in 'U' value is reflected directly by a change in heat loss. For example if a wall has a 'U' value of 2·0 and by insulating it you achieve a 'U' value of 1·0, then the new value is

$$\frac{1·0}{2·0} \times 100 = 50 \text{ per cent of the original.}$$

The heat loss through this wall is reduced by 50 per cent in this case.

Your walls lose about 25 per cent of the total heat of the house. If you reduce this by the 50 per cent we calculated, then 50 per cent of 25 per cent is:

$$\frac{25}{100} \times 50 = 12.5 \text{ per cent}$$

So you could reduce the heat loss from the entire house by 12.5 per cent if you insulate all the walls (using this example).

Working Out Cash Saved

Once you know roughly how much heat you can save, then find what percentage that is of your total bill.

Taking the above example: if your fuel bill is £200 a year, 12.5 per cent of it is:

$$\frac{£200}{100} \times 12·5 = £25$$

So you save about £25 a year with this insulation.

Strictly speaking you should work this out as a percentage of your *heating* bill, but most people do not know what they pay for lighting etc., and as the figure is approximate it is sufficient to take your total fuel bills as a basis for the calculation.

Working Out the Return on Your Investment

An accurate calculation is very difficult as it needs to take into account, among other things, the change in cost of fuel and the change in value of money invested in insulation over the period of return. However, the following simplification gives a reasonable estimate.

■ Obtain a total costing for the insulation you require (by adding up everything you have to buy to do the work).

■ Work out from the estimates in the relevant chapter the possible reduction in heat-loss and therefore the cash you may save annually.

■ Divide the total cost of the work by the annual saving and the answer is approximately how many years it takes to repay the outlay in saved fuel. For example, if the total cost of wall insulation is £200 and the annual saving is £25:

$$\frac{£200}{25} = \text{eight years}$$

Then *you* have to decide if it is worth the outlay.

One final point. All the calculations assume that you are saving fuel. That is, we expect you to keep your house at the temperature it is now, while using less fuel because of improved insulation. However, you can use the insulation to achieve a higher inside temperature with the same amount of fuel. In this case you will not save anything, neither will you get your money back in time — you will just be warmer.

3. Exposed Areas

The problem of damp penetrating walls is increased in exposed areas. This problem can be worsened by filling cavity walls with an insulating material. People living in severely exposed areas should be aware of the Local Authority Regulations on this (contact your Local Council Offices) and should ask for a written guarantee from the insulating firm. The guarantee should state that the walls are in a suitable condition for cavity insulation.

The map shows exposure to wind and rain:
Heavy shading — severe exposure;
medium shading — moderate exposure;
white areas — sheltered.

4. Temperature Differences

The map below shows what the average temperature difference is between the inside and the outside of houses in Great Britain during the normal eight-month heating period.

Remember these are not actual air temperatures but temperature *differences*

This is worked out from the number of 'degree days'. The calculation is: 18°C minus average temperature of outside air for each day heat was required divided by 240.

The figure of 18°C (65°F) is the temperature at which most people keep their houses, and this figure is divided by 240 as this is the number of days in the normal eight-month heating period.

The final temperature at which we arrive is the average difference and therefore says nothing about the extremes of temperature a house may suffer; it is, however, a useful indication of the problem insulation may have to cope with. For example if you live in an area with a difference of over 13°C (24 °F), then 100 mm (4 in.) loft insulation will certainly be worthwhile.

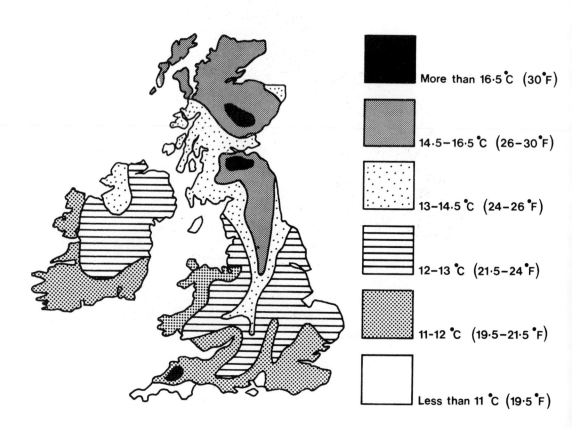

More than 16·5 °C (30 °F)

14·5–16·5 °C (26–30 °F)

13–14·5 °C (24–26 °F)

12–13 °C (21·5–24 °F)

11–12 °C (19·5–21·5 °F)

Less than 11 °C (19·5 °F)

5. Fuel Consumption Tariffs

Gas

For the householder there are two possible ways of paying for gas. These are the Domestic Credit Tariff and the Domestic Prepayment Tariff. The Prepayment Tariff is purely for those houses still fitted with a money in the slot gas meter. As the Gas Board have to cover the cost of emptying and servicing these meters, gas sold through them is sold at a higher rate than on the Credit Tariff. It is therefore in your interest to ask the Gas Board to change you over to the Credit Tariff. Most people are on the Domestic Credit Tariff, and their gas is charged in the following ways:

■ A standing charge is levied each quarter. This is a small charge to cover the costs of providing the gas supply. It is charged whether or not you consume any gas that quarter.

■ The charge is for the quantity of gas that you use. The first 52 therms of gas are charged at about 5p per therm more than the rest of the gas used. This is rather like a discount for buying wholesale. In practice most people use more than the initial 52 therms per quarter. (NB: 1 therm=100,000 British Thermal Units (Btu) of heat.)

The average price of 1 therm of gas is therefore not the same as the charge for 1 therm. This can however be calculated as follows:

$$\text{average price of one therm} = \frac{\text{total amount due per quarter}}{\text{total number of therms used per quarter}}$$

Though the Gas Board charge for the number of therms used, the gas meter actually measures the number of m^3 of gas used. To convert from one to the other, the Gas Board work out a 'declared Calorific Value' for the gas, which is the amount of heat measured in British Thermal Units that you will get if you burn 1 m^3 of gas. They then use the following formula:

$$\frac{\text{number of } m^3 \times \text{calorifc value}}{100\ 000}$$
$= \text{number of therms}$

The calorific value of the gas is always shown on the bill, and may change slightly from one bill to the next.

Electricity Bills and Tariffs

The normal tariff is the General Domestic Tariff. In addition to this there is the White Meter Tariff and the Off-peak Tariffs. These last two are designed primarily for those with electric night storage heaters and immersion heaters for hot water. If you do not use either of these then you will be on the General Tariff, and there is no advantage to you the others.

The General Domestic Tariff

The electricity is charged in the following way:

■ The first 72 units that you use each quarter are charged at the high price of over 6p per unit. This is to cover the administration and other costs of running the service.

■ The remaining units are charged at a much lower price.

■ There is sometimes a 'fuel adjustment' charge. This is to take into account small variations in the cost of the fuel that the Electricity Board has to buy in order to make electricity. They work out how much they have spent on fuel, and for each 1p above or below £20 per tonne that this works out to be, they then alter your bill up or down by 0·00046p for each unit used.

The average price of one unit of electricity therefore depends on how much electricity you use. It can however be calculated as follows:

average price of one unit=
total amount due per quarter−
total number of units used per quarter.

The White Meter and Off-peak Tariffs
Both of these tariffs enable you to buy electricity at a cheap rate during the night. The Electricity Board install a different meter but you have to install a time-clock and a separate wiring system so that the devices using this cheap electricity can be turned on and off automatically at the right time.

With the white meter you are charged a 'day rate' for all electricity used during the day, and a 'night rate' for all that you use at night. Instead of charging a high rate for the first so-many units used, they cover the service costs by charging a fixed quarterly amount.

With this system it is possible to have night storage heaters turned on for a boost period during the day, though you will be paying the day rate for this.

The off-peak tariff electricity is available only during the night, so no daytime boost is possible. This tariff is really intended for industrial users but it is possible to have this tariff in a house if you wish. Prior to March 1970 the White Meter Tariff did not exist, and the Off-peak Tariff allowed for daytime boost periods. Consumers who were already on this tariff at this time still get this, but all new installations are as outlined above.

The decision as to which tariff is best depends upon how much power you wish to use at night, and of course upon the current charges, so we suggest you consult your local Electricity Board.

6. Units and Metric Conversions

Length

1 inch=25·4 millimetres (mm) 1 mm= 0·039 in.

1 foot=0·340 metres (m) 1 m=3 feet 3·4 in.

Weight

1 pound (lb)=0·45 kilogrammes (kg) 1 kg=2·2 lb.

Energy

The main unit of energy and heat is the 'joule'.

1 joule is the energy you get from 1 watt of power used for one second

1 kilojoule (kJ)=1000 joules (J)

1 megajoule (MJ)=1000000 joules (J)

1 British Thermal Unit (Btu)=1·05 kJ. 1 kJ=0·94 Btu.

1 kilowatt hour (kW/h)=3·6 megajoules (MJ). 1 MJ=0·28 kW/h.

1 therm=105·5 MJ. 1 MJ=0·0095 therms.

'U' values

The metric unit for this is watts per square metre, degrees centigrade $(W/m^2, °C)$.

The imperial unit is British Thermal Units per square foot, hour, degrees fahrenheit $(Btu/ft^2, h, °C)$.

1 $Btu/ft^2 h, °F$=0·176 $W/m^2, °C$
1 $W/m^2, °C$=5·67 $Btu/ft^2, hr, °F$

For most purposes it will be found to be accurate to use the following;

Imperial 'U' value=metric 'U' value÷6
Metric 'U' value=Imperial 'U' value×6

If you are using more than one insulating material together, it is not possible to find the 'U' value of the combination by simply adding the individual 'U' values. A rather complicated method is needed for this calculation.

Temperature Conversion Chart:
Fahrenheit to Centigrade (Celsius)

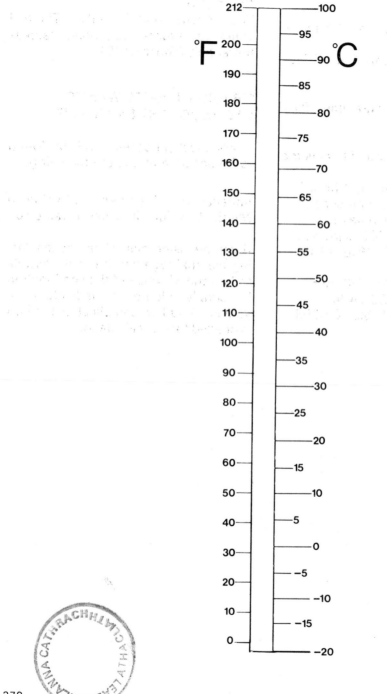